75 CLASSIC RIDES
NORTHERN
CALIFORNIA

75 CLASSIC RIDES
NORTHERN
CALIFORNIA
THE BEST ROAD-BIKING ROUTES

Bill Oetinger

MOUNTAINEERS
BOOKS

To Kathy

MOUNTAINEERS BOOKS

Mountaineers Books is the publishing division of The Mountaineers, an organization founded in 1906 and dedicated to the exploration, preservation, and enjoyment of outdoor and wilderness areas.

1001 SW Klickitat Way, Suite 201, Seattle, WA 98134
800.553.4453, www.mountaineersbooks.org

Printed in China

Distributed in the United Kingdom by Cordee, www.cordee.co.uk
First edition, 2014
Copy editor: Jane Crosen
Design: Heidi Smets
Additional design and layout: Jennifer Shontz, redshoedesign.com
Cartographer: Pease Press Cartography
Cover photograph: *Dropping off Campmeeting Ridge on Meyers Grade Road (Ride 17)* (Darell Dickey)
Frontispiece: *Climbing Old La Honda Road in the Santa Cruz Mountains (Ride 34)* (Tim Aikin)
All photographs by the author unless otherwise noted.
Photographs on pages 24, 27, 31, 105, 117, 129, 156, 166, 208, 276, and 278 by Nancy Yu, Ride Chronicles, yurides.wordpress.com
Photograph on page 305 by Jof Hanwright, www.scout911.com

Library of Congress Cataloging-in-Publication Data
Oetinger, Bill.
  75 classic rides Northern California : the best road-biking routes / Bill Oetinger.
    pages   cm.
  Includes index.
  ISBN 978-1-59485-784-3 (ppb)
1. Cycling—California, Northern—Guidebooks. 2. California, Northern—Guidebooks. I. Title.
  GV1045.5.C22O735 2014
  796.6'409794—dc23

                                          2013033484

ISBN (paperback): 978-1-59485-784-3
ISBN (ebook): 978-1-59485-785-0

CONTENTS

CENTRAL VALLEY

GOLD COUNTRY

With your purchase of this book, you also get access to our easy-to-use, downloadable cue sheets:

» Go to our website: www.mountaineersbooks.org/ClassicRidesNorCA.
» Download a complete set of mileage cue sheets for all 75 rides in this book.
» When you open the document on your computer, enter the code "Hopland10" when prompted.

It's our way of thanking you for supporting Mountaineers Books and our mission of outdoor recreation and conservation.

MAP LEGEND

——— Featured Route

- - - - Route on Bike Path

······ Route Variation

- - - - - Other Bike Path

——→ Route Direction

↩ Turnaround

═══ Freeway (Limited Access)

——— Highway

——— Secondary Road

⑤ ⑧⓪ ②⑧⓪ Interstate Highway

⑨⑦ ①⓪① US Highway

① ②⓪ ①②⑧ State Highway

⑥② County Road

①②③ Forest Road

S Start (and Finish for loops and out-and-back rides)

F Finish (for one-way rides)

❶❷❸ Stages (Rides 73-75)

■ Point of Interest

▲ Peak

) (Pass

○ Town

⊟ Bridge

) (Tunnel

Park

Water

State Boundary

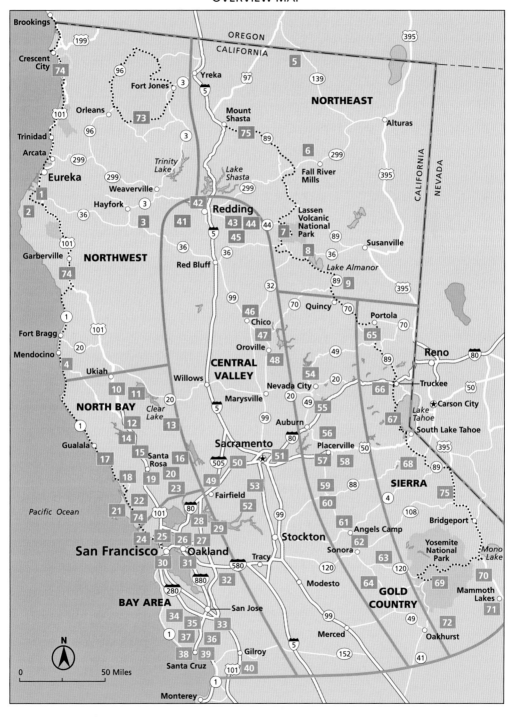

RIDES-AT-A-GLANCE

NO.	RIDE	DIFFICULTY RATING	DISTANCE (IN MILES)	ELEVATION GAIN (IN FEET)	TIME (IN HOURS)	POINTS OF INTEREST
1	Lunch in Ferndale	Moderate	30	1500	2–4	Quiet roads and a charming, historic village
2	Tour of the Unknown Coast	Epic	98	8700	6.5–10	The most remote coast in California
3	Hayfork–Wildwood Loop	Challenging	46	3800	3–4	Forests and meadows in the middle of nowhere
4	Mendocino Meandering	Moderate/ Challenging	20, 46, 64	1600–5400	4–6	Three loops in the coastal hills south of Mendocino
5	Tule Lake–Lava Beds National Monument	Moderate	54	1500	4–6	Lava Beds National Monument and nearby Tule Lake
6	Fall River Loop	Moderate/ Challenging	61	2500	4–6	Pretty rivers, fields of peppermint, deep forest
7	Lassen Lollipop	Challenging	42	3800	3–5	Lassen Volcanic National Park and nearby roads
8	Almanor Out–and–Backs	Moderate	42	1900	3–4	Tiny wooded roads north of Lake Almanor
9	Indian Valley– Antelope Lake	Challenging	89	4500	5.5–8	A lovely, tranquil region; can be split into rides of 35 and 54 miles
10	Hopland–Boon-ville–Ukiah Loop	Challenging	66	4400	4.5–6.5	Rugged ridges of southern Mendocino County
11	Kelseyville Two–Looper	Challenging	15, 41, 56	up to 5000	1–5	Longer and shorter options in the hills above Clear Lake
12	The Geysers Loop	Challenging	47	3800	3–4.5	Classic loop over the highest road in Sonoma County
13	Knoxville–Butts Canyon Loop	Challenging/ Epic	82	5500	5–7	Hilly, remote loop in northern Napa and southern Lake counties
14	Wine Country Loop #1	Easy/ Moderate	31	1200	2–3	Dry Creek Valley and Alexander Valley vineyards
15	Wine Country Loop #2	Moderate	50	2000	3–5	Russian River Valley, Alexander Valley, Dry Creek Valley
16	Pope Valley Loop	Moderate	35	2500	2.5–4	The quiet side of Napa County, away from the tourists
17	King Ridge– Coleman Valley Loop	Challenging/ Epic	71	8000	5–6	High ridges, coastal hills, spectacular scenery . . . a legendary ride
18	Santa Rosa– Sebastopol Bike Trails	Easy	20	400	2–3	Mellow meander on Sonoma County bike paths
19	Sonoma–Napa Chutes and Ladders	Challenging/ Epic	52, 81	8500	5–8	Complicated, steep journey through two counties

NO.	RIDE	DIFFICULTY RATING	DISTANCE (IN MILES)	ELEVATION GAIN (IN FEET)	TIME (IN HOURS)	POINTS OF INTEREST
20	Up and Down Napa Valley	Moderate/ Challenging	45, 63	1400, 2500	3–6	The definitive Napa Valley tour
21	To the Lighthouse	Challenging	44, 62	2700, 4400	4–6	Exploring Point Reyes National Seashore
22	Sonomarin Borderlands	Challenging	66	4300	4.5–7	Pastoral valleys, beautiful bay, and high ridgelines
23	The Carneros District	Moderate	43	1700	3–4.5	Historic town of Sonoma and nearby Carneros vineyards
24	Mount Tamalpais and More	Challenging	48	5200	3.5–6	Mill Valley, Muir Woods, Marin County coast, Mount Tam
25	San Francisco to the Ferries	Moderate	13, 26, 37	up to 1900	1–4	Over the Golden Gate Bridge to ferries sailing back to the city
26	Berkeley Waterfront	Easy	12	Flat	1–2	Bay shore bike trails and nearby neighborhoods
27	Berkeley Hills	Moderate/ Challenging	56	4500	3.5–5	Classic route through the wooded parklands above Berkeley
28	Contra Costa–Carquinez	Moderate	38, 50	2300	3–5	Suburban bike trails and an obscure loop along Carquinez Strait
29	Mount Diablo Loop	Challenging/ Epic	65	6100	4–6	Morgan Territory and the south–north ascent of the mountain
30	San Francisco Parks	Moderate	16	1100	1.5–3	Golden Gate Park, the Presidio, and Lands End
31	Alameda Old and New	Easy	14	Flat	1–2	Old town Alameda and Bay Farm Island
32	Mount Hamilton Loop	Epic	110	9200	7–10	Calaveras Reservoir, Sierra Road, Mount Hamilton, San Antonio Valley
33	Coyote Creek Loop	Moderate/ Challenging	28, 32	2200	2–4	Classic South Bay bike trail and nearby roads
34	Old La Honda–Tunitas Creek	Challenging	68	6100	5–6	Northern Santa Cruz Mountains and coast
35	Big Basin–Bear Creek Loop	Challenging	62	up to 8000	4–6	Deep redwood forest, big climbs, and wild descents
36	Almaden Two–Looper	Moderate/ Challenging	52	2800	3–5	Two loops in the hills south of San Jose
37	Santa Cruz Mountains	Challenging	66	7000	4.5–6.5	Hilly, tangled journey through the heart of the Santa Cruz Mountains
38	Santa Cruzin'	Easy	20	Nearly flat	3	Promenade along the beach frontage of Santa Cruz and Capitola
39	Corralitos–Highland Loop	Challenging	54	4500	4–5	Southern Santa Cruz Mountains

NO.	RIDE	DIFFICULTY RATING	DISTANCE (IN MILES)	ELEVATION GAIN (IN FEET)	TIME (IN HOURS)	POINTS OF INTEREST
40	San Juan Bautista–Elkhorn Slough Loop	Moderate	45	3200	3.5–4.5	Quiet back roads and a wonderful mission compound
41	Platina Out–and–Back	Challenging	71	6100	5–7	An obscure, delightful road southwest of Redding
42	Sacramento River Trail Loop	Moderate	37	2000	3–5	Turtle Bay, Sundial Bridge, Shasta Dam, Keswick Dam
43	Millville Loop	Moderate	41	2600	3–5	Rocky foothills along the eastern edge of the Central Valley
44	Ponderosa Lollipop	Challenging	52	4500	4–5	Farther up into those rocky hills, with more woods
45	Shingletown Shuffle	Challenging	35	3200	2.5–4	Short but steep; quiet hilly roads just right for riding
46	Easy Chico	Easy	27	Flat	2–3	Two lazy loops, one outside town, one in Bidwell Park
47	Essence of Wildflower	Challenging	64	3900	4–6	Best parts of the Chico Wildflower Century
48	LaPorte–Forbestown Loops	Challenging	38, 44, 63	up to 4800	4–6	Two loops and three options in the foothills southeast of Oroville
49	Winters Wooden Wiggles	Moderate/Challenging	27, 69	1300, 4200	4–5	Long and short loops west of Winters, including Wooden Valley
50	Davis Bike Loop	Easy	12	Flat	1–1.5	Circumnavigation of the bike-friendly city of Davis
51	American River Trail	Moderate	57	1200	4–6	Beautiful trail from Sacramento to Lake Natoma and back
52	Sacramento Delta Loop #1	Moderate	56	Flat	3.5–5	Southern Sacramento–San Joaquin Delta, out of Rio Vista
53	Sacramento Delta Loop #2	Easy/Moderate	32	Flat	2–3	Northern Sacramento–San Joaquin Delta, closer to Sacramento
54	Lunch in Nevada City	Challenging	68	up to 5600	6	A hilly trek to a famous gold mining boomtown
55	Iowa Hill–Foresthill Loop	Epic	55	7500	4.5–6	Steep, daunting journey into the canyon of the American River
56	The Mother Lode Loops	Challenging	61, 66	5800, 6500	4.5–6	Wildly steep ups and downs out of Coloma, the original gold discovery site
57	Plymouth–El Dorado Loops	Challenging	40, 57	4000–5000	3.5–5.5	Rolling gold country foothills
58	Fiddletown Loops	Challenging	47, 51	4000, 4500	3.5–5	Rolling roads, but with the infamous Slug Gulch on the long route
59	Sutter Creek Figure-8	Moderate/Challenging	50	4500	3–5	Two loops (22 and 28 miles) out of quaint old town

NO.	RIDE	DIFFICULTY RATING	DISTANCE (IN MILES)	ELEVATION GAIN (IN FEET)	TIME (IN HOURS)	POINTS OF INTEREST
60	Jackson Loops	Challenging/ Epic	61, 75	6700, 7500	4.5–7.5	Long and short loop out of Jackson; ruggedly hilly
61	Angels Camp Loop	Challenging	41	4600	3–5	Murphys, Sheep Ranch, Old Gulch, Calaveritas, Dogtown
62	Sonora–Columbia Loop	Challenging	49	4700	3–5	Pretty loop visiting Columbia State Historic Park
63	Wards Ferry– Cherry Lake Loops	Epic	90, 109	11,500, 14,000	6–10	Massive climbs and descents in the most spectacular mountain scenery
64	Coulterville Loops	Challenging/ Epic	34, 56, 73	3900–7300	5–8	Three options in the southern Gold Country hills
65	Portola–Gold Lake–Yuba Pass Loop	Challenging	61	4200	4–5	Half High Sierra granite and half open valleys
66	Truckee Out–and–Backs	Moderate/ Challenging	up to 44	2100	4–5	Donner Lake, Donner Summit, and Truckee River Trail
67	Lake Tahoe Out–and–Back	Moderate/ Challenging	25, 49	up to 3200	2–6	Along west shore of lake
68	California Alps Out–and–Backs	Challenging	65, 73	up to 8500	5–7	Alpine Lake via Ebbetts Pass and Pacific Grade, plus Grover Hot Springs
69	Yosemite Valley	Easy/ Moderate	21	up to 1000	2–4	Roads and trails around the magnificent valley
70	June Lake Loop	Easy/ Moderate	28	1700	2–3	June, Gull, Silver, and Grant lakes
71	Mammoth–Mary– Minarets	Challenging	40	3900	4–5	Two adventures out of Mammoth Lakes
72	Bass Lake–Grizzly Loop	Challenging	76	7100	5–7	Around Bass Lake and High Sierra granite, spectacular
73	Marble Mountains Loop	Challenging	168	12,700	3 days	A loop along wild rivers and over high mountains
74	California Coast	Challenging	448	30,000	7 days	From Oregon to San Francisco, on or near the coast
75	California Peaks	Challenging/ Epic	548	34,000	9 days	From Shasta to Yosemite, in the Cascades and Sierra

Climbing Coleman Valley Road in the coastal hills of Sonoma County (Ride 17) (Darell Dickey)

ACKNOWLEDGMENTS

Writing a cycling guidebook is a bit like going on a group ride. Yes, you have to pedal your own bike, but the task is made easier and more enjoyable by the company of those around you, drafting in a pace line, sharing bike lore, helping to fix a flat...

So I want to say *"Chapeau!"* to at least a few of the folks who have shared this long ride with me. I want to salute the many members of the Santa Rosa Cycling Club who have given me the opportunity to plan and lead so many rides and tours over the years. You are the crash-test dummies who have tried out all my routes for the first time, trusting me to have gotten things right.

Writing about club rides and tours follows directly from that, and writing for Bike Cal.com is the next link in that same chain. Traveling to other parts of the state with my club mates for centuries and doubles and tours has expanded my horizons, bringing all sorts of great roads and fascinating regions to my attention. It all flows downstream from involvement with the club.

Then there are the friends who have assisted directly with this book, advising me about obscure back roads I would not, could not, have found on my own. I asked for your help, and you said yes: opening your homes to me and then taking me out on wonderful rides; or patiently answering my email queries. Thanks to all of you who share my passion for finding the road less traveled: Linda and Sid Fluhrer, Rich Fuglewicz, Jean Cordalis, Margie and John Biddick, Kirk Beedle, Robin Dean, Tom Hiltz, Craig Robertson, Mike DeMicco, Donn King, Rick Sawyer, Frank Pedrick, Darell Dickey, Paul McKenzie, Bob Stolzman, Craig Gaevert, Gordon Stewart, Joe and Arlene Morgan. Thanks also to those who have shared their photos for use in this book. And thanks to my editors, Margaret, Janet, and Jane, who patiently guided me through the process of building a book, and who gently sanded the rough edges off my copy.

Thanks to my folks, Bill and Annis, for teaching me the rudiments of proper English usage, and for always encouraging me to be curious and to never settle for ordinary.

Finally, last but most definitely not least, profound gratitude to my wife and best pal, Kathy, who has supported me in my mercurial enthusiasms for all these years; who graciously allowed me to turn so many of our vacations into tour-planning odysseys, taking notes for me as we wandered endlessly along little lanes better suited to bikes than cars. Reviewing her notes later, I might find that, on a long descent, she had written, *"Wheeeeee!!!"* That about sums it up.

Views to infinity are the standard bill of fare on the western flank of the Santa Cruz Mountains (Ride 39).

INTRODUCTION

I cannot claim to have ridden all over the world, but my two-wheeled travels have taken me through most of the states in the American West and to other states and foreign countries farther afield. All of those bike adventures have been worthwhile and some have been wonderful. But in the end, when it comes to day-in, day-out cycling excellence, I channel Dorothy: I click my bike shoe heels together and repeat: "There's no place like home!"

Home, in my case, is Northern California. I've been riding here for many, many years, and I have yet to exhaust the possibilities for biking exploration and fun, for scenic sensory overload, for climbing challenge and dancing descents. If I had to boil the region's best attributes down to their fundamentals, I would say there are two things that stand out: variety and climate.

This variety expresses itself in two ways. First of all, there is the broad diversity across all of Northern California, from the moist, mossy redwood forests of the northwest to the rugged, granite minarets of the High Sierra, from the sheep and dairy pastures of the coastal hills to the deep, steep river canyons of the Gold Country. Sleepy pioneer villages, with one foot still in the nineteenth century. Bustling urban stews, with coffee bars, bistros, bookstores, and bike stores on every block (and bike trails around every corner). Rolling, oak-dotted grasslands, green in the winter, golden in the summer. The corduroy rows of vineyards and the patchwork quilt of farm fields. It's a jumbo-size sampler pack of everything the American West has to offer.

But you don't have to drive (or ride) halfway across the state, moving from one landscape to another, to experience that variety. Yes, of course, some of the extremes may be many miles apart. But more frequently, even at the relatively low speed of bike travel, you can sample several different environments in quick succession. In just one easy ride from the foot of my driveway, I can visit vineyards, redwoods, apple orchards, sheep-cropped hilltops, rivers, seashore, and an assortment of small towns. It's a biking buffet, a smorgasbord of scenic treats . . . a movable feast.

And then there's climate. To be sure, there are some parts of Northern California that are buried under snow for half the year, and a few other areas that may be as hot as a sauna now and then. But most of the region is temperate, and most cyclists, with just a dollop of dedication, can ride the whole year round. For a few months—between November and March—we may have to throw on a few extra layers and may still feel a bit nipped around the nose and toes, but we can keep riding. While other parts of the country are locked up in the deep freeze of winter or dismally wet and gray, as another rainy front swarms ashore, we are still out there, logging our miles and stretching out our smiles.

It all adds up to something approaching cycling paradise. But even paradise will be a muddled maze if you don't know your way around it, and that's where this book comes into play. By sharing these seventy-five rides with you, I hope to eventually provide you with a working understanding of what this great state (okay, half state) has to offer.

Each one of these rides is worth doing and—I hope!—each description and mileage log is accurate and functionally useful. But beyond the specific nuts and bolts of each ride, I hope these pages serve as inspiration for you: I hope they prime the pump of your curiosity and wanderlust, encouraging you to not only do these exact routes, but to use them as gateways to other routes on other roads nearby.

That brings me to my one big disclaimer: so many roads, so little time! Or, more to the point in the context of this book: so many roads, so few pages! I could have filled another hundred pages with roads and rides, had the publisher allowed it. Settling on these seventy-five rides has been a challenging process of subtraction and compromise. In the interest of offering a balanced portfolio of easy, moderate, and hard rides, and an even spread of rides throughout Northern California, I have had to leave out many a tasty road. If you are local to the area and wonder why I left out your favorite backyard back road, be assured I didn't overlook it. I almost certainly knew about it, considered it, and ultimately had to pass it by, for any number of reasons.

But those roads haven't dried up and blown away, simply because they didn't make the final cut in this book. They're still out there, and once you learn your way around the roads that are in the book, you can begin improvising new routes of your own.

GEOGRAPHY

Citizens of California have been talking about splitting the state in two ever since this long, lanky chunk of real estate was added to the union in 1850. Many different "borders" have been proposed as dividing lines, based on political, philosophical, agricultural, and commercial interests. I'm a resident of Northern California, but I've cycled extensively in Southern California too, and have a pretty good feel for the roads and rides down there. I puzzled long and hard over where to draw the southern border for this book. My final decision takes into account the dynamics of specific roads and regions on either side of the border, and also reflects an attempt at balance between the two halves of the state. I've left somewhat more than half the land mass in the south, but I believe there are more good bike roads concentrated in the north, so the split feels about right.

I have divided Northern California into seven regions. Across the top of the state are two huge, remote, lightly settled sectors: Northwest and Northeast. Wedged in between them and running almost the length of the state is the vast Central Valley, comprised of the drainages of the Sacramento and San Joaquin rivers and all their tributaries and deltas.

In the west, clustered around San Francisco Bay, are the North Bay and Bay Area regions. The Bay Area includes all the communities and countryside around San Francisco Bay, but it also includes the Santa Cruz Mountains—the high, wooded spine of the San Francisco peninsula—and the coastal zone west of the mountains. North of the Bay Area, the North Bay embraces the wooded hills, vineyards, dairy lands, and coastline of Sonoma, Napa, and Lake counties and the northern half of Marin County. Added together, these two regions still occupy fewer square miles than any of the bigger, emptier regions to the north, and yet they account for nearly half of all the rides in the book. The reason is simple: more people, more towns, more roads (and bike trails), and, by the way, some of the most spectacular scenery in the state as well.

In the east, the Gold Country and Sierra regions are first cousins: the Gold Country occupies the foothills of the mountains farther east. Any dividing line between "foothills" and "mountains" is going to be a fuzzy line, but for all their similarities, there are plenty of differences too.

If you study the master map of Northern California, you may feel that some areas are underrepresented, in particular Northwest, Northeast, and Sierra. For the most part, this is true and inevitable. Those regions, although packed with gorgeous scenery, simply have fewer roads with which to create "classic" rides. But don't forget the three multiday tours passing through those areas. If the individual stages on those tours are added in, their total

Cruising through the vineyards in Alexander Valley, Sonoma County (Ride 15) (Kurt West)

ride counts become quite respectable, and the spread of nice rides throughout all the regions looks reasonably balanced.

GETTING STARTED

I'm going to guess most of you browsing this book have at least a little cycling experience. You may not be grizzled old campaigners, but you at least have some rudimentary understanding of how to ride a bike … more expertise than what you had when your dad let go of your saddle and you wobbled off down your neighborhood street as a kid. But how much more expertise you have, I can't know. So I will run a few basics past you, just in case.

Contrary to what some people might think, you do not learn everything you need to know about riding a bike when you take that first wobble down your childhood street. Yes, you can probably stay upright from then on, most of the time, but there are numerous subtle skills that good riders acquire over the years that make cycling safer, more efficient, and more enjoyable. You can pick up some of these skills simply by riding and getting better at it, while some skills may be learned from others.

If you're a rookie rider, still well down the learning curve, consider these suggestions.

» Join a bike club. If you live anywhere close to a city of any size, there will be bike clubs nearby. Some are going to be better than others, but any halfway decent one will bring you into contact with other riders, many of whom will be experienced and skilled. (It isn't a given that all bike club members are skilled or responsible, but you will quickly figure out which ones are.) There are clubs geared to racing and others to touring or recreational riding, and many offer rides and mentoring for novices.

Once you start going on club rides and watching other riders, your cycling skill set will expand by leaps and bounds. Don't be afraid to ask your new mates questions. Remember: The only dumb questions are the ones you don't ask.

» Take a class. There are three sorts of bike classes I recommend. First is a basic skills clinic: how to ride efficiently, alone or in a group; how to descend and climb and corner; how to participate in a pace line. Then there are classes about traffic: knowing the rules of the road and how cyclists interact with motor vehicles and pedestrians. Finally, there are bike maintenance classes, teaching everything from how to change a tire right on up to advanced bike wrenching. Good bike clubs will sponsor some of these classes and clinics, and bike shops offer the maintenance sessions.

» If you can't find clubs or classes near you, head for the Internet or subscribe to good bike periodicals. The amount of good information out there is almost limitless.

RIDING ETIQUETTE AND SAFETY

While you're honing your bike skills, don't lose track of the basic rules of the road. Bicyclists have the same rights and are subject to the same rules and responsibilities as the operators of motor vehicles. For starters, that means you ride with traffic and not against it. You stop at stop signs and red lights, yield for pedestrians in crosswalks, and so forth. Do on your bike what you would do in your car—assuming you're a responsible driver—and that includes the things you should *not* do, such as talking on your phone or texting.

Midway along the magnificent ascent of Mount Tamalpais in Marin County (Ride 24) (Darell Dickey)

Rolling along next to Lake Hennessey in the hills above Napa Valley (Ride 16)

Don't dart through traffic in sudden, unpredictable ways. Never assume the drivers around you have seen you. Watch the "body English" of the drivers to anticipate what they're going to do or whether they've seen you. This includes noticing drivers in parked cars who might be about to open a door in your path. Try to see the big picture, all around you, staying awake to new developments all the time. (I recommend wearing a rear-view mirror, mounted to your glasses or helmet. I've worn one for years and wouldn't think of riding without it.)

Smooth and steady are good watchwords for riders. Be predictable in all the right ways. This is true not only for working in traffic, but for working in a group ride. If you've never been in a pace line, try it out. Take it easy at first and watch the other, more experienced riders. The most important rule is this: Never do anything sudden, either accelerating or slowing. Whether you're pulling on the front or drifting to the back, keep it steady. When a good pace line is working well, it's a thing of beauty and makes the ride faster, more efficient, and more fun. But it takes a little getting use to. Be patient and observe, then put it all into practice.

On bike trails, cyclists are the fastest users on those "roads," occupying the niche cars do on highways. Never hammer on a bike path. Dial it back a notch or two. Exercise the patience and courtesy with walkers and birders and roller-bladers that you hope motorists will accord you. When approaching walkers from behind, slow down and call out,

"Bicycle!" in a cheery, loud-enough voice. It's a word that can't be mistaken for any other and it gives folks all the information they need to make the right decision.

Staying awake and in the moment isn't just for traffic. Be thinking ahead at all times, even on a quiet country road. There are booby traps galore out there, from loose gravel to wet spots to roadkill to broken glass to potholes to open-range cattle. You name it, it's out there somewhere, waiting for you. All that said, don't fall into the timid trap: don't be so frazzled and fearful about the dangers around the next bend that you ride all day in a state of borderline panic. A tense, nervous rider overreacts and makes poor decisions. Improve your skills until you're comfortable on the bike, then relax and enjoy the ride. A competent rider is a confident rider. And never forget: overall, in spite of the assorted perils, cycling is a relatively safe activity.

THE BIKE

I'm no expert on bikes and would never presume to tell you what kind of bike to ride. I find one I like and stick with it for years, and have only owned a few over a long cycling life. I've made the same progression many other riders have: from steel to titanium to carbon fiber. But I'm not a bike geek, poring over stats or stressing over grams. I just want it to work well, to move me down the road efficiently.

If you're in the market for a bike, and especially if you're new to this and unsure about how to proceed, bear these thoughts in mind. Do your research, of course. Test as many bikes as you can get your hands on and chat with others about their bikes. But above all, find a bike that is compatible with who you are and how you plan to ride. Don't let some racer boy clerk in the bike store talk you into buying an expensive, state-of-the-art racing

Pastoral and peaceful: Butts Canyon Road in Southern Lake County (Ride 13)

bike when all you want to do is ride comfortably at touring speed.

Make sure the bike comes with gearing appropriate to your physical strength and your agenda. These days, compact chain rings are all the rage; two rings of fifty and thirty-four teeth have taken the place of the classic setups of fifty-two or fifty-three and thirty-eight or thirty-nine. Compact chain rings, coupled with the right cluster of cogs in back, allow you to climb almost any hill without blowing a gasket.

Find a saddle that makes your hinder parts happy. Don't shy away from hard, skinny saddles that make you think you'll be sitting on the sharp end of an ax blade. Those saddles may actually be more comfortable, in the long run, than some cushy tractor-seat model. However, if you're just getting started on this voyage of discovery, don't overthink this or try to reinvent the whole deal. Use the saddle that comes on your new bike. It's probably a decent saddle. Only if it proves uncomfortable, after quite a few miles, do you need to contemplate a change.

Once you've found a bike that's right for you, have someone who knows what they're doing give you a bike fitting. It might be included in the purchase price of your bike or it might cost extra, but in either case, you should do it. Sitting on a bike and pedaling, hour after hour, can be effortless and pleasant, or it can be an acute form of torture resulting in long-term injuries. How you're positioned on the bike can make all the difference between those two poles.

Your bike should have two water bottle cages and the bottles that go in them. You should mount a seat bag and carry at least one spare tube, a patch kit, tire iron, and a pump or other mechanism for inflating a tire. Some sort of small, multipurpose tool for minor bike repairs is a good idea too. (Racer wannabes often use itty-bitty seat bags barely big enough for one spare tube. It's a style statement. I prefer one big enough to carry my

tools and tubes, with room left over to stash my vest or arm warmers, so I don't have to stuff them in my jersey pockets.) The point about tools and tubes is: you may be way out in the country, all by yourself, when you get a flat or have a mechanical. You need to be self-sufficient. And for the rare occasions when you can't fix whatever has gone wrong, you should have a cell phone.

One last thought about buying a bike or any other bike gear: Shop locally. Unless you live hours away from a good bike shop, you should forget about the online and catalog buys. Sure, there might be better deals out there in cyberia, but that's a penny-wise, dollar-foolish game. You want to establish a good rapport with the folks in your local shop, and buying your gear there helps keep the shop in business and pays the wages of the skilled mechanics working in the back room...the folks who can make your bike run like a Swiss watch.

Speaking of which, some of you may be adept at your own bike cleaning and maintenance. If you are, good for you and good for your bike. If you're not, you really want a good shop mechanic on your side. Whether you do it yourself or have it done, keep on top of bike maintenance. Your bike will love you for it and repay you with years of delightful riding.

YOU AND YOUR KIT

There is a reason why cyclists dress the way they do: those clothes are designed for the task and work well. Never think of riding more than a few miles in anything but decent cycling shorts with proper padding in the crotch. If you don't believe me, go ahead and try it. Your rear end will very quickly send a mission statement to headquarters, leaving you in no doubt about the discomfort, down there where the sun don't shine. The debate will rage forever between the bib-shorts faction and the waistband-shorts faction. I prefer the latter, but many of my friends swear

One of California's great roads, Highway 1, heads north between Muir Beach and Stinson Beach (Ride 24). (Nancy Yu)

by bibs. The only way you'll figure out which you prefer is to try them both.

Jerseys with pockets in the back make sense. Some jerseys are better than others, but the basic concept is sound. They should be constructed of some miracle fabric that wicks away moisture. Some folks don't wear padded cycling gloves, but I can't imagine riding without them. Arm warmers and knee warmers and wind shell vests are almost essential, at least if you ride when it's nippy in the morning. Undershirts of some wicking material or of merino wool are useful too, as are full tights, a rain jacket, and long-fingered gloves for winter riding. Almost all cyclists wear some sort of eyewear. You'll understand why the first time a bug hits you in the eye. You don't have to break the bank, buying all this gear at the outset. Get a decent pair of shorts and a good jersey and then, over the course of a few rides, let your body tell you what else it needs.

I haven't mentioned two of the most important parts of your bike kit: helmet and shoes. Years ago, none of us wore helmets. Now, the practice is almost universal, and helmet design and fit have improved immensely. I hope there's no debate about this one! I calculated once that I have spent about 14,000 hours on my bike, and of those many hours, I have only needed my helmet twice, for about three seconds each time. But had I not had the helmet on during those two short moments of mayhem, I would quite likely be dead now.

Good cycling shoes won't save your life, but they can certainly improve your life while you're pedaling down the road. Most good shoes connect to the pedals with click-in cleats, a cyclist's version of a ski binding. They may take a little getting used to, but once you're comfortable with them, you'll never want to use anything else. A decent shoe and a good cleat–pedal connection improve both your efficiency and your comfort immeasurably. I suggest you shop for shoes that have the cleat recessed into a rubber sole so that you can walk in the shoes when not on the bike. They may be a tad heavier than pure racing shoes, but unless you're really racing, who cares?

FUELING

Cycling is one of the few sports where eating and drinking are an integral part of the activity. If your ride is long enough and you fail to keep fuel in the tank, you will quite literally run out of gas. It's not pretty when that happens, and no experienced rider wants to go there. So a huge industry has grown up around the process of keeping riders fueled up on their rides, from energy drinks to syrupy gels to fancy (read: expensive) energy bars.

Some people will tell you these nutritional additives are essential on any ride of more than a few miles, but I won't be one of them. I subscribe to a simple philosophy for bike fueling: eat what you normally eat and drink what you normally drink. On shorter rides—up to 40 miles—I usually eat nothing at all. On longer rides, I have a banana or two and a few whole-wheat fig bars, plus, perhaps, whatever munchies seem appealing from a corner store along the route. And I drink only water. I'm not recommending my approach, nor am I trying to shoot the whole sports energy industry in the kneecap. I'm just telling you what I do. On my very hardest rides—a few a year—I do use some of the energy supplements. But most of the time, my fueling is minimalist.

HOW TO USE THIS BOOK

Each ride description begins with a thumbnail summary of that ride, including a rating for level of difficulty, distance, elevation gain, riding time, best seasons, directions to the start, and notes on pavement and traffic. The same information appears in the Rides-at-a-Glance chart in the front of the book.

DISTANCE

Mileage is the only measure here that does not contain some level of subjectivity. This book of seventy-five rides contains twenty-seven under 40 miles, fifteen over 70, and seventy-one between 41 and 70 miles. (Yes, that adds up to well over seventy-five rides. There are nineteen stages on the multiday tours to count, and there are many rides that have longer and shorter options.)

Lying at the center of a web of great biking roads, the town of Tomales is a popular spot for rest stops on North Bay club rides (Ride 22). (Kurt West)

I've attempted to offer a wide spread of rides, with something for everyone. It's a bell curve, with the largest sampling between 45 and 65 miles: rides long enough to give average cyclists a good workout but not to the point of being death marches. And while I personally enjoy long rides, I also appreciate the pleasure of simply cruising along for a handful of miles, enjoying the scenery and chatting with my riding companions. I don't believe a ride needs to be a huge undertaking to be considered a "classic ride" in the context of this book.

ELEVATION

You'd think feet of elevation gain would be as easy to track as miles, but after years of experiments with different altimeters, with GPS and online mapping sites, I've decided this is still a work in progress. (I used to be obsessive about elevation data, but I've backed away from that lately. When my most recent altimeter died last year, I did not upgrade to a newer, fancier model. I replaced it with an old, bare-bones cyclometer I found in my spare-parts bin, and I now only check elevation gain online.) The figures in this book are a melding of past stats collected on rides and the figures generated by the online mapping site ridewithgps.com, but with this caveat: I believe the online figures are inflated by a good deal of "noise," so I dial those numbers back a bit. In the end, I've taken all the data I could find and have shuffled it around and produced my best guesses. I've spent enough time studying this to accept my numbers as plausible, but even so, please take them with a grain of salt. Note that with a few of the flattest rides, I have omitted elevation profiles.

RIDING TIME

Estimating riding time is of course hugely subjective and elastic. Pro racers can average over 30 mph for a 200-K stage and over 25 mph for an entire stage race. But the folks reading this book are unlikely to be riding at that tempo. Our recreational pace is more likely to average around 15 mph, even if we throw in some snappy pace lines in the mid-20s. By the time we add in a couple of coffee breaks or a mid-ride lunch stop, our elapsed times will be considerably longer. I've used 15 mph (or a little above) as the high side for most of these time windows and around 10 mph for the low end.

BEST SEASONS

Time of year is an important consideration. Weather patterns vary widely over Northern California, from the foggy coast to the alpine peaks, with many places in between that will range from well below freezing in the winter to triple digits in the summer. My recommendations are well thought out and generally accurate. But even in my recommended best seasons, the weather can change dramatically from one day to the next or even from one side of a ridge to the other. On the 2012 Terrible Two double century, in mid-June, riders were seeing temperatures on their bike thermometers of over 125 degrees Fahrenheit in some inland canyons around noon, but two hours later, out on the coast, it was closer to 75 degrees. Two hours, 30 miles…50 degrees difference! That was, admittedly, an extraordinary day, but even under more normal conditions, you should not expect one "best season" suggestion to be accurate for every day or throughout many, varied microclimates. Use my guidelines as a starting point, but check the local forecast before heading out.

ROAD CONDITIONS

Pavement and traffic vary even more than the weather. I may occasionally note that the pavement will be good and traffic will be light all day, but more commonly, any given ride will be a mix of good and bad: silk-smooth paving, then patches and potholes; quiet back roads, then a busy highway.

I do try to avoid high-traffic roads. No one likes traffic. But cars and trucks and RVs are

Heading north toward historic Pierce Ranch in Point Reyes National Seashore (Ride 21) (Nancy Yu)

all part of our cycling world, and if we have to mingle with them to get where we need to go, we will do so. You cannot be terrified of traffic and enjoy cycling. Sooner or later, you have to make your peace with it. I believe all cycling—heck, all of living, really—is predicated on the assumption of some level of risk, be it from traffic or from potholes or gravel on a funky old road. I expect you, the reader/rider, to be willing to accept and manage that risk.

GETTING THERE

In these days of easy-to-use mapping programs on your phone or in your car, you may not need these directions. But we're listing them anyway, and their most important information may not be how to get there

but where to park your car when you arrive. I favor parking lots at schools and parks, although in some small towns, things are so relaxed you can park anywhere.

DIFFICULTY

Rating difficulty is perhaps the most subjective yardstick of all. One person's moderate ride will be another person's monster sufferfest. With that in mind, I will try to define the terms used to rate the challenge of each ride. Difficulty is not simply defined by distance. Climbing is a factor too, and the steepness of the grades may be more crucial than simple elevation gain. A half mile at over 12 percent will feel harder than 3 miles at 4 percent. In some respects, these ratings also define a mindset: the more challenging rides assume a more robust, experienced, self-reliant approach. It doesn't mean you have to be a hard-core warrior to tackle them, but you have to at least be ready for whatever the day may bring.

» **Easy** rides are usually under 25 miles, nearly flat, and run in parks or on bike paths, away from traffic. There are exceptions to these standards, but that's my guiding premise. I won't say that all Easy rides are suitable for children or absolute beginners. Some are; some aren't.

» **Moderate** rides are usually under 45 miles, but not all rides of that distance are Moderate. In general, this level assumes a rider has some experience and at least decent fitness and a comfortable attitude about climbing (and descending).

» **Challenging** rides are for self-sufficient, fit, experienced riders. They will be hilly and possibly remote. Mileage varies from 40 to 70, but again, distance is only part of the equation: climbing will be significant as well. You don't have to be fast to do the harder rides. These are not races. You just have to be fit and competent.

» **Epic** rides are really just Challenging rides on steroids. They will appeal to the same riders, and the only difference might be an increase in the level of preparedness ahead of time and energy management during the ride. They will be long and the climbing will be extensive and often steep. There are only three century-length rides in the book, but they are all hard rides...definitely *not* entry-level centuries. In general, if you see the Epic tag on one of these rides, you can be sure you're in for a serious day.

Many rides are listed as "Moderate/Challenging" or "Challenging/Epic." In some cases, this reflects longer and shorter options, one at each level. In other cases, with just one distance listed, it means the ride falls in between those ratings.

A NOTE ABOUT SAFETY

Safety is an important concern in all outdoor activities. No guidebook can alert you to every hazard or anticipate the limitations of every reader. Therefore, the descriptions of roads, trails, routes, and natural features in this book are not representations that a particular place or excursion will be safe for your party. When you follow any of the routes described in this book, you assume responsibility for your own safety. Under normal conditions, such excursions require the usual attention to traffic, road and trail conditions, weather, terrain, the capabilities of your party, and other factors. Keeping informed on current conditions and exercising common sense are the keys to a safe, enjoyable outing.

—*Mountaineers Books*

NORTHWEST

Redwood groves as magnificent as any cathedral; three hundred miles of rugged coastline; vast tracts of wilderness, carved into deep canyons by wild rivers; remote ranches running sheep and dairy herds…this is the northwest corner of California. Cities, people, and paved roads are all in short supply. But what roads there are lead to great cycling adventures.

1 LUNCH IN FERNDALE

Difficulty:	Moderate
Time:	2 to 4 hours
Distance:	30 miles
Elevation gain:	1500'
Best seasons:	All year, although November through April may be rainy
Road conditions:	Most roads are low traffic. Pavement varies.

GETTING THERE: From downtown Eureka, take Hwy 101 south approximately 8 miles to the College of the Redwoods exit (exit 698). Follow the off-ramp to a right on Tompkins Hill Rd. and proceed to the entrance to the college, approximately 1 mile from Hwy 101.

If 18 miles to Ferndale (including one stiff climb) doesn't seem like enough work to whet your appetite for lunch, consider starting from downtown Eureka, following the route of Stage 3 on our California Coast multiday tour (Ride 74) to the point where this route begins. That would add 10 miles each way for a 50-mile day.

The goal today—the big payoff—is the village of Ferndale. But with any bike ride, it's as much about the journey as it is about arriving, so let's talk about how to get there. The first 7 miles head south along Tompkins Hill Road, a small highway—flat, smooth,

and straight—for the first 2 miles. Then it hits a couple of miles of lumpy rollers, and at mile 4, a steep climb: 650' up in 1.5 miles, averaging 8 percent with a few spots up into the low teens. That'll get your heart rate up! This ride would be considered "Easy" except for this climb.

Tompkins Hill begins in the flat, verdant dairy lands near the Eel River. Most of the climb bends back and forth across open, grassy hillsides, with some nice views across the valley. Scattered groves of fir and broadleaf trees appear at the higher elevations. While the quality of the road becomes increasingly

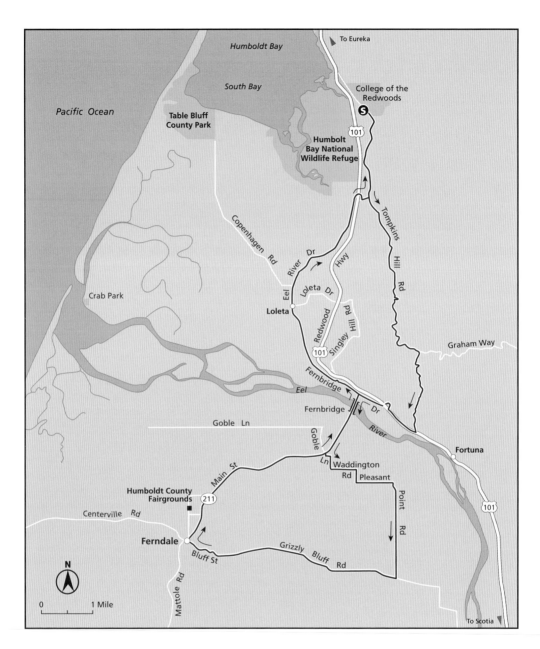

funky on the climb, things are marginally better on the 2-mile descent off the south side of the ridge as the single lane widens and the pavement improves, making for a reasonably smooth, frisky downhill.

The descent ends smack up against Highway 101 and you have to zoom up the on-ramp onto the freeway, but only for half a mile to the next exit, to Fernbridge and Ferndale. (This is allowed and there are wide shoulders.) Fernbridge Drive leads to Fernbridge, that is, the bridge of that name, crossing the Eel River. Built in 1911, it is a handsome span, now a protected historic structure. However,

The entire town of Ferndale is a California Historical Landmark because of its many spectacular Victorian structures. (Nancy Yu)

nobody took bikes into account when they built it, and the lanes are narrow for the half-mile crossing, with no shoulders. But cyclists and motorists have, for the most part, learned to share this old relic.

Rather than taking this main road into Ferndale, we'll sneak up on the town via a series of dinky roads out across the pastures east of town. Turn left onto Goble Lane at mile 9.9, just after crossing the bridge, and follow the route for 8 miles to the backdoor entrance to town.

Ferndale has been the hub and heartbeat of the Eel River agricultural region for 150 years. Much of the town was built during the latter half of the nineteenth century, and the commercial buildings on the main streets of town are almost all superb examples of the best Victorian architecture of the era. So too are many of the houses—both modest and grand—that line the neighborhood streets. Somehow, the town escaped most of the dubious benefits of progress in the twentieth century. Then, in the 1960s and '70s, the locals looked around at their beautiful village and realized they were living in a time-capsule treasure. Steps were taken to ensure that it would stay this pretty and unspoiled forever. And so far it has, with the entire town now registered as a California Historical Landmark. Although most of the downtown businesses now make their living off tourists and every third house on the quiet side streets seems to be a B&B, Ferndale remains a pleasant, low-key village, with locals still outnumbering visitors.

There are a number of good spots for lunch along Main Street. Find one, kick back, and soak up the town's charm. After lunch, head out the other end of town on the main drag, back toward the old bridge over the river. Now go left (north) on Fernbridge Drive. Turn left onto Eel River Drive and roll through the pastures, past the little town of Loleta. Just beyond the town, the road tilts up into an easy climb: 250' in a bit less than a mile. It wouldn't look like much of a hill at all except that everything else around here is as flat (and green) as a billiard table. There's a mile-long descent off the other side of this little bump and then just 2.5 flat miles to the finish, unless you're riding back to Eureka.

Starting at the college or in Eureka... either way, it's a nice ride. The butch climb over Tompkins Hill makes it feel as if you've really done something, and the visit to quaint, picturesque Ferndale wraps the ride up in a big, elaborate Victorian ribbon.

MILEAGE LOG

0.0	From College of the Redwoods driveway, left on Tompkins Hill Rd.
5.6	Summit
7.2	Right on Hwy 101
7.7	Exit toward Fernbridge Dr.
8.6	Left over Eel River on Fernbridge (Hwy 211)
9.9	Left on Goble Ln.
10.0	Right on Waddington Rd.
11.0	Left on Pleasant Point Rd.
13.7	Right on Grizzly Bluff Rd.
17.1	Bear left on Bluff St.
17.9	Right on Main St. (Hwy 211); downtown Ferndale (lunch)
18.0	After lunch, continue on Hwy 211 out of town, back over Fernbridge
22.7	Left on Fernbridge Dr.
23.2	Left on Eel River Dr.
25.0	Pass town of Loleta
27.9	Cross Hwy 101 on overpass to left on Hookton Rd.
28.0	Left on Tompkins Hill Rd.
29.9	Right into College of the Redwoods and finish

2 TOUR OF THE UNKNOWN COAST

Difficulty:	Epic
Time:	6.5 to 10 hours
Distance:	98 miles
Elevation gain:	8700'
Best seasons:	May through October
Road conditions:	Everything from freeway shoulders to town streets to remote country roads. Pavement varies from excellent to poor.

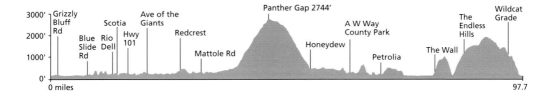

GETTING THERE: From Eureka, head south on Hwy 101 approximately 14 miles to the Fernbridge, Ferndale exit. Turn right (south) on Hwy 211 and drive 3.8 miles to a right on Van Ness Ave. Turn left on 5th St. and left again into the Humboldt County Fairgrounds. Or continue straight on Hwy 211 into Ferndale if you are staying in town.

One of my favorite centuries in California is the Tour of the Unknown Coast (TUC), held each year in May, starting and finishing in the historic village of Ferndale, south of Eureka. For several years, I created the graphics for the event. As part of my compensation each year, I was given an entry in the ride and a weekend at one of the best B&Bs in town, the Gingerbread Mansion. I came to know the town and the ride well over those years, and I've been a big fan ever since.

The charming town is at least part of the attraction with this ride. (For more about Ferndale, see Ride 1.) The TUC promoters like to call this big ride the hardest century in the state. I don't know if it's the hardest, but it's a challenge, for sure, and it might be the most beautiful. It visits one of the only sections of California coast without a major highway nearby, hence the name Unknown Coast.

The ride begins at the fairgrounds because that's where the official century begins, but you could start anywhere in town. Head east and south out of town, starting with 7 miles across flat pastures on Grizzly Bluff Road and 4 miles of small hills through the woods next to the Eel River on Blue Slide Road. Mile 13 finds you in the town of Rio Dell, heading for a crossing of the river and a transit of the curious town of Scotia. This is a classic old company town built around the massive Pacific Lumber Company mills. Follow Main Street through town and jump onto the wide shoulder of Highway 101 South.

After 4 miles, leave the highway at the Pepperwood exit and head south along the Avenue of the Giants, the scenic byway through Redwood National Park, amid the tallest trees on Earth. There are several waysides for stopping and communing with these paragons of the plant world. The town of Redcrest comes up at mile 27, the last spot for food and fluids for another 27 miles.

At mile 31, the Avenue of the Giants bears left, but you bear right on Mattole Road, following the sign to Honeydew. A long, gentle climb through deep forest in Bull Creek Basin leads to the first serious climb of the day: 2400' in 7 miles to 2744' Panther Gap, an average grade of more than 6 percent. It's a long, medium-hard slog, up out of the redwoods into broadleaf forest and out across open hillsides. I don't think the summit is marked, but you'll know when you're on the other side of the ridge, beginning with 3 miles of gentle downhill and then more than 5 fast miles snaking down into the lovely, remote valley of the Mattole River. All that lively diving ends at an old, wooden-deck bridge and a turn past the Honeydew store at mile 53.4.

Beyond Honeydew, the road heads northwest along the valley of the river, winding its way downstream toward the tiny town of Petrolia—downstream, but not always downhill. There are a few small climbs along this stretch, two of which are a mile long and 400' high.

If you're attracted to this remote, beautiful loop but feel such a big ride is more than you want, consider turning it into a two-day tour. If you can figure out how to transport camping gear out here, there is a nice county campground at mile 61.5, with a good swimming hole in the river. And there is one inn out here too, in Petrolia: the Petrolia Guest House. The town of Petrolia offers one last chance for food and water at about mile 68. After that, the second of those 1-mile climbs clears the last coastal ridge before an easy 3-mile descent to the beach… the real unknown coast.

The road runs north along the empty, pristine (but sometimes windswept) beach for 6 miles before clambering back over the ridge on a climb notorious in the lore of the century ride: the Wall. It climbs 800' in 1.5 miles, a 10 percent average, but there are spots well above 15 percent. It's fierce. Another mile of uphill stair steps leads to a descent that is even steeper than the Wall: almost 1000' down the rabbit hole in 1.5 miles (12 percent). This wild plunge bottoms out in the valley of the

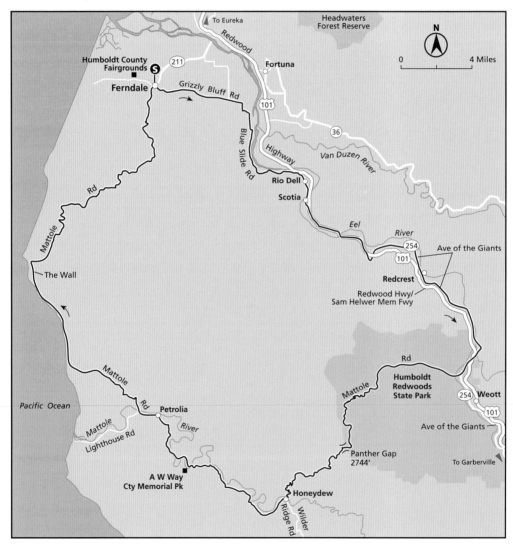

Bear River, and then you have to confront the last climbs of the day, what the century organizers call the Endless Hills: first, 1400' up in 4 miles, then 1 flat mile, and finally 400' up in another 1.5-mile pitch. None of it is brutal, but it can feel endless, late in the day.

At long last, a summit of sorts is crossed, and you can look forward to 7 miles of mostly downhill dancing on Wildcat Grade, all the way back to Ferndale. There are several dips and uphill blips in there too, but most of the time, it's rip city. Once this wild descent ends, all that's left is the run back to the fairgrounds or to your lodgings in the town. Now your only challenge is figuring out which of the restaurants in this charming village is going to be given the job of replenishing all those calories you burned up today.

MILEAGE LOG

0.0	From Humboldt County Fairgrounds, left (south) on 5th St.
0.7	Left on Bluff St.
1.6	Right on Grizzly Bluff Rd.; becomes Blue Slide Rd., then Belleview Ave.
13.1	Right on Wildwood Ave., town of Rio Dell
14.0	Cross Eel River to Main St., town of Scotia
16.0	Jog left, then right to head south on Hwy 101
20.0	Take exit 674, follow sign to Pepperwood and Ave. of the Giants
20.2	Left under highway on Ave. of the Giants (Hwy 254)

Long and sometimes steep climbs, including the Wall above Cape Mendocino, make this loop a very big challenge. (Bill Bushnell)

26.9	Town of Redcrest
31.1	Right on Mattole Rd.; follow sign to Honeydew; Redwoods scenic waysides at miles 32.4 and 35.5
45.0	Panther Gap summit (2744')
53.4	Left to stay on Mattole Rd.; Honeydew store
61.5	A. W. Way County Memorial Park and campground
67.9	Town of Petrolia; Petrolia Guest House
97.0	Jog right on Ocean Ave. to left on 5th St.
97.7	Finish at Humboldt County Fairgrounds

3 HAYFORK–WILDWOOD LOOP

Difficulty:	Challenging
Time:	3 to 4 hours
Distance:	46 miles
Elevation gain:	3800'
Best seasons:	Late spring and early fall
Road conditions:	Some highway miles may be busy, but most roads are quiet; pavement is good.

GETTING THERE: From I-5 at Red Bluff, take Hwy 36 west 54 miles to the Wildwood Rd. junction. Park in the Wildwood Store lot.

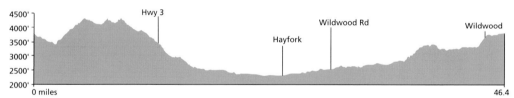

I led a club tour through this remote region a few years ago, riding on highways 3 and 36. Everyone liked the route, but we missed Wildwood Road, one part of this loop. I didn't know the road at the time. Now that I do know it, I've combined it with our old tour miles, creating a nice, mid-size loop with a moderate level of challenge, exploring a (mostly) pristine mountain wilderness.

I begin the loop at the Hwy 36/Wildwood Road junction because this is the nearest point to the outside world, Red Bluff and Interstate 5, with a large parking lot in front of the Wildwood Store. But you could just as easily start on Hwy 3 in the town of Hayfork, near Weaverville.

Starting from Wildwood, you get the worst of the climbing checked off in the early miles. After a 2-mile descent, Hwy 36 tilts uphill for 900' in 3 miles. That's a little over 5 percent and is an accurate measure of what to expect: a steady grind, but never a leg-breaker. Over the top, the next 4 miles bounce along the ridgeline, with two more half-mile climbs and the balance either level or mildly downhill, all amid handsome fir and madrone forest, with

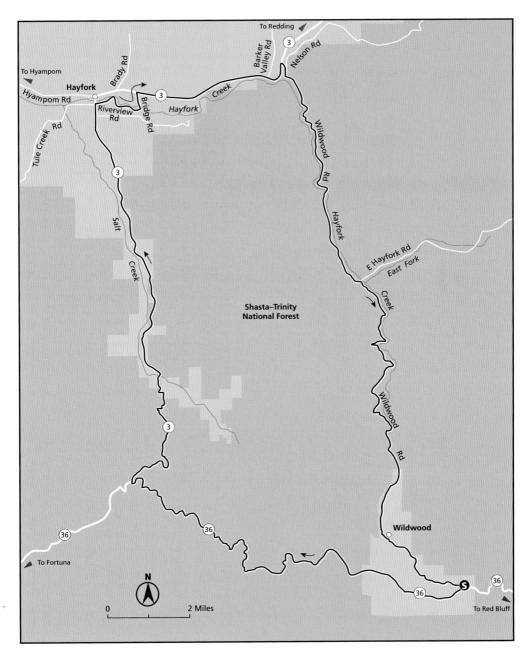

To Redding

To Hyampom

Hayfork

Brady Rd

Hyampom Rd

Riverview Rd

Bridge Rd

Hayfork Creek

Barker Valley Rd

Nelson Rd

3

3

3

Tule Creek Rd

Salt Creek

Wildwood Rd

Hayfork

E Hayfork Rd

East Fork

Creek

Shasta–Trinity
National Forest

3

Wildwood Rd

Wildwood

36

36

36

36

36

S

To Fortuna

To Red Bluff

N

0   2 Miles

a good sampling of rocky outcrops thrown in. Hwy 36 is a useful connector between I-5 at Red Bluff and Hwy 101 at Fortuna, so it will have some traffic; you won't have it all to yourself. But my impression from past visits is that it will be tolerable.

By mile 9, the ridge-running is over and you grab onto 7 miles of lively downhill excitement, carving around one curve after another, all on good pavement. Other than two flats, it's mostly fast fun. The first 3 miles are on Hwy 36, and then you sweep around

Wildwood Road: quiet, pretty, and remote...made to order for back-road biking.

a corner onto Hwy 3 and keep dropping for another 4 miles into a pretty valley along Salt Creek. At the bottom of the descent, the valley opens up and meadows appear along the left side of the road. For 7 miles, you roll down the valley, through the trees, on a lazy, slightly downhill run.

When you start seeing homes and ranch compounds, instead of true wilderness, you'll know you're approaching the town of Hayfork, just at the midpoint of the ride. Hayfork is a rusticated, unsophisticated backwater, and its main drag, straggling along the highway for 3 miles, is not exactly picture-postcard material. I've plotted a bypass around most of the town on a couple of quiet side roads. You pass the high school on this detour, a possible spot for water. The town's biggest market—Hayfork Discount—is on Hwy 3 on the far side of town, after the route returns to the highway (so you won't miss it if you're in need of chow).

Beyond the market, back in the country, 3 more level miles along Hwy 3 bring you to a right turn onto Wildwood Road and the run south to the finish. Wildwood is a wonderful

cycling road: almost 18 miles long, meandering through a deep wilderness of fir, pine, and oak forest, almost always near Hayfork Creek. It carries so little traffic, you have to wonder why it's even here. And yet, for all that remoteness, it is nicely paved. It includes two moderate climbs of 3 miles and 1 mile, and the balance is rollers or mild uphill (almost flat). Sometimes the seemingly endless colonnades of forest trees back away to the nearest ridge and leave the road tracking across open, cattle-cropped meadows. It's beautiful, peaceful, and empty. The miles on Hwy 36 are good; the miles on Hwy 3 are better. But the miles on Wildwood are the best.

The tiny hamlet of Wildwood pops up at about mile 44. It's so small, it makes Hayfork look like a big city. If there are any public services besides the post office, I missed them. But 3 miles farther south, the Wildwood Store sits at the end of the road, and it's nice to know it's here at the end of the ride, with big coolers full of chilled beverages and ice cream bars, and shelves full of chips: all the basic food groups.

0.0	West on Hwy 36
12.1	Right on Hwy 3
23.1	Right on Riverview Rd. (bypass around Hayfork)
24.5	Left on Bridge Rd.; Valley High School (water) at 24.7
24.9	Right on Hwy 3; Hayfork Discount (store) at 25.5
28.8	Right on Wildwood Rd.
43.7	Town of Wildwood
46.4	Finish at Hwy 36 junction; Wildwood Store

4   MENDOCINO MEANDERING

Difficulty:	Moderate/challenging
Time:	4 to 6 hours (long route)
Distance:	20, 46, 64 miles
Elevation gain:	1600' to 5400'
Best seasons:	All year, although winter may be rainy
Road conditions:	Pavement varies from excellent to mediocre. Traffic may be busy on Hwy 1 and Hwy 128. Back roads will be quiet.

GETTING THERE: Most visitors approach Mendocino from the south on Hwy 1, approximately 3 hours from Santa Rosa. From Hwy 1, head west into Mendocino on Main St. Park anywhere.

This ride offers three loops of increasing distance and climbing challenge. All stage out of the iconic village of Mendocino, and the town is as much an attraction today as any of the backcountry bike miles.

Mendocino prospered in the nineteenth century, with lumber and fishing paying the bills. It slumbered for many decades before finding a second wind as an artists' colony in the latter half of the twentieth century. It was a feisty bohemian enclave in the sixties, but more recently, since becoming a trendy mecca for the rich and famous, it has become too precious and pricey for starving artists to actually live here anymore. They've mostly decamped to the hills or up the highway to more affordable Fort Bragg.

All three loops begin by heading south on Highway 1, but there is one little detour almost immediately: turn right on Brewery Gulch Road, just after crossing the bridge over the Big River. Put a foot down and look back north across the cove to Mendocino. Seldom has a town been more advantageously situated for having its picture taken, with the elegant, spare Victorians along the front rank of Main Street standing shoulder to shoulder, facing out to sea, like a row of wedding cakes in a baker's window.

Brewery Gulch provides a half-mile detour after the view, and then you settle in for a run south on Hwy 1. The highway along the bluffs above the ocean is by no means flat. It dips into and climbs out of several coves

Mendocino: picturesque, bohemian, trendy, charming, and a perfect spot to begin and end a ride. (Jef Poskanzer)

and arroyos in the 10-mile run down to the Navarro River.

The shortest of these routes diverges early and cuts northeast on little roads through the woods near the town of Albion. The middle route departs at the Navarro River, heading inland on Hwy 128, next to the river.

The longest loop crosses the river and begins a 6-mile, 1100' climb, first with 1 more mile on Hwy 1 and then with 5 miles on remote

Cameron Road, amid dense forest and banks of native rhododendron. At the top of Cameron, turn left on Philo–Greenwood Road. This hilly road tumbles along a high, forested ridgeline, constantly tilting up or down. There are at least ten mini-summits between miles 17 and 29, adding up to over 1500' of gain, but also including numerous short descents. Finally, one last descent turns into the real deal, dropping 1200' to the Navarro

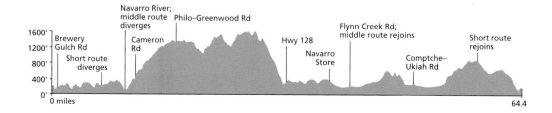

River in 3 hectic miles. After crossing the river on an elderly, one-lane bridge, climb briefly and turn north on Hwy 128, where 6 miles of jumbo rollers through vineyards and orchards lead to the Navarro Store at mile 38, your first shot at food since early in the ride.

After the store, the road settles into an easy run through the redwoods to Flynn Creek Road, where the middle route rejoins after its level cruise upstream along the Navarro River. Flynn Creek Road is a quiet byway with minimal traffic and pleasant, woodsy scenery. It gains 500' in a series of small pitches along its namesake creek, interspersed

with little descents. The last descent ends at the Comptche–Ukiah Road junction. Turn left here and head for the coast. Just west of Comptche, the road drops a bit and settles in alongside the Albion River for a few almost level miles. All of this country is remote, quiet, and pretty...little streams and big trees, lovely valleys and lonely farms.

At mile 52, the road bends up and away from the Albion River in a series of short climbs, up out of that river drainage and down the other side of the ridge into the Big River watershed. This is a superb stretch for cycling, and it only gets better as you begin

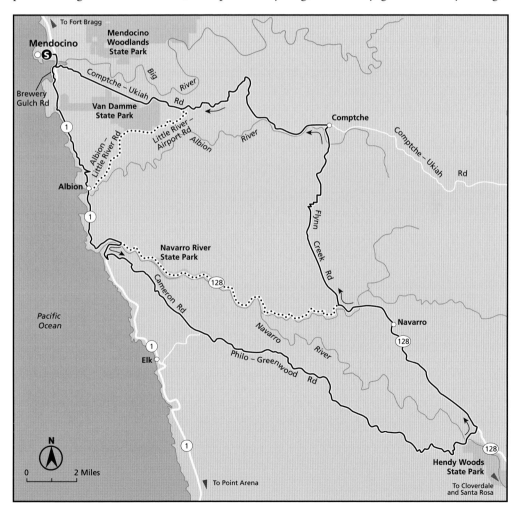

the descent toward the coast and Mendocino. Over the final 6 miles, you drop 900', with 1 mile of gentle uphill in the middle. It's a fun descent, with enough slinky bends to keep it entertaining, but not so steep or tricky that you can't spare a glance at the beautiful river in the canyon on your right, and—teasing glimpses through the trees—the enchanting sight of Mendocino, shining white in the sun, on its bluff overlooking the ocean.

Head back into Mendocino, park the bike, and begin the balance of your day: exploring the charming town. In spite of its reputation as "Spendocino," it's still a wonderful place to visit and be a tourist. Those in control have made sure they didn't kill the goose laying all the golden eggs; anyone seeking fast-food franchises or outlet malls must look elsewhere. Here, everything is tastefully in character with the pioneer Victorian heritage of the town, with an indulgent nod to the bohemian ambience that gives it that creative panache. Best of all for cyclists, there is no shortage of cafés and watering holes for a post-ride refresher.

MILEAGE LOG

0.0	East on Main St.
0.2	Right on Hwy 1
0.8	Right on Brewery Gulch Rd.
1.3	Right on Hwy 1
6.8	Short route diverges left on Albion–Little River Rd.; other routes stay on Hwy 1

Short route:

6.8	**Left on Albion–Little River Rd.**
10.0	**Bear right on Little River–Airport Rd.**
13.2	**Left on Comptche–Ukiah Rd.; rejoin other routes (see mile 57.9)**

10.5	Middle route diverges left on Hwy 128; long route stays on Hwy 1

Middle route:

10.5	**Straight on Hwy 128 before bridge across Navarro River**
22.1	**Left on Flynn Creek Rd.; rejoin long route (see mile 40.8)**

11.5	Left on Cameron Rd.
17.2	Left on Philo–Greenwood Rd.
32.3	Left on Hwy 128
38.0	Navarro Store
40.8	Right on Flynn Creek Rd.; middle route rejoins
49.2	Left on Comptche–Ukiah Rd.; Comptche Store
57.9	Short route rejoins
63.7	Right on Hwy 1
64.2	Left on Main St., into Mendocino
64.4	Finish

NORTHEAST

In this most remote, least populated corner of Northern California, over half of the region lies within national forests. Mount Shasta (14,162') and the rugged peaks of Lassen Volcanic National Park mark the southern tail of the Cascades, while to the east lies a vast, arid emptiness of plateau, prairie, pine forest, and rangeland. Biking here is a beautiful journey to the far side of nowhere.

5   TULE LAKE–LAVA BEDS NATIONAL MONUMENT

Difficulty:	Moderate
Time:	4 to 6 hours
Distance:	54 miles
Elevation gain:	1500'
Best seasons:	May through October
Road conditions:	Most roads are low traffic. Pavement varies.

GETTING THERE: From Hwy 97 at the Oregon border, take Hwy 161 east for 19.4 miles to Hwy 139. Drive 3.6 miles south on Hwy 139 to town of Tulelake. Turn right on Main St. and follow it 0.6 mile to the high school.

The phrase "out in the tulies" means being off in the middle of nowhere, about as far from civilization as you can be. Whoever coined the term may well have had Tule Lake in mind. Not only is the lake home to the tule grasses mentioned in the phrase, it is indisputably off in the middle of nowhere. Just 3 miles south of the Oregon border and even farther from a city or an interstate or much of anything else, it is certainly the most remote venue for a ride in this book. Which begs the question: why would anyone come all the way out here to do a ride? The answer: Lava Beds National Monument, a geological wonderland just a few miles south of the lake (and the nearby town of Tulelake). This is a ride in two parts, each with distinctly different characters: a nearly flat circuit around Tule Lake (33 miles), and an out-and-back exploration of Lava Beds National Monument (21 miles).

The ride begins in Tulelake and heads south along Highway 139. These first miles are the least interesting of the ride, over with quickly. Once you turn off onto the little roads (County Roads 111 and 120) that circle the lake, things improve.

Tule Lake and the patchwork quilt of farm fields around it are within the boundaries of a national wildlife refuge, an important stopover on the flyway for migratory birds. Geese and swans and other winged travelers use the lake and the leftover grain in the fields for refueling on their long journeys. The land around the lake is nearly table flat, with only a few rollers here and there to break things up. There are almost no trees, aside from a few cottonwoods and other shade or windbreak trees around the few farm compounds.

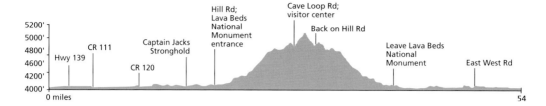

Any flat fields not given over to agriculture are covered in sage or other low scrub. The horizon is limitless.

That changes as you turn away from the lake and head south on Hill Road into the national monument at mile 19. Great masses of volcanic rock begin to dominate the landscape, and the road begins lumping up and down over these chunky lava flows. In the 9 miles between the park entrance and the

Rock, rock, and more rock in this volcanic wonderland…the most remote ride in the book (Kathy Oetinger)

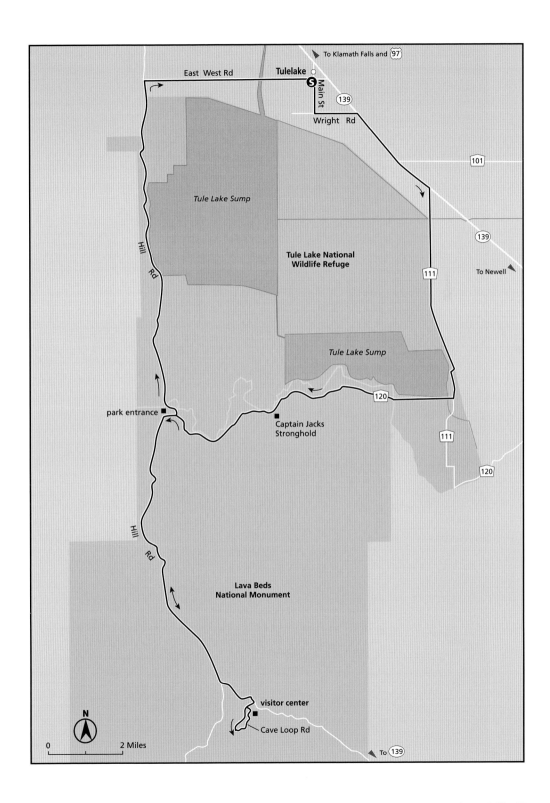

To Klamath Falls and (97)

East West Rd

Tulelake

S

Main St

(139)

Wright Rd

(101)

Tule Lake Sump

Tule Lake National
Wildlife Refuge

(139)

111

To Newell

Hill Rd

Tule Lake Sump

120

park entrance

Captain Jacks
Stronghold

111

120

Hill Rd

Lava Beds
National Monument

visitor center

Cave Loop Rd

N

0   2 Miles

To (139)

highest point of the ride, you will gain over 1000' in a series of pitches. This lava-covered landscape is here because of the many eruptions of the Medicine Lake shield volcano to the south. While it is considered dormant now, the last eruption was only 1100 years ago, a blink in geologic time. The landscape looks bleakly beautiful, rugged and raw in a primordial way, unlike anything else visited on rides in this book.

Turn right at mile 28 onto Cave Loop Road, which visits some of the park's most interesting attractions—its caves. The overlapping lava flows are honeycombed with lava tube caves. So far, over seven hundred of them have been discovered, the densest concentration of caves in the United States. To explore the caves, you'll need sturdy shoes and a flashlight, and a change of clothes. You can either park your car at the nearby visitor center (worth a visit) and modify the ride accordingly, or drive back from Tulelake after the ride. Either way, allow time for a little caving.

The visitor center will also give you an opportunity to learn about the Modoc Indians, the region's first inhabitants. They were forced off their land by settlers, but did not go quietly, and the famous Modoc War of the 1870s is well documented at the center. Captain Jacks Stronghold, which you passed on CR 120 at mile 15.6, is the site of the most important battle of that conflict.

After Cave Loop Road, return north on Hill Road, descending through the lava fields and on along the west side of the lake. Here, the road runs between the lakeshore and a massive, humpback bluff rising up along the west side of the road. This part of the landscape is definitely not flat! Turning east across the top of the lake, now closing the loop back to Tulelake, you leave the bluff and any other hilly topography behind and head out into the farm fields. East West Road is as flat as a frypan and as straight as a ruler—a classic, western American geography of roads and fields platted out along section lines.

The town of Tulelake is not exactly a booming, sophisticated metropolis. You're not going to find trendy bistros or cafés serving up mochas here. But there is a classic burgers-and-fries drive-in on Main Street, and that might be just the ticket after a ride through this far-off corner of the state.

MILEAGE LOG

0.0	From school parking lot, south on Main St.
0.2	Left on Wright Rd.
1.8	Right on Hwy 139 S.
4.6	Right on CR 111; follow signs to Lava Beds National Monument
10.3	Right on CR 120
15.6	Captain Jacks Stronghold historical site
18.9	Bear left on Hill Rd., through national monument entrance
28.1	Right on Cave Loop Rd.
28.2	Visitor center (water)
29.3	Highest point on Cave Loop Rd.
30.4	Left on Hill Rd.; retrace route out of national monument
39.7	Left to stay on Hill Rd.; leave national monument
49.1	Right on E. West Rd.
53.6	Right on Main St.; town of Tulelake
54.0	Finish at school parking lot

6 FALL RIVER LOOP

Difficulty:	Moderate/challenging
Time:	4 to 6 hours
Distance:	61 miles
Elevation gain:	2500'
Best seasons:	May to October
Road conditions:	Most roads are low traffic. Pavement is good.

GETTING THERE: From I-5 at Redding, drive 70 miles east on Hwy 299 to the town of McArthur. Turn left on Grove St. and proceed one block to the Inter-Mountain Fairgrounds.

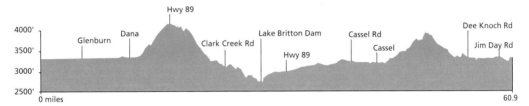

The Fall River Valley is a wonderful little treasure, dozing peacefully off in the middle of nowhere, 60 miles southeast of majestic Mount Shasta. The Pit River and Fall River—both prime fly-fishing waters—flow lazily through the valley, where the acres not given over to cattle ranches are planted in fragrant fields of peppermint. It's home to bald eagles, osprey, hawks, and sandhill cranes, all of which can be seen along this route. Cyclists can be spotted here too, from time to time. They run a nice century up here in July, and this loop is carved out of the best parts of that ride, including the start/finish at the fairgrounds.

From the fairgrounds, head west and north along McArthur Road. For the first 12 miles, it stays as close to level as anything in the mountains can, as it wanders across the flat, fertile valley. After that, the road ramps up into a 4-mile grade climbing out of the valley to a forested tableland, where it tees into Highway 89. This climb is never difficult,

always an easy grade. Turn left on Hwy 89 and head south. The highway is almost level for 2 miles before sloping downhill for 5 fast miles on a grade of around 6 percent. This stretch has recently been repaved and is now smooth as silk and is the fastest descent on the ride.

At the bottom of the hill, watch for a right turn on little Clark Creek Road. This delightful detour off Hwy 89 wraps around the perimeter of McArthur–Burney Falls State Park and Lake Britton, a large reservoir impounding the waters of the Pit River, Hat Creek, and Burney Creek. Clark Creek climbs briefly—offering nice views over the lake—and then launches into a snappy descent. It starts out gradually but soon becomes steep and twisty for most of 3 miles. The descent ends in a level run along the shore of the lake, including riding across the top of Lake Britton Dam, an interesting Art Deco–style structure built in the 1920s. After the dam, there is an easy 1-mile climb,

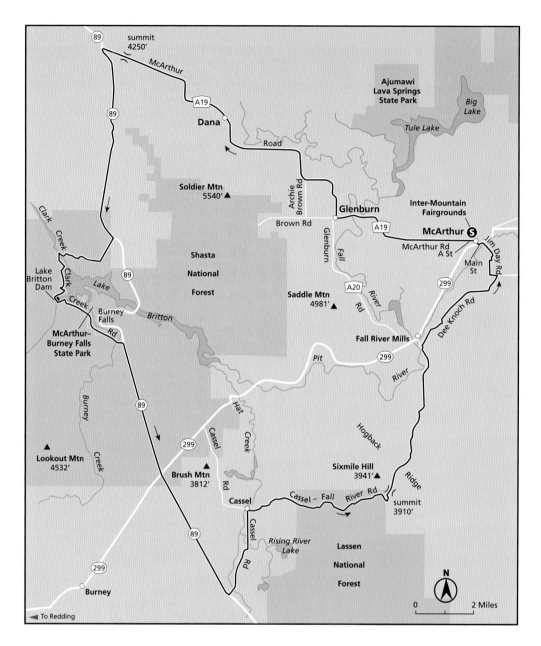

and after another couple of level miles, the road returns to Hwy 89.

Turn right on Hwy 89 and head south for 9 miles. This is the least interesting portion of the ride. The highway is arrow straight and nearly flat, with nothing for scenery but walls of fir and pine.

But things will improve as soon as you turn left onto Cassel Road. For the rest of the ride, you'll be on quiet back roads undulating over constantly changing terrain. Moderately challenging climbs and wiggly descents are mixed together with large helpings of rollers and dipsy-doodles, sometimes in a pretty

A mirror-smooth pond on the Rising River is typical of the scenery on this quiet loop. (Robin Dean)

forest of mixed hardwoods and firs and sometimes out across sprawling meadows. It's a landscape into which bikes fit comfortably. There is a spot I love on Cassel Road where it crosses the Rising River, a tributary of Hat Creek: the waters are backed up in a little mirror-smooth pond near a country home, and the setting of pond and home is so pretty...I always stop or at least slow down here to take in the beautiful picture.

After passing through the one-store town of Cassel and turning right on Cassel–Fall River Road, you begin a mostly uphill section known as Sixmile Hill. This ascent has a few steep pitches that will get most riders out of the saddle, if only briefly. The last half-mile is the steepest, perhaps touching 10 percent, before the road tops out along Hogback Ridge, where the views off the hilltop are quite expansive and grand.

As is only fair, the payoff after the climb is an entertaining descent. It isn't all downhill, all the time—the descent is much like the climb that preceded it: a mix of ups and downs— but there is more down than up for a while. While you descend, spare a glance to your left for pretty vistas over the wild Pit River, down in its rocky canyon below the road.

Right at the bottom of this mostly downhill run, turn right on Dee Knoch Road. (If you cross a bridge and roll up into the town of Fall River Mills, you missed the turn.) Dee Knoch is a pleasant, pretty lane. It skirts a wide meadow, often in sight of an old meandering irrigation canal known as the Knoch Ditch. The road is up along the high rim of the meadow, and there are pretty views spilling away to the north, all down the length of the valley, with the Pit River in the middle distance.

Just before mile 59, the road comes to a T, with more of Dee Knoch bearing off to the right and Jim Day Road turning left. Take Jim Day and roll downhill to a crossing of the Pit River, then uphill into the town of McArthur, back to the fairgrounds. And that'll do it: a simple but highly entertaining loop around a lovely, peaceful region.

MILEAGE LOG

0.0	Right on A St.; leave fairgrounds; becomes McArthur Rd.
5.1	Right in town of Glenburn to stay on McArthur Rd.
17.0	Left on Hwy 89
23.9	Right on Clark Creek Rd.
28.1	Cross Lake Britton Dam
31.5	Right on Hwy 89
35.7	Cross Hwy 299
40.6	Left on Cassel Rd.
43.7	Right on Cassel–Fall River Rd.; town of Cassel
49.6	Summit
55.0	Right on Dee Knoch Rd. (before crossing bridge into Fall River Mills)
58.8	Left on Jim Day Rd.
60.5	Right on Main St. in town of McArthur
60.7	Left on A St.
60.9	Right to finish at fairgrounds

7 LASSEN LOLLIPOP

Difficulty:	Challenging
Time:	3 to 5 hours
Distance:	42 miles
Elevation gain:	3800'
Best seasons:	July through September
Road conditions:	Traffic is moderate; pavement is good.

GETTING THERE: From I-5 at Red Bluff, drive 41 miles east on Hwy 36 to Mineral. Turn right on Hwy 172 and go 4 miles to Mill Creek Resort.

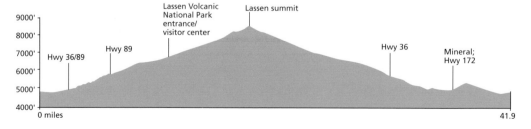

Several miles of these wiggly-worm hairpins make the road through Lassen Volcanic National Park feel like a classic col in the French Alps.

Lassen Volcanic National Park is one of the great treasures of Northern California, especially noteworthy for its volcanic heritage. And for cyclists, Highway 89, which runs through the park, is as good a biking road as you are likely to find. The loop at the bottom of this lollipop is a real treat as well. The whole ride is pretty much top-quality cycling entertainment from start to finish.

The ride starts and ends at Mill Creek Resort, a family-run facility with rustic cabins and a homey restaurant. It's very quiet and laid-back, with a nice swimming hole in Mill Creek.

The resort is on Hwy 172, south of the national park. Head east for 3 miles, then turn uphill toward the park on Hwy 36/89.

This is the beginning of one giant climb, all the way to 8512' Lassen summit, 16 miles and 4000' away. That sounds daunting, but it is actually quite manageable. The average gradient is about 4 percent, and most of the time it holds steady in that range. There are long, nearly level sections and short pitches that might touch 7 percent. Yes, of course, it's a challenge, but I have led tours here with many moderate riders involved, and all crossed this summit in good shape.

Let the climb take as long as it has to, and stop to check out the sights along the way. There are various scenic attractions on this run up the mountain, including the Sulphur Works, a region of steaming fumaroles and hot, bubbling mud pots. It's right alongside

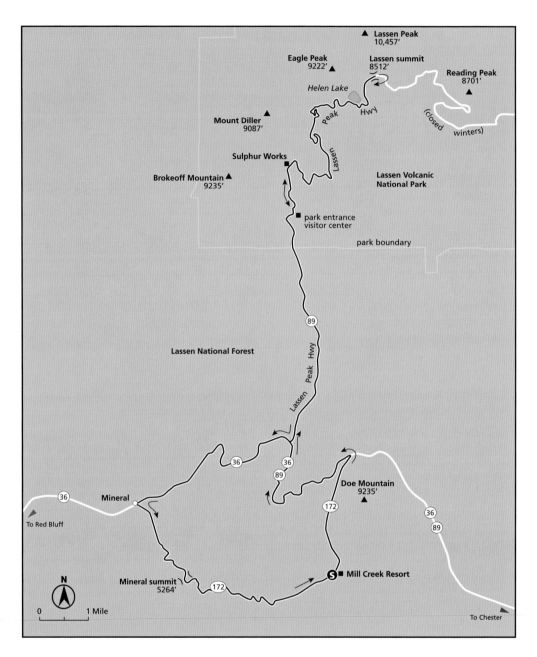

the road and easy to explore. The Sulphur Works is thought to be the original vent for ancient Mount Tehama, an immense volcano that blew its top 600,000 years ago, like Mount St. Helens, only bigger. Lassen Peak last erupted in 1916, and until Mount St. Helens lost her head, that had been the most recent volcanic eruption in the contiguous United States.

The borders of the park enclose miles of pristine wilderness, but the park exists to preserve the various volcanic and geothermal wonders associated with Lassen Peak, or perhaps more accurately with the late Mount Tehama. Many of the rugged peaks in the park's high country are remnants of the original volcano, the ragged fringe of its exploded caldera. However, 10,457' Lassen Peak is not. It's considered the world's largest plug dome volcano: a vent formed in the remnants of Tehama's collapse, spewing out assorted volcanic material that over time built up a cone 2000' high before becoming plugged. Lassen is the southernmost peak in the long string of volcanoes that make up the Cascades.

It may seem to take forever, but eventually you will get to the summit. This is the highest paved road in the Cascade Range, and the snow can be 40' deep here some years. It is often so deep that the road can't be cleared until mid-July or occasionally even later. I've ridden over the top in mid-August between 20'-high walls of snow and blue ice.

I put the route's turnaround at the summit, but the view isn't all that great there. If you have a little extra energy, descend the north face for a bit until views open up to the south and east, out across Lake Almanor.

Heading south from the summit, the road twists and turns in carsick loops as it wriggles its way down the mountain. The descent is pretty much uninterrupted madness for 16-plus miles. Not only is the road a superb, E-ticket ride in terms of its twists and turns, but the pavement is generally superb as well, silky smooth and free of potholes or other booby traps.

When Hwy 89 tees into Hwy 36 outside the park, the route turns right and heads west on Hwy 36, logging 4 more miles of downhill fun before bottoming out in the small town of Mineral. Right in the middle of town, turn left on Hwy 172.

How did such a remote back road end up with an official state highway number? It's almost as if the engineers at the highway department decided to build a road just for cyclists and threw in all the things we like: zero traffic, pretty meadows and leafy woods, a short, mildly challenging climb, and a descent much longer than the climb up to it. Add in smooth pavement, perfectly banked corners (a lot of them), and a downhill that's steep enough to be fast and fun, but not so steep that you have to be braking all the time. I know Caltrans doesn't build roads just for bikers, but that's what this little gem feels like.

After a flat, 1-mile run along beautiful Battle Creek Meadow leaving Mineral, the road climbs for a little over a mile to Mineral Summit and then topples off the other side in a delightful downhill of 3.5 miles, leveling out near the finish at Mill Creek Resort. The sweet little descent is the perfect finale for a nearly perfect ride.

MILEAGE LOG

0.0	From Mill Creek Resort, east on Hwy 172
2.8	Left on Hwy 36/89
6.4	Right on Hwy 89 toward Lassen Volcanic National Park
11.6	Park entrance and visitor center
12.6	Sulphur Works (wayside for geothermal activity)
18.8	Lassen summit (8512'); turn around and retrace, or explore beyond summit
26.0	Leave park
31.2	Right on Hwy 36
35.7	Town of Mineral; left on Hwy 172
37.9	Mineral summit (5264')
41.9	Finish at Mill Creek Resort

8 ALMANOR OUT-AND-BACKS

Difficulty:	Moderate
Time:	3 to 4 hours
Distance:	42 miles
Elevation gain:	1900'
Best seasons:	May through September
Road conditions:	Traffic is light; pavement is good.

GETTING THERE: From the junction of Hwy 36/89, drive 2.5 miles east to Chester. Turn right on Willow Way, then right again on 1st Ave. to the Chester Library parking lot.

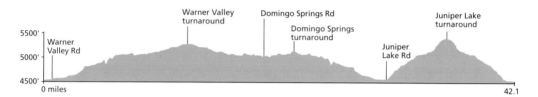

We did this ride on a club tour a few years ago without having checked it out ahead of time, taking someone else's word that it was worth doing. While it isn't the greatest ride in the world or even in this book, I was pleasantly surprised at how nice it turned out to be. If you happen to find yourself at Lake Almanor, looking for a good ride, you could do a lot worse than this one.

The route combines three dead ends near the town of Chester, on the north shore of the lake. You could ride them in any order, but this is how we did them, and it works well. All three point northwest, nosing up into the wilderness below Lassen Volcanic National Park. The scenery consists of forests of tall ponderosa pines running along the roads, except where the occasional subalpine meadow opens up the vistas a little. Each runs along the valley of a stream—the headwaters of the Feather River, Warner Creek, and Benner Creek—although the creeks are not often visible from the roads. The roads look alike and ride alike, with the same pavement. Some

might say that sameness is a problem, but it's a nice sort of problem to have: 40-plus miles of quiet byways through pristine forest, with no traffic, smooth pavement, and every so often a pretty meadow, backed by beautiful views of Lassen Peak off in the west.

The route tackles the roads in this order: Warner Valley, Domingo Springs, Juniper Lake. Each climbs from its beginning to its end. Warner Valley is the longest climb. There are lumpy rollers and stair steps all the way, a few of them mildly steep. But the total gain is only 750' in 12 miles, hardly a climb at all. Domingo Springs is even smaller: less than 200' up in 2.5 rolling miles. Juniper Lake is the most serious ascent, but even this is modest: 800' up in 5 miles. This last hill is at least a concentrated-enough gradient that it will turn into a snappy descent on the way back.

At the end of Domingo Springs Road, you will find that namesake spring: a grotto really, with a pretty pool below a rocky cliff, with split-rail fences around the water. There is a hose bib by the fence where you can fill your

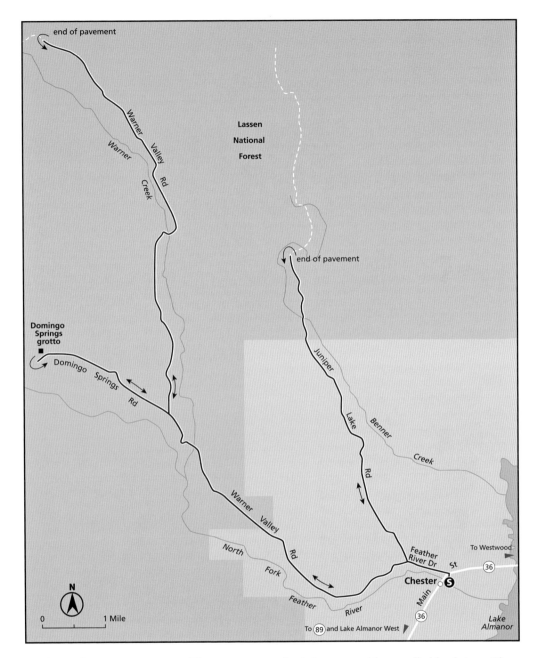

bottles with pure spring water. This comes up at mile 22, about halfway through the ride, making it a good spot for a break and a highlight of the route.

Once you've climbed Juniper Lake and wrung every last ounce of fun out of the final descent and have rolled back into Chester, there is one more treat in store. Just to the west of the finish, on Highway 36, in the heart of Chester, is an old-fashioned ice cream parlor, with a soda fountain along one wall, complete with the old chrome stools.

It's called the Lassen Gift Company because it has a lot of floor space dedicated to selling souvenir kitsch. But the main attraction, at least for hungry cyclists, is the fountain. The cheerful folks at the counter will whip up any ice cream treat you desire: cones, sundaes, malts, floats, shakes, splits. If the 42 mildly hilly miles today have put an edge on your appetite, you might want to make a stop here before leaving town.

MILEAGE LOG

0.0	From Chester Library, left (north) on 1st Ave.
0.2	Slight left on Feather River Dr.; cross Hwy 36; Forest Service sign, "WARNER VALLEY"
0.8	Left on Warner Valley Rd.; follow signs to Drakesbad
6.3	Bear right to stay on Warner Valley Rd. at Domingo Springs Rd. junction
13.0	End of pavement; turn around and retrace
19.7	Right on Domingo Springs Rd.
22.4	Domingo Springs grotto (water); turn around and retrace
25.1	Right on Warner Valley Rd.
30.6	Left on Juniper Lake Rd.
35.9	End of pavement; turn around and retrace
41.2	Left on Feather River Dr. into Chester
41.9	Cross Hwy 36 to 1st Ave.
42.1	Finish at Chester Library

Smiles all around on this exploration of the forest north of Lake Almanor (Doreen Carey)

9 INDIAN VALLEY–ANTELOPE LAKE

Difficulty:	Challenging
Time:	5.5 to 8 hours
Distance:	89 miles
Elevation gain:	4500'
Best seasons:	May through September
Road conditions:	Traffic is light; pavement is good.

GETTING THERE: From Lake Almanor, drive 15 miles south on Hwy 89 to Arlington Rd. (6 miles north of Hwy 70). From this junction drive 4.7 miles east on Arlington Rd. to Taylorsville. Park anywhere.

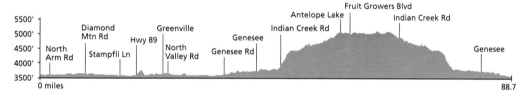

I've led three tours through Indian Valley, and all of those rides have been wonderful. I love this quiet patch of mountain country. This can be one big, fairly ambitious ride, or it can be two rides of 35 and 54 miles apiece. The shorter ride explores Indian Valley and is about as easy as a ride can be, with minimal climbing. The longer ride is a run up to Antelope Lake, looping around the lake and descending back to the valley.

Head north out of Taylorsville on Nelson Road for a mile, then jog right (east) on North Arm Road to a loop around a little side valley, the drainage of Lights Creek. Diamond Mountain Road brings you back "down" the valley, although the road is really almost flat. For all 11.5 miles around this loop, the roads hug the rim of the valley, with open, short-grass cattle range on the left and hills thatched in dense fir and pine forest rising steeply on the right.

Back in Indian Valley, Stampfli Lane cuts directly west across the valley to Highway 89 for a 3-mile run north toward Greenville.

This section of state highway is the only part of the route that might carry some traffic. It also includes the only significant climb in the Indian Valley portion of the ride: 200' in 1 mile, with a matching descent off the north side. A little detour on Hideaway and Round Valley roads, before reaching town, gets you off Hwy 89 at the first opportunity and bypasses some commercial clutter. The detour brings you right into the center of town, riding along quaint old Main Street. At 22 miles, it's a good spot for a break.

Beyond Greenville, one of the best parts of this ride awaits: a 12-mile run on North Valley Road. The lovely little lane bumps along the eastern edge of the valley, with the valley floor along Indian Creek rolling away to the right of the road and wooded hills crowding in on the left. This is cycling the way it's meant to be: a quiet road with decent pavement and no traffic; green, grassy meadows; scattered stands of oak and pine; lazy little meandering streams; handsome old barns and funky little bridges; and on the far side of the

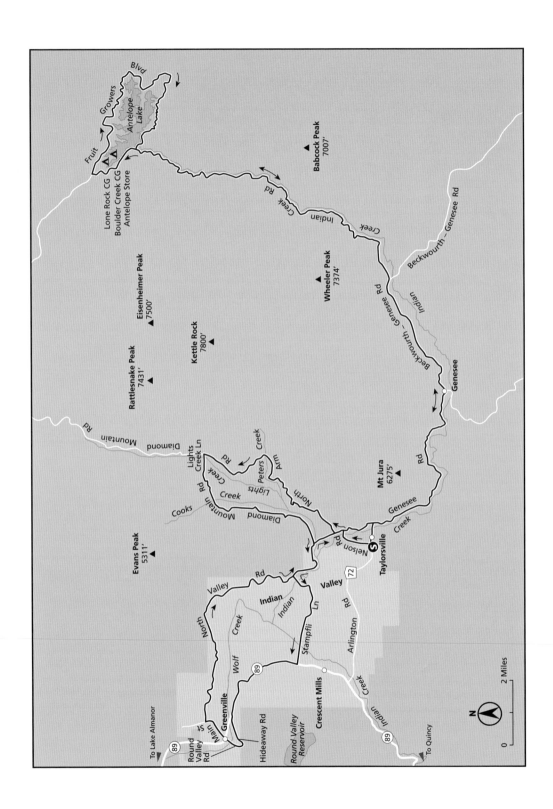

Growers
Blvd
Fruit
Antelope
Lake
Lone Rock CG
Boulder Creek CG
Antelope Store

Babcock Peak
7007'

Indian Creek Rd

Creek

Beckwourth – Genesee Rd

Eisenheimer Peak
7500'

Wheeler Peak
7374'

Beckwourth – Genesee Rd

Indian

Rattlesnake Peak
7431'

Kettle Rock
7800'

Genesee

Diamond Mountain Rd

Lights Creek Ln

Creek

Peters Arm

Mt Jura
6275'

Genesee Creek

Cooks

Creek

Mountain Rd

Diamond

North Lights Creek

Rd

Nelson Rd

Taylorsville

S

Evans Peak
5311'

North Valley Rd

Indian

Indian

Valley

Ln

Stampfli

Arlington Rd

72

Wolf Creek

89

Greenville

Main St

Hideaway Rd

Round Valley Reservoir

Crescent Mills

Indian Creek

89

To Lake Almanor

89

Round Valley Rd

To Quincy

N

0   2 Miles

Genesee

This tranquil cruise down Indian Valley comes very close to cycling perfection.

valley, majestic mountains shouldering along the western horizon. The road is almost flat, with just a few little lumps that won't get you out of the big ring but might get you out of the saddle.

This dreamy run takes you back past the Lights Creek valley and down to a junction with Genesee and Arlington roads. Turning right on Arlington will take you straight into Taylorsville to complete the easy, 35-mile cruise around Indian Valley. Turning left on Genessee will point you toward Antelope Lake. The first 10 miles are more of the same easy riding along the valley, with just a bit more in the way of uphill rollers hinting at the hills to come. At mile 40, you pass through the pretty pioneer settlement of Genesee. There is a store here, although I've never seen it open.

This is beautiful country: shady forest alternating with open meadows, with impressive displays of big High Sierra granite up in the hills. Along most of the journey to Antelope Lake, Indian Creek is never far away.

The bulk of the climbing begins at mile 44.5, with the toughest pitch first: 650' in 1.5 miles (8 percent). After that little beast, 9.5 more miles of rolling, uppity humps add another 650' before arriving at the lake, right at the dam where Indian Creek flows out and down the canyon. There are restrooms here and an information kiosk. As you loop around the lake, near mile 58, you'll pass a little store near Boulder Creek and Lone Rock campgrounds, your only access to food out here.

Ride around the lake in the clockwise direction, turning right on Fruit Growers

Boulevard. (Fruit Growers Boulevard? Excuse me? This is high in the Sierra Nevada. No one grows fruit here. And this meandering mountain lane is hardly a boulevard.) Once you've rounded the lake, return to Indian Creek Road and the 11-mile downhill—both rolling and steep—back to the valley. Finally, there are the last 11 miles along the tranquil valley floor, back through Genesee and on to Taylorsville…a mellow way to wind down at the end of what has been a long but relatively easy and absolutely gorgeous ride.

MILEAGE LOG

0.0	North on Nelson Rd.
1.1	Left on North Valley Rd.
1.4	Right on North Arm Rd.
7.6	Left on Lights Creek Ln.
8.0	Left on Diamond Mountain Rd.
12.9	Right on North Valley Rd.
14.5	Left on Stampfli Ln.
17.6	Right on Hwy 89
20.8	Left on Hideaway Rd.
21.8	Right on Round Valley Rd.
22.1	Cross Hwy 89 to Main St.; town of Greenville
23.4	Right on North Valley Rd.
34.1	Left on Genesee Rd. (or right on Arlington to Taylorsville to complete 35-mile ride)
40.1	Town of Genesee
40.3	Becomes Beckwourth–Genesee Rd.
44.5	Becomes Indian Creek Rd.
55.6	Bear left on Indian Creek Rd. at Fruit Growers Blvd. junction; Antelope Lake
57.4	Right on Fruit Growers Blvd.
57.9	Access road on right for Antelope Store
66.6	Left on Indian Creek Rd.
77.7	Becomes Beckwourth–Genesee Rd.
81.8	Becomes Genesee Rd.
82.0	Town of Genesee
88.0	Left on Arlington Rd.
88.7	Finish in Taylorsville

NORTH BAY

No other area in California has so many bike-friendly back roads, nor as much scenic variety. Hundreds of miles of rugged coastline, thousands of acres of premier vineyards, redwood and bay forest, oak-dotted grasslands, sheep-cropped ridge tops...it's all here, north of the Golden Gate. It is justifiably famous as a cycling utopia.

10 HOPLAND–BOONVILLE–UKIAH LOOP

Difficulty:	Challenging
Time:	4.5 to 6.5 hours
Distance:	66 miles
Elevation gain:	4400'
Best seasons:	May through October
Road conditions:	Traffic is light on most of these roads, although a few may be busier. Pavement varies from average to very good.

GETTING THERE: From central Santa Rosa, drive 52 miles north on Hwy 101 to Hopland. Park anywhere. The route begins one block north of the junction with Hwy 175.

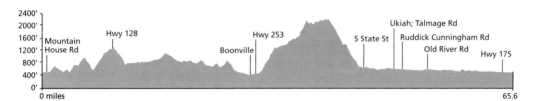

This is a big, clockwise loop through the hills and valleys of southern Mendocino County, beginning and ending in the village of Hopland, along Highway 101. There are a few challenging climbs, all of them bundled with fun descents, and also many miles that are flat or rolling. Scenery is a mix of vineyards, orchards, and huge expanses of semiwilderness (woods and meadows).

Begin this loop on Mountain House Road, heading out of Hopland in a southeasterly direction. It starts out dead flat but soon tilts up into the first of five climbs, each one a little

longer than the one before. Altogether, you climb almost 1400' along the 9-mile length of this road. It's nice climbing, surrounded by oak and bay laurel, with open hilltops and little ponds here and there. There is very little traffic, with just the occasional local rancher to interrupt your solitude.

The only climb on Mountain House not followed by a descent is the last one, which is also the longest: 700' up in 2 miles. At the summit, turn right on Hwy 128 and head northwest toward Boonville. In less than a mile, the road tips off the ridgeline and

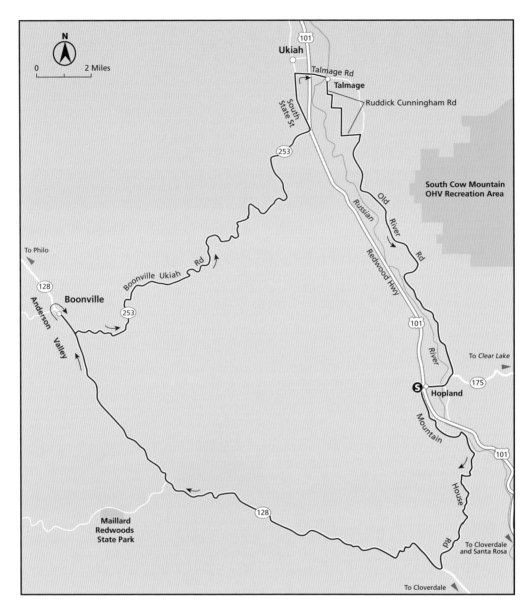

slithers down into the valley, dropping over 500' in 1.5 miles. It's a good downhill, with nicely banked corners, a smooth surface, and just the right grade. The only thing that might make it less than ideal is traffic. Hwy 128 is the main route from the Bay Area up to trendy Mendocino, so on weekends it can get a bit tiresome. Most of the time it won't

be an issue, and in any event there are roomy shoulders along much of the road.

The run north along Hwy 128 eventually ends up in beautiful Anderson Valley. This area has been renowned for its apple production for nearly a hundred years and still has some orchards and fruit stands going strong, although now vineyards blanket some of the hills where apples used to flourish. The terrain up the length of the valley is rolling, with a few husky climbs and zippy descents that stretch the definition of "roller." Between Mountain House and Boonville, you go downhill more than up, losing 900' and gaining only 400'. It's generally easy, pleasant riding.

Boonville is at the heart of Anderson Valley. Falling at a useful midpoint on the drive to Mendocino, it has been a way station for travelers for many years and is currently enjoying a period of vibrant prosperity, with shops and cafés, including a nice brewpub, catering to the passing throng. The heart of town is most of a mile past the junction with Hwy 253, so you have to do a little out-and-back into town to find water and food.

Hwy 253 presents the biggest challenge on this otherwise moderate loop: a 6.5-mile climb with 1700' of gain. It's divided into three sections: first a substantial climb of 2 miles, then an almost level *intermezzo*

of 3 miles, and finally another climb of 1.5 miles. That easy middle section makes the whole package manageable. There are three more mildly rolling miles traversing the hillside after that summit, with lovely views out across empty ridges and canyons. Finally, at around mile 40, you get your payback for all that climbing: two descents, back to back, with just a tiny uphill bump between them. Each is 2 miles long and about 8 percent, with good pavement. They can be full-tilt fliers, as fast as your skills and your nerves will allow.

At the bottom, the road rolls out alongside Hwy 101, and we have our only dud miles of the loop: 3-plus miles into and through the southern fringe of the city of Ukiah, a band of commercial clutter. It's a little ragged but tolerable, and it does offer a few stores for finding food or water.

Cross over Hwy 101 and the Russian River, and leave town behind on Ruddick Cunningham Road and Old River Road. From

Even on a grey day, the hills of Mendocino County along Mountain House Road can still be beautiful. (Kendra Markle)

the base of the big descent, through Ukiah, and all the way south along the valley, the last 20 miles of the ride are about as flat as anything in this region can be. (Several years ago, the Masters National Championships were staged near here, and Old River was used for the time trial, because it's so nearly flat and so traffic-free.) Running south down the valley, densely wooded hills rise up steeply on the east side of the road. Here again, the broad valley floor was once covered in wall-to-wall orchards, but now vineyards are moving in

and elbowing the old fruit trees aside.

Bend west at the bottom of the loop, back across the valley to Hopland. As this town's name indicates, hops were the main crop before orchards and vineyards, so there really ought to be a brewery here. There used to be a good one—the home of Red Tail Ale—where we always ended our rides, but the brewery relocated to Ukiah, just off our route. However, there are other cafés in the village for after-ride refreshments.

MILEAGE LOG

0.0	From central Hopland, go south on Hwy 101
0.2	Right on Mountain House Rd.
9.3	Right on Hwy 128
28.1	Straight (past Hwy 253 junction) into Boonville
28.9	After break in Boonville, retrace route to...
29.7	Left on Hwy 253
46.6	Left on South State St.
48.8	Right on Talmage Rd.; city of Ukiah
50.0	Right on Ruddick Cunningham Rd.
53.5	Right on Old River Rd.
64.3	At traffic circle, take second right on Hwy 175
65.5	Right on Hwy 101 in Hopland
65.6	Finish

11 KELSEYVILLE TWO-LOOPER

Difficulty:	Challenging (or less so with the shorter options)
Time:	1 to 5 hours, depending on the route
Distance:	15, 41, or 56 miles
Elevation gain:	Up to 5000'
Best seasons:	Spring or fall; midsummer can be hot
Road conditions:	Some highway miles may be busy, but most roads are low traffic. Some roads are well paved and some not so well, but all are at least decent.

GETTING THERE: From the junction of Hwy 29 and Lakeport Blvd. in Lakeport, take Hwy 29 south for 6.3 miles to a left on Bell Hill Rd. Turn right from Bell Hill Rd. onto Main Street, heading into the center of Kelseyville. Park anywhere.

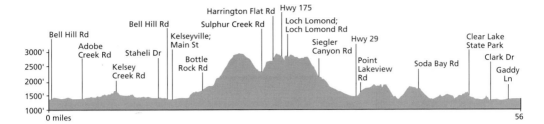

Kelseyville is a sleepy village southwest of Clear Lake, out in the middle of pear and walnut orchards, with vineyards striping the nearby hillsides. There is a hint of tourist and big-city sophistication about the place, but mostly it remains a quiet, homey town, where agriculture is still a common topic of conversation on Main Street.

To begin the short loop, head west on Main Street, turn left at the edge of town, cross Highway 29, and continue on Bell Hill Road, following flat, section-line zigzags through a mix of vineyards, orchards, woods, and a scattering of country homes. Turn left on Adobe Creek Road, which begins as a straight road but soon meanders up and down over little folds in the woods-and-meadows landscape. It blends seamlessly into Kelsey Creek Road and is soon rolling along through the woods with the rocky creek on the right and occasional rocky cliffs on the left. This is a delight for cycling: easy rolling topography, decent pavement, no traffic, and dreamy scenery.

Bear left on Staheli Drive for a very short climb. Level out and roll back to Bell Hill Road, cross Hwy 29, and turn right, back into Kelseyville, to complete the little loop at about mile 15.

To continue to the big loop, top off your water and then head east out the other side of town, bearing right on Live Oak Road. This begins with a small climb, followed by near-flats on Cole Creek and Bottle Rock roads. But around mile 19, Bottle Rock tilts up into a serious challenge: 1100' up in 3 miles (6 percent). It's not the biggest hill you'll ever do, but it is definitely hard work. Scenery along the way is dense forest and rock cliffs, often with glassy black obsidian sparkling in the rock faces.

Over the top, you get some payback on that climb with a fast, sinuous 2.5-mile descent into a pretty valley. But the climbing resumes almost immediately after a left turn on Sulphur Creek Road. This ascent through broadleaf forest gains 600' in a bit less than 2 miles, with a half mile of near-flat in the middle; some pitches may touch 10 percent. After that flat spot, bear right on Harrington Flat Road, finishing the balance of the climb on this road. Descend to Hwy 175, turn left, and head for the town of Loch Lomond, where there is a little country market at mile 28.

This is where the shortcut shoots back down the hill to Kelseyville. If you are opting for this route, simply stay on Hwy 175 and enjoy a delightful downhill cruise through the trees. It's one of the sweetest, smoothest descents around: never too steep, but plenty fast enough to be fun. At the end of Hwy 175, turn left onto Hwy 29 and roll out the last miles back to Kelseyville, including one last half-mile climb amid all the downhill high-jinks. With the little Kelsey Creek loop to start, this yields a ride of 41 miles.

If you're staying with the long course, turn right on Loch Lomond Road at the store, hump up and down along the forested ridgeline, then topple off the edge on a steep plunge: about 700' down in one white-knuckle mile. There is a brief flat at the bottom, and then the descending continues after a left onto Siegler Canyon Road. While the Loch Lomond descent might be too steep to be really fun, this one is just about perfect: one slinky bend after another for 4 miles along a pretty creek. It starts out steep enough to get you rolling—perhaps 5 percent—and at the bottom rolls out along the creek on a grade that is still downhill, although you'll have to be pedaling to keep things lively. In the spring, the grassy hillsides will be a spectacular display of blossoming blue lupine.

When Siegler Canyon tees into Hwy 29, turn left, uphill, on the busy highway. This is not great riding, but there is a decent shoulder and it will be over quickly when the route turns right after half a mile onto Point Lakeview Road. This begins a long flirtation with Clear Lake, which will put in appearances over the remainder of the ride, either as a far-off panorama (now) or up close (later). Clear Lake is the largest natural freshwater lake entirely within California. That carefully worded claim excludes larger salt lakes,

reservoirs, and Lake Tahoe (half of which is in Nevada). Whatever its claims to fame, it is a beautiful lake.

This run north along the west shore could best be described as up and down. There are any number of modest climbs and two fast descents of about a mile and a half apiece. Scenery varies from those distant or close-up views of the lake to transits of mobile home parks to little towns and scattered rural-residential settlements, with a few segments in the forest that are as pretty as the nearby lake, unspoiled by the dubious benefits of progress.

Turn right from Point Lakeview onto Soda Bay Road, just at the top of one of the fast descents. Soda Bay will take you almost all the way to the finish. Just past Clear Lake State Park, bear off left on Clark Drive and begin a last, flat run through the farm fields, away from the lake and back to Kelseyville.

Kelsey Creek Road is a hidden treasure up in Lake County, visited by few but cherished by all who discover it.

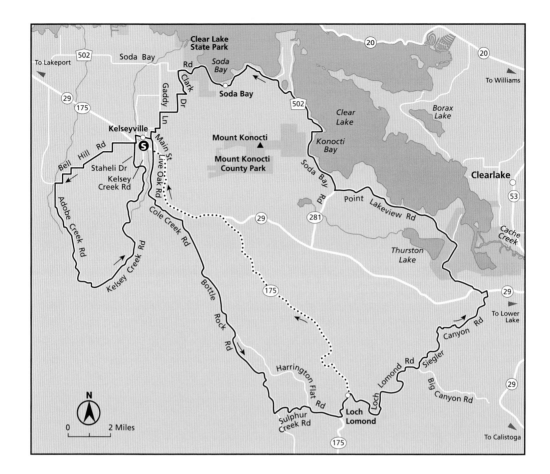

MILEAGE LOG

0.0   West on Main Street in Kelseyville

0.2   Left on Bell Hill Rd.

0.4   Cross Hwy 29 to continue on Bell Hill Rd.

3.9   Left on Adobe Creek Rd.

7.9   Straight on Kelsey Creek Rd.

12.9   Left on Staheli Dr.

13.9   Right on Bell Hill Rd., recross Hwy 29

14.2   Right on Big Valley/Main St. into Kelseyville; end of short loop

14.5   Continue east on Main St. for long loop

14.8   Right on Live Oak Rd., cross Hwy 29

17.5   Right on Cole Creek Rd.

18.1   Right on Bottle Rock Rd.

25.3   Left on Sulphur Creek Rd.

26.5   Bear right on Harrington Flat Rd.

27.6   Left on Hwy 175

28.3	Right on Loch Lomond Rd.; town of Loch Lomond (shortcut stays straight on Hwy 175 and Hwy 29 back to Kelseyville)
32.3	Bear left on Siegler Canyon Rd. at Big Canyon Rd. junction
36.4	Left on Hwy 29
36.9	Right on Point Lakeview Rd.
43.8	Right on Soda Bay Rd.
52.6	Left on Clark Dr.
54.7	Left on Gaddy Ln.
55.3	Left on State St. in Kelseyville
55.7	Right on Main St. to finish

12 THE GEYSERS LOOP

Difficulty:	Challenging
Time:	3 to 4.5 hours
Distance:	47 miles
Elevation gain:	3800'
Best seasons:	All year, although winter may be rainy, even snowy
Road conditions:	Most roads are low traffic. Surfaces vary from decent to patches of gravel.

GETTING THERE: From downtown Santa Rosa, drive 24 miles north on Highway 101 to the Canyon Rd. exit. Turn right on Canyon, then right on Geyserville Ave., and drive 0.1 mile to Geyserville Elementary School.

The loop around "The Geysers" (as locals refer to it) is one of the best and most classic of all Sonoma County rides. It is challenging and remote, and there is no source of water all around the backcountry side of the loop. Although only 47 miles long, this route is a serious challenge.

While it becomes remote and borderline-brutal later on, it begins quite tamely, heading north from Geyserville along rolling roads near Highway 101, through the vineyards at the top end of Alexander Valley. With most of the traffic on the highway, your road will be quiet.

This route makes use of a seasonal bridge across the Russian River, open only from June through September. There is an alternate route open year-round, and both options are explained in the mileage log. Both lead to Geysers Road at about mile 11.

Geysers Road explores a wild, rugged stretch of country, with the road sketched

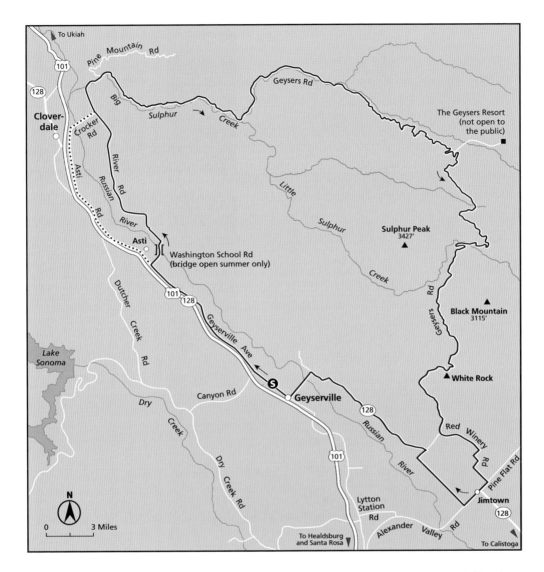

tentatively along the rocky mountain slopes and canyon walls. Frequent earthquakes and winter weather pound on this hilly, unstable terrain, and the local road crews can barely stay abreast of the carnage. It's a rare year when there isn't a landslide somewhere along this road, usually mended with a truckload of gravel.

The main ascent of the Geysers is divided into three sections, each with its own personality. First is an 8.5-mile section with numer-

ous ups and downs in the narrow defile of Big Sulphur Creek canyon. None of these climbs is particularly long, though some are steep for short stretches. In between are level runs and descents, the final one dropping to an old iron bridge over the creek. The canyon is beautiful, and you should take the time to slow and peer over the edge into its rocky depths.

Beyond the bridge, the second section of climb settles into a steady 4.5-mile, 800' grade that is never steep. It is almost entirely shaded by leafy trees and is quite pretty, with little brooks splashing down to the road to join the bigger creek below.

At a junction with Geysers Resort Road, the road turns hard right. That "Resort" name gives you a hint of how this active geothermal area was originally exploited in the nineteenth century: folks came to take the steaming waters. Now the area is closed to public access and given over to producing power from geothermal steam, the largest such project in the country. You can't fail to notice the miles of pipes snaking over the otherwise empty hills and the steaming power plants off on distant ridges.

The third leg of the Geysers climb begins after that hard right, and this is the nasty one: over 750' in 1.5 miles. It's an unrelenting wall for the entire distance and will leave most strong cyclists gasping for air. Once at the top, there is a mercifully flat section where one can recover before climbing a few smaller, less steeply canted hills.

There is an actual summit to Geysers Road at around 2700', but it doesn't announce itself very clearly. Following those last small

Geysers Road is the highest road in Sonoma County, and one of the wildest and most remote. (Georg Ockenfuss)

climbs, you eventually find yourself hurtling downhill big time, and by that you may surmise you're on the other side of the mountain, but you're not quite done with the climbing. After a fast descent of 2 miles, the road tilts up again for another climb of over a mile, followed by another good descent and still another small climb, all the while surrounded by some of the prettiest, emptiest country, with rarely a mailbox, let alone a house, to indicate any human element in this vast, rumpled wilderness.

Finally, around mile 27, you arrive at a last summit, beyond which lies nothing but downhill for 4 miles off the southern face of the mountain. The road is well engineered and the pavement is generally good, lending itself to full-tilt fliers. But just because I say it's a ripper descent doesn't mean you can throw caution to the wind. There are many technical turns and cattle guards to catch you out, and from time to time, the same gremlins washing out sections of pavement on the north end

of the road will lay booby traps here as well, some of them extremely tricky. Also, spare a moment on the way down to check out the view: it's spectacular, taking in Alexander and Russian River valleys and more.

Once this wonderful downhill comes to an end, turn left on Red Winery Road. Down out of the mountains now, the balance of the route travels mildly rolling roads through thousands of acres of some of the best vineyards in the world. You could bear right here on Geysers Road and right again on Hwy 128 to shorten the route by a few miles, but after all those hilly miles with no water stops, you could be a bit parched at this point, and the loop around Red Winery swings you past the Jimtown Store, a bike-friendly watering hole described in more detail in Rides 14 and 15.

After a stop at the store, it's a simple matter of cruising north the last 7 miles through Alexander Valley on Hwy 128, back to Geyserville, a nice wind-down after the tough walk on the wild side that is the Geysers.

MILEAGE LOG

0.0	From Geyserville Elementary School, left on Geyserville Ave.
3.1	Becomes Asti Rd.
4.7	Right on Washington School Rd.
5.1	Cross Russian River on gravel "summer crossing" bridge; becomes River Rd. This is a seasonal bridge, only open from June through September.

In other seasons:

4.7	**Stay on Asti Rd. past "Bridge Closed" signs at Washington School Rd.**
9.3	**Right on East 1st St. (near town of Cloverdale); becomes Crocker Rd.**
10.0	**Bear left onto River Rd.; rejoin main route (see mile 9.7)**

9.7	Bear right to stay on River Rd.
10.7	Bear right (essentially straight ahead) on Geysers Rd.
23.6	Right to stay on Geysers Rd. at Geysers Resort Rd. junction
26.8	Summit (high point on ride and highest road in Sonoma County: 2700')
36.1	Left on Red Winery Rd.
38.4	Right on Pine Flat Rd.
38.8	Right (straight ahead) on Hwy 128
39.0	Jimtown Store
39.3	Right to stay on Hwy 128 at Alexander Valley Rd. junction
45.9	Right on Geyserville Ave. in town of Geyserville
46.6	Finish at Geyserville Elementary School

13 KNOXVILLE–BUTTS CANYON LOOP

Difficulty:	Challenging/epic
Time:	5 to 7 hours
Distance:	82 miles
Elevation gain:	5500'
Best seasons:	Late spring and fall
Road conditions:	Most roads are low traffic, but a few miles are busier. Pavement varies.

GETTING THERE: From Silverado Trail in Napa Valley (north of St. Helena), drive 10 miles east on Deer Park Rd. and Howell Mountain Rd. to the town of Pope Valley. Park at the grange hall.

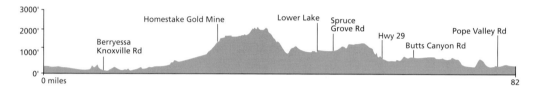

In Ride 16, I refer to Pope Valley as "the quiet side of Napa County, the part the tourists rarely see." This loop begins and ends at Pope Valley but goes even farther away from the wineries and limos and tour buses of mainstream Napa, out into a remote wild patch of Napa County wilderness, plus a remote corner of Lake County. Combined with the long miles and the chunky topography, that remoteness makes this a loop for only fit, self-sufficient riders.

Head east out of Pope Valley into Pope Canyon, crossing broad meadows that can be a riot of wildflowers in the spring. Two little climbs at miles 8 and 9 carry you over the ridge and down into the valley that is home to Lake Berryessa. Turn left on Berryessa Knoxville Road and head north, away from the lake and away from pretty much everything else.

This is the most remote, wildest part of the loop. The road starts out with two wide lanes, guardrails, and good engineering, but a few miles along it loses its stripes, narrows to one fat lane, and the paving deteriorates. The little road crosses Eticuera Creek many times,

and several of those crossings are fords: in the wet season, into April, the stream flows over the road rather than under it. It can be quite deep in the wetter months, almost impassable. But even if it's only damp, be aware that the surface may be slimy, a slip-'n'-slide for bikes.

This is empty country: nothing out here but rocks, oaks, pines, redbud, and grassy hillsides, and all the critters that call this wilderness home. Traffic is almost nonexistent. For 18 miles, the road climbs gently in the creek canyon. At about mile 28, the grade tilts up into something more substantial. For the next 11 miles, the road mostly goes up, sometimes only a little and sometimes as steeply as 10 percent. There are a number of little saddles in there, but climbing dominates. It adds up to a fairly husky challenge.

Rather suddenly, in the middle of this section, the road regains its stripes and wide lanes, and the nearby landscape changes considerably. You have arrived at the sprawling Homestake Gold Mine. This is not an historic artifact from the Gold Rush. Its heyday was just a few years ago. Between 1985 and

Riding through several fords along Eticuera Creek is part of what makes this ride such a walk on the wild side.

2002, a billion dollars' worth of gold dust was extracted from big open pit mines here. Now, with the mining over, the site has become a 7000-acre natural preserve. The 300 miners who toiled here have been replaced by a small staff of ecologists working on the remediation of the site. (Mining is often a messy and sometimes ugly business, but in this case, the mine's owners were above-average conscientious about their environmental responsibilities, and the site is in pretty good shape.)

Finally, at mile 39, the climbing comes to an end—for a while—and you hurl yourself off the ridge on a screaming 3.5-mile descent. That drops you into the bottom of a canyon, where you have another climb of 1.5 miles before you can settle down for a long, easy run across Morgan Valley and up into the town of Lower Lake at mile 47. This is the

best spot on the ride for food and fluids.

The main road west from Lower Lake is busy Highway 29. It's okay to ride, but not ideal. Fortunately, there is an alternative that does come pretty close to being ideal: Turn off Hwy 29 just out of Lower Lake on Clayton Creek Road. This little lane takes you to Spruce Grove Road, a real hidden treasure. For 10 miles, it meanders through the empty hills on a mildly uphill run. There are a few homes and ranches out here, but not many. The scenery is more of what we've been seeing all day: shady woods and grasslands. The pavement is much better than anyone would expect on such a minor road. It's almost perfect for cycling, and yet few riders even know it's here.

The last 2 miles are a fast, smooth descent skirting the scattered residential community

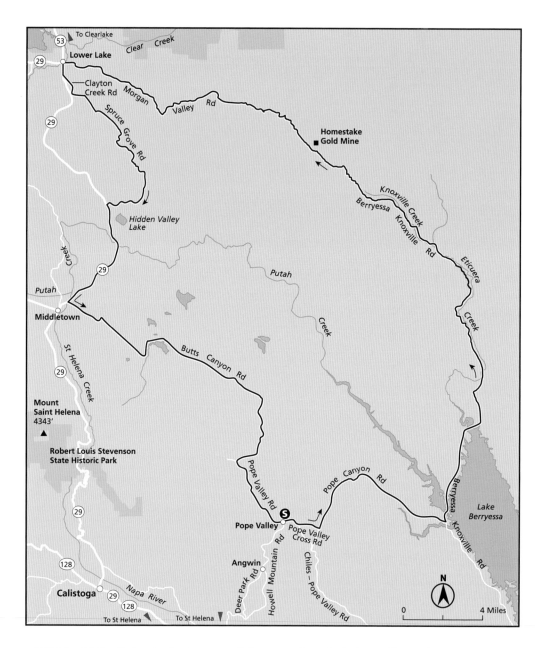

of Hidden Valley Lake. At the bottom of this flier, turn left on busy Hwy 29, following the main drag for almost 6 miles to the turn onto Butts Canyon Road near Middletown. Hwy 29 isn't a great bike road, but it has recently been repaved and has decent shoulders.

Butts Canyon Road is another nice bike road, with light traffic and nice scenery. It begins with 4 flat, straight miles through open horse and cattle ranches. Another 4 miles of rollers past a pretty lake lead to a 3-mile descent into the road's namesake canyon. Then you have one last bit of work to do: a 1-mile climb out of the rugged canyon.

Over the top of that little summit, a wiggly 1.5-mile descent returns you to lovely Pope Valley, with just 5 mellow miles left to roll out down the valley to the end of the ride.

MILEAGE LOG

0.0	From Pope Valley Grange, left (south) on Chiles–Pope Valley Rd.
0.8	Left on Pope Valley Cross Rd.
1.8	Left on Pope Canyon Rd.
10.2	Left on Berryessa Knoxville Rd.
33.3	Becomes Morgan Valley Rd.
47.5	Left on Hwy 29; town of Lower Lake
48.1	Left on Clayton Creek Rd.
49.2	Left on Spruce Grove Rd.
58.0	Left on Hwy 29
63.7	Left on Butts Canyon Rd.
78.4	Becomes Pope Valley Rd. at Aetna Springs Rd. junction
82.0	Finish at Pope Valley Grange

14 WINE COUNTRY LOOP #1

Difficulty:	Easy/moderate
Time:	2 to 3 hours
Distance:	31 miles
Elevation gain:	1200'
Best seasons:	Year-round; midwinter may be rainy
Road conditions:	Traffic is generally light. Pavement varies from subpar to very good. Some of these roads have wide shoulders, but most do not.

GETTING THERE: From central Santa Rosa, drive 14 miles north on Hwy 101 to the central Healdsburg exit, which merges onto Healdsburg Ave. At the signal, bear left on Vine St., which becomes Grove St. Park at Healdsburg City Hall.

This is the definitive "wine country" ride. There are other, longer routes through Sonoma County's vineyards (including Rides 12 and 15), but this is the one that provides the simplest, most accessible sampling of what the area has to offer. There are a few hills, but all are either short or, if longer, gradual.

The start/finish is in the small city of Healdsburg (HEELDS-burg), which has, in recent years, become the hub of all wine-related tourist activity in Sonoma County. It's at the heart of one of the best wine-producing regions, but it is also an attractive town in its own right, with many tree-lined streets of fine old homes and a vibrant downtown arrayed around its classic town square. It has grown into its role as ground zero of the wine country, with many inns and restaurants and shops catering to the visiting hordes. And yet

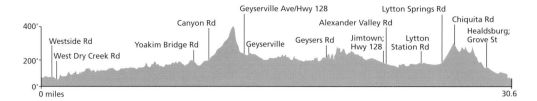

in spite of the influx of tourists, it retains its own small-town charm.

The ride begins at Healdsburg City Hall on Grove Street, a couple of blocks from the plaza. Head out of town on Westside Road and in 1 mile turn right onto West Dry Creek Road. This is where the ride really begins.

West Dry Creek Road plays host to cyclists in large groups and small on almost every day of the year. Touring companies all feature it in their "wine country" packages. Centuries and triathlons and fund-raising rides use it, as do club rides on a regular basis. It's easy enough for beginners but still interesting for

West Dry Creek Road is probably the most popular cycling road through Sonoma County's wine country. (Kirby James)

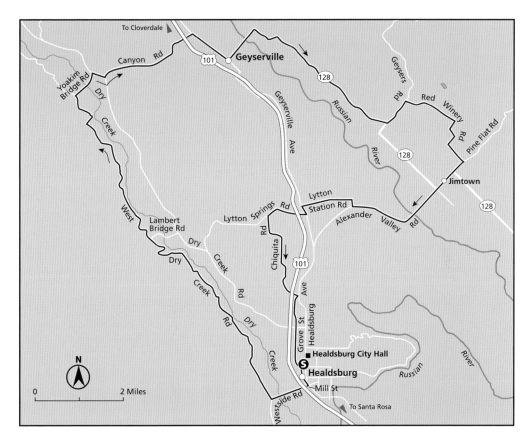

To Cloverdale

Canyon Rd

Yoakim Bridge Rd

Dry

Creek

101 Geyserville

Geyserville Ave

128

Russian

River

128

Geysers Rd

Red

Winery Rd

Pine Flat Rd

128

Jimtown

128

West

Lambert Bridge Rd

Dry

Dry

Creek Rd

Creek Rd

Dry Creek

Lytton Springs Rd

Chiquita Rd

101

Lytton Station Rd

Lytton

Alexander Valley Rd

River

Grove St

Healdsburg Ave

Healdsburg City Hall

Healdsburg

Russian

Mill St

Westside Rd

To Santa Rosa

N

0   2 Miles

veterans. It tumbles along its mildly up-and-down course for 9 miles, heading north up the valley. On the right side of the road are wall-to-wall vineyards; on the left, a steep ridge, heavily wooded.

Turn right on Yoakim Bridge Road and cross the valley to Dry Creek Road. Turn right and jog south to Canyon Road. Canyon is the biggest climb of the day. It is never difficult, never steep. The entire road is 2.3 miles long and the 200' climb takes up quite a bit more than half that total, for the descent into Alexander Valley on the other side is shorter and steeper. That means this climb is long and lazy. The downhill is almost dead straight, so riders who feel bold enough can schuss down the grade at a good clip.

At the bottom, turn right on Geyserville Avenue (Highway 128) and roll into Geyser-ville, a sleepy village that hasn't changed much over the years. There are a few new homes and commercial spaces, but anyone who lived here in 1940 would recognize the town today. Cruise to the center of town and turn left to continue south on Hwy 128, crossing the Russian River on a long, new bridge. This road is similar to West Dry Creek. There are no significant climbs or descents, and the rollers here are smoothed out compared to those in the other valley. What little ups and downs there are will be soft and easy. As far as wine-related impressions, Alexander Valley and Dry Creek Valley are much the same. Local enologists may quibble over subtle differences in microclimate or *terroir,* but from the seat of a bike, it all looks similar.

Leave Hwy 128 for a left turn onto Gey-sers Road, then bear right onto Red Winery

Road, a quiet bypass off Hwy 128. The scenery is exactly the same on Red Winery as it is on Hwy 128: vineyards sprawling away across the valley on the right; wooded hills rising up steeply on the left. At its southern end, Red Winery tees into Pine Flat Road; turn right and return to Hwy 128. Turn right (literally, straight ahead) on Hwy 128 and roll down to a rest stop at the bike-friendly Jimtown Store, where there are bike racks and a hose bib up the side alley with a sign inviting cyclists to refill their bottles. There is comfortable seating on the big porch out front, and on any sunny day the benches will be filled with cyclists.

After a stop at the store, head west on one more short section of Hwy 128. Then, when Hwy 128 turns north, carry on straight ahead on Alexander Valley Road. Cross the Russian River again and follow a mildly uphill grade to a right turn onto Lytton Station Road. Turn right again in a little over a mile on Lytton Springs Road, cross under Hwy 101, and begin a small climb. At the summit, turn left on Chiquita Road and begin descending, gently, through more vineyards. There are two short but rather steep uphill bumps on Chiquita, each followed by a descent. They are probably the two steepest pitches on the entire ride, but are both very short.

At the bottom of the last descent, you pass the Healdsburg city limit sign. Over the course of the 2 miles on Chiquita, the density of residential properties has been steadily increasing, until now it looks fairly suburban, in a relaxed, unregimented way. Chiquita tees into Grove Street, where the route turns right and heads south into the city proper. Grove is a quiet, low traffic alternative to Healdsburg Avenue, the busy main drag through town. In this northernmost section, it passes some light industry and condo complexes. Then it enters a pleasant, shady neighborhood of older, handsome homes, and finally tilts downhill slightly and rolls out in front of City Hall, where the ride began.

MILEAGE LOG

0.0	From City Hall parking lot, right on Grove St.; becomes Vine St.
0.4	Right on Mill St.; becomes Westside Rd. at edge of town
1.2	Right on West Dry Creek Rd.
10.0	Right on Yoakim Bridge Rd.
10.7	Right on Dry Creek Rd.
10.9	Left on Canyon Rd.
13.2	Right on Hwy 128 (Geyserville Ave.) into town of Geyserville
14.1	Left to stay on Hwy 128 at stop sign in center of Geyserville
18.6	Left on Geysers Rd.
19.3	Right on Red Winery Rd.
21.6	Right on Pine Flat Rd.
22.0	Right (actually straight ahead) on Hwy 128
22.3	Jimtown Store
22.5	Straight on Alexander Valley Rd. (Hwy 128 turns right)
24.6	Right on Lytton Station Rd.
26.0	Right on Lytton Springs Rd.
26.8	Left on Chiquita Rd.
28.9	Right on Grove St. into Healdsburg
30.6	Right into Healdsburg City Hall parking lot and finish

15 WINE COUNTRY LOOP #2

Difficulty:	Moderate
Time:	3 to 5 hours
Distance:	50 miles
Elevation gain:	2000'
Best seasons:	All year, but May and October are best
Road conditions:	Traffic varies; pavement does too.

GETTING THERE: From central Santa Rosa, drive 8 miles north on Hwy 101 to the Shiloh Rd. exit. Take Shiloh east 0.7 mile to Esposti Park.

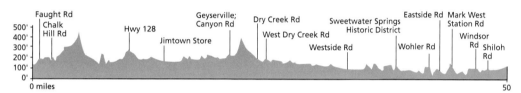

This is one of two Sonoma County Wine Country loops and is the longer and more ambitious of the two. There is some overlap between the two routes; check Ride 14 to see how they're intertwined.

This ride stages out of Esposti Park, near the suburban fringe of Windsor, half a mile east of a sprawl of big-box stores near the Highway 101 off-ramps. Begin by heading away from that sprawl on Shiloh Road and then Faught Road, which rolls along the edge of the valley for a mile, with vineyards below the road on the left and wooded hills rising up on the right. Turn right on Chalk Hill Road. Chalk Hill is one of the county's many wine appellations, and the pretty hills are often carpeted in rows of vines. Not every acre is given over to grapes, though. The road winds through the dappled shade of oak, sycamore, laurel, and other broadleaf trees, and there are horse ranches here as well.

Chalk Hill climbs very gently, with numerous flats along the way, to a little summit, gaining 400' in 3 miles. The descent beyond this summit is short but fun, as you toss away

all that gain in 1 mile. After that frisky downhill, there are no big climbs or wild descents, but also almost nothing that is remotely flat, just modest, lumpy rollers, again and again.

At mile 10, Chalk Hill tees into Hwy 128. Head north on this smooth, rolling, lightly traveled highway, descending into Alexander Valley, another prestigious wine region. Sometimes the road rolls down the middle of the valley, with vines on either side, and sometimes it rubs along the east side of the valley, with vines sprawling away on the left and oak-studded hills rising up steeply on the right.

The Jimtown Store awaits at mile 13.6. This quaint old market is a popular stop for cyclists in the wine country, with benches and bike racks in front and a water spigot up the alley at the side. Inside is an intriguing store, including an excellent deli-style lunch counter with a changing menu of delicious cuisine.

After a break at the market, continue on Hwy 128, north along the valley to the town of Geyserville. Here, the route climbs over a ridge and descends into Dry Creek Valley. A

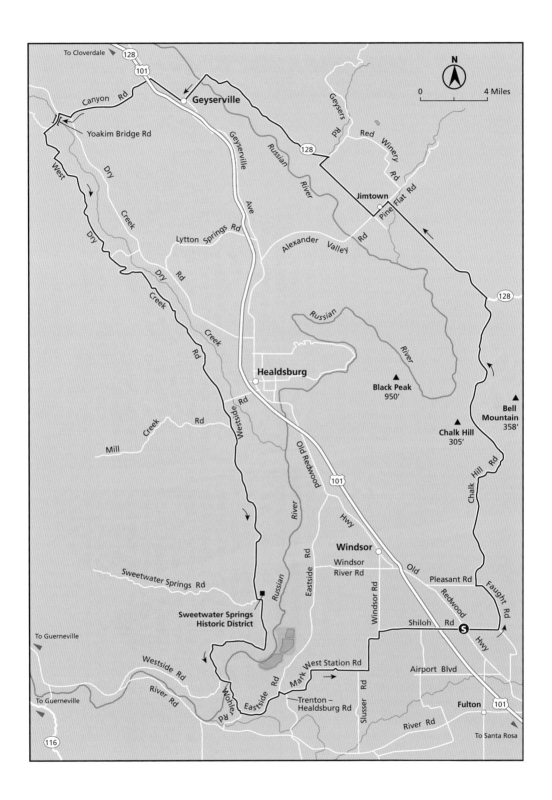

N

0   4 Miles

To Cloverdale
128
101

Canyon Rd

Geyserville

Yoakim Bridge Rd

West

Dry

Dry

Creek

Geyserville Ave

Russian River

128

Geysers Rd

Red Winery Rd

Jimtown

Pine Flat Rd

Lytton Springs Rd

Alexander Valley Rd

Dry Creek Rd

Creek Rd

Russian River

128

Creek Rd

Mill Creek Rd

Healdsburg

Black Peak 950'

Bell Mountain 358'

Chalk Hill 305'

Westside Rd

Old Redwood

Chalk Hill Rd

101

River

Hwy

Windsor

Windsor River Rd

Old Redwood

Pleasant Rd

Faught Rd

Sweetwater Springs Rd

Russian River

Eastside Rd

Windsor Rd

Shiloh Rd

S

Sweetwater Springs Historic District

To Guerneville

Westside Rd

River Rd

Wohler Rd

Eastside Rd

Mark West Station Rd

Slusser Rd

Airport Blvd

Hwy

Fulton

101

To Guerneville

Trenton– Healdsburg Rd

River Rd

To Santa Rosa

116

A stop at the bike-friendly Jimtown Store is an essential part of any ride through Alexander Valley. (Darell Dickey)

quick jog across the valley floor brings you to a run south down the valley on West Dry Creek, a great cycling road. It is narrow and winding, has slightly bumpy pavement, is forever dancing up and down over an endless series of little hills, and carries almost no traffic. What it does carry are legions of cyclists. This is quite possibly the most popular cycling road in the area and one of the most popular in the state. It's the sort of road you would create, were you to sit down and design the perfect back-road cycling experience. As a consequence, it is featured in the catalogs of every company that runs catered cycling vacations. It is used for centuries and triathlons, and it plays host to an endless parade of weekend club rides and visits from individuals out for a spin among the vines.

West Dry Creek Road tumbles along its rolling course for 9 miles down the picturesque valley. For the most part, the valley floor to the left is all vineyards, while on the right the steep hills are covered in dense fir and oak forest. At mile 33, the road tees into Westside Road. Westside is almost as nice as West Dry Creek. The scenery is every bit as good and the road is perfect for cycling—more pleasant little ups and downs through the trees and vines—and the only marks against it are a slight increase in traffic and some spots with lousy pavement. You're on Westside for another 9 miles.

Midway along the road is the Sweetwater Springs Historic District, a wide spot in the road highlighted by the grand old hop kiln at Hop Kiln Winery. Hearty, dark hops used to be a major crop in Sonoma County before Prohibition and big brand-name beers wiped out the little brewers. There are numerous old hop-drying barns in the area, and this stately stone structure is one of the finest examples.

There is one small climb toward the end of Westside: up about 100' in half a mile through a shady wood. On the downhill side of this little ridge, be alert for a left turn onto Wohler Road. Wohler crosses the Russian River on a rusty old truss bridge and then descends to a junction with Eastside Road. Turn left here and climb gently to a right turn onto Trenton–Healdsburg Road, followed almost immediately with a left onto Mark West Station Road.

Mark West Station begins with a small downhill through a dense thicket before breaking out into rolling pastures. After two small climbs, the road levels out and connects to Windsor Road, along the backside of Sonoma County Airport. Finally, turn right on the last road of the day. Shiloh Road begins out in the country but soon enters a zone of development spreading out from the Hwy 101 corridor. Over the course of 2 flat, straight miles, it passes a golf course, a time-share condo complex, and a shopping center. Just beyond this brief zone of clutter, the ride returns to Esposti Park.

MILEAGE LOG

0.0	From Esposti Park, left on Shiloh Rd.
0.7	Left on Faught Rd.; becomes Pleasant Rd. (briefly)
2.0	Right on Chalk Hill Rd.
10.1	Left on Hwy 128
13.6	Jimtown Store
13.8	Right to stay on Hwy 128 at Alexander Valley Rd. junction
20.4	Right on Geyserville Ave. in town of Geyserville (still also Hwy 128)
21.3	Left on Canyon Rd.
23.5	Right on Dry Creek Rd.
23.8	Left on Yoakim Bridge Rd.
24.4	Left on West Dry Creek Rd.
33.2	Right on Westside Rd.
41.9	Left on Wohler Rd.
42.9	Left on Eastside Rd.
44.1	Right on Trenton–Healdsburg Rd.
44.2	Left on Mark West Station Rd.
46.7	Straight on Windsor Road at Slusser Rd. junction
47.9	Right on Shiloh Rd.
50.0	Finish at Esposti Park

Difficulty:	Moderate
Time:	2.5 to 4 hours
Distance:	35 miles
Elevation gain:	2500'
Best seasons:	All year, although winter may be rainy
Road conditions:	Pavement is usually good. Silverado Trail may be busy, but smaller roads are quiet.

GETTING THERE: From Hwy 29 in St. Helena, 20 miles north of city of Napa, take Pope St. east for 0.3 mile to Jacob Meily Park.

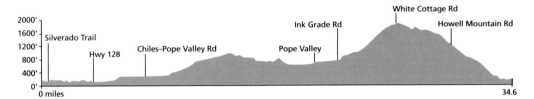

This is a journey to the quiet side of Napa County, the part the tourists rarely see: Pope Valley, only one ridge away, but a world apart.

The ride begins in St. Helena, at the heart of Napa Valley's world-famous wine region. But it won't stay in the valley for long. After a rolling run south on the wide shoulder of Silverado Trail, turn left on Sage Canyon Road (Highway 128) and say good-bye to the tourist hordes. A brief, level run through the trees leads to an easy climb to the shore of Lake Hennessey, the reservoir holding Napa's drinking water. As reservoirs go, this one is quite nice, doing a passable imitation of a natural lake. The road follows the pretty contours of the lake to a junction with Chiles–Pope Valley Road. Bear left onto this delightful road.

For a mile or so the road is level, until it encounters Chiles Creek and begins a gentle climb up the creek's rocky canyon. It's a nearly ideal cycling road, even if it is an uphill, with the pretty creek dancing along next to the road in the dappled shade of alders and sycamores. After the climb in the canyon, the road continues north, still climbing gently. From Lake Hennessey onward, you climb for most of 5 miles, but much of that is little more than false flat, never difficult. After those lazy climbs, the road rolls up and down through long meadows and scattered woods. In the spring, the meadows are splashed with gaudy displays of wildflowers, many varieties in great profusion. It's quite a show. There is very little in the way of development in Pope Valley: gravel drives leading off to ranches in the hills are the only evidence of settlement. It's empty and peaceful.

At 17 miles, you climb the only hill of any size (since the canyon). After this little bump, cruise downhill to the village of Pope Valley and its little store: your only food and drink depot around the entire loop. Right across from the store is Howell Mountain Road. Even though you may see Howell Mountain on the mileage log, you do not want to take

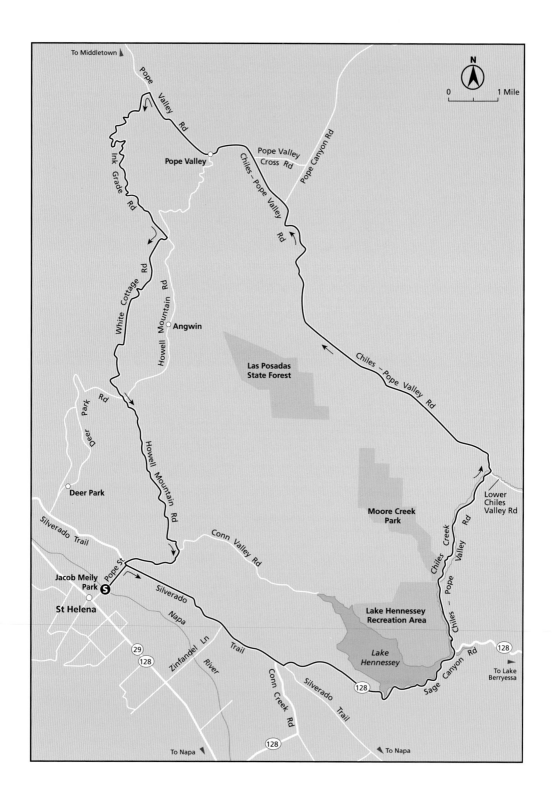

To Middletown

N

0   1 Mile

Pope Valley Rd

Pope Valley

Ink Grade Rd

Pope Valley Cross Rd

Pope Canyon Rd

Chiles – Pope Valley Rd

White Cottage Rd

Howell Mountain Rd

Angwin

Las Posadas State Forest

Chiles – Pope Valley Rd

Deer Park Rd

Howell Mountain Rd

Deer Park

Moore Creek Park

Lower Chiles Valley Rd

Silverado Trail

Conn Valley Rd

Chiles Creek Rd

Pope St

Jacob Meily Park

St Helena

Silverado

Napa

River

Trail

Conn Creek Rd

Silverado Trail

Chiles – Pope Valley Rd

Lake Hennessey Recreation Area

Lake Hennessey

Sage Canyon Rd

128

To Lake Berryessa

Zinfandel Ln

29

128

128

To Napa

128

To Napa

Pope Valley in the spring means quiet roads and green meadows sprinkled with the confetti colors of wildflowers.

this section of road. It climbs very steeply for over 2 miles—a brutal pitch—and besides, it carries most of the traffic. No, there is a better option. Head north on Pope Valley Road and turn left on Ink Grade Road.

Ink Grade is a wonderful road. It carries almost no traffic and although it climbs the same hill as Howell Mountain, it does it in a much more civilized manner, rationing the elevation gain out over a couple of extra miles so that it's never too steep, as it meanders back and forth across the hillside through broad-leaf forest. Toward the top, the leafy canopy shifts to fir and pine, and there are occasional mossy rock walls overhanging the one-lane road. It's so pleasant, you may be inclined to overlook the fact that it's the longest climb of the day: 1000' in 4 miles.

The ascent isn't quite over when you turn right on White Cottage Road at mile 26. You have to climb for another small fraction of a mile and then—from the high point on the ride—you begin the first of several snappy

descents. White Cottage runs for 4 mostly downhill miles to a junction with Howell Mountain. Cross directly from White Cottage to Howell Mountain and continue the wild descent.

Unlike the busier section of Howell Mountain over in Pope Valley, this run is almost deserted. It's old and slightly funky and narrow. For 4 miles, it's all tangled up in an endless series of slinky S-bends, slithering down the wooded slope of Conn Valley. Some of the pavement is new and smooth, but some has enough cracks and bumps to require your fullest attention. The grade isn't steep enough to make this a white-knuckle descent, nor to require much braking. If you're a skilled descender, you might almost—*almost*—do the whole thing without braking at all. It's one of my all-time favorite descents.

This excellent road rolls out to Silverado Trail, just across from Pope Street and the short run back to the park where the ride began. The town of St. Helena is one of the hottest of Napa Valley's hot spots when it comes to tourist services, with cafés and bistros in every block along the main drag. But the best spot might be Velo Vino on the south end of town: a shop opened by the founder of Clif Bar and dedicated to his twin passions: wine and cycling. How very Napa Valley!

MILEAGE LOG

0.0	From Jacob Meily Park, left on Pope St.
0.6	Right on Silverado Trail
3.9	Left on Sage Canyon Rd. (Hwy 128)
7.7	Left on Chiles–Pope Valley Rd.
20.1	Village of Pope Valley
21.7	Left on Ink Grade Rd.
25.9	Right on White Cottage Rd.
29.6	Straight on Howell Mountain Rd.
34.0	Cross Silverado Trail to Pope St., toward St. Helena
34.6	Finish at Jacob Meily Park

17 KING RIDGE–COLEMAN VALLEY LOOP

Difficulty:	Challenging/epic
Time:	5 to 6 hours
Distance:	71 miles
Elevation gain:	8000'
Best seasons:	March through October
Road conditions:	Some highway miles may be busy, but most roads are low traffic. Most are well paved but some are quite primitive.

GETTING THERE: From Sebastopol, drive 5.5 miles west on Bodega Hwy Turn right on Bohemian Hwy and go north 4 miles to Occidental. Park in the public lot in the center of town.

This loop includes all the marquee attractions on the by-now famous King Ridge Gran-Fondo. That big event puts around 5000 riders on this course each October. These roads have also appeared in pro races and have been written up in pretty much every cycling magazine out there. (I've written a few of those articles myself.) One writer called this loop, "God's cycling theme park." It definitely plays to rave reviews. Is it as good as everyone says it is? Ride it and find out . . .

Our trek begins in the village of Occidental and gets going quickly with a rollicking, 3-mile downhill on Bohemian Highway, all snappy bends through the redwoods along Dutch Bill Creek. Another 3 easy miles bring you rolling down to the town of Monte Rio on the Russian River. Cross the river, turn left on River Road, and head downstream to a right on Austin Creek Road. Head upstream on a rolling run alongside the creek, deep in the redwoods. Austin Creek and Cazadero

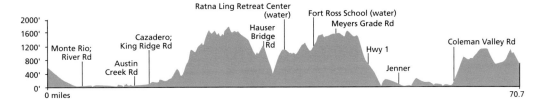

Highway lead to the village of Cazadero, the gateway to King Ridge and the last spot for water before heading into the remote hills. (There are two sources for water in the hills, noted on the mileage log.)

King Ridge begins with 4 miles of chunky ups and downs along the creek, and then the hard work begins around mile 20 with a stiff climb of 1.3 miles, a mile of uphill rollers, and another steep climb of 1 mile. At this point, you've reached the real world of King Ridge, the part everyone raves about. You're now riding along the ridgeline, with views off one side or the other, to the west out over the far Pacific and to the east across rank on rank of empty, serried hills. The vegetation ranges from redwood, oak, and bay laurel, to open meadows of waving grass. Every inch of this ride is beautiful, but up on the ridge the vistas are so sublime, even hardened hammerheads slow down and smile.

In addition to all the buffed-out climbing on King Ridge, there are also a number of exciting descents. If we were riding this road in the opposite direction, our cyclometers would record 1400' of gain, and for you that translates into 1400' of twisting, busy fun.

Eventually, King Ridge ends at a junction with Hauser Bridge Road around mile 32. Hauser is intense: a wild, corkscrew, free-fall, culminating in a 20 percent plunge to a one-lane, iron-grate bridge over the Gualala River. Pavement on this descent ranges from mediocre to dreadful, so you need to treat it with respect.

After the bridge, you have to climb back out of the canyon into which you just dropped: a steep pitch of 1.7 miles, followed by 5 miles of more moderate ups and downs (mostly ups) along Seaview Road. This leads to a junction with Fort Ross Road, coming up from the coast. The route merges onto Fort Ross and, half a mile later, departs Fort Ross to continue straight on Meyers Grade.

Throughout the climbs on Hauser and Seaview, the road has been in the trees—close-up scenery without any views—but once up on Fort Ross and Meyers Grade, you emerge onto a ridge above the ocean with views to forever. But you may forget to notice the view, once you begin the hair-raising, 16 percent descent to Hwy 1.

The beat goes on when you turn onto Hwy 1, with another couple of miles so dizzily twisted the locals call it Dramamine Drive. The grade isn't as steep as the pitch on Meyers Grade, but is perhaps more fun because you can really let it rip. Drop all the way to the beach, climb a small hill, traverse the cliff face above the crashing surf, arriving in a couple of miles at the mouth of the Russian River and the town of Jenner, at mile 53, a good spot for a break.

Head south from Jenner on Hwy 1. This run down the coast is great fun, diving into and climbing out of numerous little canyons where small streams plunge to the beach. At mile 60.6, leave the coast for the last big challenge of the day: the hilly run back to Occidental on Coleman Valley Road. The turn onto Coleman Valley is easy to miss. It's not well marked and comes in the middle of a little downhill.

The worst comes first on Coleman Valley, as the road kicks up 800' in the first 1.5 miles, clawing up the steep hillside before leveling

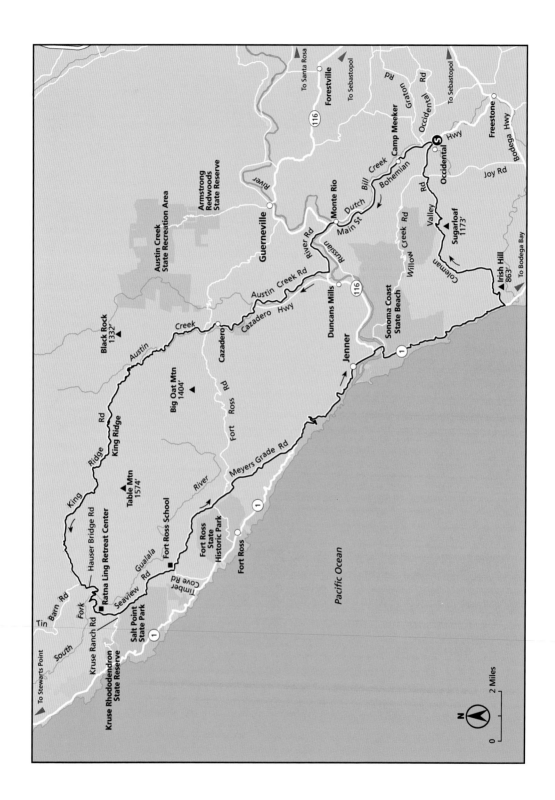

To Santa Rosa

Forestville

To Sebastopol

116

Armstrong Redwoods State Reserve

Austin Creek State Recreation Area

River

Guerneville

Monte Rio

Main St

Dutch Bill Creek

Camp Meeker

Bohemian

Graton

Rd

Occidental

Rd

To Sebastopol

Freestone

Bodega Hwy

Occidental Hwy

S

Joy Rd

Valley Rd

Sugarloaf 1173'

Willow Creek Rd

Coleman

Irish Hill 863'

To Bodega Bay

River Rd

Russian

River Rd

Austin Creek Rd

Cazadero Hwy

Duncans Mills

116

Sonoma Coast State Beach

Jenner

1

Creek

Black Rock 1332'

Austin

Cazadero

Ross

Rd

Big Oat Mtn 1404'

Fort Ross

Rd

Meyers Grade Rd

Ridge

Rd

King Ridge

King

Table Mtn 1574'

River

Fort Ross School

Fort Ross State Historic Park

Fort Ross

1

Pacific Ocean

Hauser Bridge Rd

Ratna Ling Retreat Center

Seaview Rd

Gualala

Timber Cove Rd

Salt Point State Park

1

Tin

Barn Rd

Fork

South

Kruse Ranch Rd

Kruse Rhododendron State Reserve

To Stewarts Point

N

0   2 Miles

King Ridge in the springtime, when the hills are green, is just about as good as it gets. (Darell Dickey)

off for a run along the ridgeline. More climbs follow—less severe—and the road tops out at 1100' among high, hilltop meadows and stately stands of oak and bay.

Give one last, backward glance to the panorama of coastline, then bomb downhill between split-rail fences on a steep, technical dive through the woods into the little valley that gives the road its name. Just beyond the old one-room schoolhouse, the road tilts up again, climbing another 200' out of this pretty pocket valley before a final, fast, smooth descent into the town of Occidental.

This charming village is home to two huge Italian family-style restaurants that pretty much define the term "carbo-loading." While you recuperate and chow down at one of the restaurants, you can rehash the ride and decide whether all the things folks say about it are true.

MILEAGE LOG

0.0	North on Bohemian Hwy; depart Occidental
5.0	Straight ahead on Main St.
6.5	Left across bridge over Russian River; town of Monte Rio
6.7	Left on River Rd. (SR 116)
9.3	Right on Austin Creek Rd.
12.9	Right on Cazadero Hwy
15.5	Town of Cazadero
16.0	Straight on King Ridge Rd.
32.2	Left on Hauser Bridge Rd.
35.0	Ratna Ling Retreat Center (water faucet for cyclists on right)
35.8	Bear left on Seaview Rd. at Kruse Ranch Rd. junction
39.3	Fort Ross School (water)
42.5	Straight on Fort Ross Rd. (Fort Ross Rd. merges from the right)
43.0	Straight on Meyers Grade Rd. (Fort Ross Rd. turns left)

47.9	Left on Hwy 1
53.0	Town of Jenner
60.6	Left on Coleman Valley Rd.
70.7	Finish in town of Occidental

18 SANTA ROSA–SEBASTOPOL BIKE TRAILS

Difficulty:	Easy
Time:	2 to 3 hours
Distance:	20 miles
Elevation gain:	400'
Best seasons:	April through October
Road conditions:	Mostly on Class 1 bike trails with good pavement. Approximately 5 miles are on public roads, some with shoulders, some without.

GETTING THERE: In central Santa Rosa, leave Hwy 101 at the Third St., "downtown" exit. Head east to a right on A St. and a left on 1st St., then proceed three blocks to the parking lot behind City Hall.

This carefree and (mostly) car-free cruise features the best of Sonoma County's bike trails system. Of the ride's 20 miles, 15 are on dedicated bike trails, entirely removed from traffic. Of the 5 miles on roads, most are on quiet country lanes. If you have the fitness to ride as much as 20 miles, you probably also have the experience to deal with the traffic on the public roads.

Depart City Hall with a left on 1st Street, then a left on Santa Rosa Avenue. Head south half a block to the entrance to the Prince Memorial Greenway, the first and fanciest of today's bike trails. The trail runs along Santa Rosa Creek, which had been "channelized" for flood control in the 1960s, turning it into

an unsightly, oversized storm drain lined with riprap and industrial refuse. In the late '80s, the city began the process of restoring the creek to something approaching its natural state, or at least to a park-like compromise with nature: trails and benches and art. Now the Greenway is one of the crown jewels of the city's park system. For cyclists, it's the gateway to a network of trails stretching out into the rural lands west of town.

At 0.7 mile into the ride, leave the Greenway with a sharp right turn up a ramp and over a bridge that connects to the Joe Rodota Trail. Signs at the junction point to the new trail. This trail runs from downtown Santa Rosa to downtown Sebastopol, a little over 6

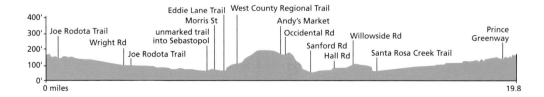

miles away. It is built along the bed of the old rail line that used to connect the cities. As is the case with most rails-to-trails conversions, the grade is gentle.

The first 2 miles of the trail pass through the city's backyard. Included in this semi-urban run are crossings of three busy streets. All have crosswalks and signals for bikes. At the last of the three crossings, Wright Road, turn left and ride down the wide sidewalk for half a block to the signal at the corner of Sebastopol Road. Cross here and continue west one block to pick up the trail again.

Say good-bye to Santa Rosa and roll out across the floodplain of the Laguna de Santa Rosa, sprawling all the way to Sebastopol. (The Laguna is the little river that drains the llano south and west of Santa Rosa, flowing north to the Russian River.) Stately old oaks

dot the nearly flat plain and thickets of creek willows crowd in around the waterway.

At mile 7, turn right on a side trail. This trail is not marked, but it is the only paved side trail you will encounter at this point in the ride. It comes up soon after you cross a long, wooden bridge over the main channel of the Laguna. This spur trail leads to Highway 12, the main highway through Sebastopol. Cross the highway at the signal and head north on Morris Street, a quiet street on the edge of town.

As Morris bends left at its northern end, look for a right on a short bike path next to the local high school. At High School Road, go left one block to the next section of bike trail. This section curves northwest, leaving town on a gently uphill grade, mostly in the shade of acacias and oaks, amid a scattering

The Prince Greenway, along Santa Rosa Creek, is the gateway to miles of bike trails heading west out of Santa Rosa.

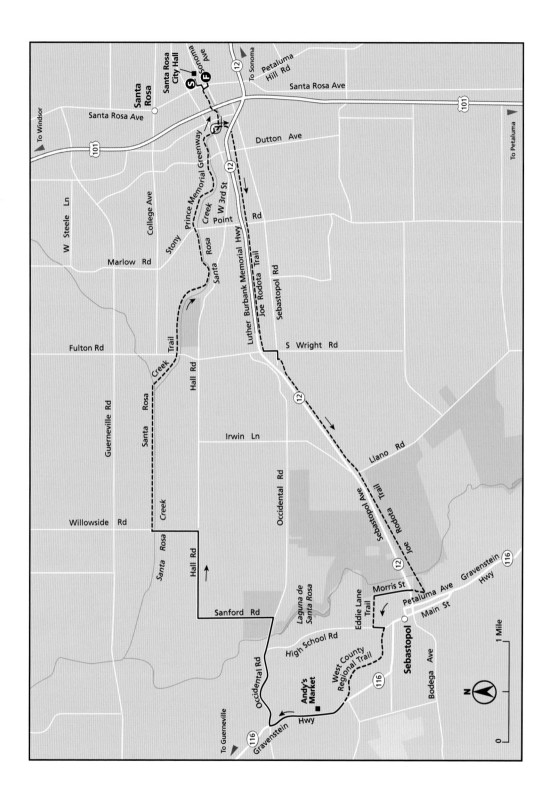

of homes along the northern edge of town. At the top of this 1-mile, 2 percent grade, the bike trail encounters Hwy 116, the other main highway serving Sebastopol. It continues alongside the highway but separate from it, now heading north.

Midway along this highway run is Andy's Market, a good spot for a mid-ride break. Andy's is a little fruit stand that grew up into a full-service market. In addition to offering excellent food, they have a patio along the bike trail, right next to a coffee kiosk.

At the north end of the Hwy 116 leg, turn right on Occidental Road and head back downhill to another crossing of the Laguna de Santa Rosa, a distance of 1 mile. Occidental is the one somewhat busy stretch of road on this ride, but almost all of it has wide shoulders. For the next 2.5 miles, the route follows Sanford, Hall, and Willowside roads on its way to the next bike trail. All three are straight and nearly flat and usually low traffic. Scenery along this stretch begins with dairy pastures along the Laguna and ends with a sprinkling of rural-residential development that manages to feel mostly rural.

Turn right from Willowside onto the Santa Rosa Creek Trail on the north bank of the creek (not the unpaved trail on the south bank). This will be your home for the remaining 6 miles of the ride. The trail runs along the top of the flood levee next to the creek, with a canopy of trees overhanging both the creek and the trail. When the trail encounters busy streets on its way into the city, it ducks beneath them on underpasses.

As the trail approaches the center of Santa Rosa, it becomes the Prince Greenway again. At the very end, take the last bike bridge over the creek to the south bank, wander through Prince Gateway Park, with its impressive rainbow trout sculpture, and then use Sonoma Avenue to reach the City Hall parking lot.

MILEAGE LOG

0.0	From City Hall parking lot, left on 1st St.
0.1	Left on Santa Rosa Ave. to right on Prince Greenway
0.7	Right on Joe Rodota Trail
3.5	Left on east sidewalk of N. Wright Rd.
3.6	Right on Sebastopol Rd. (follow signs for trail)
3.8	Left to pick up trail again
6.9	Right on unmarked trail (0.2 mile beyond long wooden bridge)
7.2	Cross Hwy 12 to Morris St.; city of Sebastopol
7.6	Right on Eddie Ln. bike trail past high school campus
7.9	Left on High School Rd. (also known as N. Main St.)
8.1	Right on Joe Rodota Trail (now also known as West County Regional Trail)
9.2	Bear right on trail, now parallel to Hwy 116
9.7	Andy's Market (mid-ride break)
10.1	Right on Occidental Rd.
11.4	Left on Sanford Rd.
12.3	Right on Hall Rd.
13.3	Left on Willowside Rd.
13.9	Right on Santa Rosa Creek Trail; becomes Prince Memorial Greenway
19.5	Right over creek on footbridge to Prince Gateway Park
19.6	Left on Sonoma Ave.; cross Santa Rosa Ave.
19.8	Left into Santa Rosa City Hall parking lot and finish

19 SONOMA–NAPA CHUTES AND LADDERS

Difficulty:	Challenging/epic
Time:	5 to 8 hours
Distance:	52 miles (challenging) or 81 miles (epic)
Elevation gain:	8500' (long route)
Best seasons:	April through October
Road conditions:	Some highway miles may be busy, but those sections have good shoulders (usually). Some are well paved and some are terrible.

GETTING THERE: Leave Hwy 101 at the Cotati/Hwy 116 exit, 7 miles south of Santa Rosa, and drive 0.4 mile south on Old Redwood Hwy into Cotati. Turn left on E. Cotati Ave. and proceed 2 miles to the campus of Sonoma State University.

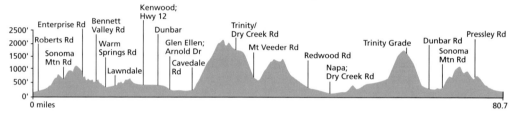

Sonoma and Napa counties are next-door neighbors on the map, but in the real world they are separated by steep, rumpled ridges running along their border. Riding over this humpbacked landscape is a challenge. This ride tackles those rugged ridges again and again. It's about as hard as an 81-mile ride can be. But there is a way to cut the ride down to 52 miles, which makes it, if not exactly easy, at least a bit more manageable.

Head south from the university along Petaluma Hill Road and turn left on Roberts Road, which turns into Pressley Road a bit past 2 miles. This is where the first climb begins. It will also be the end of the last descent, as the first 9 miles of the ride are also the last 9 miles: a simple retrace.

Two small climbs and two smaller descents on Pressley lead to a right turn onto Sonoma Mountain Road. This little road may not look like much in the elevation profile, but it is hard work, with a series of short but sometimes steep pitches climbing through beautiful woods and meadows. At mile 8, it topples off the ridge and becomes a steep, technical downhill. After a first tricky descent on Sonoma Mountain, there is more of the same on Enterprise Road: short, kinky drops mixed in with little uphill bumps, all of it amidst broadleaf forest, hilly vineyards, and palatial country estates.

Turn right onto Bennett Valley Road and zip downhill to a left on Warm Springs Road. You are now in Sonoma Valley, otherwise known as the Valley of the Moon. Warm Springs and the roads that follow—Lawndale and Schultz—are all quiet back roads through the same sort of scenery: vineyards, woods, and comfortable country homes tucked back in the trees.

After a brisk descent, Lawndale tees into Highway 12. This will be the busiest road of the ride, and you will be on it for a little over 3 miles, south through the town of Kenwood

The wickedly steep and twisted roads in the hills along the Sonoma-Napa border are challenging, as climbs or descents. (Georg Ockenfuss)

and out into vineyard-covered hills. There are decent shoulders along the busy highway, but it's still nice to finish this run and bail out onto Dunbar and Henno, two little lanes with no traffic. By the time you finish with Henno Road, at mile 24, you are approaching the village of Glen Ellen, where there is a nice market: time for a break.

Head south out of Glen Ellen on Arnold Drive, tack left across the valley on Madrone, then nip south on Hwy 12 to reach Cavedale Road. Get your climbing gears ready: you'll need them for the next few miles on this tough old road. Cavedale gains 2000' in 5 miles. It's a stair-step climb, with many pitches under 4 percent but a few well over 15 percent. Those steep ramps are all near the top. Each one is short, with little, false-flat resting spots in between. Collectively, the whole hill is daunting. Scenery is often just trees and shrubs enclosing the road, but occasionally vistas open up over the valley, even all the way south to San Francisco Bay.

There is more of Cavedale after the sum-mit: a couple of sketchy descents on lousy pavement and one more little climb. The road tees into Trinity Grade Road at mile 35, where there is a fire station with a hose bib handy to cyclists. This junction is your deci-sion point: turn right and carry on over the hill, down into Napa Valley, or turn left and descend Trinity Grade, back into Sonoma Valley. The first choice is the 81-mile option; the second is the 52-mile alternative.

The long option climbs gently to the sum-mit on Trinity, where the road name changes to Dry Creek. Roll over the top and launch off on a wild descent: 2 miles long, often steep and twisty. The pavement is fine, so there is a tendency to want to drill it, but the corners are just too tight, too tricky.

Turn right onto Mount Veeder Road and start climbing again: 800' in 3 miles. The middle mile is almost level, so the climbing is packed into the other 2 miles, mostly into this first one: perhaps 500' in a mile. Most of this road runs under the shade of a dense forest of oak, fir, and bay. Over the top, you

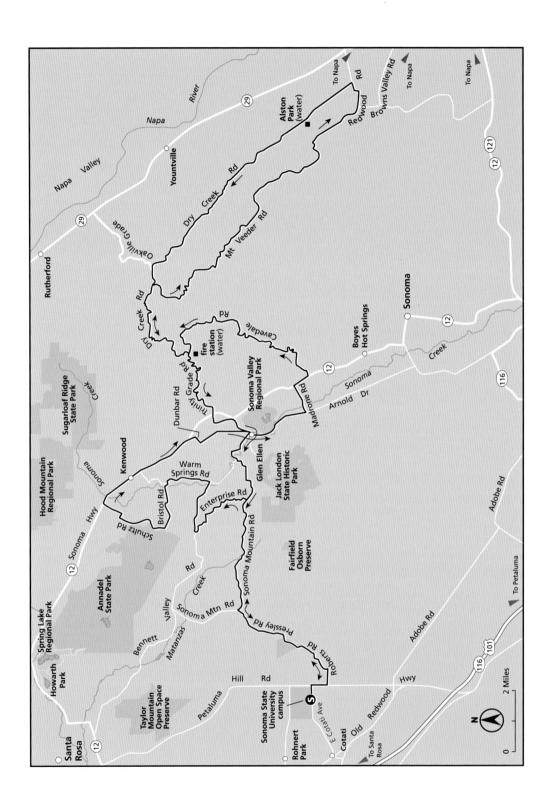

are treated to a ripper of a downhill: 1200' in 6 miles. The first 3 miles are fast and frantic; the second 3 are swift roll-out.

Near the bottom of the hill, the road name changes to Redwood, but you carry on straight ahead into the suburban fringe of the city of Napa. For 2 miles—50 to 52—Redwood Road and Dry Creek Road will run through tract neighborhoods, but soon you will leave that behind and head out into the hill country again. There is a park on the left side of the road at mile 51.4 where you can fill your bottles.

Dry Creek Road? Yes, the same Dry Creek as the hairy descent into the valley a few miles back. Now you have to climb back up that same pitch. But before you do that, you have to get there along this lower section of the road, which runs for about 10 miles, slowly gaining elevation over a series of rollers. This part is never difficult, but the big climb is looming out there, just around the corner: 1100' up in 2 miles (10 percent). It's a very hard 2 miles.

It eases a bit at the top, and then—as Trinity Grade again—finally tips downhill. This descent is even better than the one on the other side of the hill: 3 miles long and as tangled up as a plate of fettuccine. At the bottom, cross Hwy 12, turn left on Dunbar and right on Arnold, heading back toward Glen Ellen. At mile 69, turn right on Warm Springs.

One rolling mile along Warm Springs brings you to a left on Sonoma Mountain. A mile and a half on Sonoma Mountain—mostly uphill, often steeply—completes the loop and brings you back to the junction with Enterprise Road. You've been here before; this is where you begin the final 9 miles of retracing the route to the finish.

Your weary legs won't be happy to learn that this retrace begins with another mile and a half of wickedly steep climbing. But after that last, painful pitch, things do get easier. There are still a few modest uphills in the final miles, but more frequently you will be going downhill. Because you will have seen this road on the way out, you should be prepared for the kinks and curves it will throw at you on the way back... sneaky little downhill wiggles that can catch you out if you're not careful. You should be used to that by now on this ride!

MILEAGE LOG

0.0	Left on E. Cotati Ave.; leave Sonoma State campus
0.4	Right on Petaluma Hill Rd.
0.9	Left on Roberts Rd.
2.3	Straight on Pressley Rd.
5.2	Right on Sonoma Mountain Rd.
9.0	Left on Enterprise Rd.
11.4	Right on Bennett Valley Rd.
13.0	Left (straight ahead) on Warm Springs Rd.
14.6	Left on Lawndale Rd.
15.6	Straight on Bristol Rd. to right on Schultz Rd.
16.9	Left on Lawndale Rd.
18.6	Right on Hwy 12
19.3	Town of Kenwood
21.9	Right on Dunbar Rd.
22.2	Right on Henno Rd.
24.1	Left on Warm Springs Rd. to right on Arnold Dr.; town of Glen Ellen

26.2	Left on Madrone Rd.
27.2	Right on Hwy 12
27.7	Left on Cavedale Rd.
35.1	Right on Trinity Grade Rd.; shortcut turns left on Trinity; water at fire station
36.7	Straight on Dry Creek Rd.; descend into Napa Valley
39.1	Right on Mount Veeder Rd.
47.4	Straight on Redwood Rd.
50.5	Suburban fringe of city of Napa
50.9	Left on Dry Creek Rd.; water in Alston Park at mile 51.4
59.9	Left to stay on Dry Creek Rd. at Oakville Grade junction
64.3	Straight on Trinity Grade Rd.
67.4	Cross Hwy 12
67.7	Left on Dunbar Rd.
68.2	Right on Arnold Dr.
69.0	Right on Warm Springs Rd.; town of Glen Ellen
70.2	Left on Sonoma Mountain Rd.
75.8	Left on Pressley Rd.
78.7	Straight on Roberts Rd.
80.0	Right on Petaluma Hill Rd.
80.5	Left on E. Cotati Ave.
80.7	Right into Sonoma State campus and finish

20 UP AND DOWN NAPA VALLEY

Difficulty:	Moderate/challenging
Time:	3 to 6 hours
Distance:	45 or 63 miles
Elevation gain:	1400' or 2500'
Best seasons:	All year, although winter may be rainy
Road conditions:	Pavement is good. Some highways may be moderately busy, but smaller roads are quiet.

GETTING THERE: From Hwy 29 10 miles north of the city of Napa, take the California Dr. exit into Yountville. Head north on Washington St. and turn right on Yount St. Turn left on Finnell Rd. into the town hall parking lot.

This is my definitive tour of Napa Valley, America's most famous and most visited wine region. On most weekends, it is thronged with wine-tasting, gourmandizing tourists to the point that it sometimes resembles a Disneyland for grown-ups. However, in spite of that, it is still a great place to visit on a bike, and this ride offers cyclists a useful route for exploring the valley while dodging most of the tourist traffic. The longer route heads north out the top end of the valley and dips a toe into Sonoma County in remote Knights

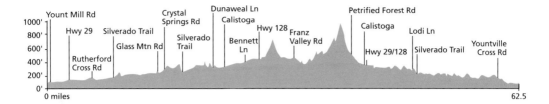

Valley, while the shorter route only goes as far "up valley" (as the locals describe it) as the town of Calistoga.

Napa Valley is a simple piece of geography: 3 miles wide and 30 miles long, hemmed in by steep hills but virtually flat on the valley floor, with nearly every inch turned to vineyards, except for the land covered by four communities spaced at 10-mile intervals along its length, from north to south: Calistoga, St. Helena, Yountville, and Napa. The valley is actually oriented along a northwest–southeast diagonal, but one tends to think of it simply running north–south. Two highways run parallel up the length of the valley: Highway 29 on the west side and Silverado

Riding past Clos Pegase winery in the northern reaches of Napa Valley on a bright, crisp April morning

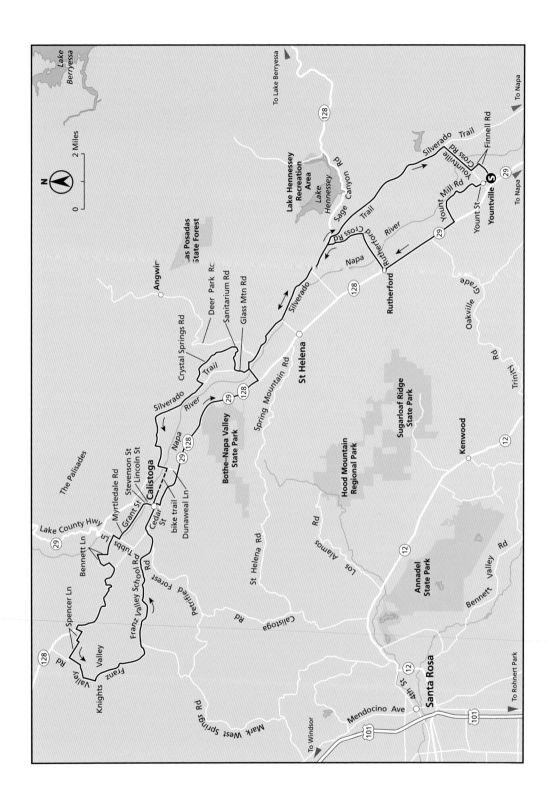

Trail on the east. Between them are several cross-valley connector roads tying the two highways together like rungs on a ladder.

The ride begins in Yountville, one of the tourist hubs in the valley, home to numerous elegant inns and trendy restaurants. Head north out of town on Yount Mill Road, a sleepy little lane through the woods, entirely devoid of all those tourist trimmings. When it ends—too soon!—head north on Hwy 29 for 3 miles to a right on Rutherford Cross Road. Hwy 29 is always busy, here in the heart of the valley, but this section has wide shoulders. North of Rutherford Cross, it becomes much less bike friendly for several miles, so cut across the valley to Silverado Trail, which avoids that busy section of Hwy 29 both out and back. To minimize the backtracking, the ride detours onto a wonderful set of side roads on the way north: Glass Mountain and Crystal Springs, a quiet 3-mile bypass.

After Crystal Springs Road, continue north along Silverado Trail for 4 miles to a left on Dunaweal and then turn right on a bike path heading into Calistoga. Scenery stays much the same all the way up or down the valley: vineyards and wineries and a smattering of rural homes in the foreground, and rugged, forested hills rising up steeply on either side. As you approach Calistoga, the valley narrows, culminating in a grand congress of rocky ramparts known as the Palisades. These hulking buttes adorn the flanks of Mount St. Helena, at 4344', the highest peak in the area.

It may be a shading of subtle stylistic than St. Helena and Yountville. There are probably just as many chic shops and nouvelle bistros here as there are down the valley, but it simply feels more rustic and laid-back. The town is famous for its spring-fed waters, both the bottled sort one drinks and the hot, curative sort one bathes in. I like to point out to other cyclists the steaming water in roadside ditches on this route: don't go off the road into that!

The short route heads down the main street of Calistoga to Hwy 29/128, where the long route returns from its hillier northern loop. That yields a ride of about 45 miles, all nearly level.

The long route heads north out of Calistoga along quiet neighborhood streets. Beyond the town, follow pretty Bennett Lane for 2 miles and then hop onto Hwy 128. Although not absolutely deserted, its traffic load is light and it's an enjoyable road to ride. Shortly after turning onto the highway, you begin a gradual climb of about a mile, at the top of which you cross over into Sonoma County.

Over the top, a smooth descent rolls out into Knights Valley, a remote, unpopulated region... very little out here but a few vineyards, empty meadows, and tall trees. Spencer Lane, Franz Valley Road, and Franz Valley School Road carve an arc through this beautiful valley, swinging around the top of the loop and heading back south into Napa County. Sometimes you're riding in leafy woods and sometimes across meadows, with views up to Mount St. Helena and the other peaks of the Mayacamas Mountains. Franz Valley and Franz Valley School climb in little fits and starts to another hilltop summit right on the county line. Beyond the summit is an excellent, 2-mile downhill: the pavement is smooth, the corners are just right, and the grade is perfect for a comfortable level of medium-speed mayhem.

The downhill ends at Petrified Forest Road, a busier highway funneling you back down to Hwy 128 near Calistoga. Directly across Hwy 128 from Petrified Forest is a road leading into a mobile home park. A short bike path from that road links to Cedar Street, a tree-lined neighborhood lane through residential Calistoga. Take this quiet bypass to see more of the town and avoid riding on the highway.

Head south out of Calistoga on Hwy 29/128. This northern section of highway is okay to ride, even better than okay. The scenery is excellent, and although there is usually some traffic, there are immense shoulders. The route sticks with Hwy 29/128 for 6 miles before turning left on Lodi Lane and crossing the valley back to Silverado Trail.

Now all that's left is a pleasant, 11-mile run south along Silverado to a right on Yountville Cross Road, with one last little detour on Finnell Road to bring you back to the start in Yountville.

MILEAGE LOG

0.0	From parking lot behind Yountville Town Hall, right on Finnell Rd.
0.1	Right on Yount St.; becomes Yount Mill Rd.
1.5	Left to stay on Yount Mill Rd.
2.9	Right on Hwy 29
5.9	Right on Rutherford Cross Rd. (Hwy 128)
8.8	Left on Silverado Trail
14.8	Right on Glass Mountain Rd.
15.6	Left on Sanitarium Rd.
15.8	Left on Crystal Springs Rd.
18.0	Right on Silverado Trail
22.1	Left on Dunaweal Ln.
22.5	Right on Napa Valley Vine Trail (bike path just past Clos Pegase winery)
23.5	Becomes Washington St.
24.0	Right on Lincoln St. (Hwy 29); town of Calistoga; short route turns left
	Short route:
24.0	**Left on Lincoln**
24.2	**Left on Hwy 29/128 south; rejoin long route (see mile 42.4)**
24.1	Left on Stevenson St.
24.3	Left on Grant St.; Monhoff Recreation Center (water, restrooms)
25.3	Becomes Myrtledale Rd.
25.9	Right on Tubbs Ln.
26.1	Left on Bennett Ln.
27.1	Left to stay on Bennett Ln.
28.1	Right on Hwy 128
31.3	Left on Spencer Ln.
32.7	Left on Franz Valley Rd.
36.3	Left on Franz Valley School Rd.
40.6	Left on Petrified Forest Rd.
41.2	Cross Hwy 128 to Cedar St., toward mobile home park
41.5	Right on bike trail link to south section of Cedar St.
41.6	Continue south on Cedar St. into Calistoga
42.3	Right on Pine St.
42.4	Left on Hwy 29/128; short route rejoins
48.6	Left on Lodi Ln.
49.1	Right on Silverado Trail
60.2	Right on Yountville Cross Rd.
61.5	Left on Finnell Rd.
62.5	Finish at Yountville Town Hall

21 TO THE LIGHTHOUSE

Difficulty:	Challenging
Time:	4 to 6 hours (full route)
Distance:	44 or 62 miles
Elevation gain:	2700' or 4400'
Best seasons:	All year, although winter may be rainy
Road conditions:	Pavement varies from good to poor. This is a national park and a tourist destination; traffic is relatively light on weekdays, heavier on weekends.

GETTING THERE: There are many approaches to Point Reyes Station: from north or south along Hwy 1; from San Rafael along Sir Francis Drake Blvd.; from Petaluma along Petaluma–Point Reyes Rd. Park anywhere in Point Reyes Station, where the ride starts.

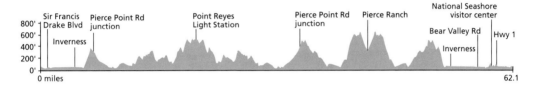

Riding through the Point Reyes National Seashore is a voyage to another land, or at least to another landmass. Everything on the far side of Tomales Bay is part of a different tectonic plate than the rest of North America. It's a transient sled of rock that first emerged from the ocean down around Mexico a few million years ago. It has been bumping and grinding its way up the coast ever since. In the great quake of 1906, it leaped northward 20 feet in a single bound. The long, thin bay is the visible evidence of the San Andreas Fault, that restless seam between the two plates. Over there, on the other side, it is, both literally and figuratively, a world apart.

The ride consists primarily of two out-and-backs: one to the Point Reyes Light Station and one to historic Pierce Ranch. You can do one or both. The adventure begins with a loop around the south end of the bay and a run up the west shore along Sir Francis Drake Boulevard to the town of Inverness. This, the sheltered side of the bay, is all leafy forest, with residential settlement back amid the trees, plus a few stores, motels, restaurants, and boating facilities.

After Inverness, you climb a moderate grade of about a mile before descending gently out onto the open, windswept bluffs by the ocean. (Windswept, for sure: this is one of the windiest spots on the California coast, and the wind will be as much of a challenge for a cyclist as any of the many climbs.) You pass the turn to Pierce Ranch near the top of that first climb. You can visit the ranch now, but I suggest you wait until the return trip from the lighthouse, after you see how much energy the hills and wind have taken out of you. There are several small climbs on the way to the lighthouse, most gaining 200' or 300' in a mile or so. In contrast to the lush woods back near Inverness, trees are sparse out here—usually a few wind-sculpted cypresses—and the landscape is quite austere.

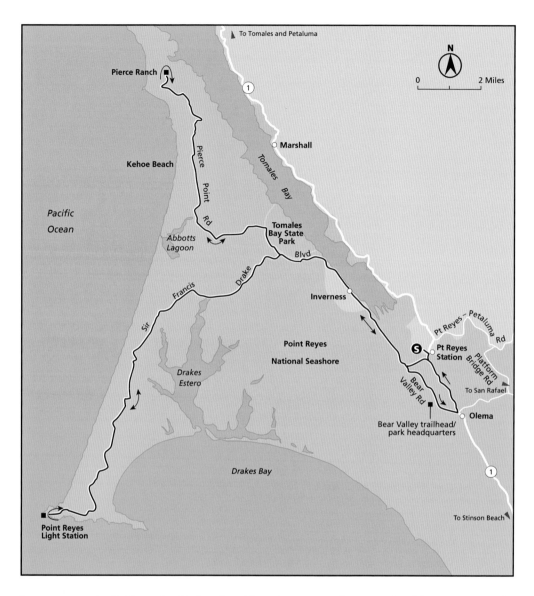

But in season the fields are freckled with wild-flowers: buttercup, poppy, iris, owl's clover, lupine. In spite of this being a national park, the hills are still grazed by cows. A handful of dairies, all over 100 years old, are spaced out along the route, with the road passing through at least two barnyards.

The steepest climb—300' in half a mile—is the last one just before the end of the road. It lifts you up to the final, rocky buttress of the peninsula as it shoulders out into the blue-green sea. The feeling of being thrust out into the vast, forever ocean is powerful and exhilarating here. In places, as you ride along the knife-edge ridge of rock leading out to the lighthouse, you can see the ocean far below off either side of the road. This is an excellent spot for whale-watching, as gray whales pass very close to the point on their migrations along the coast. If you drive a car here, you must park and walk the final half mile, but you can ride your bike all the way to the viewpoint overlooking the lighthouse. After your visit to the end of the world, you retrace the route, with each climb becoming a descent and each descent a climb.

If you do visit Pierce Ranch on the way back, you're in for a treat. Established in 1859, this prosperous farm escaped any unfortunate "improvements" and survived in more or less original form until the Park Service set about a careful restoration. Now it stands as a classic example of a nineteenth-century California farm complex. Large barns, farmhouses, milking and calving sheds, a smithy, a bunkhouse, even a one-room schoolhouse; all are beautifully preserved, deployed around a central courtyard. The only modern touches are a few information placards...no guided tours, no tourist facilities. For the most part, it feels like a place time passed by, quiet and serene, a window onto another, earlier world.

To ride to and from Pierce Ranch takes some doing. From Sir Francis Drake Boule-vard, you climb a small hill and then descend gradually for 5 miles, from 400' down to near sea level at Kehoe Beach. (It's quite likely that you will see herds of elk in this area.) You then climb over 400' in about a mile. After a brief run along the ridgeline, with gorgeous views in all directions, you begin the descent to the ranch, down about 250'. The return trip, like the one from the lighthouse, turns the tables on the topography: ups become downs, etc.

Back down at bay level, Inverness and its little grocery store arrive at mile 54, your first shot at store food on the entire ride. Beyond Inverness, down at the south end of the bay, there is one more loop to do: down Bear Valley Road through the inland heart of the national park. You could skip this little embellishment and scoot straight back to the finish, but it's a worthwhile add-on: a lovely road through a Garden-of-Eden forest, with a possible stop at the park visitor center, if that interests you. A short run north on Highway 1 returns you to Point Reyes Station, where bakeries and bistros await.

The vista overlooking Drakes Estero is typical of the wonderful scenery in Point Reyes National Seashore. (Nancy Yu)

0.0	East on B St. in Point Reyes Station
0.2	Right on Hwy 1
0.3	Right on Sir Francis Drake Blvd.
4.2	Town of Inverness
6.7	Continue straight on Sir Francis Drake Blvd. at Pierce Point Rd. junction
20.2	Point Reyes Light Station (water); turn around and retrace route
33.8	Left on Pierce Point Rd.
42.8	Pierce Ranch; turn around and retrace route
51.8	Left on Sir Francis Drake Blvd.
53.9	Town of Inverness
57.5	Right on Bear Valley Rd.
59.3	Entrance (to the right) to Point Reyes National Seashore visitor center
59.8	Left on Hwy 1; village of Olema to the right
62.0	Left on 4th St. in Point Reyes Station
62.1	Finish

22 SONOMARIN BORDERLANDS

Difficulty:	Challenging
Time:	4.5 to 7 hours
Distance:	66 miles
Elevation gain:	4300'
Best seasons:	All year, although winter may be rainy
Road conditions:	Pavement varies from excellent to poor. Main highways may be busy, but smaller roads are quiet.

GETTING THERE: From the center of Sebastopol, take Bodega Hwy west for 5.5 miles. Turn right on Bohemian Hwy and go north 4 miles to Occidental. Park in the public lot in the center of town.

Sonomarin? What's that? It's a splice of Sonoma and Marin counties. This ride is half in one and half in the other: the borderlands. But it's more than just a cute name. The region really is unique, not quite like the rest of Sonoma County and not at all like most of Marin. It's a special place, and just about perfect for cycling.

The hills have a soft, rounded feel and are generally free of dense forest. There are iso-lated stands of eucalyptus and cypress, with willows down along the creeks, but most of the hills wear only grasses and wildflowers. The bulk of this stage runs through prime dairy country, and your constant companions will be grazing Holsteins, placidly convert-ing those hillside grasses to butterfat. Herds of sheep also call these hills home, but few humans do. The ranches are large and the towns are small.

Begin by heading south on Bohemian Highway on a smooth, sinuous downhill through the trees. Once the descent peters out, roll through meadows and woods to the quaint village of Freestone, a designated historic district. After 1 mile of busy, no-shoulder Bodega Highway, escape on a quiet byway to the town of Valley Ford. Head south out of Valley Ford along Middle Road, crossing the border into Marin County. Double back on Marsh Road to Franklin School Road. A climb and descent lead to a left on Whitaker Bluff Road.

Stop up on the bluff just after the turn. It's a lovely spot, with the Estero de San Antonio scrawling lazy loops along the valley below.

Highway 1 along Tomales Bay in northern Marin County (Bill Bushnell)

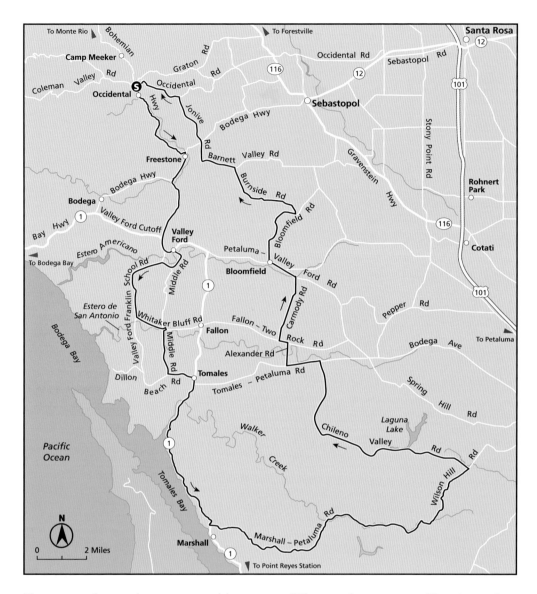

Sheep graze the meadows, egrets and herons stalk the shallows, and hawks circle overhead. After Whitaker Bluff, head south to the town of Tomales, home to an excellent bakery and deli, with comfortable chairs along the street. At 17 miles, it's the perfect spot for a break. On any weekend, you'll find a few of your velo fellows taking their ease here, soaking up the sun, munching pastries, and swapping bike yarns.

When you leave town on Hwy 1, you drop into a little valley and follow it west to Tomales Bay. Out along the bay, the road begins humping up and down, in and out of coves and sloughs. You'll ride alongside this beautiful, unspoiled bay for 7 miles to the north edge of the village of Marshall. Turn left—inland and uphill—just before the town. This is Marshall–Petaluma Road, known in local cycling parlance as the Marshall Wall. I think "wall" may be overstating it in this case. You are in for a good climb, but only 700' in 3 miles, including some flat spots where you can relax. You're climbing across an open hillside, and the lack of trees means an unobstructed panorama when you break out onto the ridge. What a view! The grassy slopes tumble down to Tomales Bay, stretched out in a long silver sweep, far below, with the mountainous, forested bulk of the Point Reyes National Seashore (Ride 21) across the water.

After goggling at the scenery from the summit, careen down the far side of the ridge for 2 miles into Verde Canyon, another remote valley filled with a lot of nothing except meadows, boulders, and old trees along the creek. The road rolls along the tranquil valley for 6 miles, often nearly level, but occasionally cresting rises that may cause you to grab a gear or two.

At the end of the valley, bear left on Wilson Hill Road. This is a bigger ascent, a medium-steep grade of 1.5 miles. Over this ridge, there is another impressive vista, this time looking inland over more grassy hills, with the city of Petaluma off in the hazy distance. At the bottom of the speedy descent, turn left on Chileno Valley Road. This is a popular cycling venue, and with good reason: it rolls through a valley of almost dreamlike beauty and serenity. For 18 miles, from the bottom of the Wilson Hill descent, through Chileno Valley and along an assortment of other little roads, the terrain remains mostly moderate. There are a few hills, the biggest being a 250' bump on Carmody Road, but overall, the workload is modest. Around mile 56, the topography becomes more challenging, gaining about 500' in 2 miles as Burnside Road stair-steps up a ridge called English Hill.

Take a break at the summit to admire the view: off to the northeast, all of Santa Rosa and its suburbs are spread out on the plain, with Mount Saint Helena and Geyser Peak looming in the distance. At 900', this is the high point of the ride. A frisky descent of a mile delivers you to a left onto Barnett Valley Road. Three short jogs of 2 miles each on Barnett Valley, Jonive Road, and Occidental Road, are all that remain. Barnett Valley bumps up and down along a ridgeline through woods and meadows. Jonive climbs steeply at first, and after a brief run across an open hillside, snuggles into thick forest, with a few apple orchards thrown in. It's pretty much the same on Occidental Road, except that this arterial is likely to have a heavier burden of traffic. Occidental climbs gently for about a mile to a final hilltop, and then there's one last, mile-long descent into Occidental. See Ride 17 for more about the town of Occidental.

MILEAGE LOG

0.0	South on Bohemian Hwy
3.4	Village of Freestone
3.7	Right on Bodega Hwy (can be busy)
5.0	Left on Freestone–Valley Ford Rd.
7.6	Left on Hwy 1
8.0	Village of Valley Ford
8.3	Right on Middle Rd.
9.3	Right on Marsh Rd.
10.2	Left on Franklin School Rd.
12.8	Left on Whitaker Bluff Rd.
14.2	Right on Middle Rd. (unmarked)
16.1	Left on Dillon Beach Rd.

17.2	Right on Hwy 1; village of Tomales
24.4	Left on Marshall–Petaluma Rd.
35.3	Bear left on Wilson Hill Rd.
37.9	Left on Chileno Valley Rd.
47.4	Left on Tomales–Petaluma Rd.
48.7	Right on Alexander Rd.
49.5	Left on Fallon–Two Rock Rd.
49.9	Right on Carmody Rd.
52.5	Left on Petaluma–Valley Ford Rd.
53.6	Right on Bloomfield Rd.; village of Bloomfield
56.3	Left on Burnside Rd.
59.6	Left on Barnett Valley Rd.
61.8	Cross Bodega Hwy to Jonive Rd.
63.9	Left on Occidental Rd.
66.1	Left on Bohemian Hwy to finish in town of Occidental

23 THE CARNEROS DISTRICT

Difficulty:	Moderate
Time:	3 to 4.5 hours
Distance:	43 miles
Elevation gain:	1700'
Best seasons:	All year, although November through April may be rainy
Road conditions:	Most roads are low traffic, but a few are busy. Pavement varies from excellent to poor.

GETTING THERE: Sonoma can be approached from Napa on Hwy 12/121; from Santa Rosa on Hwy 12; from Petaluma on Hwy 116. Once at the downtown plaza in Sonoma, take 1st St. E. to the parking lot behind the Vallejo Barracks.

The Carneros District is the southernmost of the viticultural regions in the North Bay. It sprawls across the low, rolling hills bordering San Pablo Bay and its vast wetlands, the northern perimeter of San Francisco Bay. The towns of Sonoma and Napa act as bookends at the western and eastern edges of the region. The ride begins and ends in Sonoma

The Carneros District is the southernmost of all the wine regions in the North Bay, with its low hills rolling right down to the wetlands bordering San Francisco Bay.

and takes a mid-ride break in Napa. There are essentially three loops to the ride: the big one around the vineyards and two smaller ones near Napa and Sonoma.

The ride begins with the loop out of Sonoma, the shortest but hilliest of the loops. After heading east on the Sonoma Bike Path, pick up Lovall Valley Road as it heads out of town. At mile 2, you leave the town behind and begin the biggest climb of the day: 500' in 2 miles. This is an easy climb up a rocky draw, with a little creek near the road. At the top of this climb, turn left on Lovall Valley Loop Road to loop around the pretty valley before heading back down to town, with the 2-mile climb now transformed into a zippy, twisty descent.

Turn left on 7th Street East and head south along the east edge of town, through a neighborhood of handsome, upscale homes. Denmark Street and Burndale Road carry you clear of the residential fringe of town and out into the true Carneros, where the corduroy rows of vines slope gently down to the wetlands and the bay, which can be seen off on the southern horizon.

Once you're done with the Lovall Valley descent, the topography becomes about as moderate as it can be. Between miles 10 and 24, the roads roll gently up and down through the vineyards, with hardly a hill worthy of the name. (Most of that run is along Ramal and Las Amigas roads.) Only when you reach the far end of the Carneros and

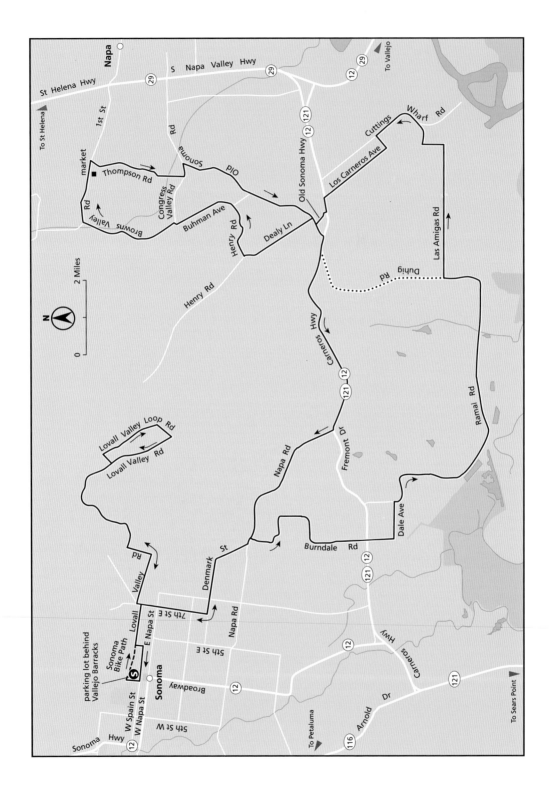

turn inland toward the city of Napa do you finally have to tackle a few climbs, and even these are minor bumps. After the second of two hills, you drop into the suburban fringe of Napa, where there is a good market for a rest stop. Just beyond the market, turn right on Thompson Road, climb another little hill, and return to the open, rolling hills of the Carneros.

Now it's time to mention the biggest bogey of this ride: 3 miles along Highway 12/121. By the time you get to this sector at mile 34, you will have already crossed this busy highway twice, so you should have a sense of how hectic it can be. In past years, I would never have considered riding on it. But it has recently been rebuilt with huge shoulders, and now I'm comfortable riding it and recommending it, at least for these 3 miles. However, if you are nervous about traffic—even when there are big shoulders—there is an alternative. Find Duhig Road on the map: that will return you to Ramal Road, where you would simply retrace your outward-bound route. Your ride will be a bit longer, but you will avoid most of the busy highway.

Hwy 12/121 includes a 1-mile climb and a slightly longer descent. Napa Road, which follows, is also rather busy but also has enormous shoulders. It begins with a gentle rise and then tilts downhill for 1.5 smooth, fast miles, back to Denmark Street, where you pick up the route through the residential fringe of Sonoma (which is all very nice riding, by the way).

Near the end of the ride, I run you around the other side of a few city blocks so that you can visit the historic downtown of Sonoma. However, the plaza and mission and stores would probably be more accessible on foot than on a bike, so you might choose to simply roll back along the bike path to the park where the ride began and then do your exploring without your bike.

On two feet or two wheels, take a little time to investigate the town. It is one of the cornerstones of California history. It was the northernmost outpost of colonial California, under Spanish and then Mexican control, until the Bear Flag Revolt of 1846, when the Yankee settlers raised their grizzly-emblazoned flag over the plaza and declared themselves independent of Mexican rule. Many of the buildings around the plaza today date from that era or shortly thereafter. Some are museums and some are shops, including the sorts of shops hungry cyclists love best: bistros and cafés and *taquerias*.

MILEAGE LOG

0.0	From parking lot, north through Depot Park
0.1	Right on Sonoma Bike Path
0.5	Jog left on 4th St. E. to right on Lovall Valley Rd.
1.1	Jog left on 7th St. E., right on Castle Rd., right again to continue on Lovall Valley Rd.
4.2	Left on Lovall Valley Loop Rd.
5.5	Right on Lovall Valley Rd.
9.5	Jog left on Castle to left on 7th St. E.
10.6	Left on Denmark St.
11.9	Cross Napa Rd. to Old Burndale Rd.
12.0	Right on Burndale Rd.
14.2	Cross Hwy 12/121 (carefully) to continue on Burndale
14.6	Left on Dale Ave.
15.2	Right on Ramal Rd.
19.2	Becomes Duhig Rd.

19.9	Right on Las Amigas Rd.
21.8	Left to stay on Las Amigas Rd. at Milton Rd. junction
22.5	Straight on Cuttings Wharf Rd.
23.2	Left on Los Carneros Ave.
23.4	Right to stay on Los Carneros Ave.
24.6	Left on Hwy 12/121 (heavy traffic; cross carefully)
24.8	Right on Old Sonoma Hwy
25.0	Right on Old Sonoma Rd.
25.2	Left on Dealy Ln.
26.3	Right on Henry Rd.
27.1	Left on Buhman Ave.
28.1	Left to stay on Buhman Ave.; into city of Napa
29.5	Right on Browns Valley Rd.
30.0	Browns Valley Market
30.4	Right on Thompson Rd.
31.8	Left on Congress Valley Rd.
32.0	Right on Old Sonoma Rd.
34.4	Right on Hwy 12/121 (heavy traffic but wide shoulder)
37.4	Right on Napa Rd.
39.6	Right on Denmark St.
40.9	Right on 7th St. E.
41.9	Left on Lovall Valley Rd.
42.4	Left on 4th St. E.
42.6	Right on Spain St.; downtown Sonoma, plaza, historic sites
43.0	Right on 1st St. W.
43.2	Right on Sonoma Bike Path into Depot Park
43.3	Right on path to parking lot
43.4	Finish

BAY AREA

Ground zero for most of the north state's population, industry, and technology, the communities around San Francisco Bay are home to hundreds of thousands of avid cyclists and cycling advocates, and the bike-support systems they engender, including hundreds of miles of bike trails. Surrounding the urban sprawl is a wonderful patchwork of parks, preserves, and watersheds available for two-wheeled exploration.

24 MOUNT TAMALPAIS AND MORE

Difficulty:	Challenging
Time:	3.5 to 6 hours
Distance:	48 miles
Elevation gain:	5200'
Best seasons:	All year, although winter may be rainy
Road conditions:	Pavement varies from excellent to fair. Traffic may be busy on Hwy 1. Back roads will be quiet.

GETTING THERE: From Hwy 101, take East Blithedale Ave. west 2 miles to downtown Mill Valley. Park in any available public space and ride to Depot Plaza.

I cannot think of another ride in this book that is so consistently beautiful and rewarding as this one. The only disclaimer I will make is that the same scenic charms that make it so appealing for cyclists also attract motorized tourists. Doing the ride on a weekday in the spring or fall, when most of the tourists are elsewhere, would greatly improve the quality of the experience.

This grand adventure begins in the pleasant village of Mill Valley, one of Marin County's prettiest towns. You'll see the best of it on a 2.7-mile, 650' climb along quiet neighborhood streets curling uphill through a charming world of cozy cottages and shady woods. Cascade and Marion are especially attractive little lanes. When you reach that first summit, you leave Mill Valley's residential fringe and spill down the other side of the ridge on a twisty plunge to Muir Woods National Monument, a preserve of old-growth redwoods. Riding directly from town into a national monument is par for the course on this ride. Most of the miles today are within

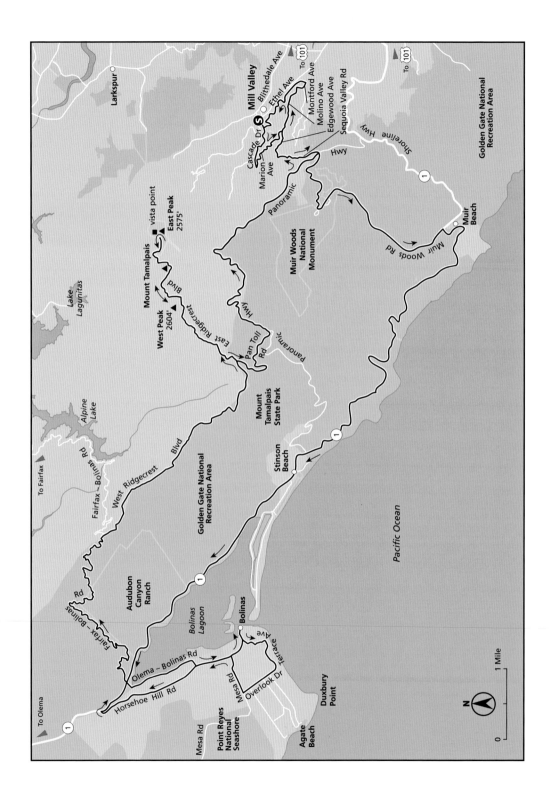

Larkspur

Mill Valley

Cascade Dr

Blithedale Ave

Ethel Ave

Marion Ave

Montford Ave

Molino Ave

Edgewood Ave

Sequoia Valley Rd

To 101

To 101

Golden Gate National Recreation Area

Shoreline Hwy

Hwy

Muir Beach

Muir Woods Rd

Panoramic

Muir Woods National Monument

vista point

East Peak 2575'

Mount Tamalpais

West Peak 2604'

East Ridgecrest Blvd

Pan Toll Rd

Panoramic Hwy

Lake Lagunitas

Alpine Lake

Fairfax – Bolinas Rd

To Fairfax

West Ridgecrest Blvd

Golden Gate National Recreation Area

Mount Tamalpais State Park

Stinson Beach

Pacific Ocean

Audubon Canyon Ranch

Bolinas Lagoon

Bolinas

Overlook Dr

Terrace Ave

Fairfax – Bolinas Rd

Olema – Bolinas Rd

Horsehoe Hill Rd

Mesa Rd

To Olema

Point Reyes National Seashore

Mesa Rd

Duxbury Point

Agate Beach

N

0   1 Mile

Ridgecrest Boulevard, on the northern shoulder of Mount Tamalpais (Nancy Yu)

the borders of state or national parks. From beginning to end, it is a landscape of pristine wilderness and spectacular natural beauty.

Beyond Muir Woods, the road continues down a peaceful, empty valley to a junction with Highway 1. Turn right and climb 1 mile to the high bluffs above the ocean. This begins a fabulous 5-mile dance along the hillside, always gently up or down, always on silky-smooth pavement, and always with the blue Pacific on display, far below. You might think this is about as beautiful as a bike ride can be, but all I can say is: you ain't seen nothin' yet!

This dreamy run ends with a descent to the town of Stinson Beach at mile 13. After the town, Hwy 1 flattens out for a level, 6-mile run along the shore of Bolinas Lagoon. This includes two left turns around the north end of the lagoon, heading toward the village of Bolinas. Both turns are without signs. All you need to know about them is that they are the first and only lefts you can make after riding along the lagoon. Quirky, offbeat Bolinas stands apart from the tide of tourists washing across the region, and does so

quite intentionally. This includes removing the street signs out on the highway pointing toward the town. But as a former resident of the town myself, I can assure you that the occasional cyclist will be welcome here, and in fact, I strongly encourage you to pursue this 7-mile *divertimento* through the town.

The general store comes up at 19.5 miles. Grab a snack and take it around the corner to the little dock overlooking the lagoon. Let the peaceful ambience settle in around you. It's a special place. After a break, complete the exploration of town: up the hill to the mesa and back down, then out around Horseshoe Hill and back to Hwy 1, where a little downhill delivers you to Fairfax–Bolinas Road.

This is the biggest challenge of the day: 2500' up in 9 miles. The task begins with 1500' in the 4 miles on this road. It's real work, but never brutal, holding steady at 7 percent all the way, looping back and forth from meadows to redwoods, usually nearly deserted. The remaining 5 miles along Ridgecrest Boulevard are broken up into small but sometimes steep pitches, as the road does what its name implies, clambering up the crest of an open ridge. You might be forgiven for thinking you've seen this road before. Its undulating curves and dipsy-doodle terrain and its eye-popping panoramas over the ocean have been the setting for dozens of car commercials, for both print and television. It may be the most filmed road in California.

West Ridgecrest, where all the commercials are staged, leads to East Ridgecrest, an out-and-back to the summit of Mount Tamalpais. The end of the road is not the highest point on the road. Beyond the high spot, there are another 2 miles of ups and downs before the end, where a wonderful vista point awaits, with the entire San Francisco Bay Area laid out at your feet like God's model train set. Whatever else you do on this ride, *do not* come to this spot without getting off your bike and walking the few yards out to the terrace where the view opens up.

After regaining that high spot on the way out, you are now ready for a big helping of gravity candy: almost 10 miles of downhill. This is a twisting, twirling whirling dervish of a downhill, most of the time on excellent pavement. There is a mile-plus of flats and a modest uphill in the middle, but the rest is as wild as you want to make it, first on Ridgecrest, then on Pan Toll Road and Panoramic Highway, and finally on Sequoia Valley Road, dropping back into Mill Valley. You came up Sequoia Valley at the start, after Marion. Now, skip Marion and stay on this nice road through Mill Valley's residential fringe, as its name changes from Edgewood Avenue to Molino Avenue, all the way down to its end. Turn left on Montford and immediately left on Ethel Avenue. Ethel, like Marion, is a tranquil, sylvan lane traversing the hillside to the center of town. A couple of turns at the very end drop you right down to the town plaza, where the ride began. Now you can explore the town, beginning, perhaps, with a pastry from the Depot Bakery, right on the plaza.

MILEAGE LOG

0.0	Left on Throckmorton Ave.
0.3	Left on Cascade Dr.
0.7	Left on Marion Ave.
1.6	Right on Edgewood Ave.
2.0	Bear left on Sequoia Valley Rd.; follow sign to Muir Woods
2.7	Straight on Muir Woods Rd.
4.3	Muir Woods National Monument visitor center
6.6	Right on Hwy 1
12.9	Town of Stinson Beach
17.3	Left on unmarked connector road toward Bolinas, across from Fairfax–Bolinas Rd.
17.4	Left on Olema–Bolinas Rd.
18.6	Left to stay on Olema–Bolinas Rd. at Horseshoe Hill Rd. junction
19.4	Left on Wharf Rd. into downtown Bolinas
19.6	Turn around at dock on Bolinas Lagoon, retrace
19.8	Left on Brighton Ave.
20.0	Right on Park Ave.
20.1	Right on Terrace Ave.
20.7	Right on Overlook Dr.
21.2	Right on Mesa Rd.
21.8	Left on Olema–Bolinas Rd.

22.4	Straight on Horseshoe Hill Rd.
24.0	Right on Hwy 1
24.5	Left on Fairfax–Bolinas Rd.
28.9	Straight on W. Ridgecrest Blvd. (Fairfax–Bolinas Rd. turns left)
32.8	Bear left on E. Ridgecrest Blvd. at Pan Toll Rd. junction
35.5	Bear right on Old Railroad Grade Trail
35.8	Mount Tamalpais vista point and turnaround (food, water, restrooms); retrace E. Ridgecrest Blvd.
38.8	Left on Pan Toll Rd.
40.2	Left on Panoramic Hwy
44.7	Left on Sequoia Valley Rd.
45.5	Straight on Edgewood Ave.
46.2	Straight on Molino Ave.
46.6	Left on Montford Ave.
46.7	Left on Ethel Ave.
47.8	Right on Ethel Ct.
47.9	Right on Throckmorton Ave.
48.0	Finish at Depot Plaza

25 SAN FRANCISCO TO THE FERRIES

Difficulty:	Moderate
Time:	1 to 4 hours
Distance:	13, 26, 37 miles
Elevation gain:	Up to 1900'
Best seasons:	All year, although winter may be rainy
Road conditions:	Many miles are on bike paths; some streets may be busy.

GETTING THERE: The routes to the San Francisco Ferry Building are as varied as the streets of San Francisco. Parking is a challenge downtown, and expensive. Riding to this start is recommended.

The basic premise of this ride is simple: Start at the Ferry Building in San Francisco, ride over the Golden Gate Bridge and onward to one of three towns with ferry terminals—Sausalito, Tiburon, or Larkspur—and catch a ferry back to San Francisco. It's a plan employed by thousands of tourists who rent bikes from outfitters in the city and follow some variation of this route. You can't help but notice them, pouring across the bridge like army ants on their matching bikes.

My route is a bit more complicated than the ones they use. I throw in a few detours that greatly improve the adventure, but at the expense of simplicity. For the most part, though, you won't go astray if you follow that river of rental-bike riders, at least through San Francisco and across the bridge.

Crossing the bridge on bikes is tricky. On weekends and after 3:00 PM on weekdays,

riders use the west walkway, having it all to themselves, with pedestrians restricted to the east walkway. Earlier on weekdays, bridge workers use the west walkway, and bikes have to share the east walkway with the pedestrians. On busy days, riding through this jostling crowd feels like being in a rugby scrum. It's also more complicated to follow the route at the north end of the bridge from the east walkway. All in all, west is best.

At the north end of the bridge, the route heads up Conzelman Road and soon climbs to vista points looking back at the bridge and the city beyond that are panoramic and iconic. You could ride all the way to the top of the headland on Conzelman—quite a big climb—but you'll get the good views on this first section, so there's no need to go higher unless you really want to. I have you hopping over the ridge and descending into a lovely valley at the first opportunity, then doubling back for a shot through Barry–Baker Tunnel. This is a long, one-lane tunnel regulated with timed lights. If there are cars waiting with you on the red, let them go first and then jump in at the back. The tunnel is well lit and downhill, so you speed through quickly. Just beyond the downhill end, turn left on Bunker Road and continue downhill into Fort Baker, once an army base but now part of the Golden Gate National Recreation Area.

After the pretty cruise through the fort, descend into Sausalito, rolling along Bridgeway into the center of this relentlessly chic tourist town. The first of the ferry terminals is right downtown. You could call it a day here and board the ferry, but I hope you continue at least to Tiburon. To do that, head north on Bridgeway—sometimes quite busy—

until you pick up the Mill Valley–Sausalito Path, a bike trail across the Richardson Bay wetlands. The next 10 miles, from Mill Valley to Tiburon, are complicated, but the log should steer you through. Highlights include the run along Seminary Drive, right down at bay level, the run along the Tiburon Linear Park trail, and the pretty cruise into Tiburon, a charming town that always reminds me of a village on Lake Como in Italy.

The Tiburon ferry comes up at mile 26. To continue to Larkspur means another 10-mile run, and a good chunk of it is on aptly named Paradise Drive. This winding, wooded lane really comes close to cycling paradise. It begins with a modest climb and then settles in on a traverse of the forested hillside, a few hundred feet above the bay. This might be the most popular biking road in Marin County. It feels like a backcountry byway, but is just minutes from most of the bigger population centers in the area, so it's usually teeming with riders.

After 8 miles, Paradise descends to bay level and you use Redwood Highway or the bike path next to it to skirt around the town of Corte Madera. This is not great riding, but it's okay: a mix of neighborhoods, shopping malls, and tidal flats. At the north end of Redwood Highway, you feed onto a path alongside Hwy 101 that crosses Corte Madera Creek and drops right down to the entrance to the Larkspur ferry terminal.

I've done variations on this bike-and-ferry excursion a number of times, and it's always fun. It's pretty much a nonstop highlight reel of famous sights and spectacular scenery the whole way, and the ferry ride at the end puts a delightful exclamation point on the day. If

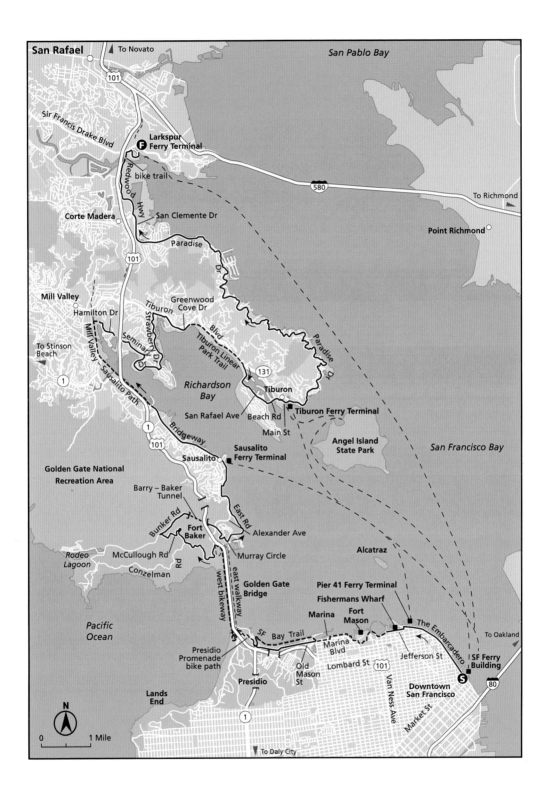

San Rafael

To Novato

San Pablo Bay

101

Sir Francis Drake Blvd

580

To Richmond

Larkspur
Ferry Terminal

bike trail

Redwood Hwy

Corte Madera

San Clemente Dr

Point Richmond

101

Paradise Dr

Mill Valley

Greenwood
Cove Dr

Hamilton Dr

Tiburon Blvd

Tiburon Linear
Park Trail

Paradise Dr

Strawberry Dr

Seminary Dr

To Stinson
Beach

Mill Valley – Sausalito Path

Richardson
Bay

131

1

Tiburon

San Rafael Ave

Beach Rd

Tiburon Ferry Terminal

Bridgeway

Main St

1
101

Sausalito

Sausalito
Ferry Terminal

Angel Island
State Park

San Francisco Bay

Golden Gate National
Recreation Area

Barry – Baker
Tunnel

Bunker Rd

Fort
Baker

East Rd

Alexander Ave

Rodeo
Lagoon

McCullough Rd

Murray Circle

Alcatraz

Conzelman Rd

west bikeway

east walkway

Golden Gate
Bridge

Pier 41 Ferry Terminal

Fishermans Wharf

To Oakland

Pacific
Ocean

SF Bay Trail

Marina

Fort
Mason

The Embarcadero

Marina
Blvd

Jefferson St

SF Ferry
Building

Presidio
Promenade
bike path

Old
Mason
St

Lombard St

101

Downtown
San Francisco

80

Presidio

Van Ness Ave

Lands
End

1

Market St

N

0   1 Mile

To Daly City

From the Marin Headlands, the views back to San Francisco are picture-postcard perfect.

you're not thrilled with the prospect of dealing with stashing your car in downtown San Francisco, consider starting the ride here, at the Larkspur ferry terminal, where there is ample parking.

One other option: From Tiburon, take the little ferry out to Angel Island in the bay, ride around the perimeter of the beautiful island—6 mostly easy miles—and then take another ferry from the island to San Francisco. You would gain an Angel but lose Paradise. Either way, it would be heavenly.

MILEAGE LOG

0.0	From the Ferry Building, head west along the Embarcadero
1.7	At Fishermans Wharf, jog left one block on Taylor St. to right on Jefferson St.
2.1	At the end of Jefferson St., continue along trail through Aquatic Park
2.3	Jog right on Van Ness Ave., left on trail through Fort Mason
2.8	Follow San Francisco Bay Trail along Marina waterfront
3.9	Follow Old Mason St. or nearby bike trail through the Presidio
5.1	Jog left on Mason Street to right on Crissy Field Ave. (SF Bike Route 2)
5.2	Right on Battery East Trail to Golden Gate Bridge (Route across bridge varies depending on day of week and time of day. This route is based on the weekend schedule, also in effect after 3:00 PM on weekdays, using the west bikeway.)
7.7	At north end of bridge, left on Conzelman Rd.
8.8	At roundabout, first right on McCullough Rd.
9.7	Right on Bunker Rd., through Barry–Baker Tunnel
10.9	After tunnel, left on Bunker Rd., following sign to Fort Baker
11.4	Right on Murray Circle, left on East Rd.

12.6	Right on Alexander Ave.; becomes South St., then 2nd St.
13.1	Right on Richardson St.; becomes Bridgeway; city of Sausalito
13.5	Sausalito ferry terminal at Vina del Mar Park
15.3	Bear right from Bridgeway onto Mill Valley–Sausalito Path
17.6	Right on bike path through Hauke Park, opposite Sycamore Ave. turnaround
17.8	Right on Hamilton Dr.
18.3	Right on Redwood Hwy, under Hwy 101
19.1	Right on Seminary Dr.; right to stay on Seminary Dr. at mile 19.2
20.6	Becomes Strawberry Dr.
21.8	Right on Tiburon Blvd. to right on Greenwood Cove Dr.
22.7	From end of road, follow Tiburon Linear Park trail along bay
24.1	Right on San Rafael Ave.
25.2	Left on Beach Rd., then bear right on Main St.
25.7	Right on Tiburon Blvd.; becomes Paradise Dr.; Tiburon ferry terminal to the right at this corner; also site of ferry terminal for Angel Island
34.2	Bear right on San Clemente Dr. or nearby bike path
34.6	Right on Redwood Hwy or nearby bike path
35.8	Bear left on bike-pedestrian path to Larkspur ferry terminal
36.1	Right on Larkspur ferry terminal access road
36.5	Finish at Larkspur ferry terminal; ride ferry back to Ferry Building

26 BERKELEY WATERFRONT

Difficulty:	Easy
Time:	1 to 2 hours
Distance:	12 miles
Elevation gain:	Nearly flat
Best seasons:	All year, although midwinter may be rainy
Road conditions:	Some roads are busy; most are not. Many miles are on bike trails. Pavement varies.

GETTING THERE: Exit I-80 at University Ave. in Berkeley. Go west to Frontage Rd. and south to parking lot next to San Francisco Bay Trail.

This is one of the shortest, flattest rides in the book. It's a lazy, slow-motion exploration of the bay shore near Berkeley. The route I've laid out works well at hitting many of the best bike trails and city streets in the area, but it is by no means the only way to explore this region. Think of it as a starter set upon which you can build and improvise. It is, for instance, possible to add miles by tooling around the Emeryville Marina at the south end of the course, or by exploring around the Golden Gate Fields horse race facilities at the north end of the course. It is even possible to follow the San Francisco Bay Trail and nearby streets all the way north along the bay to Richmond, doubling or tripling the miles

This impressive bike bridge spans Interstate 80 before descending to Aquatic Park in Berkeley.

you'd cover on this little ride. The point is exploring: noodling along at a comfortable speed, with your head swiveling around like an owl's to take in all the varied scenery along the way.

I begin the ride with a circumnavigation of the César Chavez Park and Berkeley Marina, jutting out into the bay. The mileage log does a rudimentary job of describing this route, but honestly, ignore the directions and just follow your front wheel. Stay as near the water as the paved paths and occasional roads allow, in and out of parks and parking lots, past hotels and restaurants, around boat basins. Do what seems to make sense and what appeals to you. There will be sights aplenty, from up-close looks at boats in the harbor to far-off vistas of San Francisco, across the bay.

After you've crossed the marina off your list, cross the bike bridge over Interstate 80. This suspension span, opened in 2002, is one of the more impressive bike structures you will ever see, with its monumental sculptures by Scott Donahue anchoring each end of the overcrossing. On the inland side, it curves down to feed onto Bolivar Drive, which runs along the east bank of the mile-long rowing basin in Aquatic Park. The road peters out after a while, but you carry on to the south along the trail through the park, eventually popping out the southern end into the city streets of Emeryville.

This part of Emeryville used to be a drab, dreary industrial belt, but it has been renovated and fancied up to an amazing degree in the last thirty years or so. Now it's a busy hive of posh hotels, upscale offices, and chic shopping malls. The route dodges the busier streets on a 1-mile cruise through the modern development, then picks up the San Francisco Bay Trail along Powell Street to cut under the freeway and get back out onto the bay frontage. Now you're heading north along the Bay Trail, right next to the water. This is the longest and simplest sector on the route: 3 miles without any turns or confusions, always with the bay on your left, with grand views over the water to San Francisco, the Bay Bridge, Golden Gate Bridge, Treasure Island...

At the north end of this run, at the gate to Golden Gate Fields, the route turns its back on the bay and heads under the freeway on

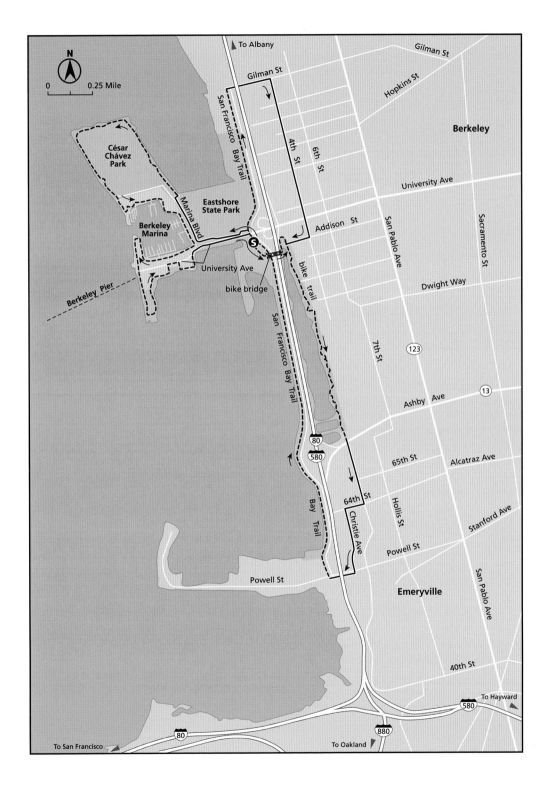

N

0   0.25 Mile

To Albany

Gilman St

Gilman St

San Francisco Bay Trail

4th St

6th St

Hopkins St

Berkeley

University Ave

César Chávez Park

Eastshore State Park

Marina Blvd

Berkeley Marina

Addison St

San Pablo Ave

Sacramento St

Dwight Way

S

University Ave

bike bridge

bike trail

Berkeley Pier

San Francisco Bay Trail

7th St

123

Ashby Ave

13

65th St

Alcatraz Ave

80

580

64th St

Hollis St

Stanford Ave

Bay Trail

Christie Ave

Powell St

Powell St

Emeryville

San Pablo Ave

40th St

580

To Hayward

80

880

To San Francisco

To Oakland

Gilman Street. (But don't forget the possibilities mentioned earlier for more miles and exploration farther north.) Gilman Street is taking you to a right turn and a run south along 4th Street, one of Berkeley's more interesting districts. Like the reinvented industrial zone in Emeryville, this street has undergone a quite astonishing transformation in recent years. Not that long ago, this too was a seamy, grimy wasteland of dilapidated factories and warehouses, with the venerable Spenger's Fresh Fish Grotto the only attraction for tourists. Now, what a difference! For several blocks, it's wall-to-wall bistros and boutiques and interior design studios, with hipsters and yuppies bustling along the busy sidewalks under the street trees or cruising by on their bikes. You can cruise by too, but you may want to break off the ride here and grab a sidewalk table for a *café* and croissant. It's a nice spot for sitting and watching the world go by.

At this point, the ride is almost done, unless you want to throw in a few more exploratory blocks in the nearby neighborhood. The basic route turns right off 4th Street onto Addison, which delivers you, in a few short blocks, back to Bolivar Drive and another crossing of the beautiful bike bridge, now in the other direction. If you followed the route exactly, your car should be waiting for you at the far end of the bridge. But as I have noted, following the directions exactly is neither essential nor encouraged today: use this little ride as a framework upon which you can construct more elaborate explorations of the area.

MILEAGE LOG

0.0	North on San Francisco Bay Trail
0.1	Left on University Ave. toward Berkeley Marina
0.4	Right on Marina Blvd.
0.7	Follow waterfront trail around César Chavez Park
2.1	Follow waterfront trail around Berkeley yacht basin
3.1	Continue along bay on Seawall Dr.
3.6	Follow bayside trail around Shorebird Park
4.3	Right on University Ave., with optional detour along bayside
4.6	Right on San Francisco Bay Trail
4.7	Right on trail up and over bike bridge crossing freeway
5.0	Continue on Bolivar Dr.
5.2	Continue on trail through Aquatic Park, heading south
6.1	Straight on Bolivar Dr.
6.2	Becomes Bay St. at Potter St. junction
6.3	Becomes Shellmound St. (city traffic)
6.7	Right on 64th St.; city of Emeryville
6.8	Left on Christie Ave.
7.2	Cross Powell St. to right on San Francisco Bay Trail
7.3	Cross under freeway, turn right to stay on trail next to W. Frontage Rd.
7.5	Bear left (north) along bayshore on San Francisco Bay Trail
10.3	Right on Gilman St., under freeway
10.6	Right on 4th St.
11.5	Right on Addison St.
11.6	Right on Bolivar Dr. to ramp to bike bridge crossing freeway
11.9	Finish

27 BERKELEY HILLS

Difficulty:	Moderate/challenging
Time:	3.5 to 5 hours
Distance:	56 miles
Elevation gain:	4500'
Best seasons:	March through October
Road conditions:	Some roads may be busy, but most are quiet. All are well paved.

GETTING THERE: From I-580 in Berkeley, take 35th Ave. east; it becomes Redwood Rd. and continues uphill to a left on Skyline Blvd. Go 0.5 mile to the parking lot of the Richard C. Trudeau Training Center.

When cyclists in the East Bay (the communities along the eastern shore of San Francisco Bay) want to escape the wall-to-wall sprawl of their cities and suburbs, their first, simplest option is to head for the hills above Berkeley, where tens of thousands of acres of forested ridges and canyons have been bundled together as regional parks, recreation areas, open space preserves, and watersheds. Much of this semiwilderness is abutted by pleasant rural-residential neighborhoods. Fortunately for cyclists, there is a nice network of mostly quiet roads meandering through the region. Ask local riders for their favorite route through these hills—as I did—and no two answers will be the same. This is one way of going about it, one I think hits most of the best roads and sights.

The ride begins on Skyline Boulevard but quickly topples off the ridge with a sassy downhill on Redwood Road through the cool, shady forest. At mile 3, turn left onto

Pinehurst Road and tackle a moderate climb of a little over a mile, followed by a descent of the same length and grade, all of it on tranquil, winding, wooded roads. After that descent, Pinehurst begins a 4-mile climb. The first 2 miles are nearly flat, winding along a narrow canyon crowded with massive redwoods (one of my favorite spots on this ride). There is even a "town" called Canyon here, or at least an old post office serving a few homes back in the trees. The second 2 miles are a real climb, wriggling up the hillside at over 6 percent.

At the top of Pinehurst, turn right on Skyline and continue climbing, now more or less up on the ridge, heading north, with wild parklands to the east and the sprawl of towns and cities to the west, spilling down to San Francisco Bay. There is a nice park wayside, with water and restrooms, near mile 11. Just uphill from the wayside, turn right on Grizzly Peak Boulevard. A little over 2 miles of lumpy

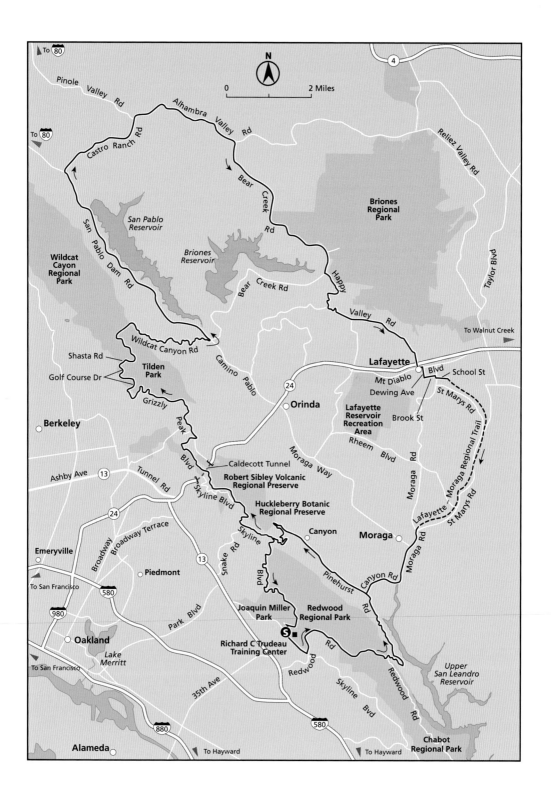

Springtime in Alhambra Valley—thoroughly rural, but just around the corner from the East Bay 'burbs (Nancy Yu)

rollers and 1-plus mile of steeper climbing bring you to the high point on the day at mile 15. From this 1670' summit, the panoramic vistas out across the bay are simply spectacular…time to put a foot down and drink it all in. And then it's time for more downhill, beginning with 2 more miles on Grizzly Peak. Turn right on Golf Course Drive on an up-and-down run—now heading inland, away from the bay—past pretty Tilden Park Golf Course. Work your way over to Wildcat Canyon Road and, after a mile of nearly level traverse through the woods, enjoy another 2.5 miles of slinky downhill to the point where Wildcat tees into San Pablo Dam Road.

This highway above San Pablo Reservoir may be the busiest and least interesting road on the ride. But it has wide shoulders and goes by quickly, ending with a 1.5-mile descent to a right turn on Castro Ranch Road. San Pablo Dam, Castro Ranch, and the two roads that

follow—Alhambra Valley and Bear Creek—carve a 15-mile, clockwise loop around two large reservoirs. Aside from two unobtrusive tract neighborhoods along Castro Ranch, the scenery around this loop is decidedly rural and agricultural. It's more open than the wooded parklands up on the peaks. Out here, it's open fields of waving grasses, with oaks scattered about.

After a little up-and-down on Castro Ranch, Alhambra Valley and Bear Creek settle into 4 miles of easy, false-flat uphill. Then you hit what local riders call The Bears: a couple of climbs between miles 33 and 36. On the far side of those humps, look for a left onto Happy Valley Road at mile 36.5. This charming little lane scrambles over a woodsy ridge on a short, sharp climb, drops off the other side on a descent that is just as tight and tangled as the climb, and then cruises gently downhill through the comfortable suburb of

Lafayette, past upscale homes set back among woods and wide lawns. Happy Valley dumps out onto Mount Diablo Boulevard in the middle of Lafayette's pleasant shopping district. There is a good market directly across the street, your first access to store-bought food on the whole loop.

After a break at the market, follow neighborhood streets for a mile to the Lafayette–Moraga Regional Trail. You'll be on this nicely developed, tree-shaded bike trail for 4.5 miles, avoiding some congested roads. When you leave the trail, hop on Moraga Road, which becomes Canyon Road in a block or so. It's a suburban boulevard for a mile, but then returns to the forested canyons of the parks and preserves. When Canyon ends, turn right on Pinehurst. Yes, the same Pinehurst you were on early in the ride. It's déjà vu time: you are going to do the same 4-mile section again, along the deep, shady canyon and up the twisting climb to Skyline. In order to tie together all the other wonderful roads on this ride, this small bit of redundancy is necessary. But, as I noted earlier, it's one of the best roads on the ride, and I doubt anyone will complain too vigorously about having to do it again, even if it is all uphill.

This time at the top, turn left on Skyline and head south. The climbing continues for another 2-plus miles, with a few flats and downhills mixed in, up on the ridgeline. The ride ends with 1 final mile of speedy downhill. I hope it also ends with you feeling as if you've had a great ride, exploring this sampler pack of the best of the Berkeley hills.

MILEAGE LOG

0.0	From Richard C. Trudeau Training Center, left on Skyline Blvd.
0.5	Left on Redwood Rd.
3.0	Left on Pinehurst Rd.
7.0	"Town" of Canyon
9.6	Right on Skyline Blvd.
11.2	Rest area with restrooms, water
11.3	Right on Grizzly Peak Blvd.
16.8	Right on Golf Course Dr.
17.7	Right on Shasta Rd.
17.9	Right on Wildcat Canyon Rd.
21.9	Left on San Pablo Dam Rd.
27.3	Right on Castro Ranch Rd.
29.5	Right on Alhambra Valley Rd.
32.2	Right on Bear Creek Rd.
36.5	Left on Happy Valley Rd.
40.7	Left on Mount Diablo Blvd.; town of Lafayette (store)
40.8	Right on Dewing Ave.
41.0	Left on Brook St.
41.3	Jog right on Moraga Rd., left on School St.
41.6	Right on Lafayette–Moraga Regional Trail
46.2	Left on Moraga Rd.; becomes Canyon Rd.
48.4	Right on Pinehurst Rd.
52.3	Left on Skyline Blvd.
55.9	Left to stay on Skyline Blvd.
56.0	Left into parking lot and finish

28 CONTRA COSTA–CARQUINEZ

Difficulty:	Moderate
Time:	3 to 5 hours
Distance:	38 or 50 miles
Elevation gain:	2300'
Best seasons:	All year, although winter may be rainy
Road conditions:	Everything from suburban boulevards to bike trails to old, decrepit country roads. Traffic varies accordingly.

GETTING THERE: From I-680 in Concord, drive 1 mile east on Concord Ave./Gallindo St. Turn left on Cowell Rd. and go 1 mile to Concord Community Park. For alternate start site: Exit I-680 at Treat Blvd., go one block east, and turn right on Oak Rd. Go three blocks south to Walden Park.

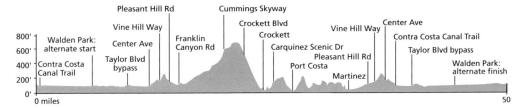

The goal of this ride is to chart a safe and pleasant path through the suburbs of the East Bay—in this case, the Concord–Pleasant Hill area—to an unusual, 20-mile loop visiting the towns of Crockett, Port Costa, and Martinez.

One way to navigate the suburbs is to use bike trails. This ride begins and ends with 12 miles on the excellent Contra Costa Canal Trail, a typical example of the trails seen all over the Bay Area. It's nearly flat for its first (and last) 6 miles as it follows its namesake canal. You may opt for the alternate start at mile 6 at Walden Park to trim the ride down to 38 miles. Between miles 6 and 12, the trail becomes more roly-poly. There are dozens of places where the path crosses streets. Most of these are quiet side streets and easy to manage. A few crossings are at busier boulevards and take some care, both with traffic and with puzzling out little kinks in the trail. The trickiest one is at Taylor Boulevard at

mile 9.7 (mile 39.9 on the way back), where you have to ride a block uphill from the trail (on the sidewalk) to cross at a signal before returning to the trail. As is the case with all suburban bike trails, this is not a place to hammer. There are too many other trail users and, occasionally, turns that are too tight for higher bike speeds.

From the end of the trail to where our little country loop begins, there is a 3-mile gap bridged by suburban roads: Center, Vine Hill, Pleasant Hill, and Alhambra Way. Center is rather ordinary, but the others are all quite pleasant, meandering through woodsy neighborhoods.

At mile 15.4, turn onto Franklin Canyon Road, leaving the suburbs behind and heading out into the countryside. This begins the biggest climb of the ride: 600' in 5.5 miles. It's never steep, but it does go on for a while. Franklin Canyon is quiet and shady. Cummings Sky-

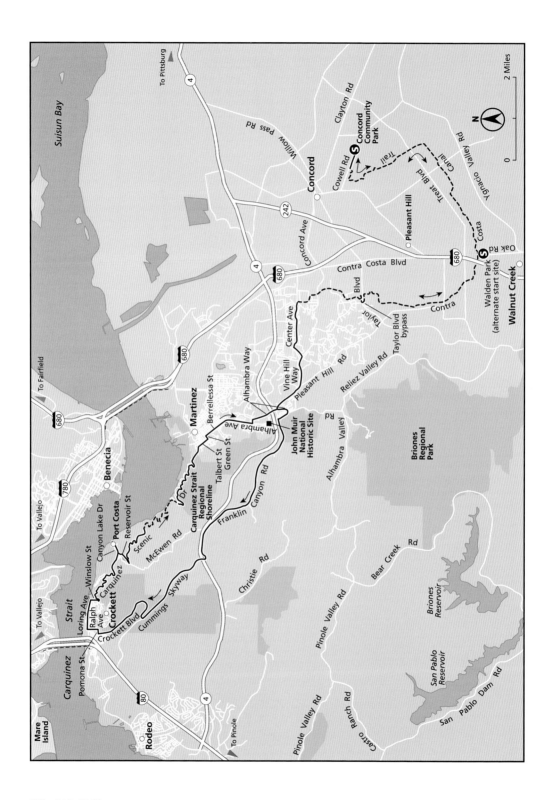

The quaint town of Crockett faces Carquinez Strait, the broad waterway connecting the Sacramento River and San Francisco Bay.

way—the top end of the climb, up on a high, bald ridgeline—is newer and wider and less bike friendly, but okay. Over the summit, the Skyway and Crockett Boulevard combine for a fast, 3-mile descent into the town of Crockett.

Crockett is one of the special points of interest on the ride. The funky old town is here because of the massive C&H Sugar refinery along the bay front. The old brick buildings dominate the town, looking like relics from the industrial revolution, which is exactly what they are (dating from 1910). Very little here appears to have changed in a good many years; the bustle of the busy Bay Area has passed Crockett by. The route heads past the refinery and follows the little road next to Carquinez Strait, the channel connecting the

Sacramento River to San Pablo Bay. Beyond the quaint town is Carquinez Scenic Drive, which traverses the hillside above the strait for 8 miles, heading to Martinez.

But before going too far along this wonderful road, there is a little detour down to Port Costa, another fascinating town. This must be the most secret, hidden-away town in the East Bay. The sleepy village snuggles down in the bottom of its wooded cove, next to the water, miles away from any hint of the modern world. At mile 27, it's about halfway through the ride, so a good spot for a break. If it's open, visit the Warehouse Café: have a beer or at least look around. To say it has a lot of character would be a howling understatement. It would be easy to skip the out-and-back into Port Costa, but I hope you don't. It's part of what makes this ride so very special.

Carquinez Scenic Drive bumps up and down constantly, mixing frisky little drops with short climbs. From the higher spots, the views across the strait are, as advertised, scenic...spectacular, even. Aside from the scenery, the main thing you need to know about this road is that 2 miles in the middle are closed to through traffic. For several years, this section has been barricaded because of landslides, although cyclists could still ride through. Now, as we go to press, the county is in the process of renovating the closed section as a bike-pedestrian trail. It is probably impassible, even for bikes, until they finish construction. If in doubt, check locally before setting out on this ride.

Another 2 miles beyond the closed section, this wild, ragged road dumps into Martinez. Not as quaint or unique as Crockett and Port Costa, it's just a nice, small town, with quiet, older residential neighborhoods. The route does a good job of getting through town and out the other side with a minimum of congestion or clutter. There is a short, optional side trip in Martinez to visit John Muir's home, a national historic site. It's noted in the log (0.5 mile round trip) but not included in the total miles. Leaving Martinez, you begin retracing the first part of the route: 3 miles of suburban roads and 12 miles on the bike trail. Concord Community Park, where the ride finishes, is the home of the city's public pool, which might be appealing after 50 miles in the saddle, if not for a swim, at least for a shower.

MILEAGE LOG

0.0	From Concord Community Park, right (west) on Cowell Rd.
0.4	Left on Contra Costa Canal Trail
6.0	Walden Park on Oak Rd. (alternate start site)
9.7	Left on sidewalk at Taylor Blvd.; cross Taylor at signal to return to trail
12.0	Left on Center Ave.
13.1	Left on Vine Hill Way
13.4	Jog right on Morello Ave.; left on Vine Hill Way
14.1	Straight on Pleasant Hill Rd.
14.9	Left on Alhambra Way
15.2	Right on Alhambra Ave.
15.4	Left on Franklin Canyon Rd.
19.8	Right on Cummings Skyway; cross over Hwy 4
21.9	Bear right on Crockett Blvd.
23.9	Right on Pomona St. to left on Ralph Ave.
24.2	Right on Loring Ave.; town of Crockett
24.7	Right on Winslow St.
25.1	Left on Carquinez Scenic Dr.
26.7	Left on Canyon Lake Dr. into town of Port Costa
27.2	Town of Port Costa; turn around and retrace Canyon Lake Dr. to...
27.4	Left on Reservoir St.
27.8	Left on Carquinez Scenic Dr.
29.0	Road closed to cars, but bikes okay
30.8	End of closed section

32.8	Right on Talbert St.; city of Martinez
33.0	Left on Green St.
33.1	Right on Berrellessa St.
33.8	Becomes Alhambra Ave.
34.4	Left on Alhambra Way
34.9	Optional out-and-back: right on Walnut Avenue to John Muir National Historic Site (0.5-mile round trip)
35.1	Bear left on Pleasant Hill Rd.
35.9	Straight on Vine Hill Way
36.5	Jog right on Morello Way, left on Vine Hill Way
36.9	Right on Center Ave.
38.0	Right on Contra Costa Canal Trail
39.9	Right on footbridge to begin Taylor Blvd. bypass to continue on trail
44.0	Walden Park at Oak Rd. (alternate finish site)
49.6	Right on Cowell Rd.
50.0	Finish at Concord Community Park

29 MOUNT DIABLO LOOP

Difficulty:	Challenging/epic
Time:	4 to 6 hours
Distance:	65 miles
Elevation gain:	6100'
Best seasons:	April through October
Road conditions:	Some suburban miles may be busy, but most roads are low traffic. Some are well paved and some not so well, but all are at least decent.

GETTING THERE: From I-680 in Concord, head east on Treat Blvd. for 1 mile. Turn right on Bancroft Rd., which becomes Walnut Ave. At mile 3.4, turn left on Oak Grove Rd., then right on Arbolado Dr. to Arbolado Park.

This is one of three big rides in what might loosely be described as the East Bay hills. The highest profile element on this ride—both literally and figuratively—is the climb and descent of 3849' Mount Diablo, a solitary peak looming over the hills of Contra Costa County. But the ride is more than just the trek to the summit. It's a circumnavigation of the mountain, a tour of some of the 90,000 acres contained within Mount Diablo State

Park and the dozens of preserves, watersheds, and farms surrounding the mountain.

The ride begins in the neighborhoods that crowd around the mountain on its more populous western flank, first with 2 miles along bike trails and then with another 8-plus miles along a series of suburban boulevards. These are the price of admission to the better miles and wilder landscape ahead. Once you shake free of the 'burbs around mile 10, you still

have 3 miles along Marsh Creek Road: a busy highway with meager shoulders. Not until you turn right onto Morgan Territory Road at mile 13 do you finally hit really bike-friendly roads.

You'll be on Morgan Territory for almost 15 miles, and every inch of that will be best-quality biking. This is a dream road, well out into the lovely, wild countryside. It starts out looking like a well-engineered highway, with two smooth lanes rolling along amid scattered country homes, but 4 miles in, the road loses its stripes, shrinks to one skinny, funky lane, and starts weaving and staggering about like a drunken sailor. Not coincidentally, it also starts climbing: 1300' up in 6 miles. Most of

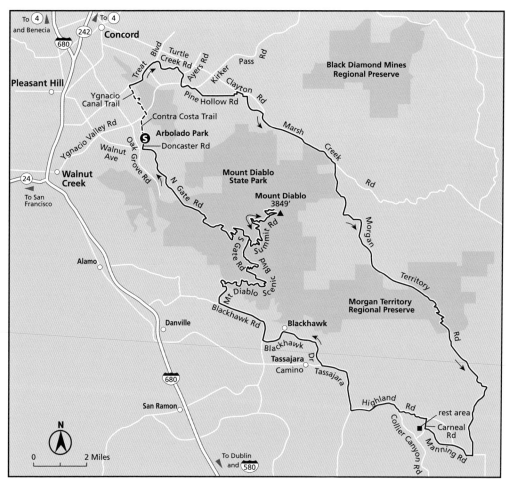

*Climbing (and descending) Mount Diablo is one of the
great bike journeys of the East Bay.* (Linda Fluhrer)

this climbing is easy and relatively painless, although there are a few spots that might flirt with 10 percent.

All of the climb, on the north face of the ridge, is in the shade of oak forest. But over the top of the ridge, around mile 22, the trees give way to open vistas across grassy hillsides, green in the winter and spring, golden in the summer and fall. For the first 2 miles, the descent dawdles along gently, but at about mile 24, life becomes more exciting. The hill slopes off more steeply and for most of 3 miles, the road carves down the open hillside in a series of long, sweeping bends. How fast do you want to go? How good are your descending skills?

At the bottom, turn right on Manning Road and begin an 8-mile meander through open, rolling farm fields that will eventually return the route to the suburbs. At the corner of Manning and Carneal roads, there is a rather surprising but welcome sight: at a remote cattle ranch, a big sign announces: "BICYCLIST FRIENDLY REST AREA." There are water fountains, vending machines, picnic tables, and even floor pumps.

At about mile 35, the suburbs return along Camino Tassajara, and in just a block or two, our route turns right on Blackhawk Drive heading through a posh neighborhood. Although this is ostensibly a gated community, my local cycling friends assure me the gate is always open. If you do find it closed, continue on Camino Tassajara to a right on Blackhawk Road, where Blackhawk Drive ends up. At mile 40.9, Blackhawk Road passes our right turn onto Mount Diablo Scenic Boulevard. This is where you begin the long ascent to the summit of the mountain. (The road becomes South Gate Road soon after you turn onto it, and I think most folks refer to all of it by that name.)

As the profile attests, this is a big climb: over 3000' of gain in a little over 11 miles. That's a 5 percent average, which ought to be manageable for most fit riders, even extended over 11 miles. But no matter how challenging, it's worth it. To use the shopworn old cliché, this is as good as it gets. There's a reason why this is all part of a huge park: it's gorgeous, alternating between shady woods and open hillsides, with the vistas growing bigger and grander the higher you go.

At mile 48.2, South Gate Road arrives at a junction with North Gate and Summit roads.

Obviously, you could plow straight ahead onto North Gate and descend from here directly to the finish, lopping 9 miles off the ride. But I hope you won't do that. Instead, follow the route up Summit Road to the end of the line, to the top of the world. The views are everything you would expect them to be, ranging out across San Francisco Bay and all the lands arrayed around it. And to think that you got here just by cranking away at those pedals…

Once you've soaked up all the vistas you can hold, it's time for a big helping of gravity candy: over 3500' down in 11 miles, mile after mile of dancing, diving, switch-backing, zigzagging bliss. At the bottom of the hill, the suburbs return for the last mile and a half of the ride. This is a nice neighborhood of quiet, tree-lined streets, an easy little roll-out to give your legs one last spin before racking the bike.

MILEAGE LOG

0.0	North from Arbolado Park on Contra Costa Trail
1.2	Bear right on the Ygnacio Canal Trail
2.3	Right on Treat Blvd.
3.7	Bear right on Turtle Creek Rd.
5.2	Right on Ayers Rd.
6.2	Right on Pine Hollow Rd.
7.9	Left on Mount Zion Dr.
8.0	Right on Clayton Rd.
8.2	Right on Oak St.; becomes Main St.
8.4	Right on Marsh Creek Rd.
12.8	Right on Morgan Territory Rd.
22.4	Summit of ridge on Morgan Territory Rd.
27.5	Right on Manning Rd.
29.7	Right on Carneal Rd.; "BICYCLIST FRIENDLY REST AREA"
30.1	Left on Highland Rd.
33.2	Right on Camino Tassajara
35.6	Right on Blackhawk Dr.
38.4	Right on Blackhawk Rd.
40.9	Right on Mount Diablo Scenic Blvd.; becomes South Gate Rd.
48.2	Right on Summit Rd.
52.7	Summit parking lot; retrace Summit Rd. downhill
57.2	Right on North Gate Rd.
64.9	Right on Doncaster Rd.
65.2	Finish at Arbolado Park

30 SAN FRANCISCO PARKS

Difficulty:	Moderate
Time:	1.5 to 3 hours
Distance:	16 miles
Elevation gain:	1100'
Best seasons:	All year, although winter may be rainy
Road conditions:	Pavement is excellent. Some city streets may be busy. Some miles are on bike trails or closed roads.

GETTING THERE: There are many ways to reach the Great Highway from all over the city. Park in public lots along the highway.

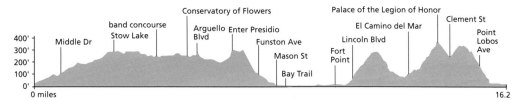

San Francisco is one of the most popular tourist destinations in the world. Millions of visitors have left their hearts here, as the old song says. The locals are rather fond of the town too. Cycling can be a little challenging, though. There are all those steep hills, and the traffic that goes with a densely packed, busy city. To be an everyday, everywhere rider in the city, you need legs of iron and nerves of steel.

But there are ways for cyclists to sample what this great town has to offer without being totally hardcore: this little loop, for example, which explores Golden Gate Park, Lincoln Park (Lands End), and the Presidio, three of the great urban parks of the world. A few blocks of city streets connect the parks, but most of the miles are in or alongside the parks. It would be hard to conjure up another big-city ride that stays so consistently verdant and beautiful.

The route I've laid out is absurdly complicated, with more than 40 lines in the mileage log covering just 16-plus miles. My goal is to run you past as many scenic attractions in the parks as possible, which results in a higgledy-piggledy wiggle of a route. But you needn't feel bound by these directions. You can use this basic loop as a rudimentary template, modifying as you see fit.

The ride begins at the Great Highway because there is so much easy parking there, but you can start anywhere around the loop. The first 5 miles through Golden Gate Park are among the most complex, but the highlights are simple: a run through the park, a loop around Stow Lake, another loop around the band concourse, past all the big museums and the Japanese Tea Garden, and a swing past the magnificent Conservatory of Flowers. If you can check those off your list, you'll have a pretty good sampler of what this grand old park has to offer.

Arguello Boulevard, connecting the park with the Presidio, represents the biggest chunk of pure urban riding: about nine city

The grand old Conservatory of Flowers in Golden Gate Park is just one of many wonders on this densely packed loop through some of the best urban parks in the world.

blocks, with the last quarter-mile a classic San Francisco hill (steep). At the top, you enter the Presidio. This has been a military installation since Spanish times, and up until quite recently was an active US Army base. Now it's all part of a huge park, with the various military buildings converted to everything from housing to movie studios to nonprofit office space. The route descends Arguello to the center of the base, near the venerable officers' club, before tacking around a few blocks of stately old officer housing. More little lanes through the base lead to a crossing of busy Richardson Avenue and a cruise past the magnificent Palace of Fine Arts and its lovely lake, the only relics left from the grand Panama-Pacific Exposition of 1915.

Just beyond the Palace, cross Marina Boulevard and pick up a series of bike trails rolling out across Crissy Field, site of a former air base along the bay, now a broad lawn crisscrossed with numerous walking and cycling trails. Our trail of choice here—the one closest to the bay—is unpaved for 1.4 miles, but is okay for road bikes.

Follow the San Francisco Bay Trail out to Fort Point to visit the Civil War–era fort tucked in underneath the south end of the soaring Golden Gate Bridge. Then double back and climb to the bike trail next to Lincoln Boulevard. The trail passes through all of the sites and facilities associated with visiting the bridge...a good spot for a break. After nipping under the highway, climb a small hill, now on Lincoln Boulevard, before topping out at a spectacular vista point overlooking the ocean. A zippy, 1-mile descent curls down the cliff face to carry you out of the Presidio and into the elegant residential enclave of Sea Cliff. After eight blocks of ritzy mansions, you enter Lincoln Park, riding uphill through its handsome golf course, with picture-postcard views back to the bridge. At the top of the climb, cruise past the majestic Palace of the Legion of Honor museum.

Several uphill blocks along Clement Street, next to the park, lead to the last summit before a mile-long plunge to sea level, past the sites of the old Cliff House and Sutro Baths and Playland by the Sea. All those fabulous tourist attractions from an earlier era are gone now, but the wooded cliffs and the windswept beach remain.

It's impossible, in this space, to list the many points of interest around this loop, or to cover their colorful histories. This little ride is packed solid with scenic and historic attractions, some spectacular, some subtle. If you're visiting San Francisco for the first time, read the available literature on the Internet, then take that knowledge out on the road, around this loop. By the time you've rolled out these few miles, you will have a much better appreciation for what makes San Francisco such a popular city, for visitors and residents alike.

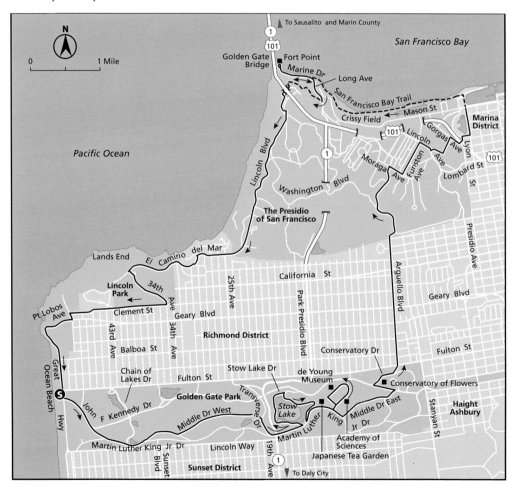

0.0	From parking lot on Great Hwy, east on John F. Kennedy Dr.
0.4	Straight on South Fork Dr. (JFK Dr. turns left)
0.5	Bear left on Martin Luther King Jr. Dr.
0.9	Left on Middle Dr. W.
1.2	Bear left to stay on Middle Dr. Sign says "NOT A THRU STREET," but bikes okay.
1.9	Continue on Transverse Dr.
2.1	Left on Martin Luther King Jr. Dr.
2.4	Left on Stow Lake Dr.
2.9	Right on Stow Lake Dr. E.
3.5	Left on Martin Luther King Jr. Dr.
3.8	Left on Music Concourse Dr. past California Academy of Sciences
4.1	Bear left around band concourse in front of de Young Museum
4.2	Left behind Temple of Music and right to return to Martin Luther King Dr.
4.4	Left on Middle Dr. E. (also known as Nancy Pelosi Dr.)
4.9	Left on John F. Kennedy Dr.
5.1	Right on Conservatory Dr., behind Conservatory of Flowers
5.3	Left on Arguello Blvd.; leave Golden Gate Park
6.5	Enter Presidio of San Francisco
7.2	Right on Moraga Ave.
7.3	Left on Funston Ave.
7.6	Right on Lincoln Blvd.
7.7	Left on Torney Ave.
7.8	Left on O'Reilly Ave.
8.0	Right on Gorgas Ave.; becomes Lyon St.
8.1	Cross Richardson Ave. to continue on Lyon St.
8.2	Right on Bay St.; Palace of Fine Arts
8.3	Left on Baker St.
8.5	Cross Marina Blvd. to the San Francisco Bay Trail
8.6	Bear left on Bay Trail (also signed as San Francisco Promenade). 1.4 miles of flat, hard dirt/gravel trails along bay. Paved Mason St. is nearby.
10.1	Right on Marine Dr.
10.4	Fort Point; turn around and retrace
10.7	Bear right on Long Ave.
10.9	Right on Battery East Trail, next to Lincoln Blvd.
11.3	Left on San Francisco Bike Route 95 through Golden Gate Bridge visitor center
11.4	Right through tunnel underneath Hwy 101
11.5	Jog left on Cranston Rd. to right on Merchant Rd.
11.6	Right on Lincoln Blvd.
13.0	Becomes El Camino del Mar; leave Presidio
14.0	Bear left on 34th Ave. in front of Palace of Legion of Honor
14.5	Right on Clement St.; becomes Seal Rock Dr.
15.3	Jog left on El Camino del Mar to right on Point Lobos Ave.; becomes Great Hwy
16.2	Finish at parking lot along Great Hwy

31 ALAMEDA OLD AND NEW

Difficulty:	Easy
Time:	1 to 2 hours
Distance:	14 miles
Elevation gain:	Flat
Best seasons:	All year, although midwinter may be rainy
Road conditions:	Some roads are busy; most are not. Many miles are on bike trails. Pavement is good.

GETTING THERE: Exit I-880 in Oakland at High St. and head south for 0.4 mile, across the bridge to Alameda. Turn left on Fernside Blvd. and drive 1 mile to Lincoln Middle School.

Say what you will about the thrill of a wild downhill, or the sizzle of a hot pace line, or the panoramic view from the top of a high summit—all parts of a great ride. But there are other, quieter pleasures to be had on a bike. In between those bigger and faster rides, one of my favorite forms of cycling enjoyment is the neighborhood crawl: a slow cruise around a fine old residential district, checking out the stately homes.

The first part of this ride is just that sort of meandering exploration of a wonderful, venerable neighborhood: a part of Alameda, on the east shore of San Francisco Bay. Alameda is an island, buffered from the rest of the East Bay not only by water but by a dense belt of freeways, rail yards, shipping terminals, and factories along the Oakland shore. Sequestered behind this wall of industrial wilderness, and connected to the mainland by only three small bridges and two undersea tunnels, it stands apart: an island, both literally and figuratively.

The island is not all lovely old neighborhoods. The western third is home to the Alameda Naval Air Station. At least another third is fairly ordinary: shopping centers and tracts of no particular distinction. But the remaining third is quite exceptional. The best part of Alameda is block after block of Victorian, Edwardian, and Arts-and-Crafts homes, usually well maintained. Some are modest but still of interest, and some are grand to an eye-popping degree. The best part is that they're so accessible, set back behind manicured lawns and gardens but seen easily from the street. It's a visual feast from the front-row seat of a bicycle.

This route through old Alameda is a bit convoluted, wandering back and forth to sample a number of nice streets on the way to Washington Park. I suggest you use it as a cue sheet for navigating, but feel free to meander along any side streets that catch your fancy. In particular, the dead-end streets heading south off San Antonio Avenue, down to a quiet lagoon, are worth a look: Bay, St. Charles, Hawthorne, and Caroline. Every one is a candy box of architectural treats.

Once you've had your fill of old Alameda, it's time for something new. The transition begins with a bike path through Washington Park, riding out along the southern side of Alameda Island beside Shoreline Drive. After 2 miles along San Francisco Bay, a few twists and turns bring you to the Bay Farm Island Bicycle Bridge and a crossing to yet another island.

Bay Farm Island was once truly an island, given over mostly to wetlands, asparagus farms, and oyster flats. Extensive landfill has now connected it to the shore near Oakland International Airport, which occupies the eastern half of the island. Most of the rest of the space is occupied with recent development: condo complexes, office parks, and a thirty-six-hole golf course. The attraction for cyclists is a pleasant bike path that circles the island, right along the bay, offering gorgeous views across the water in all directions. The view of San Francisco, glittering in the distance like a hoard of jewels, is especially fine.

I suggest circling the island in the counter-clockwise direction. At the southeastern end of this loop, you bump up against the back fence of the airport and follow that boundary—on Harbor Bay Parkway—back up to the north side of the island. While the parkway is fine for cycling—not too much traffic—there is a bike trail on the west side of the road, next to the golf course, if you prefer that. At the north end of the parkway, cross Doolittle Drive and pick up another bike path around the edge of Shoreline Park, which returns you to the bike bridge over the estuary. Back over the bridge, there is just one last, half-mile run back to the school where the ride began.

From the bike trail around Bay Farm Island in Alameda, the views across the bay to San Francisco are spectacular.

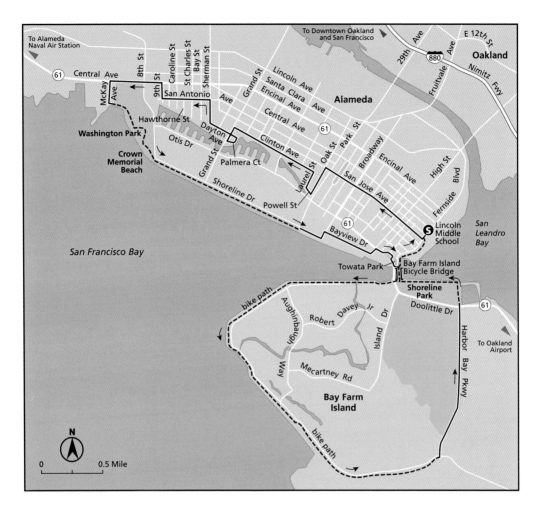

"Old" Alameda and "new" Bay Farm Island are as different as they can be. But they both share the same island ambience: that sense of being somewhat apart from the bustle of the busy Bay Area around them. Whether that apartness is expressed along quiet, tree-lined neighborhood streets or out along the bike trails next to the bay, the feeling is real and special.

MILEAGE LOG

0.0	From Lincoln Middle School, left on Fernside Blvd.
0.1	Right on San Jose Ave.
1.1	Left on Oak St.
1.3	Right on Powell St.
1.4	Right on Laurel St.
1.5	Left on Clinton Ave.
2.3	Left on Grand St.
2.4	Left on Palmera Ct.

2.5	Left on Dayton Ave.
2.7	Right on Sherman St.
2.9	Left on San Antonio Ave.
3.3	Right on 9th St.
3.4	Left on Central Ave.
3.9	Left on McKay Ave. into Washington Park; follow bike path through park
4.8	Continue along bike path parallel to Shoreline Dr.
6.3	Jog left on Broadway to right on Bayview Dr.
6.8	Right on Otis Dr.
6.9	Right on Peach St. into Towata Park
7.0	Follow bike path under Otis Dr. (Hwy 61)
7.2	Hard left onto Bay Farm Island Bicycle Bridge
7.3	Right on bike path around shoreline perimeter of Bay Farm Island
10.7	Merge onto Harbor Bay Pkwy., move toward left turn lane
11.2	Left to continue on Harbor Bay Pkwy.
12.6	Cross Doolittle Dr. to bike path around Shoreline Park
13.2	Right across Bay Farm Island Bicycle Bridge
13.4	Follow bike path beside Fernside Blvd.
13.7	Finish at Lincoln Middle School

32   MOUNT HAMILTON LOOP

Difficulty:	Epic
Time:	7 to 10 hours
Distance:	110 miles
Elevation gain:	9200'
Best seasons:	April through October
Road conditions:	Some roads are busy; most are not. Pavement is good.

GETTING THERE: From I-580 in Livermore, head south on Livermore Ave. for 2.5 miles to Robertson Park.

This is a huge ride, one of the longest and hardest in the book. I've done these roads, in one direction or the other, as part of the Devil Mountain Double, the 125-mile Mount Hamilton Challenge, and on several club rides. This route is manageable for a fit but approximately average rider (if I can do it, so can a lot of you). It is also the better (easier) way to go around the loop. It's a fantastic ride,

and your efforts will be rewarded with wonderful scenery and cycling adventures.

The ride starts at a park in Livermore, and though suburban, this unavoidable section includes some miles on nice bike trails. From mile 10 through the rest of the loop, with one short exception, you'll be riding in deep country or at least in rural-residential neighborhoods.

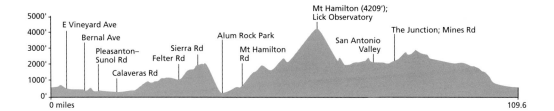

With that first suburban run behind you, a pleasant, level cruise along Pleasanton–Sunol Road leads to the first marquee attraction of the ride: Calaveras Road. After 4 flat miles passing tree farms, it settles into a beautiful, 10-mile meander through the woods, often overlooking Calaveras Reservoir. At its far end, a left on Felter Road introduces a more ambitious uphill: 1000' of stair-step climbs in 6 ridge-running miles. Felter becomes Sierra Road midway along this section. You might be familiar with Sierra Road from the Tour of California. Its ferocious ascent has been featured in almost every edition of the stage

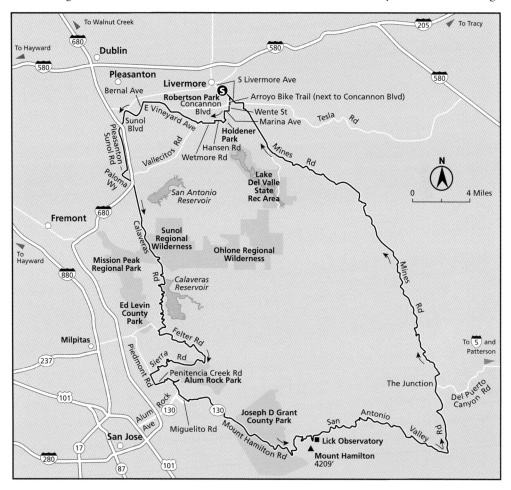

When Lick Observatory looms on the horizon, you know you're almost done with the long climb to the 4209' summit of Mount Hamilton. (Bill Bushnell)

race; it is also a dreaded challenge late in the Devil Mountain Double. But—good news— our route is doing it in the opposite direction, coming up the relatively easy backside of the ridge and descending the infamous wall (1800' down in 3.5 miles). That's an 11 percent average for quite a distance, so take your time and stay safe. And take the time to look at the view: the entire San Francisco Bay is laid out below you in a breathtaking panorama.

At the bottom of this hairy descent, the route dips back into the suburbs for 1 mile before heading into Alum Rock Park. This run through the wooded park includes an old road closed to cars, essentially a bike path now.

Beyond the park, one more mile of hillside suburbs sees you clear of civilization, and by mile 45 you are on Mount Hamilton Road, embarked on the long ascent to the summit.

This is a big climb. The summit is 4000' higher than Alum Rock Park, where things begin to tilt uphill. Those two points are over 20 miles apart, and many different things happen to the topography in between, including some downhills and some very gradual uphills. But there are also some tougher sections approaching 10 percent. Overall, it's a big project, pedaling your bike up to Lick Observatory, at 4209'. You should stop at the observatory, not only to top up your water but to take in the view. This is the highest paved road in the Bay Area, and the views go on forever. I should mention the views on the way up the hill as well: one of the prettiest landscapes you could imagine, with grassy meadows, oak forest, and vistas out across endless hillsides and canyons, all pristine and perfect.

The views off the backside of the mountain, beyond the summit, are just as nice. But you may have to pay more attention to your line and your bike handling than the scenery. The main descent is 5 miles and is always steep—up to 13 percent—and very tangled and twisty. You're descending into a wonderful wilderness called the San Antonio Valley. Okay, it's not a true wilderness: there are a few homes and ranches out there, and even one store—at the Junction—where you can buy food. But the overall impression is of wildness and emptiness and Mother Nature looking her best. In the main valley, a pretty little creek ripples along near the road. In the spring, the meadows are splashed with confetti sprinkles of wildflowers. It really is enchanting. If there is a heaven for cyclists, it's going to look a lot like this.

After the Junction, the road name changes to Mines Road. The landscape changes too. While still nice for riding, it's not as idyllic as San Antonio Valley. The canyon narrows and the pretty meadows are squeezed out by rocky hills covered in scrub and digger pines. And while the valley had been mostly level, there are now two climbs to tackle. Compared to Hamilton, these are tiny bumps, but coming up between miles 80 and 85, when you may be a trifle worn down, they could drag a little.

Beyond those two bumps, the final 25 miles of the ride are both easy and delightful. For one thing, they're almost all downhill. And for another, the scenery perks up again: more oaks and broadleaf woods and grassy hillsides, as the road slithers down the canyon of Arroyo Mocho on smooth new pavement. The ride finishes up with a nearly level cruise to the outskirts of Livermore, amid horse pastures and vineyards. The last 2 easy miles follow the same nice bike trail used at the start of the ride, a lazy way to close the loop: while your legs enjoy a mellow spin-down, your mind can hit "Replay" and savor the highlights of this epic journey.

MILEAGE LOG

0.0	From Robertson Park, right on South Livermore Ave.
0.2	Right on Arroyo Bike Trail, next to Concannon Blvd.
0.6	Left on Wente St. (or adjacent bike trail)
1.1	Right on Marina Ave. (or adjacent bike trail)
1.4	Bear left on bike trail (away from Marina Ave.)
2.1	Right on Holdener Park access road
2.2	Left on Hansen Rd.
2.9	Left on Arroyo Rd.
3.0	Right on Wetmore Rd. (or adjacent bike trail)
4.0	Left on Vallecitos Rd.
4.3	Right on East Vineyard Ave.
8.4	Left on Bernal Ave.
10.3	Left on Sunol Blvd.
11.6	Becomes Pleasanton–Sunol Rd. after crossing under I-680
15.3	Left on Paloma Wy. (Hwy 84)
16.0	Becomes Calaveras Rd. after crossing under I-680
30.3	Left on Felter Rd.

34.5	Bear right on Sierra Rd.
40.2	Left on Piedmont Rd.
40.9	Left on Penitencia Creek Rd. into Alum Rock Park (water)
43.0	Right on Alum Rock Ave.
43.9	Straight on Miguelito Rd.
44.8	Left on Mount Hamilton Rd. (Hwy 130)
62.2	Mount Hamilton summit (4209'); Lick Observatory (water); also known as San Antonio Valley Rd. on far side of summit
80.5	Becomes Mines Rd. at Del Puerto Canyon Rd. junction; food, water at store at junction
108.5	Left on Tesla Rd.; becomes South Livermore Ave.
109.6	Finish at Robertson Park

33 COYOTE CREEK LOOP

Difficulty:	Moderate/challenging
Time:	2 to 4 hours
Distance:	28 miles (32 with optional out-and-back)
Elevation gain:	2200'
Best seasons:	All year, although midwinter may be rainy
Road conditions:	Some roads are busy; most are not. Many miles are on bike trails. Pavement is good.

GETTING THERE: In San Jose, exit Hwy 101 at Tully Rd. Head west on Tully for 0.8 mile to the Tully Community Branch Library parking lot, also the trailhead of the Coyote Creek Trail.

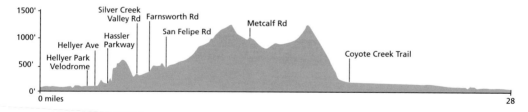

All around San Francisco Bay, the land is carpeted by urban and suburban development. The three big cities of San Francisco in the west, Oakland in the east, and San Jose in the south are joined by over thirty smaller cities to form one vast, uninterrupted metroplex. Much of this sprawl is not what anyone would think of as great cycling country: too many freeways and broad, fast boulevards, and way too much traffic. That's the bad news.

The good news is that hundreds of thousands of avid, active cyclists live in those communities, and they all hunger for places to ride that are fun and safe. To be sure, there are great roads in the hills all around this wall-to-wall sprawl by the bay. (We feature many

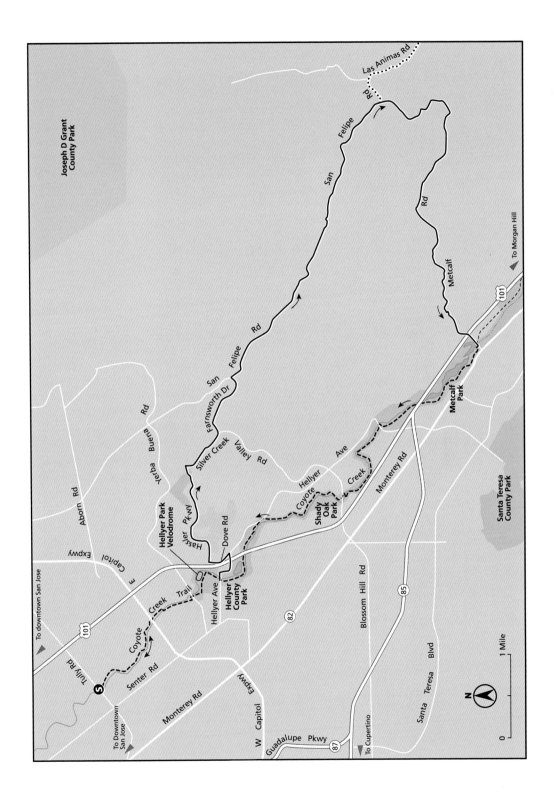

Coyote Creek Trail is one of the oldest, longest, and best-thought-out trails in the Bay Area.

of them in this chapter.) But how do those myriad riders get around down on the heavily developed valley floor? How do they get out to the nice rural roads nearby? Over the course of many years, in many different neighborhoods, through many political battles, the answer has come to be bike trails. All of those active—in some cases activist—cyclists have pushed for trails with enough will and weight that the communities have responded and the trails have been built, pretty much wherever they could be squeezed in. They run through parks, along creeks and canals, by the bay. They vault over freeways and burrow under boulevards, giving riders blessed relief from the motorized hordes.

I can't possibly describe or plot routes along them all, so I've chosen Coyote Creek Trail as my official representative of the breed. I do use bike trails on other rides, but I think of this one as special. It's pretty much the granddaddy of all Bay Area trails and it lives and functions deep in the densest, darkest heart of suburban sprawl: south San Jose. It is the prototype against which all subsequent trails are measured.

I had initially thought to offer this simply as an out-and-back along the 18-mile length of the trail, but I decided instead to incorporate a 10-mile section of the trail into a loop—using some suburban roads and some really sweet country roads—to illustrate how trails can be of service to riders, not only for their own merits but as gateways out of the sprawl and into the countryside beyond.

This ride begins at the northern end of the Coyote Creek Trail and uses 3 miles of it before heading for the hills. Along that first section, it passes Hellyer Park Velodrome, the only full-size cycling track in Northern California. Stop and check it out, but don't ride your road bike on the track. That's against the rules, and the track riders take a dim view of such interlopers.

Leave the trail just after crossing under Hellyer Avenue. Take this road east, over Highway 101 and up into a new subdivision on Hassler Parkway. This is a seriously steep climb, 440' in 1 mile. That's 8 percent, but the bottom half is well over 10 percent. It's the only element in this otherwise moderate ride that earns it a "challenging" rating. Two more suburban boulevards follow: Silver Creek Valley and Farnsworth Drive. All three of these roads, although obviously suburban, are pleasant and reasonable for cycling.

At the far end of Farnsworth, things become really nice. San Felipe and Metcalf roads, between miles 7.4 and 18, are just about perfect biking back roads. San Felipe climbs gently for 4 miles, then descends for 2, always in the dappled shade of leafy woods or across rolling, grassy meadows. Just past mile 12, the loop bears right on Metcalf. San Felipe continues to the left as a dead end, becoming Las Animas Road around the next bend. If you want a bit more than 28 miles, consider adding an out-and-back on this dead end. It's almost 4 miles round-trip, every inch of it perfect for cycling.

After an initial 2-mile descent on Metcalf, the road kicks up into a 2-mile climb: easy, rolling terrain at first, then a steeper section near the top. Once over the open ridge, there is a huge descent on tap: 1000' down in 2 miles (9 percent). If you like descending, you'll love this fast, frantic downhill, one wiggly corner after another.

Roll out across Hwy 101 at the bottom, and just past a large pond, turn right onto the Coyote Creek Trail. You'll be on the trail for the final 10 miles of the ride, heading north on a meandering run alongside Coyote Creek. Although tract neighborhoods and technology parks and shopping malls are sometimes only a few yards away on either side of the trail, most of the time they remain out of sight behind the trees, or off in the distance. It feels as if you are riding in the woods, or at least in a park.

Navigation is simple: follow the trail all the way to the Tully Road trailhead. I've noted a few tricky turns in the log, but mostly, it's just a case of rolling along and enjoying a lovely, peaceful, car-free environment...the magical miracle of a good bike trail.

MILEAGE LOG

0.0   From the Tully Community Branch Library parking lot, head south on Coyote Creek Trail
1.0   Right to ride under Capitol Expwy.
2.4   Left to ride under Yerba Buena Rd.
2.8   Hellyer Park Velodrome
3.1   Ride under Hellyer Ave.; left on spur trail to Hellyer Park access road
3.2   Right on Hellyer Ave.
3.6   Left on Dove Rd.
4.0   Right on Hassler Pkwy.
5.7   Right on Silver Creek Valley Rd.

6.4	Left on Farnsworth Dr.
7.4	Right on San Felipe Rd.
12.3	Right on Metcalf Rd.; optional out-and-back on San Felipe Rd. and Las Animas Rd. (3.8 miles round-trip)
18.1	Right on Coyote Creek Trail
22.0	Hard left to ride under Silver Creek Valley Rd.
25.5	Right to stay on trail after riding under Yerba Buena Rd.
26.3	Left to stay on trail after riding under Capitol Expwy.
28.0	Finish at Tully Rd. parking lot

34 OLD LA HONDA–TUNITAS CREEK

Difficulty:	Challenging
Time:	5 to 6 hours
Distance:	68 miles
Elevation gain:	6100'
Best seasons:	All year, but winter may be rainy
Road conditions:	A few highway miles are busy, but most roads are quiet; pavement is good to excellent.

GETTING THERE: From I-280, take the Woodside Rd. exit and head west 1 mile into Woodside. Park at Woodside Elementary School.

This has to be one of the best rides in the book, consistently entertaining from start to finish. It's one of two circuits I put together that explore the Santa Cruz Mountains from starts on the populated east side of the range (see also Ride 35).

This is a challenging ride because of its climbing, but all of the harder hills are in the big loop. It's possible to skip the smaller loop to Pigeon Point, but its 400' of easy gain adds almost nothing to the overall challenge. If you're fit enough to do the climbing on the big loop, you can add the small loop with no trouble. Those 17 miles are so nice it would be a shame to skip them.

The ride begins in the quietly affluent town of Woodside, and the first miles travel along the pretty back streets of town to the base of Old La Honda Road. This must be one of the most popular roads in this region for getting out of the suburbs and up into the mountains, and with good reason: it's a classic bike road, one wide lane climbing through beautiful, leafy woods, and no traffic. It's a

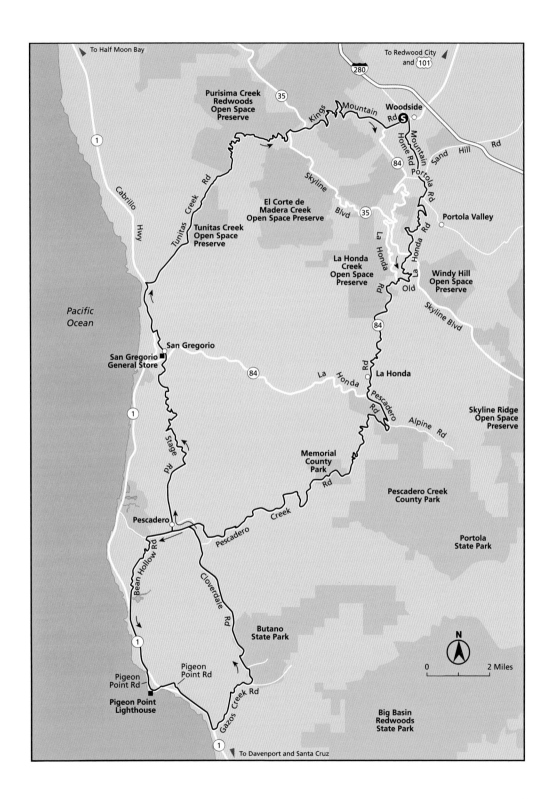

Old La Honda Road is one of the highlights on this ride packed full of highlights. (Nancy Yu)

stout climb: 1300' in 3.5 miles (7 percent). At the summit, it crosses Skyline Boulevard and begins a long descent to the town of La Honda: 1300' down in 6 miles, half on tiny, twisty Old La Honda and half on wider, somewhat busier La Honda Road (Highway 84).

Just beyond town, turn left on Pescadero Road, and in a mile, right on Pescadero Creek Road. This road includes a 2-mile, 600' climb and a 2-mile, 800' descent, all on smooth pavement and in a lovely forest of redwoods and deciduous trees, with occasional spots where the sightlines open up to distant vistas over the ocean.

At about mile 18, the serious downhill bottoms out, and this begins the coastal part of the ride: rolling or flat miles in the low hills near the beach or in nearby valleys. Between miles 18 and 56, the roads only climb above 250' for three small summits. The rest of this section is as easy as can be, but that doesn't make it boring. These are wonderful roads, dream cycling.

The town of Pescadero comes up at mile 26, a good spot for a break. Continue on Pescadero Creek Road for a straight, flat run down the valley to a left on Bean Hollow Road, a pretty little lane curling south toward Hwy 1. Head south on the coast highway, but don't miss the next turn for a 2-mile run along Pigeon Point Road, including a visit to the towering Pigeon Point Lighthouse at mile 32. Another short run on Hwy 1 brings you to a left—inland and slightly uphill—on Gazos Creek Road and Cloverdale Road. These two delightful byways bend back north up a secluded valley, all the way back to the town of Pescadero, closing the small loop. These roads are great: no traffic, smooth pavement, and wonderful scenery.

From Pescadero it only gets better. Stage Road, heading north from town, is a nearly perfect cycling road. It runs for 8.5 miles up another secluded valley with scenery that is sublime. The three small climbs mentioned earlier—the ones just a bit over 250'—are all on the north end of this road. Each is moderately challenging, but each comes bundled with a snappy descent. In between two of those hills, at mile 50, is the historic San Gregorio General Store, a popular watering hole for cyclists, with bike racks out front. This is an obvious spot for another break.

From the north end of Stage Road, a short run on Hwy 1 leads to the last and largest climb of the day: Tunitas Creek Road (often used in the Tour of California). It is a big ascent, 2000' in 9.5 miles. More precisely, it breaks out this way: 3 miles of gentle false flat to start, 3.5 miles of serious work (7 percent, the same as Old La Honda), and finally 3 miles of fairly easy uphill to Skyline Boulevard. The bottom section is in an open valley—still in that coastal zone—and the rest is in deep redwood forest. All of it is one lane wide and as quiet as can be. Yes, it is work, but what a nice place to have to work.

Over the top, you can cash in your chips with one of the best descents around: 4.5 miles of slinky, silky curves on beautifully paved Kings Mountain Road, winding through shady woods all the way down to Woodside, with just a half mile through town at the bottom to cool out before the finish. I'm not exaggerating when I say this is one of the best downhills I've ever done, anywhere. It puts an exclamation point on a ride worthy of exclamation points.

MILEAGE LOG

0.0	From Woodside Elementary School, right on Woodside Rd.
0.4	Right on Mountain Home Rd.
2.4	Right on Portola Rd.
2.6	Right on Old La Honda Rd.
6.5	Cross Skyline Blvd. (Hwy 35) to continue on Old La Honda Rd.
9.1	Left on La Honda Rd. (Hwy 84)
12.5	Town of La Honda
13.1	Left on Pescadero Rd.
14.2	Right on Pescadero Creek Rd. at Alpine Rd. junction
26.0	Town of Pescadero; short route turns right on Stage Rd.; main route stays on Pescadero Creek Rd.
26.7	Left on Bean Hollow Rd.
29.2	Left on Hwy 1
31.3	Right on Pigeon Point Rd.
32.0	Pigeon Point Lighthouse
32.3	Cross Hwy 1 to continue on Pigeon Point Rd.
33.1	Left on Hwy 1
34.6	Left on Gazos Creek Rd.
36.7	Left on Cloverdale Rd.
42.1	Left on Pescadero Creek Rd.
42.6	Town of Pescadero; right on Stage Rd.
50.0	San Gregorio General Store
51.1	Right on Hwy 1
52.7	Right on Tunitas Creek Rd.
62.1	Cross Skyline Blvd. to Kings Mountain Rd.
67.2	Left on Woodside Rd. into town of Woodside
67.7	Finish at Woodside Elementary School

Difficulty:	Challenging
Time:	4 to 6 hours
Distance:	62 miles
Elevation gain:	Up to 8000'
Best seasons:	April through October
Road conditions:	Some roads may be busy, but most are low traffic and bike friendly. The more remote roads are narrow, with little or no shoulders. Most are well paved.

GETTING THERE: From San Jose take Hwy 17 south (from either I-280 or Hwy 85) to the Los Gatos, Saratoga, exit on Hwy 9. Head west on Hwy 9; turn left on University Ave., left on Miles Ave., and left into the parking lot of the baseball field next to the Los Gatos Creek Trail.

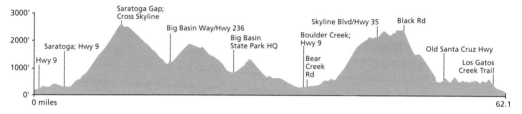

When cyclists in the South Bay want to escape the suburban sprawl, they head for the Santa Cruz Mountains, the rugged, forested ridgelines that form the high backbone between the ocean and the southern reaches of San Francisco Bay. There are many fine roads in these hills and many ways to string them together into good rides. This loop and Ride 34 are my two choices for rides beginning in the South Bay suburbs and heading west.

The ride begins in Los Gatos and knocks off 4 flat, boulevard miles first, heading north to the village of Saratoga. These are pleasant miles, but it's still nice to get them out of the way at the start. Turn left in Saratoga, following the signs for Highway 9. Ride through the town's affluent shopping district and out into the country. By mile 5, you've left the town behind and have embarked on a 7-mile, 2100' climb to Saratoga Gap. This long ascent aver-

ages around 5 percent with some variations up and down, but compared to some roads in these steeply wrinkled hills, it's a steady grade. Scenery is always good: broadleaf forest shading the road from start to finish.

At the summit, Hwy 9 crosses Hwy 35 (Skyline Boulevard). Carry on over the top and down the other side, following signs for Big Basin and Boulder Creek. Crossing the ridge means moving from the inland to the coastal environment: fog, ferns, and dense stands of redwoods. Now, amid that lush landscape, you get a nice return on your big climbing investment: 6 miles of winding downhill on smooth pavement, often with sweeping views out across the wooded ridges and canyons of Castle Rock State Park. At the bottom of this dreamy descent, Hwy 9 turns left, while our route stays straight ahead onto Hwy 236, better known as Big Basin Way.

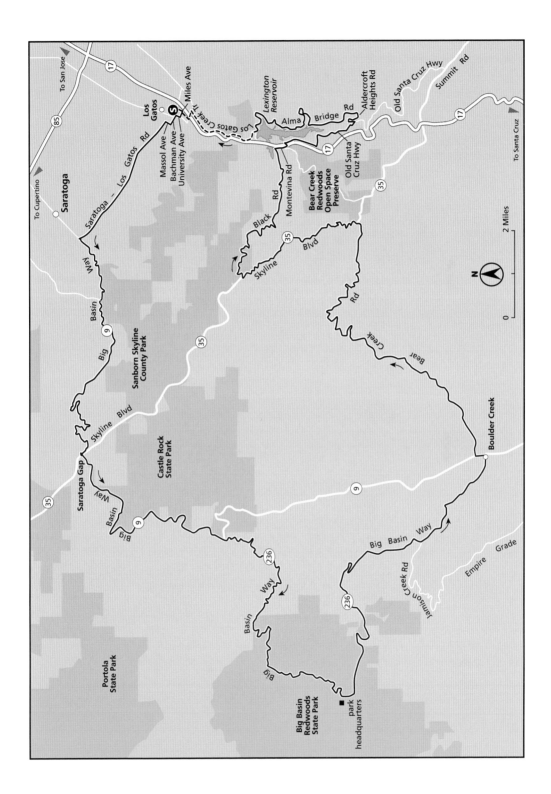

To San Jose

17

85

To Cupertino

Saratoga

Saratoga – Los Gatos Rd

Massol Ave
Bachman Ave
University Ave

Los Gatos

Miles Ave

Los Gatos Creek Tr

Lexington Reservoir

Alma Bridge Rd

Aldercroft Heights Rd

Old Santa Cruz Hwy

Summit Rd

17

To Santa Cruz

Black Rd

Montevina Rd

Bear Creek Redwoods Open Space Preserve

Old Santa Cruz Hwy

35

Skyline Blvd

35

Big Basin Way

9

Saratoga Gap

Skyline Blvd

35

Sanborn Skyline County Park

Castle Rock State Park

Bear Creek Rd

Boulder Creek

9

Big Basin Way

9

Big Basin Way

236

236

Jamison Creek Rd

Empire Grade

Portola State Park

Big Basin Way

Big Basin Redwoods State Park

park headquarters

N

0   2 Miles

Riding amid the redwoods in Big Basin Redwoods State Park: quiet, beautiful, and nice pavement too

Welcome to Big Basin Redwoods State Park. The route will be within the park and its old-growth forest for the next 11 miles, and they are some of the best miles of this ride. Hwy 236 starts out looking like a real highway but soon narrows to one fat lane and begins wriggling along between the massive trees crowding the road. The park transit begins with an easy climb: 700' up in 3 miles. This is followed by 5 miles of wonderful downhill, all on this tiny, tangled twist of road, threading among the towering trees. At the bottom, just past mile 25, deep in the heart of the most magnificent grove of red-

woods, you arrive at park headquarters, a good spot for a break. There is a handsome old log lodge and restrooms.

Leaving the park means an easy 2-mile climb and then a 6.5-mile descent to the town of Boulder Creek. Only the first 2 miles are true downhill, with the balance being lazy roll-out. Scenery remains much the same as in the park: redwoods mixed with leafy trees, with a moderate increase in human presence—residential and commercial—as you approach the town. Boulder Creek comes up at mile 35 and effectively marks the midpoint of the ride. There is a decent market right on the corner where Hwy 236 tees into Hwy 9. Turn left on Hwy 9 and go about a quarter-mile to a right on Bear Creek Road.

Bear Creek Road is one of the biggest challenges on this ride. It starts out with 4.5 miles of gently rolling uphill, but then chugs up the wooded hillside in a steep, unrelenting grade of 3 miles, gaining 1200', followed by 2 more miles at an easier but still uphill pitch. Those 3 miles average 7 percent, but some spots will exceed 10 percent. Bear Creek is challenging in another way too: traffic. There is a fair bit of it, and the road is lacking shoulders more often than not. It can be a tight fit. However, local cyclists assure me they do this road all the time. No one would claim it as a favorite road, but riders put up with it to connect the other pieces in this loop. I can tell you I was happy to see the signs for the left turn off this road and onto Hwy 35, Skyline Boulevard.

Farther north, Skyline is a busier, faster highway, but down here, at its southern end, all of that goes away. For 4 enchanting miles, this dinky, one-lane road tumbles and rambles along an up-and-down, back-and-forth wiggle through oak and madrone forest, all free of traffic. You could hardly dream up a road more suited to cycling…hilly cycling, anyway. At mile 48.4, just where Skyline straightens out, widens, and regains its stripes, looking like a legitimate, numbered state highway again, our route turns right on Black Road and drops down the rabbit hole on a wickedly steep plunge. Black is 4.5 miles, top to bottom: first a 1.5-mile plummet, then 1 flat mile, and finally another 2-mile flier. Both descents hit 15 percent in places…an intensely busy few minutes.

At the bottom of this brake-burner, you're less than 4 miles, in a straight line, from the finish in Los Gatos. But it will take over 9 miles to get there along our route, looping around Lexington Reservoir on a series of quiet, meandering back roads and, finally, along a section of the Los Gatos Creek Trail, which runs right past the parking lot where you started. The trail is gravel in a few spots, but easy to ride on a road bike. These late miles are as nice as the rest of the roads on this great loop. It all adds up to a wonderful adventure. If you can manage this much climbing, you will be in bike heaven on this ride.

MILEAGE LOG

0.0	From baseball field parking lot, right on Miles Ave.
0.1	Right on University Ave.
0.3	Left on Bachman Ave.
0.5	Right on Massol Ave.
0.7	Left on Saratoga–Los Gatos Rd. (Hwy 9)
4.1	Left on Big Basin Way (Hwy 9); town of Saratoga
11.4	Cross Skyline Blvd. (Hwy 35) to continue on Big Basin Way (Hwy 9); summit
17.5	Straight on Big Basin Way, now Hwy 236 (Hwy 9 turns left)
25.8	Headquarters, Big Basin Redwoods State Park
34.9	Left on Hwy 9; town of Boulder Creek
35.2	Right on Bear Creek Rd.
44.5	Left on Skyline Blvd. (Hwy 35)
48.4	Right on Black Rd.
52.9	Right on Montevina Rd.
53.2	Left on Bear Creek Rd., cross over Hwy 17
53.3	Right on Old Santa Cruz Hwy
55.3	Left on Aldercroft Heights Rd.

55.9   Left on Alma Bridge Rd.
60.0   Right on Los Gatos Creek Trail
61.9   Cross Hwy 17 on trail, turn right to continue on trail
62.1   Right on Miles Ave. to baseball field parking lot and finish

36 ALMADEN TWO-LOOPER

Difficulty:	Moderate/challenging
Time:	3 to 5 hours
Distance:	52 miles
Elevation gain:	2800'
Best seasons:	All year, although midwinter may be rainy
Road conditions:	Some roads are busy; most are not. Some miles are on bike trails. Pavement is good.

GETTING THERE: In San Jose, exit Hwy 85 at the Almaden Expwy. and drive south 0.8 mile. Turn left on Coleman Rd., cross Las Alamitos Creek, and turn right on Winfield Blvd., then right into Almaden Lake Park.

This is the southernmost ride in the immediate Bay Area (the suburban sprawl around San Francisco Bay). Its two loops dangle like Christmas tree ornaments off the bottom edge of San Jose. The route dodges around the edges of the suburbs in a few spots, but most of it is out in the country. The best parts of the ride are very good indeed.

The ride stages out of Almaden Lake Park and as it heads out, it makes use of a bike trail through the park to avoid a busy boulevard. By the time you've crossed the creek above the lake, that busy street has settled down to something more appropriate for bikes. You're on its wide shoulder for 2 miles before turning onto Hicks Road, where, quite suddenly,

you leave the 'burbs behind and pedal out into deep, leafy countryside.

You also begin climbing. This ride would be rated Moderate were it not for one climb on this road. You can see it sticking up like a dunce cap on the elevation profile. The ascent begins gradually but kicks up into a short, steep pitch to the dam at Guadalupe Reservoir. (This is the first of five reservoirs along the route today.) After a level run along the lake, you hit the hard part, and it is very hard: 750' in a bit over a mile. That's a 14 percent grade...for a mile. *Ouch!*

The descent off the other side is just as long and just as steep, a real plunge down the rabbit hole. At the bottom, you can let your rims

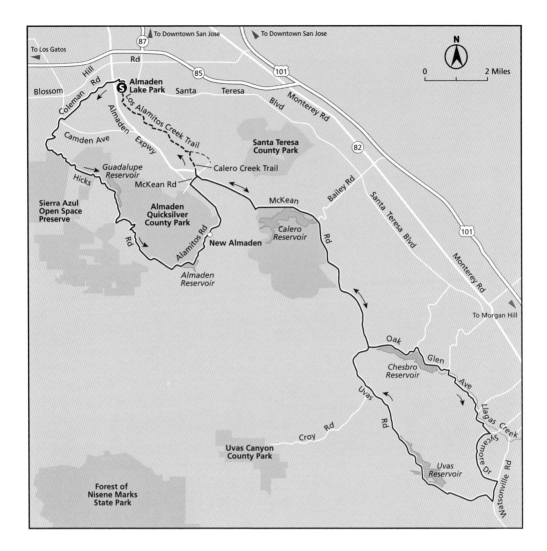

cool off with an easy run alongside Almaden Reservoir. Beyond that dam, the road slopes gently downhill, through the rural community of New Almaden. Finishing off the first loop, the road bends back north to the ragged fringe of suburbia at around mile 15. Turn right on McKean Road and right again to stay on the same road to head back out into pretty country again. Just after that second turn, there is a school on the left that may be your best shot at water for the entire ride. There are no stores anywhere on this ride, so bring enough pocket food for the duration.

McKean is the connector road between the two loops and so is ridden twice, heading south and again returning north. It climbs gently to Calero Reservoir, and after a level run near the lake, ramps up into a 1-mile climb: not too hard, but perhaps a bit tedious. A smooth, simple descent leads to a turn onto Oak Glen Avenue and another level run past Chesbro Reservoir. This begins the southern loop, and as nice as some of the roads have been so far, I think they're even better here. Past the reservoir, Oak Glen wiggles downhill through the woods alongside

Almaden Reservoir is one of five lakes this little ride passes.

Llagas Creek, with prosperous country estates tucked back in the trees nearby. After a right onto Sycamore Drive, it's more of the same: quiet miles in the dappled shade of broad-leaf forest. There is a short but sharp summit on Sycamore, with the last half mile being real work.

The bottom of the little descent from that summit represents the southernmost point on this ride. From here, at mile 32, you head back north on Uvas Road, another delight-ful byway. It too is nicely accessorized with its very own lake. As before, the road climbs gently to the lake, runs level along its shore for a while, then climbs again, this time gen-tly, before a short descent closes the loop and

brings you back to the McKean–Oak Glen junction. Now you have the return trip on McKean to do, where the biggest challenge will be the summit near Calero Reservoir. After that, the final 10 miles are either down-hill or level.

McKean brings the route back to the sub-urbs at about mile 48. The final 4 miles sneak through the tract neighborhoods on another nice bike trail: first a short section of the Calero Creek Trail and then a longer run on the Las Alamitos Creek Trail, which takes you all the way to the park where the ride began. There are a couple of turns to watch out for along this trail run, which are noted on the mileage log.

MILEAGE LOG

0.0	From Almaden Lake Park, take bike trail north, underneath Coleman Rd.
0.6	Right on bike trail spur up to Coleman Rd.; cross creek on bike bridge
0.8	Leave bike trail and continue west on Coleman Rd.
2.8	Jog right on Camden Ave., left on Hicks Rd.
6.5	Guadalupe Reservoir

9.1	Summit (1405')
10.8	Left on Alamitos Rd.; Almaden Reservoir
12.5	Becomes Almaden Rd. at community of New Almaden
14.8	Right on McKean Rd.
15.1	Right to stay on McKean Rd.; school on left after turn (water)
18.3	Calero Reservoir
23.7	Left on Oak Glen Ave.; Chesbro Reservoir
26.8	Right to stay on Oak Glen Ave. at Llagas Rd. junction
29.4	Right on Sycamore Dr.
31.5	Right on Watsonville Rd.
32.0	Right on Uvas Rd.
34.1	Uvas Reservoir
41.7	Straight on McKean Rd.
48.3	Cross Harry Rd. to Calero Creek Trail
49.1	Left on Camden Ave. to cross creek
49.2	Right on Las Alamitos Creek Trail
50.6	Right over bridge to stay on trail through Pfeiffer Park
52.3	Finish in Almaden Lake Park

37 SANTA CRUZ MOUNTAINS

Difficulty:	Challenging
Time:	4.5 to 6.5 hours
Distance:	66 miles
Elevation gain:	7000'
Best seasons:	April through October
Road conditions:	Some highway miles may be busy, but most roads are low traffic and bike friendly. Most are well paved, but a few are quite primitive.

GETTING THERE: From Hwy 1 in Santa Cruz, take the 41st Ave. exit and proceed south 1 mile to a left on Jade St. Go 0.25 mile to Jade Street Park.

This is one of four big rides set in the Santa Cruz Mountains and along with Ride 38, is one of two with a start on the coastal side of the range. As the elevation numbers suggest, it's a hard ride, with some serious climbing challenges. However, the hardest work is over by mile 40 and the last third of the ride is mostly downhill or level. Navigation is also going to be a challenge, with quite a few turns to puzzle out.

The ride begins at Jade Street Park in Santa Cruz, a regular start venue for local club rides. It takes 2 miles to clear the city, and then the route turns onto North Rodeo Gulch Road, leaves the suburbs behind, and begins an easy, 4-mile, 750' ascent. As it climbs away from town, the road loses its striping, narrows, and begins twisting up the lushly wooded hillside. Over the top, the course follows a pretty, rolling downhill run for 5 miles along Mountain

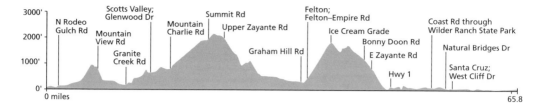

View Road and Branciforte Drive to a right turn onto Granite Creek Road, where the uphill exercise resumes.

After a 3-mile climb, Granite Creek Road brings you to the town of Scotts Valley. Getting through town entails a mile-plus of neighborhood streets and busy boulevards, but by mile 15 most of that is behind you. Uphill from the high school on Glenwood Drive, it's deep country again, and it's going to get deeper the higher you go. Glenwood climbs for a mile beyond town, then traverses the hillside for another mile through the forest before arriving at the next turn: Mountain Charlie Road. Turn uphill here and begin a long but not too difficult ascent: 1200' up over 4 miles (6 percent).

Mountain Charlie has to be one of the most primitive, sketchy excuses for a paved road one is likely to find. Its one narrow

Climbing into the mist on remote Mountain Charlie Road (Nancy Yu)

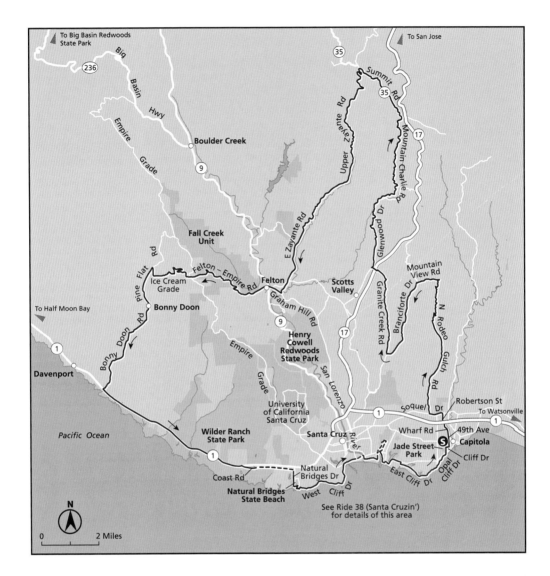

lane bumbles up the hillside in a higgledy-piggledy way...like a hound on the scent of a rabbit, coursing back and forth through the woods. This is all wonderful stuff for a cyclist, at least if you enjoy climbing. Traffic is almost nonexistent, although there are houses tucked away in these remote woods, so you may run into a few locals. Mountain Charlie ends with 1 level mile before teeing into Summit Road (Highway 35). Turn left here and chug up a steep climb for most of a mile.

Summit Road starts out looking like a real highway—wide lanes, stripes, guardrails—but that doesn't last long. It soon reverts to one wide lane, but still with smooth pavement. Over the top, it's a rolling, mildly downhill run through the woods. Then, at mile 25, turn left and head downhill on Upper Zayante Road. The next 2.5 miles are a steep, technical corkscrew down the rocky, wooded canyon. The single lane is wide enough to allow for uphill traffic, but only barely; take care.

There is 1 mile of gentle uphill after that wild descent, followed by another mile of steep descent and then almost 7 miles of gradual roll-out down the valley, toward the town of Felton. Riding through Felton involves 1 mile of busy boulevards: Graham Hill Road on the way into town and Felton–Empire Road on the way out, which ceases to be busy as it leaves town.

Felton–Empire may be the toughest climb of the day: 1600' up in a little less than 4 miles. That's an 8 percent average, and it is all of that and, occasionally, quite a bit more. It's a grinder. On the bright side, it is the last serious climb of the day, ending near mile 40, where Felton–Empire crosses Empire Grade and becomes Ice Cream Grade. Ice cream, indeed: you will feel as if you've earned a big bowl of dessert after eating your spinach on that last climb. And you get a first helping right away, with a mile-plus plunge on this road. Another mile of mild uphill follows, and then the real fun begins: over 4 miles of nonstop, satin-smooth downhill on Pine Flat and Bonny Doon roads, from 1700'

almost all the way to sea level…flying on two wheels.

This sweet run ends around mile 48 when Bonny Doon tees into Hwy 1. Turn left on the coast highway and roll out 7 level miles back to the outskirts of Santa Cruz. The last 2 of those miles leave Hwy 1 and run through Wilder Ranch State Park on park access roads and bike trails. This leads directly onto Mission Street, into Santa Cruz. Turn right on Natural Bridges Drive and head into and through Natural Bridges State Beach. When you pop out the far end of the park at mile 56.4, you have arrived at Cliff Drive, which, true to its name, runs along the cliff above the ocean, pretty much all the way to the finish of the ride.

This last run along the cliff is replicated almost exactly in the following Santa Cruzin' ride, so see Ride 38 for a blow-by-blow description of how to navigate the final 9 miles along the Santa Cruz waterfront. It's a beautiful way to wind down at the end of a challenging day, with laid-back miles along the beach.

MILEAGE LOG

0.0	From Jade Street Park, right on Jade St. to right on Topaz St.
0.2	Left on 49th Ave.
0.5	Bear left on Wharf Rd.
1.2	Straight on Robertson St. (under Hwy 1)
1.5	Left on Soquel Dr.
2.0	Right on N. Rodeo Gulch Rd.
7.4	Left on Mountain View Rd.
8.3	Left on Branciforte Dr.
11.3	Right on Granite Creek Rd.
14.5	Left on Granite Creek to cross over Hwy 17
14.7	Right on Scotts Valley Dr.; town of Scotts Valley
14.8	Left on Glenwood Dr.
17.5	Left on Mountain Charlie Rd.
22.6	Left on Summit Road (Hwy 35)
25.0	Left on Upper Zayante Rd.; becomes East Zayante Rd.
35.8	Right on Graham Hill Rd. into town of Felton
36.3	Cross Hwy 9 to Felton–Empire Rd.
39.9	Cross Empire Grade to Ice Cream Grade

42.5	Left on Pine Flat Rd.
44.1	Straight on Bonny Doon Rd.
47.8	Left on Hwy 1
53.7	Right on Coast Rd. through Wilder Ranch State Park
54.3	Right on bike trail parallel to Hwy 1
55.3	Straight on Mission St. (suburbs of Santa Cruz)
55.5	Right on Natural Bridges Dr.
55.9	Enter Natural Bridges State Beach, follow road through park
56.4	Exit park, straight on West Cliff Dr.
59.0	Bear right on Beach St., past Municipal Wharf and amusement park
59.7	Right on San Lorenzo Riverway bike trail over old railroad trestle
59.8	Right on E. Cliff Dr., then right to stay on E. Cliff Dr.
60.2	Jog left on Seabright Ave., then right on Atlantic Ave.
60.5	Left on Mariner Park Way; follow bike trails and other waterside roads around Woods Lagoon yacht basin
61.3	Right on Brommer St.; follow path along yacht basin
61.8	Right on Lake Ave.
62.1	Bear right on 5th Ave.
62.2	Becomes E. Cliff Dr. at roundabout; follow E. Cliff Dr. through many turns
64.7	Becomes 41st Ave. briefly, then right on Opal Cliff Dr.
65.5	Jog left on Portola Dr. to right on 47th Ave.
65.7	Left on Topaz St.
65.8	Left on Jade St. to finish at Jade St. Park

38 SANTA CRUZIN'

Difficulty:	Easy
Time:	3 hours
Distance:	20 miles round trip
Elevation gain:	Nearly flat
Best seasons:	All year, although midwinter may be rainy
Road conditions:	Some roads are busy; most are not. Pavement is good.

GETTING THERE: From Hwy 1 in Santa Cruz, take Swift St. south. Drive 0.3 mile, then turn right on Delaware Ave. and go 0.4 mile. Turn left on Swanton Blvd. and drive 0.4 mile to a parking lot near the entrance to Natural Bridges State Beach.

Great rides don't have to be epic adventures logging mega miles or summiting monster mountains. Our bikes work just as well for a casual cruise through town, especially rewarding when the scenery along the way is as nice as on this promenade along the beach in Santa Cruz.

This is essentially an out-and-back from one edge of Santa Cruz, through town, out the other side and onward to the next-door

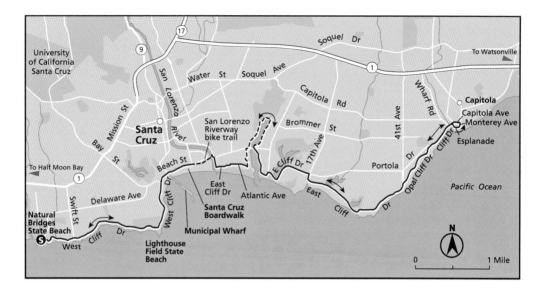

town of Capitola. The return trip retraces the route from there, although it's not quite that simple. There are a number of one-way streets along the beach frontage, mostly heading the way we go on the outward-bound half of the ride. Coming back, in some spots, you can dodge the wrong-way one-ways by using bike paths next to the road. In other spots, you may have to be a little more creative. Rather than burdening you with overly finicky directions, I am going to count on you to be able to figure out these little puzzles when you get to them. But that should be the most complicated challenge you have today. Aside from a few tricky corners, this ride is easy and enjoyable.

This ride is "nearly level" in the sense that there are no climbs longer than a quarter-mile or higher than 50', but there are a few in that range. It isn't as flat as a pancake. But overall, the climbing challenge is minimal.

One of the nicest sections of this short ride comes in the first 2.6 miles along West Cliff Drive. The road hugs the cliff over the ocean, 40 or 50 feet above the surf. On the inland side of the road, handsome homes stake out their precious plots of ocean-view frontage. In the midst of this run, you pass through Lighthouse Field State Beach, with the lighthouse out on a point, looking picturesque. The lighthouse serves as the Santa Cruz Surfing Museum, just above the popular Steamer Lane point break.

When this nice run along the cliff ends, bear right on Beach Street and descend to sea level in front of the vast complex of tourist attractions anchored by the Santa Cruz Boardwalk amusement park. This will appear tacky or colorfully fun to you, depending on how much you like corny carnival kitsch. Just in front of the grand old Giant Dipper roller-coaster, bear right onto the San Lorenzo Riverway bike trail and cross an old railroad trestle to East Cliff Drive.

The next few miles are complex for navigation. The general idea is to stay as close to the water as possible. Much of this is on one section of East Cliff Drive or another, but there are plenty of little kinks and quirks along the way to keep you on your toes and consulting the mileage log. One of these detours involves a loop inland around the Woods Lagoon yacht basin. It's a bit complicated, but if you just keep the lagoon on your right all the way around, you will eventually come back to the ocean and more of Cliff Drive.

Cruising past the lighthouse on Cliff Drive in Santa Cruz (Linnea Biddick)

This portion of Cliff Drive isn't always out along the cliff. The ocean views come and go. Sometimes the road meanders back through residential neighborhoods. The homes vary from rather ordinary to stunning, with the overall effect being quite nice. The roads are always fairly quiet and bike friendly.

The final miles of Ride 37 (Santa Cruz Mountains loop) follow this route from Natural Bridges State Beach to the corner of Opal Cliff Drive and Cliff Drive. At that intersection, the longer ride departs this course.

This route continues on one last section of Cliff Drive, descending into the village of Capitola. Immediately after crossing Soquel Creek, turn right on Esplanade and make a slow loop around the heart of this charming downtown. Yes, it is a tourist destination, but it's a very nice one. And you are, after all, a tourist... a cycle-tourist. This little loop should offer up any number of likely spots for a relaxed *al fresco* lunch. After lunch, you can retrace the route, including the few spots where you will have to improvise minor adjustments to the course to finagle your way around those one-way sections. It can be done, and I'm pretty sure you can do it!

MILEAGE LOG

0.0	From parking lot of Natural Bridges State Beach, right on W. Cliff Dr.
2.6	Bear right on Beach St., past Municipal Wharf and amusement park
3.3	Right on San Lorenzo Riverway bike trail over old railroad trestle
3.4	Right on E. Cliff Dr., then right again to stay on E. Cliff Dr.
3.8	Jog left on Seabright Ave., then right on Atlantic Ave.
4.1	Left on Mariner Park Way; follow bike trails and other waterside roads around Woods Lagoon yacht basin
4.9	Right on Brommer St.; follow path along yacht basin

5.4	Right on Lake Ave.
5.7	Bear right on 5th Ave.
5.8	Becomes E. Cliff Dr. at roundabout; follow E. Cliff Dr. through many turns
8.3	Becomes 41st Ave. briefly, then right on Opal Cliff Dr.
9.0	Right on Cliff Dr.
9.4	Right on Esplanade in town of Capitola
9.6	Bear left on Monterey Ave.
9.7	Left on Capitola Ave.
9.8	Left on Stockton Ave.
9.9	Straight on Cliff Dr. to retrace route to start

39 CORRALITOS–HIGHLAND LOOP

Difficulty:	Challenging
Time:	4 to 5 hours
Distance:	54 miles
Elevation gain:	4500'
Best seasons:	April through October
Road conditions:	Some roads may be busy, but most are quiet. Most are well paved, but a few miles are rough.

GETTING THERE: In Capitola, leave Hwy 1 at the Bay Ave. exit and drive south on Bay for 0.75 mile. Turn left on Monterey Ave. and go 0.25 mile to New Brighton Middle School.

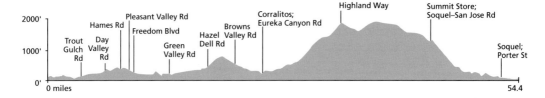

This is the southernmost ride in the Santa Cruz Mountains. All of the rides in this lush, coastal range are delightful, and this one is no exception. Considering how high it climbs and how spectacular the views are from the high points, the ride is not all that difficult. Stronger riders will call it moderate rather than challenging.

It would take half my allotted copy space to describe all the turns in the first 5 miles, getting clear of the suburbs in Capitola and Aptos, so I will simply say: follow the mileage log through the local neighborhoods, under Highway 1 and up to Soquel Drive. When you turn left on Trout Gulch at mile 3.5, you leave the regimented suburbs behind and climb into a wooded, hillier neighborhood that looks more rural than suburban, although it is still all residential properties under the tree cover. This is true for the roads that follow, Valencia and Day Valley: comfortable, sprawling rural-residential spreads

The biggest climb of the day is deep in the redwoods on Eureka Canyon Road. (Margie Biddick)

in a pleasant, woodsy setting, with apple orchards here and there.

Turn left on Freedom Boulevard and almost immediately left onto more quiet, rural lanes: Hames and Pleasant Valley roads, both very nice. This little detour returns to Freedom Boulevard, and this time you stay on the busier road for a little over a mile. (It's not *that* busy and it has wide shoulders.) Short links on Corralitos, Varni, and Pioneer roads wander through rolling and flat farm fields to a left onto Green Valley Road at mile 14. A quick look at the map will tell you that you could have skipped this whole, funny goose-neck appendage on the east end of the loop by taking either Hames or Corralitos straight to the village of Corralitos. But you don't want to do that. These are great miles out here, great roads. Green Valley, Hazel Dell, and Browns Valley are all worth whatever time and energy it takes to include them.

Green Valley Road starts off with more of the almost-flat farm fields and apple orchards

of the previous roads, but soon pushes uphill into woods and dense forest. By the time you turn left onto Hazel Dell, you are deep in the redwoods. Hazel Dell begins with a 2-mile climb that has some steep spots, but over that little summit it's all gently downhill for the balance of Hazel Dell and Browns Valley. At its far end, Browns Valley Road leaves the forest behind and returns to orchards and horsey pastures and farm fields before rolling into the village of Corralitos at mile 25. This is a perfect spot for a break. There is a little park and a country store on the corner.

Now turn right on Eureka Canyon Road and begin the biggest climb of the day: 1600' up in 9 miles. Before I rode this, I expected it to be a bit of a leg-breaker, but in fact it turns out to be one of the easiest "big" climbs I can recall. The first 5 miles are gentle uphill rollers and false flats. Then, back in the cool, shady redwoods, the heart of the climb scrambles up the canyon for almost 3 miles at pitches between 5 and 8 percent. A short, nearly flat

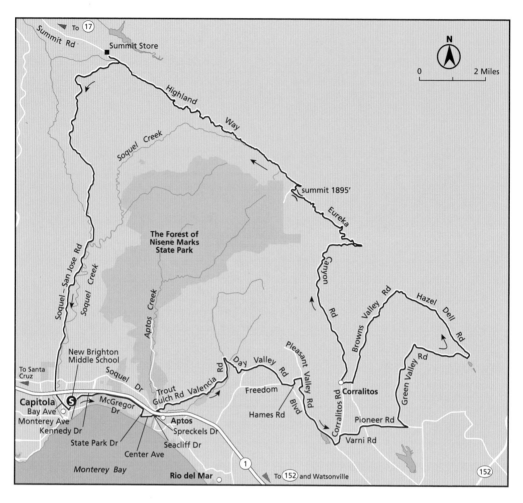

section follows, and then 2 miles at about 6 percent finish the package. This last section breaks free of the forest and offers up sweeping panoramas across the ranks of hills and out over the ocean.

The road name changes to Highland Way right at the 1895' summit (mile 34), where you turn away from the views—for the moment—and head inland on a 2-mile descent through the forest. Most of the Eureka Canyon climb is well paved, but up at the top it deteriorates to a rather sketchy stretch of patches and potholes, and this rough surface continues through the technical descent. It's not terrible, but you do need

to pay attention and watch your line. After the descent, Highland offers up one more, mellow climb—300' up in 1.5 miles—and then a rolling run traversing the hillside for 3 miles, including more panoramic vistas out over the distant ocean.

At about mile 40, Highland tilts downhill on a sweet descent of a bit over a mile, now with good pavement. At the bottom, the road comes to a junction with Summit Road and Soquel–San Jose Road. You are, in a few minutes, going to head downhill on Soquel–San Jose Road, but first I suggest you go straight on Summit, just up around the next bend, to the Summit Store at mile 41.8. Eureka

Canyon and Highland have both been remote and unpopulated in the extreme—the proverbial middle of nowhere—so it may come as a bit of a surprise to find this market here, so high up in the hinterlands. It's no funky little country store. It's fancy and full-service and even has a nice patio off to the side, with picnic tables and shady umbrellas, another great spot for a rest stop.

After that restorative break, it is almost all downhill from here over the final 13 miles of the ride, most on well-paved Soquel–San Jose Road. There are many flats and even a few climbs on the way down the mountainside. You can't coast all the way. But downhill dancing will occupy most of your time from the store down to the towns by the ocean. In particular, the section between miles 42 and 48 is a fast, smooth flier. The final 7 miles are less exciting, as you head back into the suburban fringe of the beach communities. Cross Soquel Drive, scoot under Hwy 1, and roll out the last mile to the school.

After the ride, consider a visit—on two wheels or four—to the charming beach town of Capitola, just downhill from the school.

MILEAGE LOG

0.0	From New Brighton Middle School, right on Monterey Ave.
0.4	Straight on Kennedy Dr.
0.7	Cross Park Ave. to straight on McGregor Dr.
2.4	Jog left on Sea Ridge Rd. to right on State Park Dr.
2.5	Left on Center Ave.
2.8	Straight on El Camino Del Mar; becomes Seacliff Dr.
3.0	Left on Spreckels Dr. (under Hwy 1)
3.2	Right on Soquel Dr.
3.5	Left on Trout Gulch Rd.
3.9	Straight on Valencia Rd. (Trout Gulch turns left)
6.6	Left on Day Valley Rd.
8.5	Left on Freedom Blvd., left on Hames Rd.
9.2	Right on Pleasant Valley Rd.
10.3	Left on Freedom Blvd.
11.6	Left on Corralitos Rd.
11.9	Right on Varni Rd.
12.8	Straight on Pioneer Rd.
14.0	Left on Green Valley Rd.
18.6	Left on Hazel Dell Rd.
21.7	Straight on Browns Valley Rd.
24.8	Right on Browns Valley Rd. at Amesti Rd. junction
25.1	Right on Eureka Canyon Rd.; town of Corralitos (store)
34.0	Straight on Highland Way
41.6	Straight on Summit Rd. at Soquel–San Jose Rd. junction
41.8	Summit Store; retrace to junction
42.0	Right on Soquel–San Jose Rd.
53.2	Cross Soquel Drive to Porter St.
53.5	Straight on Bay Ave. (under Hwy 1)
54.2	Left on Monterey Ave.
54.4	Finish at school

40 SAN JUAN BAUTISTA–ELKHORN SLOUGH LOOP

Difficulty:	Moderate
Time:	3.5 to 4.5 hours
Distance:	45 miles
Elevation gain:	3200'
Best seasons:	Year-round, although winter may be rainy
Road conditions:	Traffic is light on most roads. However, there is one challenging crossing of a busy highway.

GETTING THERE: From Gilroy, take Hwy 101 south for 10 miles, then Hwy 156 east for 3.5 miles, following signs to San Juan Bautista and Hollister. Exit Hwy 156 into San Juan Bautista with a left at The Alameda. Turn right on Washington St. to the Mission San Juan Bautista.

As this is the southernmost ride in our "state" of Northern California, it's appropriate that it should stage out of a village that feels as if it might be down along the border. Much of that Spanish California ambience derives from the 1797 Mission San Juan Bautista, one of the largest of the California missions. It still serves as the parish church for the charming village of the same name, which abuts the mission compound. I'll have more to say about the town and the mission when the ride is over.

Head south out of town on The Alameda, crossing Highway 156 and bearing right onto Salinas Road, which becomes San Juan Grade Road. Just a bit more than a lane wide and looking almost as ancient as the mission, this little byway curls up the ridge for 4 miles, gaining about 800', then slithers down the other side for almost the same distance. Pavement on the climb is an elderly slapdash of patches and cracks, but just before the sum-

mit, newer, smoother pavement appears for the slinky downhill. Scenery along the way is a whole lot of lovely emptiness: rolling, grassy hillsides and shady glades of oak.

After the downhill, turn right on Crazy Horse Canyon Road. After 4 miles, cross over Hwy 101 and go a half mile to a left on Echo Valley Road. (Note: The overpass at Hwy 101 is under construction and impassible until 2015.)

For the next 5 miles, you will be following a series of four mostly quiet roads (Echo Valley, San Miguel Canyon, Paradise, and Walker Valley) through a rural-residential landscape. It's definitely country and pleasantly so, but there are homes and small ranches along all of the roads. There is one short climb on Paradise, but most of these miles are rolling or gently downhill.

At its western end, at mile 20, Walker Valley tees into Elkhorn Road. Turn right here and head north along this pretty road. Elkhorn Road travels through the Elkhorn

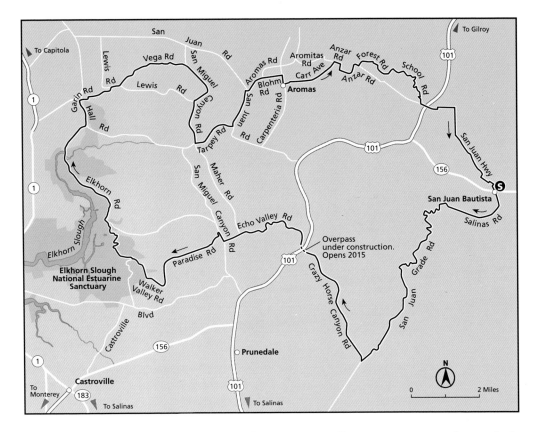

Slough National Estuarine Sanctuary for most of the next 5 miles, often with the tranquil estuary in view on the left side of the meandering road.

At the northern end of Elkhorn, turn left across busy Hall Road and look for a right turn onto tiny Garin Road. Over the next 7 miles, along Garin, Lewis, Vega, and San Miguel Canyon roads, you will be treated to a mix of nearly perfect bike roads, with smooth pavement and light traffic through rural-residential countryside. Mostly this is meadows and woods of oak and eucalyptus, but in a few spots the vistas open up to flat fields of produce, stretching off toward the Central Valley: commercial agriculture on a grand scale.

Four more roads, not quite so perfect, bring you to the sleepy village of Aromas. After 15 miles of gently rolling roads, with hardly a hill worthy of the name, leaving town on Carr

Avenue will reacquaint you with your little chain ring: a stiff climb of a bit over 500' in a mile.

Over the top of the wooded ridge on that little hump, Carr tilts downhill and rolls out across a meadow before bearing right onto Anzar Road (a seamless transition from one road to the next). Anzar is another delightful bike road, and if it were our only option here, we would be happy to ride it almost all the way to the finish. But there is an even nicer bypass: Take a left on Forest Road and enjoy the simple pleasures of Forest and School roads, as lively a pair of back roads as you would ever want to find. This little 3-mile *divertimento* is mostly up for the first mile and down for the other 2, and that descent is well worth the price of admission of the first climb. When School tees back into Anzar, 3 flat miles—1 on Anzar and 2 on San Juan

After the ride, take time to visit the Mission San Juan Bautista, one of the best of the California mission compounds.

Highway—deliver you back to San Juan Bautista. The highway has recently been rebuilt with wide, smooth shoulders.

With bike rides, we always say that getting there should be at least half the fun and sometimes almost all of the fun. But this charming little village is going to make the case for being at least half the fun, all by itself. To begin with, there is the handsome old mission. Although it has been restored a time or two, it is not over-restored; it still

retains a fine patina of age, and this extends to the historic nineteenth-century structures arrayed around the grassy plaza across from the mission, all worthy of a visit. Then there is the town, a block away, for the most part as quaint as the mission and plaza. Best of all perhaps, for hungry, thirsty cyclists: there are a number of attractive cafés and a cute ice cream parlor along Main Street. As nice as this ride is, the town may be the best part of the whole package.

0.0	From Mission San Juan Bautista, left (west) on 2nd St.
0.1	Right on Franklin St.
0.2	Left on The Alameda, cross Hwy 156, leave town
0.7	Right on Salinas Rd., becomes San Juan Grade Rd.
4.6	Summit
9.2	Right on Crazy Horse Canyon Rd.
13.0	Cross Hwy 101, continue on Crazy Horse Canyon Rd. (Note: Hwy 101 overpass under construction until 2015)
13.5	Left on Echo Valley Rd.
16.0	Right on San Miguel Canyon Rd. (CR G12)
16.2	Left on Paradise Rd.
18.7	Right on Walker Valley Rd.
20.0	Right on Elkhorn Rd.
25.4	Left on Hall Rd.
25.8	Right on Garin Rd.
27.2	Right on Lewis Rd.
27.4	Left on Vega Rd.
29.7	Bear right on San Miguel Canyon Rd.
32.2	Left on Tarpey Rd.
33.5	Left on San Juan Rd.
34.6	Right on Aromas Rd.
35.3	Right on Blohm Rd. into town of Aromas
35.8	Right on Carpenteria Rd.
36.0	Left on Carr Ave.
37.6	Right on Anzar Rd.
38.7	Left on Forest Rd.
39.2	Right on School Rd.
41.7	Left on Anzar Rd.
42.8	Right on San Juan Hwy
44.3	Straight on 1st St. into San Juan Bautista
44.9	Right on Monterey St.
45.0	Left on 3rd St. (main street of town)
45.3	Left on Mariposa St.
45.4	Finish at Mission San Juan Bautista

CENTRAL VALLEY

The vast, flat farm fields of this region are never going to be considered a cyclist's dream, but if you know where to ride, there are delightful treasures to be found here, from serpentine treks along the delta levees to runs along rivers to scrambles into the wooded foothills on either side of the valley floor.

41 PLATINA OUT-AND-BACK

Difficulty:	Challenging
Time:	5 to 7 hours
Distance:	71 miles
Elevation gain:	6100'
Best seasons:	Spring and fall; summer may be hot
Road conditions:	Traffic is low and pavement good on all roads.

GETTING THERE: From downtown Redding, head west on Placer St., which becomes Placer Rd., for 7 miles to a right on Swasey Rd. Park at Grant School.

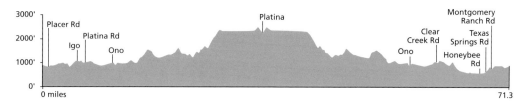

Personally, I don't have anything against out-and-backs. I think of them as deflated loops, with the outward-bound and return legs of the loop very close together. They are often low traffic (in the case of dead ends), and the dynamics are different in each direction: the climbs become descents and the scenery looks different the other way around. Besides, bike rides should always be about the journey: getting there is half the fun and getting back is the other half. So who cares if it's all on the same road?

And yet I have mostly avoided out-and-backs in this book because I have learned over the years that many people do not share my appreciation for them. In the case of this ride, though, I am making an exception. Platina Road is a wonderful bike adventure, and I had initially thought to incorporate it into a loop. But the other roads in the loop turned out to be either busy or boring. So in the end I decided to package it as an out-and-back, with a small loop on one end to vary the fare just a little. Platina is definitely good enough to be done twice, once each way.

The ride starts at a school on the southwest side of Redding, just out into the exurban, rural belt beyond town. The lowest elevation

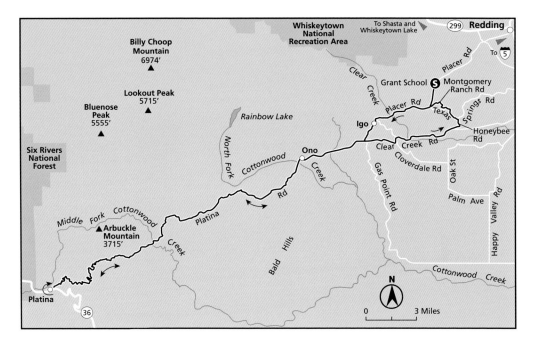

on the ride—under 900'—is near the start, and highest—over 2400'—is near its midpoint. So it's fair to assume the route climbs on its outward-bound leg and descends coming home. While that is correct in broad outline, the actual profile is much lumpier, with many small ups and downs along the way. It never stays the same for long, except for one notable exception, which I'll get to presently.

The scenery is somewhat uniform throughout. It's a classic foothills landscape of rolling, grassy meadows, with woods of oak and other broadleaf trees in profusion. There are a few ranches along the route, but mostly, this is empty country, all of it beautiful and wild. As frosting on the cake, this lightly traveled road winding through the back of beyond has very good pavement.

Platina Road takes its name from a native alloy of platinum that was mined in these hills. There was also a silver strike here, and the two little towns along the route—Igo and Ono—were founded during that boom. Local lore offers some colorful anecdotes as to how the towns came by their odd names. Most have to do with the limited English language skills of the Chinese immigrants who were part of the silver mining heyday. Igo is still a viable small town, but Ono is little more than a wide spot in the road. There is a store at our turnaround at the old stage stop of Platina at mile 33, and that will probably be your best shot at food and fluids today.

One of the most interesting features on this ride is nicely illustrated by the profile. Check out that flattop haircut it has: after all the lumpy ups and downs, it simply flattens out for 5 miles. There is a little up-down-up near the turnaround, and then the same 5 flat miles begin the return trip. Those 10 level miles do not equate with having climbed onto a flat mesa, as one might see in southern Utah. It is instead a traverse across a south-facing hillside, where the road engineers found a contour line they liked and stuck with it, as if they were building an aqueduct. But what makes it special is not the engineering; it's the view: off the south face of the hillside, the world falls away across endless empty valleys and ridges, far off into the hazy

Amazingly good pavement for such an obscure, lightly traveled road in the absolute middle of nowhere

distance. While there are forests covering all the distant hills, there aren't so many trees near the road, so the vistas are entirely unobstructed and panoramic.

Once past this level section (on the return leg), the road suddenly plunges back down into the valley. The predominantly uphill run on the first half of the ride is now turned around into a busy downhill dance, albeit with all of those lumpy ups and downs mixed in. I've added a little loop at the end—9 miles on Clear Creek, Honeybee, Texas Springs, and Montgomery Ranch roads—to keep it from being a pure out-and-back and simply because the roads are here and are

worth doing. This is back in the rural residential fringe near Redding, with prosperous estates and white-fenced horse paddocks in evidence.

This ride is unlikely to ever find a place in some cycle-touring company's catalog of must-do rides. It's too obscure. But if you happen to find yourself in Redding, hankering after a good day on the bike, you could do a lot worse than to explore this out-of-the-way trek through Igo, Ono, and Platina. The precious metals in these hills may have been played out long ago, but the wild, empty countryside, and the road winding through it, remain as wonderful hidden treasures.

0.0	From Grant School, left on Swasey Rd.
0.2	Right on Placer Rd.
5.4	Left to stay on Placer Rd. in town of Igo
6.6	Right on Platina Rd.
10.6	Town of Ono
33.3	Right on Hwy 36
33.6	Turnaround and rest stop at Platina Store; retrace to Hwy 36
33.9	Left on Platina Road
56.6	Town of Ono
60.6	Straight on Clear Creek Rd.
66.7	Left on Honeybee Rd.
67.5	Left on Texas Springs Rd.
68.5	Right on Montgomery Ranch Rd.
69.9	Right on Placer Rd.
71.1	Left on Swasey Rd.
71.3	Finish at Grant School

42 SACRAMENTO RIVER TRAIL LOOP

Difficulty:	Moderate
Time:	3 to 5 hours
Distance:	37 miles
Elevation gain:	2000'
Best seasons:	Spring and fall
Road conditions:	Most of this ride is on bike trails. The road miles are quiet, with little traffic. Paving is excellent throughout.

GETTING THERE: From I-5 in Redding, take Hwy 44 west approximately 1 mile, following signs to Turtle Bay and the Sundial Bridge. Park in the first lot on the right.

In simplest terms, this is a journey from the Turtle Bay Exploration Park, near Redding, along the Sacramento River Bike Trail, all the way up to and across Shasta Dam, and back. But it is much more than a simple bike ride, much more complex, taking in several fascinating structures, parks, and a museum.

There is, first of all, the park and the now iconic Sundial Bridge. Turtle Bay Exploration Park covers 300 acres on both banks of the river and includes bird refuges, botanical gardens, and a superb natural history museum. Connecting the two halves of the park is the Sundial Bridge, a dramatic suspension bridge for pedestrians and cyclists. Designed by Spanish architect Santiago Calatrava and completed in 2004, it has put both the Turtle Bay complex and the city of Redding on the world map. Together, the bridge and the museum have become probably the biggest

tourist destination between Sacramento and the Oregon border. The river trail was completed in 2010.

Begin by looping around the bird refuge and heading upstream along the south bank of the river to the bridge. This approach to the bridge offers some nice viewpoints for seeing the graceful span from a flattering angle. Once you've taken a few photos of this most photogenic structure, ride across on its green glass surface. How often do you get to ride along a glass road?

Continue upstream, passing through handsome parks and eventually moving out into a natural landscape. It's never a good idea to hammer on a bike trail, and that is especially true of this 5-mile section. Although well paved and engineered, it is simply too twisty and constricted for faster bike speeds, and there are too many other trail users. This is a place for dawdling along, enjoying the scenery, which is wonderful.

At mile 5, cross the river on a new bike bridge. From here on, the trail heads north along the west bank, following the old railroad grade, uphill in this direction. It's usually a constant, easy grade. However, in a few spots, the trail has to leave the old grade, and when it does, it can be steep for short pitches: over 10 percent. Most of the steep stuff is near Keswick Dam. This is a smaller dam just upstream from the bike bridge. A rolling, up-and-down section follows for 2-plus miles, and then the trail returns to the steady, almost-level railroad grade and stays that way for 8 miles, running beside the smooth, still waters of Keswick Reservoir, looking more like a lazy river than a lake.

At mile 17, at a campground, the trail becomes Coram Road, a wide, smooth road curling up the hillside to the top of Shasta Dam. This is a real climb, gaining 470' in a mile and a half, a steady 5 percent grade. When the climb ends, you're on the top of the huge dam, where a wide road runs across to the other side. In the wake of 9/11, all sorts of security was added around the dam, so that you now see a guardhouse, barriers across the road, and big signs prohibiting this and that. But it's all mostly for show, at least if you're a cyclist. Just wave to the guard, work your way past the barriers, and cruise out onto the dam.

This is an enormous, impressive structure. It's the ninth tallest dam in the United States—second tallest when it was completed in 1945—and is considered a great engineering achievement. Stop midway across the dam and look over the downstream side. It's a long way down. There is a visitor center on the east end of the dam, worth a visit.

One option at this point is to simply retrace the bike trail to the start. But I suggest you turn it into a bit of a loop by continuing along the east side of the river on local roads, beginning with Highway 151 (Shasta Dam Boulevard). This quiet road climbs 400' in 2 miles from the dam to the high point of the ride, passing a nice vista point along the way, overlooking the dam. Beyond the summit, it descends for 2 smooth, winding miles, dropping almost 600'. Turn right on Lake Boulevard and roll along this quiet highway for 4-plus miles to a right turn onto Quartz Hill Road. This is probably the least interesting section of the ride, but it's pleasant and easy.

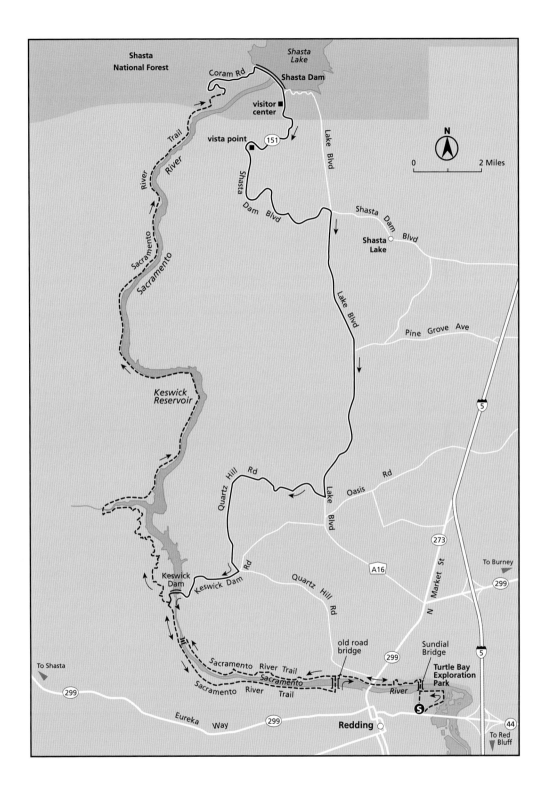

Shasta
National Forest

Shasta Lake

Coram Rd

Shasta Dam

visitor ■
center

vista point ■

(151)

N

0   2 Miles

Shasta

Dam

Blvd

Shasta   Dam

Blvd

**Shasta
Lake** ○

River   Trail

River   River

Sacramento

Sacramento

Lake Blvd

Pine   Grove   Ave

Keswick
Reservoir

Quartz   Hill   Rd

Oasis   Rd

Lake

5

To Shasta ▽

Keswick
Dam

Keswick Dam   Rd

Quartz   Hill   Rd

A16

273

Blvd

To Burney ▽

Sacramento   River Trail

old road
bridge

299

Sundial
Bridge

**Turtle Bay
Exploration
Park**

299

Sacramento

Sacramento   River   Trail

River

Eureka   Way

299

Redding ○

Ⓢ

N Market St

5

To Red
Bluff ▽

44

Follow the glass brick road across the iconic Sundial Bridge and out along the Sacramento River Trail, all the way to mighty Shasta Dam.

The fun picks up again when you turn onto Quartz Hill. An up-and-down run across the rocky butte delivers you to a right turn onto Keswick Dam Road. A short, swift descent leads to a crossing of this smaller—but still very big—dam. (It only seems small compared to Shasta.) Back on the west bank, pick up the river trail again and head downstream. On the return leg, do not cross over the bike bridge you used on the way out; stay on the west bank almost all the way to the finish. This stretch of trail, dead flat and straight, runs through broadleaf forest until mile 35, where you turn left and cross the river on an old highway bridge, now exclusively for bikes and walkers. On the far side, loop around onto the main trail again and follow it back to the Sundial Bridge and the park.

Ideally, after the ride, you will have enough time to explore the park's various attractions: the lovely arboretum and the excellent museum, where you can have lunch on the terrace overlooking the river and that magnificent bridge.

MILEAGE LOG

0.0	From parking lot, right on Sacramento River Trail
0.9	Right across Sundial Bridge
1.1	Bear left off bridge to continue on trail
3.5	Left on Harlan Dr. (part of the trail)
5.1	Cross footbridge over river to right on trail, also known as Shasta Rail Trail
5.8	Cross Keswick Dam Rd., stay on trail
16.7	Right on Coram Rd.
18.5	Right on Shasta Dam Blvd., cross Shasta Dam
19.2	At roundabout, continue straight on Shasta Dam Blvd.; visitor center to right

23.1	Right on Lake Blvd.; town of Shasta Lake
27.5	Right on Quartz Hill Rd.
30.4	Right on Keswick Dam Rd.
31.6	Cross Keswick Dam
31.8	Left on Sacramento River Trail (Shasta Rail Trail)
35.0	Left across river on old road bridge
35.3	Follow trail off bridge, left underneath bridge to retrace route toward Sundial Bridge
36.8	Right across river on Sundial Bridge
37.0	Right off bridge, follow main path out of park, left through parking lot
37.3	Finish in parking lot

43 MILLVILLE LOOP

Difficulty:	Moderate
Time:	3 to 5 hours
Distance:	41 miles
Elevation gain:	2600'
Best seasons:	Spring and fall
Road conditions:	Traffic is low and pavement good on all roads.

GETTING THERE: From I-5 at Redding, head east 11 miles on Hwy 44 to a left on Old 44 Dr. Go north 1 mile on Old 44, right on Whitmore Rd., and left on Brookdale Rd. to Millville Elementary School.

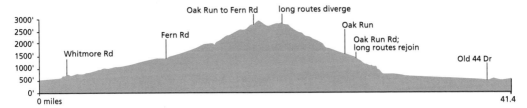

This is a simple, relatively easy ride from the eastern edge of the Central Valley up into the nearby foothills. It was recommended to me by a friend in Redding as a nice loop near that city. There are two slightly longer options that can be taken, up in the hills, padding the miles out a bit, but for reasons I'll explain when we get there, the shortest loop is the default setting.

Begin by heading east on beautiful Brookdale Road, a quiet little lane through shady woods. Several miles on Whitmore Road follow, still heading east, climbing gently into the foothills. Whitmore passes through a classic western American landscape: mile after mile of empty ranch lands, grasses riffling in the breeze, oaks scattered about, and the higher mountains around Lassen Volcanic National Park marching along the far horizon.

Climbing will predominate early on: 2350' up in the first 19-plus miles. That's a bit over 2 percent on average. There are numerous

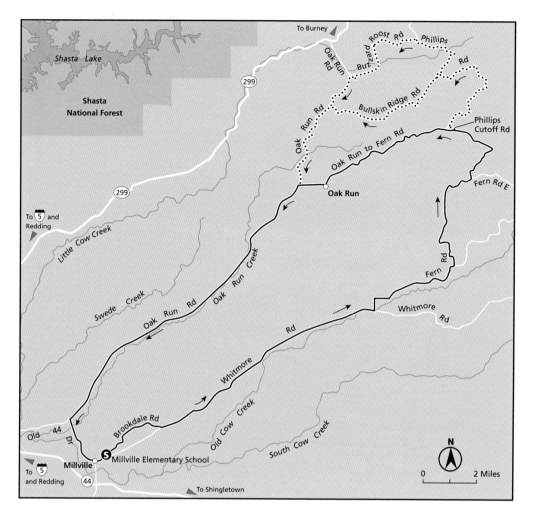

flats and occasional steeper bits, but overall the grade is fairly constant and rarely difficult.

Fern Road, coming up at mile 11, continues the gentle uphill progress across rock-strewn meadows, with well-kept ranch compounds here and there behind old stone walls. (This 7.7-mile portion of Fern Road is also part of Ride 44.)

Turn left on a road with the slightly odd name of Oak Run to Fern Road, which means the road runs between Fern Road and the town of Oak Run. Up here the open, rocky meadows give way to mountain forest of ponderosa pine.

The high point on the ride comes up just past mile 19. A half-mile descent and a gentle, 1-mile uphill follow, and then it's pretty much all downhill for the last 20 miles of the ride. But before you launch off into that long descent, consider this: just at the point where the long descent begins, side roads diverge that offer options for extending the ride. Both loops depart the same way, heading farther uphill into the pine forest on Phillips Cutoff Road and Phillips Road. Doubling back on Bullskin Ridge Road yields a loop of 49 miles; continuing to Buzzard Roost Road fattens the loop to 52 miles. All of these miles are nice, and all are easy enough. I chose to focus this ride on the shortest option because the only place out here to find water and food is at the little store in Oak Run. If you do either of the longer loops, you miss the town by a mile. Riding off-course from the longer loops into the town would add a 2-mile round-trip to the day's total. Or, if you can do 50-something miles on the water you carried with you from the start, you can skip the town entirely.

Back to the basic route and the descent to the finish: A great deal of the descending is gradual—almost false flats, really—but there are a few sections that are seriously downhill. The 9 miles between miles 21 and 30 will be the most fun, dropping 2000' on smooth pavement. It's never too steep or technical. Most of this is along either Oak Run to Fern Road or Oak Run Road. In this context, I'm assuming "run" is used the way they do in Appalachia, to refer to a mountain stream. But it might as well be describing your down-hill free fall, just a long, sweet run: hang on and have fun! Both of the longer options add more climbing, but they also extend the long run of downhill.

Very near the top of the basic loop, you leave the mountain pines behind and return to the open, rocky, oak-dotted grasslands that slope down toward the flat valley floor. The last 11 miles of the ride roll out easily through those meadows, out across the valley, heading back to the little village of Millville, where the ride began. These are not thrilling miles, but they are pleasant enough, and are a mellow way to spin out your legs after the long climbs and descents earlier in the loop.

Quiet little back roads through the foothills southeast of Redding

0.0	From Millville Elementary School, left on Brookdale Rd.
2.4	Left on Whitmore Rd.
11.0	Left on Fern Rd.
18.7	Left on Oak Run to Fern Rd.
26.5	Town of Oak Run
27.4	Left on Oak Run Rd.
39.0	Left on Old 44 Dr.
40.9	Straight on Whitmore Rd.
41.1	Left on Brookdale Rd.
41.4	Left into school

44   PONDEROSA LOLLIPOP

Difficulty: Challenging
Time: 4 to 5 hours
Distance: 52 miles
Elevation gain: 4500'
Best seasons: Spring and fall
Road conditions: Traffic is low and pavement is decent.

GETTING THERE: From I-5 in Redding, take Hwy 44 east for 25 miles to a left on Ponderosa Way. Go half a mile to Black Butte Jr. High School.

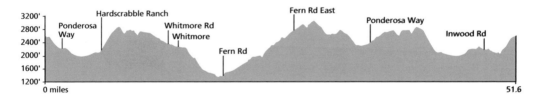

I stumbled upon Ponderosa Way while scouting two other rides in this book (43 and 45). It ties those two loops together and shares roads with both of them. This ride can be combined with the Shingletown Shuffle (Ride 45) for an epic ride of 80 miles. After reading the write-ups on both rides, you can think about splicing them together. It's a tantalizing prospect.

This ride begins just as the Shingletown ride does, with a 2-mile descent on Ponderosa to the Inwood Road junction. While that ride bears off left on Inwood, this one turns right on Ponderosa. For the next 4 miles, it bumps along amid green pastures and scattered stands of oak and pine, first for 2 mildly downhill miles and then for 2 mildly uphill miles. The road is quite primitive: just one wide lane, with no stripes, and yet with reasonably good paving. There are a number of tiny, one-lane bridges with white-washed

Several of these simple, white-washed wooden bridges on Ponderosa Road make it feel as if you're riding back in time to an earlier era.

wooden railings, quaint throwbacks to earlier times...easy to imagine them being crossed in a Model T or a horse-drawn wagon.

After one of the prettiest of these little bridges, crossing Bear Creek in front of Hardscrabble Ranch, the road rather suddenly tilts uphill in a serious way, gaining 700' between miles 6 and 8 (6 percent, with a few spots near 10 percent). It's the steepest climb of the day, but at only 2 miles, is not all that difficult. Over the summit, the road descends for most of the next 11 miles. There are two short climbs in the first 2 miles after the summit, digging up out of creek bottoms, but overall, it's easy downhill.

Ponderosa tees into Whitmore Road. There is a fire station just before the corner, a good place to look for water, either now or when you pass this spot on the way back (mile 35). Turn left and head west to the town of Whitmore, which comes up at about mile 15 and consists of little more than a school and a country store (your only food source today). After a nearly level mile through town, Whitmore Road tips downhill again, losing 900' between miles 15 and 19. That's the end of the downhill for a while. When the descent bottoms out, turn right on Fern Road and begin climbing. The uphill will continue for most of the next 10 miles, gaining around

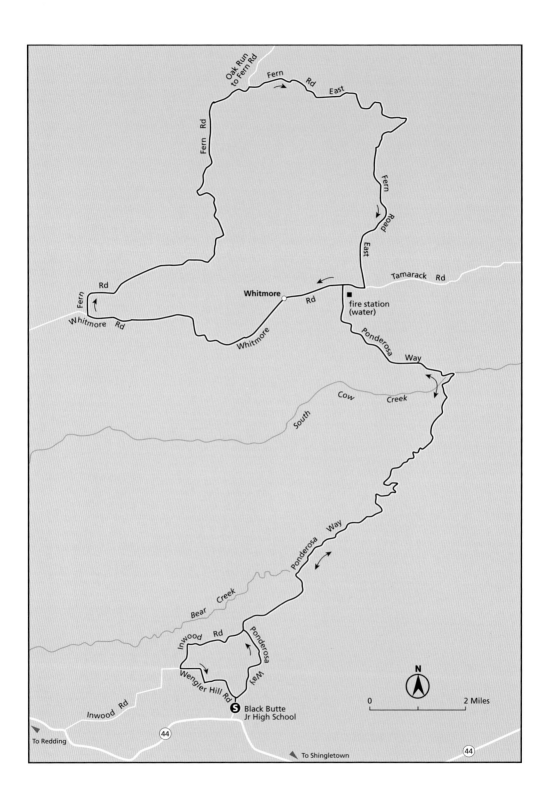

1700' over that span. But it's almost never steep and includes a number of flats and even a few downhill dips to break things up. Scenery along most of this run is classic California foothills: grassy meadows dotted with uncountable zillions of rocks and boulders, with scatters of pine and oak here and there. Only in the last miles before the summit does that open landscape give way to mountain pine forest. All around this Fern loop are ranches that look comfortably prosperous. In a few cases, they appear to go well beyond the definition of working ranches and enter the realm of palatial trophy spreads…a great deal of wealth on display.

Fern Road becomes Fern Road East at a junction with a road bearing off to the left. Continue straight ahead, with still 2 miles to the ultimate summit (but with a little downhill mixed in). Finally, head downhill quite steeply for a mile and a half, into a pretty pocket valley with a little lake alongside the road. After a short climb out of the valley, the downhill resumes, this time for about 2 miles. A mile of easy roll-out at the bottom of the hill returns you to the Ponderosa Way junction and that fire station, where cold water might be looking pretty good at this point.

Now it's retrace time: back south along the lumpy length of Ponderosa. First, 5 miles of easy, rolling uphill through the pine forest, back to the big summit, including those 2 descents into creek gullies and the slightly steeper walls climbing out of them. Then the big payback: the descent that was such a steep climb on the way north. Finally, there are the 2 miles of gentle downhill and 2 miles of gentle uphill to the Inwood Road junction, almost to the finish.

This is the point where you would depart to do the Shingletown Shuffle, if you have taken it upon yourself to double down on the routes today: west and south along Inwood and on around that hilly loop. Even if you don't plan to tackle those bonus miles, I suggest you dawdle down Inwood for a little while, rather than simply retracing the last 2 miles of Ponderosa to the school. The little loop at the end of this ride gives you a 2-mile taste of this pleasant road. Then turn left on another little lane, Wengler Hill Road, which doubles back east, ending up almost exactly at the school.

The Fern–East Fern loop, at just 21 miles, wouldn't add up to much of a ride on its own. But coupled with the Ponderosa miles, it makes a dandy day, pretty much everything you might want out of a ride. Unless, that is, you want even more, in which case you can graft on the Shingletown Shuffle and have a really big day.

MILEAGE LOG

0.0	From Black Butte Jr. High School, left on Ponderosa Way
1.9	Right on Ponderosa Way at Inwood Rd. junction
13.6	Left on Whitmore Rd.; fire station (water)
14.7	Town of Whitmore
19.5	Right on Fern Rd.
27.2	Straight on Fern Rd. E. at Oak Run to Fern Rd. junction
34.8	Right on Whitmore Rd.
35.3	Left on Ponderosa Way; fire station (water)
48.1	Right on Inwood Rd.
49.8	Left on Wengler Hill Rd.
51.4	Right on Ponderosa Way
51.6	Finish at school

45 SHINGLETOWN SHUFFLE

Difficulty:	Challenging
Time:	2.5 to 4 hours
Distance:	35 miles
Elevation gain:	3200'
Best seasons:	Spring and fall
Road conditions:	Some highway miles may be busy, but most roads are low traffic and bike friendly. All are well paved.

GETTING THERE: From I-5 in Redding, take Hwy 44 east for 25 miles to a left on Ponderosa Way. Go half a mile to Black Butte Jr. High School.

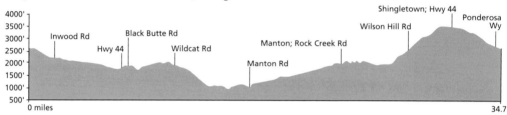

This ride may only be 35 miles, but it packs a pretty good punch for that distance. Note too that it can be combined with the nearby Ponderosa Lollipop ride (Ride 44) for an epic 80-mile day.

Both rides begin with a moderate descent, heading north on Ponderosa Way for 2 miles to a junction with Inwood Road. The Lollipop ride turns right here and heads farther north on Ponderosa, but this ride bears off left on Inwood, a delightful country lane passing through woods, meadows, and even a few vineyards. In spite of being a tiny, out-of-the-way road, it has excellent pavement. In this direction, it's mostly a gently rolling downhill for 5 miles, all the way to its end, where it tees into Highway 44.

Turn left onto the wide shoulder of the highway and climb easily for half a mile to a right on Black Butte Road, which drops steeply into a ravine and then scrambles up the far side before settling into a lumpy traverse across an open hillside. Just before mile 11,

Black Butte veers off to the right, but you continue straight onto Wildcat Road, a wonderful road that begins with a twisting descent of 3 miles (dropping almost 1000'), all on nearly new black-satin pavement. This is about as much fun as you can have on a bike, and my only complaint about it is that it doesn't go on twice as long. If you like descending, grab onto this wildcat's tail and hang on!

A mile and a half of mildly downhill roll-out at the bottom of that crazy descent leads to a junction with Manton Road. Turn left and begin a long climb toward the town of Manton. This looks grim at first, beginning with a half mile of hard work on an open, bleak hillside. But that passes and the rest of the "climb" is just an 8-mile false flat through sprawling ranch lands, not hard work at all. Ah, but wait: you're not getting off that easily. Beyond Manton, the real climb is lurking. This is the big pull up to the village of Shingletown, and it includes some wickedly steep pitches.

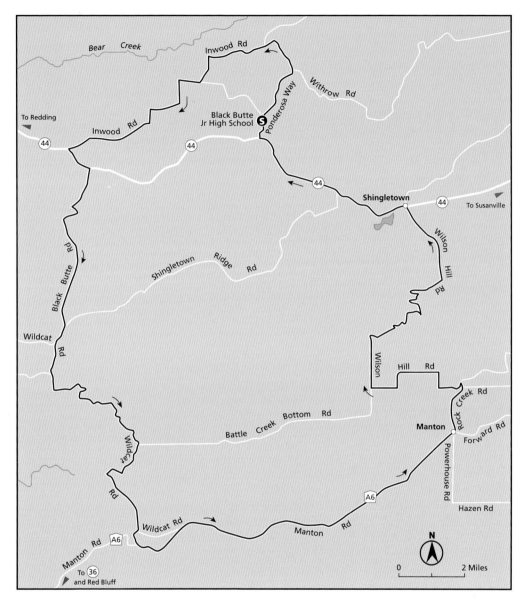

There is a quaint old store in Manton—almost the only thing there—and at mile 23, it makes a good spot for a break. Turn left at the store on Rock Creek Road and left again on Wilson Hill Road a mile later. It's 3 miles from Manton to the start of the climb, all of it across the same rocky tableland as the long run up to the town. That changes around mile 26: the road narrows to one lane and begins curling up the hillside, 1600' of gain in 4 miles. This works out to a 7 percent average, but it's not that simple. The grade changes frequently, varying between 2 and 15 percent. In a way, that's a good thing, as the near-flats allow for little breathers between the steeper pitches. As you climb, the landscape shifts from those dry, austere ranch lands through a pretty zone of shady, broadleaf wood, and

Rock Creek Road drops into this little gorge before beginning the long, steep ascent to Shingletown.

finally to a high-country forest of ponderosa pine. Some of the hardest, steepest sections are out in the open amidst scattered oaks. If it's hot, these bits will seem really bake-oven.

Over the top, the road descends briefly to Shingletown on Hwy 44. The town serves as a way station for motorists heading up to Lassen Volcanic National Park. There are many roadside services, including gas stations, restaurants, and a little supermarket. All that remains of the ride is a 3-mile, mostly downhill glide along the wide shoulder of the highway, back to Ponderosa Way.

Now then, what about combining this spunky little ride with the Ponderosa Lolli-pop? Read about that ride too and consider it. I highly recommend it, if you have the fitness for 80 hilly miles. I think it works best if you do the other ride first and this one second, but that does mean the steep climb on Wilson Hill, on this ride, will come up between miles 72 and 76. If you do this one first, because of the way the routes connect, the ride grows to 84 miles. Pick your poison: a nasty climb near the end or 4 extra miles. Either way, it's a great ride. Beautiful scenery throughout, good pavement, virtually no traffic (except for the few miles on Hwy 44), challenging climbs and too-much-fun descents…what's not to like?

MILEAGE LOG

0.0	From Black Butte Jr. High School, left on Ponderosa Way
1.9	Straight on Inwood Rd. (Ponderosa Way turns right)
6.8	Left on Hwy 44
7.3	Right on Black Butte Rd.
10.8	Straight on Wildcat Rd.; signs says, "MANTON 11"
16.4	Left on Manton Rd.

23.1	Left on Rock Creek Rd.; town of Manton
23.9	Left on Wilson Hill Rd.
31.2	Left on Hwy 44; town of Shingletown
34.4	Right on Ponderosa Way
34.7	Finish at school

46 EASY CHICO

Difficulty:	Easy
Time:	2 to 3 hours
Distance:	27 miles
Elevation gain:	Very little
Best seasons:	Spring or fall
Road conditions:	Mostly low traffic or paths through a park. Pavement is good.

GETTING THERE: In downtown Chico, park at Rosedale Elementary School, ten blocks west of Broadway on 2nd St.

This is really two rides, and you can do them all in one chunk or in two smaller installments of 14 and 11 miles. The first part is a loop out into the almond groves west of town. This is one of the few rides in our Central Valley section that doesn't turn its back on the flat valley floor and head for the foothills. This one embraces the flatness and rolls along the quiet farm roads through the almond trees. It even includes a run alongside the Sacramento River, the main waterway down the Central Valley.

From Rosedale Elementary School, head north and west out of town. After 2.6 miles of quiet city streets—Bidwell Avenue is especially nice—turn left on Oak Way and head west out into the orchards along straight, flat roads. Some are one lane wide and feel peaceful and out of the way. Others are two lanes and feel a bit busier. River Road, between miles 6 and 9, is the one with the scenic river frontage. Chico River Road is a straight and potentially busier highway—although still relatively quiet—between miles 9 and 11. After that, 4.5 miles of tiny roads through

the orchards bring the route back into town, completing the "country" loop.

The second loop is an exploration of Bidwell Park, right in the heart of town. Connecting the two loops is a 1-mile link along 1st Street, a mostly quiet city street running in front of the Chico State campus, including one four-block section closed to cars. The campus is handsome: sort of a small-scale version of a classic Ivy League school, with the stately old brick buildings and enormous trees shading broad lawns. Follow 1st as far as it goes, to the corner of Orient Street, then turn left into Bidwell Park at mile 16.7.

Created in 1905, Bidwell Park is the third largest city park in California and one of the largest in the country. It is, quite simply, one of the best urban parks you will ever visit, anywhere. But don't take my word for it. Ask Robin Hood and his merry men. Remember the classic Hollywood movie *The Adventures of Robin Hood*, with Errol Flynn, Basil Rathbone, and Olivia de Haviland? Remember all those scenes in lush, gorgeous Sherwood

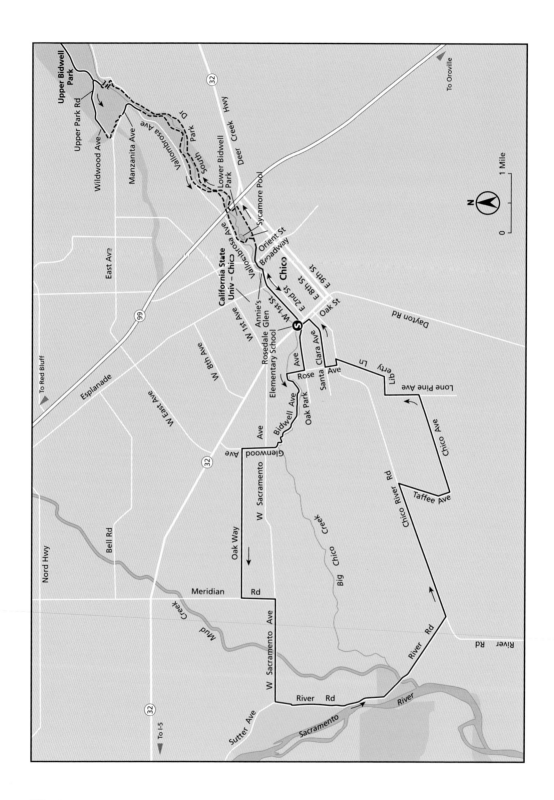

Crossing the bike bridge over Sycamore Pool in Bidwell Park (Brooke Parks)

Forest? Robin and Friar Tuck having their tussle in the creek? The merry outlaws swinging out of the trees to ambush the sheriff's men? Well, all of that was filmed in Bidwell Park in 1937. Big Chico Creek and the wonderful forest that worked so well in the film are still here, still as grand and magnificent as ever, with more towering sycamores and oaks than you'll find anywhere this side of an old English wood. The park includes a network of trails and roads perfect for easy riding. Some are closed to cars, but even the roads open to cars are quiet, with low speed limits. Walkers and cyclists rule here.

In simplest terms, the route follows South Park Drive, crossing under several city streets and highways along the way. As South Park Drive leaves the upper end of Bidwell Park, look for a bike-trail bridge that crosses the creek on the left. This isn't marked, but you can count up the 4 miles from entering the park or note when you pass under Manzanita Avenue. The trail over the bridge is less than half a mile beyond Manzanita.

Cross the creek and follow the road on the north bank to a junction with Wildwood Avenue. The route turns left and heads back toward town, but it's worth noting that a right turn would take you much deeper into the wilder, hillier reaches of Upper Bidwell Park. The paved road runs for a few miles, then continues as gravel. Most of the time it's near the creek, and there are spectacular swimming holes along this stretch of deep canyon, down among the rugged basalt cliffs.

The route heads west on Wildwood to Manzanita Avenue, where you jog south for half a mile to get back to Lower Bidwell Park. There is a paved trail on the east side of the road that covers over half that distance, but eventually, you have to get on the road for about a quarter-mile. At a roundabout with Vallombrosa Avenue, take the trail into the park.

Head west through the park along Peterson Memorial Way. This looks just like South Park Drive and is its companion road on the other side of the creek. There are pretty swimming holes along this section of creek too, not as deep and spectacular as the ones in the wilds of Upper Bidwell, but still nice. There are many picnic areas in shady glades near the water. The biggest and most official of all the swimming holes is Sycamore Pool, a broad, shallow pond behind a small dam on the creek.

The route hugs the shore of the pond and then crosses the creek on a little bridge above the dam. Follow the trail until it connects to South Park Drive. Then it's just a matter of retracing the outward-bound route through the west end of the park and along 1st Street, back through downtown Chico. If you weren't prepared for a picnic in the park, consider a lunch in any of several good bistros or cafés near the college.

MILEAGE LOG

0.0	From Rosedale Elementary School, left on Oak St.
0.1	Left on Oak Park Ave.
0.7	Right on Rose Ave.
0.9	Left on Bidwell Ave.
2.3	Jog left on W. Sacramento Ave., right on Glenwood Ave.
2.6	Left on Oak Way
4.6	Left on Meridian Rd.
5.0	Right on W. Sacramento Ave.
6.4	Left on River Rd.
9.2	Left on Chico River Rd.
11.1	Right on Taffee Ave.
11.9	Left on Chico Ave.
13.2	Left on Lone Pine Ave.
13.7	Right on Liberty Ln.
14.6	Jog left on Chico River Rd. to right on Rose Ave.
14.8	Right on Santa Clara Ave.
15.5	Left on Oak St. (past start site at school)
15.7	Right on 1st St. into downtown Chico, past Chico State campus
16.7	Left into Bidwell Park at Annie's Glen, corner of 1st and Orient streets
18.2	Left on S. Park Dr.
19.8	When South Park Dr. exits park, bear left on bike trail
20.1	Ride under Manzanita Ave. on trail
20.5	Left on trail across footbridge over Big Chico Creek
20.8	Left on Wildwood Ave., or go right for bonus miles deeper into Upper Bidwell Park
21.7	Left on trail parallel to Manzanita Ave., just before roundabout
22.0	Exit park at second roundabout and head east on Manzanita Ave.
22.3	At third roundabout, enter Bidwell Park on bike trail parallel to Vallombrosa Ave.
22.5	Left on Peterson Memorial Way
25.0	Left on Vallombrosa Ave. near Sycamore Pool
25.0	Quick left on footbridge over creek; follow trail to S. Park Dr.
25.1	Right on S. Park Dr.; signs say "ONE WAY" the other direction, but bikes okay
25.3	Right on trail through Annie's Glen
25.6	Right on 1st St. through downtown, past campus
26.6	Left on Oak St.; finish at Rosedale Elementary School

47 ESSENCE OF WILDFLOWER

Difficulty:	Challenging
Time:	4 to 6 hours
Distance:	64 miles
Elevation gain:	3900'
Best seasons:	Spring or fall
Road conditions:	Some miles may be busy, but most are quiet. Some are well paved and some not so well, but all are at least decent.

GETTING THERE: From downtown Chico, drive 1 mile south on Broadway and Park, then turn left on 20th St. and proceed 0.6 miles to the Sierra Nevada Brewery.

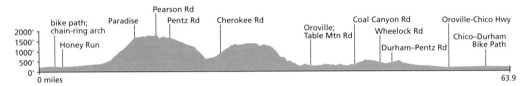

The roads on this loop comprise the best roads on the popular Wildflower Century, staged by the Chico Velo bike club on the last weekend in April each year. I've pared their century route down to a loop I think is the essence of the Wildflower.

Operating on the premise that a ride this good deserves a hearty, celebratory lunch afterward, I am starting and finishing it at the Sierra Nevada Brewery, which has a huge brew pub on the premises. No trip to Chico is complete without a visit to Sierra Nevada, so I'm making that visit easy for you.

Begin by turning right on 20th Street. This is not a great street for bikes. Over its first mile, it passes shopping malls, crosses a freeway, and just generally runs with the bulls...the motorized bulls. However, the road always sports wide shoulders, and the worst of the mess is over after that first mile.

Once clear of town, 20th leads to a bike path across an open, rocky meadow. At its beginning, the path passes under an elegant arch shaped like giant chain rings, emblematic of this town's love affair with cycling. The path leads to Honey Run, the most famous road in the region. It's the opening movement in the Wildflower Century, and on that Saturday in April, it is a river of riders flowing uphill around its many curves. After a rolling run upstream along Little Butte Creek, Honey Run begins its main ascent at mile 9 and carries on in full uphill mode for exactly 4 miles, gaining 1300'. That's an average of 6 percent, a reasonably accurate measure of what to expect. Scenery along the way is leafy woods, with rock cliffs and an occasional break in the foliage, opening up vistas across the canyon to rugged basalt buttes.

At the top, Honey Run pops out suddenly into the town of Paradise. Follow the route along a neighborhood street to a nice park where water is available. Then head east on Pearson Road to a right turn on Stearns Road. Stearns and De Mille roads together form a little bypass off the main drag and off the

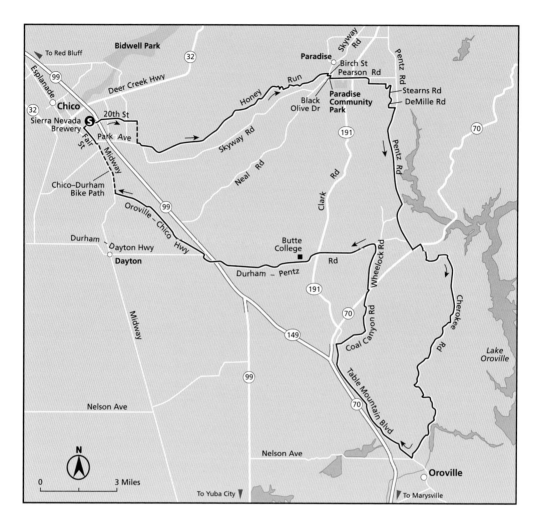

Wildflower route as well. They are too narrow and twisty for 3000 riders but are great fun for a few riders looking to get off the beaten path. When De Mille tees into Pentz Road, turn right. Pentz is all about descending. The 5-mile downhill begins gently but picks up speed as it goes along, ending with a wide-open screamer of over a mile.

After a mildly uphill roll-out, Pentz tees into busy Highway 70. Cross the highway carefully, then turn left and head uphill for half a mile to Cherokee Road, where the climbing continues: 600' in 2.5 miles. At the top of this moderate climb, Cherokee wan-ders across the more or less flat top of Table Mountain, another of the signature basalt buttes one sees everywhere here (this is Butte County). In the spring, the meadows up here are carpeted in wildflowers, hence the name of the ride. But even if the flowers aren't doing their thing, it's still beautiful, with oak and manzanita eking a hardscrabble living in the rocky soil.

At around mile 30, the road falls off the edge of the "table" and begins another 5-mile descent. This one drops 1100', and while some of it is only rolling and even includes a few uphill bumps, there are other places where it's about as much fun as a descent can be, slithering down the rocky hillside through the oak forest. Occasionally, if you can spare a glance from this wild ride, you may catch impressive views off the left side of the road, out over Lake Oroville.

When this dizzy descent ends, you're in the town of Oroville. Turn right on Table Mountain Boulevard and ride along the flat, straight city street for a little over a mile. Although you're in a big town, you won't find any stores or schools or parks right along the route where water can easily be had. There is a gas station and mini-mart in the middle of nowhere at about mile 50.

That fun descent on Cherokee drops you out of the high country and back down to the floor of the valley, and there you will stay for the duration. These miles aren't literally flat, but compared to Honey Run, Pentz, and Cherokee, they may seem so. All of the rest of the roads are much the same, rolling across open, rocky meadows, with patches of woods here and there. Some of the roads are smaller and scaled to the speed of bike travel (Coal Canyon, for one). Others are bigger highways where bikes feel a bit out of their element. After the excitement of the hills, it may seem a little ho-hum, but it's all good: easy, mellow miles, rolling back to town.

At around mile 58, the mix of meadows and woods gives way to almond orchards, and the route will run among these shady old groves right up to the edge of Chico. Midway, the last country road heading into town, has the very nice Chico–Durham Bike Path running parallel to it. The path is easy to find and easy to ride. It takes you right into town, where a right on East Park and a left on Fair will deliver you to 20th, just a couple of blocks from Sierra Nevada Brewery. Time for lunch!

If you ever needed proof that Chico is a bike-friendly community, look no further than this chain-ring gateway on a bike trail heading out of town.

0.0	From Sierra Nevada Brewery, right on 20th St.
2.1	Right on bike path through chain-ring arch
3.0	Bear left on bike path parallel to Skyway Rd.
3.2	Left on Honey Run Rd.
13.0	Jog right on Skyway to left on Birch St.; town of Paradise
13.3	Right on Black Olive Dr. or straight into Paradise Community Park (water)
13.3	Left on Pearson Rd.
15.9	Right on Stearns Rd.
16.9	Straight on De Mille Rd. (Stearns turns left)
17.7	Right on Pentz Rd.
24.0	Left on Hwy 70
24.5	Right on Cherokee Rd.
36.6	Right on Table Mountain Blvd.; town of Oroville
42.6	Right on Coal Canyon Rd.
45.9	Cross Hwy 70 to Wheelock Rd.
47.8	Left on Durham–Pentz Rd.
55.0	Cross Hwy 99 on overpass, straight on Durham–Dayton Hwy
55.5	Right on Oroville–Chico Hwy
60.4	Right on Chico–Durham Bike Path (parallel to Midway)
62.7	Jog right on East Park Ave. to left on Fair St.; back in Chico
63.5	Right on 20th St.
63.9	Right into Sierra Nevada Brewery and finish

48 LAPORTE–FORBESTOWN LOOPS

Difficulty:	Challenging
Time:	4 to 6 hours
Distance:	38, 44, or 63 miles
Elevation gain:	Up to 4800'
Best seasons:	Spring or fall
Road conditions:	Some highway miles may be busy, but most roads are quiet. Some are well paved and some not so well, but all are at least decent.

GETTING THERE: Exit Hwy 70 at Oroville. Take Oroville Dam Blvd. (Hwy 162) east for 1.7 miles. Turn right on Olive Hwy (still Hwy 162) for 1 mile, then right on Foothill Blvd. and go 2 miles to the start of the ride.

This ride heads from the nearly flat Central Valley up into the nearby hills to the east. While many of its miles cover easy, rolling terrain, there is one 17-mile section that is mostly uphill and sometimes quite steeply so. There is, of course, a corresponding downhill

after all that hard work: the last 17 miles of the ride.

Begin at the corner of Foothill Boulevard and Oro–Bangor Highway. There is a business here with a large parking lot. They allow the Chico Velo bike club to stage a rest stop on this lot, so we can guess they won't mind a cyclist leaving a car here now and then. Head south on Oro–Bangor Highway. The first 3 miles are a perfect bike road: slightly more than one lane wide, smoothly paved, and meandering through the woods. After crossing Foothill, this little road picks up a center stripe and looks more like a real highway, but it remains a quiet, pretty road, well suited to cycling.

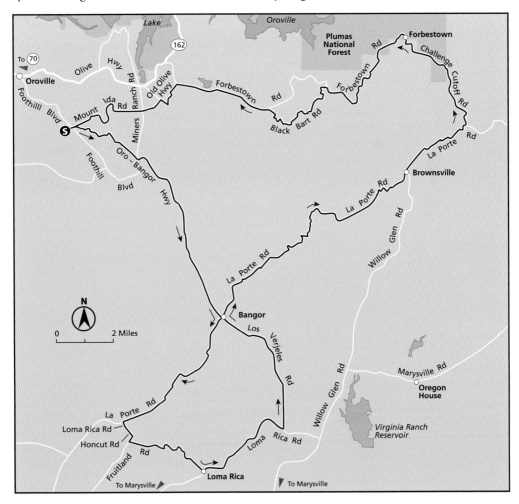

At 9.6 miles, you come to La Porte Road. As you can see from the map, there is a smaller loop at the bottom of the bigger loop, both meeting at this junction, which is the dot on the map labeled Bangor. To shorten the stage to 44 miles but retain all the hardest climbing (and wildest descending), turn left on LaPorte instead of right, skipping the little loop. To shorten the ride to 38 miles, avoiding all of the hard climbing, do the little loop, then retrace Oro–Bangor Highway to the start. This would yield a pleasant, moderate ride, with delightful scenery along tranquil, rolling roads.

To begin the little loop, turn right on La Porte and head south through meadows and scattered woods to a left on Loma Rica Road, which almost immediately becomes Honcut Road. At mile 16, Honcut tees into Fruitland Road, which in 3.2 miles tees into Loma Rica Road. No, not the little bit of it you were on a couple of miles ago; this is an entirely different road, but with the same name. You will be on this Loma Rica for about 4 miles, all of it through the same rolling, grassy meadows dotted with old oaks and chunky boulders.

Expect more of the same lovely scenery and mildly lumpy terrain along the 5 miles of Los Verjeles Road. This pleasant road completes the little loop and brings you back to Bangor. To continue the full route, turn right on La Porte. The road begins with a modest uphill of over 2 miles, then a descent of 1 mile, then 5 miles of mild climbing. But at mile 36, the word "mild" no longer applies. The next mile gains 550' in a series of wicked, switchback pitches through the forest. That's an average of 11 percent, with short sections a bit steeper. After that husky little chug, it eases off considerably. There are still 9 miles to the ultimate summit of the day, but the climbs are never too hard. There are even some flats and dips mixed into the generally uphill trend.

There are three turns during those 9 miles. First, La Porte comes to a junction with Wil-low Glen Road, where you turn left at the stop sign. It feels like a turn onto a new road, but it's still La Porte in the direction you're heading. This junction is at the center of the village of Brownsville, and there is a nice bakery on this corner. It's your first shot at munchies and water since a little store in Bangor. Turn left onto Challenge Cutoff Road and left again onto Forbestown Road. While La Porte was a smaller, funkier road during its steep climb, the roads that follow—from the Willow Glen junction onward—are all paved and engineered to a higher standard. Midway up the steep ascent, you left the grassy meadows and oak trees behind and climbed into a mountain landscape dominated by dense stands of ponderosa pine.

Once the final summit is reached along Forbestown Road at 46 miles, it is almost all downhill to the finish: 3000' over 17 miles. There are a few tiny uphill bumps and flats mixed in, just to keep your legs limber, but mostly, it's down, down, and more down. It would have been simplest to leave the route on Forbestown Road for the first 13 of those miles, but there is a little side road that's an improvement over the main highway: Black Bart Road runs for 3.6 narrow, twisty, car-free miles alongside the main road. It requires left turns onto and off of it, but I think it's worth it.

Back on Forbestown and rolling out the long descent, keep an eye peeled for a left onto Old Olive Highway. Unlike fast, well-engineered Forbestown, this road and Mount Ida Road, which follows, are dinky, kinked-up little lanes, still rolling downhill, but now around tightly tangled corners…more fun for a cyclist than the big highway. Don't miss the left onto Mount Ida. It rolls gently downhill through a scattering of rural-residential properties on the outskirts of Oroville. At its end, it merges back into the first road of the day, Oro–Bangor Highway, and you retrace one short section to the corner of Foothill, where this nice ride began.

Fruitland Road is typical of the quiet little lanes on this ride out of Oroville.

MILEAGE LOG

0.0	From its intersection with Foothill Blvd., right on Oro–Bangor Hwy
0.2	Bear right on Oro–Bangor Hwy at Mount Ida Rd. junction
9.6	Right on La Porte Rd.; town of Bangor
15.2	Left on Loma Rica Rd.
15.4	Straight on Honcut Rd.
16.0	Left on Fruitland Rd.
19.2	Left on Loma Rica Rd.
23.1	Left on Los Verjeles Rd.
28.1	Right on La Porte Rd. (town of Bangor...again)
38.2	Left to stay on La Porte Rd. at Willow Glen Rd. junction; town of Brownsville
40.9	Left on Challenge Cutoff Rd.
43.7	Left on Forbestown Rd.
49.9	Left on Black Bart Rd.
53.5	Left on Forbestown Rd.
56.9	Left on Old Olive Hwy
58.1	Left on Mount Ida Rd.
61.3	Left on Mount Ida Rd. at Oakvale Rd. junction
62.3	Straight on Oro–Bangor Hwy
62.5	Finish

49 WINTERS WOODEN WIGGLES

Difficulty:	Moderate/challenging
Time:	2 to 3 hours (short); 4.5 to 6 hours (long)
Distance:	27 or 69 miles
Elevation gain:	1300' or 4200'
Best seasons:	Spring and fall
Road conditions:	Most roads are low traffic and bike friendly, but a few are busier. Most are well paved.

GETTING THERE: Exit I-505 at Grant Ave. (Hwy 128) and head west 1 mile to town of Winters. Turn left on Railroad Ave. and proceed four blocks to the Winters Community Center.

This ride is typical of our Central Valley offerings: it flirts with the flat valley floor but spends most of its time in the foothills nearby. The ride begins and ends in the charming town of Winters, near its attractively spruced-up downtown. Roll out of town to the south on a handsome bike bridge over Putah Creek.

Follow Winters Road for the first 5 miles, initially through orchards and then out across flat farm fields next to I-505. These miles are

It doesn't take long on this ride to leave the flat farm fields behind and begin wandering through the woods on pretty Cantelow Road. (Nancy Yu)

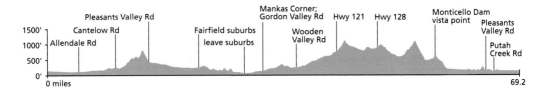

1500'
1000'
500'
0'
0 miles

Allendale Rd
Cantelow Rd
Pleasants Valley Rd
Fairfield suburbs
leave suburbs
Mankas Corner;
Gordon Valley Rd
Wooden
Valley Rd
Hwy 121
Hwy 128
Monticello Dam
vista point
Pleasants
Valley Rd
Putah
Creek Rd

69.2

a little dull, frankly, but things perk up over the next 5 miles, along a series of quiet lanes north of Vacaville. The farm fields give way to gently rolling hills, with small ranches and country homes scattered about. And then, with the third 5-mile section, things really improve. Miles 10 through 15 are taken up with Cantelow Road, and this sweet little lane pretty much defines good cycling. It's the first significant spike on the elevation profile: 4 miles of easy, stair-step climbs and dips and 1 mile of fast descent. The flat, featureless valley, just a few miles back, seems like a distant memory here, as the road meanders through pretty woods and meadows.

At the bottom of that frisky descent, Cantelow tees into Pleasants Valley Road, where the long route turns left and the short route turns right. The short route is simple: head north on Pleasants Valley to Putah Creek Road, where it rejoins the long route. That run up Pleasants Valley is flat, easy, and pretty. It includes a run past Putah Creek Road to Solano County Park, where water and restrooms are available. If you think the long loop is too much today but the short loop is not enough, consider an out-and-back to Monticello Dam. (North across the creek from the county park, then west along the creek up to the vista point above the dam.) This would add 11.4 miles (round-trip) to the 27-mile loop and would include a modest climb to the vista point, which of course turns into a nice little descent on the way back.

The longer route, heading south on Pleasants Valley, Cherry Glen, and Lyon roads, cruises along on a mildly downhill run through pretty, wooded countryside for 9 miles. But in the last half mile of Lyon, that changes: for the next 4 miles, you'll be working through the suburban fringe of the city of Fairfield. Although these boulevard miles through the tracts are not terrible, they're not exactly dream miles either. But there is no way to make this loop work without them. And it's in a good cause, because when you pop out the other side of the 'burbs at mile 29, you're headed for more good back-road riding.

Point your bike west and north toward Mankas Corner, a little village at the junction of Gordon Valley and Wooden Valley. These two quiet valleys, side by side, are made to order for cycling: quiet, low traffic roads through shady woods and the occasional vineyard. The only thing that might give you pause is the elevation profile: aside from one 1.5-mile saddle, it tilts up for 15 miles. Most of this climbing is easy. The grades through the two valleys rarely exceed 2 percent. Only in the last of those 15 miles, after turning from Wooden Valley onto Highway 121, is there anything steeper, and that is a final, 1-mile pitch at about 6 percent.

You'll be on Hwy 121 and 128 for most of 21 miles. In spite of carrying two different highway numbers, they function as one road. They are the main route to Lake Berryessa, a popular destination for boaters, so they can carry an uncomfortable burden of traffic, at least on summer weekends. In the off-season or on weekdays, that shouldn't be much of a problem. This is the hilliest part of the course, as much as 1000' above the valley floor. Between miles 41 and 58, there are five climbs and five descents, some big, some smaller, with the descents generally longer

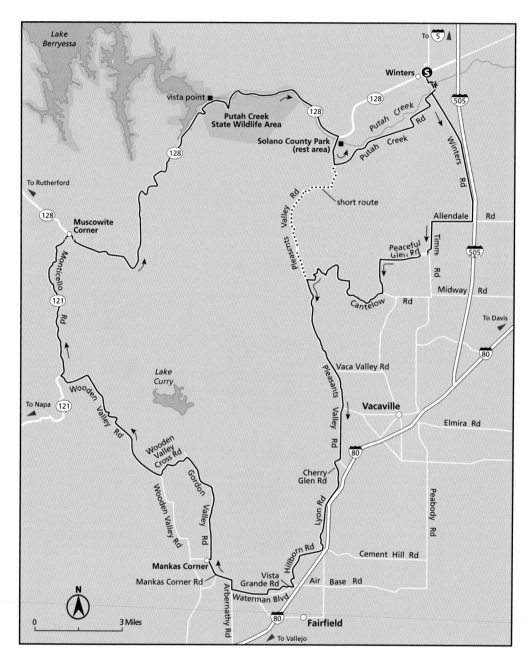

than the climbs, as you head out of the hills and back to the valley. Before the last descent, there is a vista point overlooking Monticello Dam at Lake Berryessa. It's a dramatic spot, with rocky cliffs soaring above the road on one side and the deep gorge below the dam on the other.

After that last descent, the final 11 miles of the ride are nearly level, as the roads meander along near wide, lazy Putah Creek. Depart

Hwy 128 near mile 63 and cross the creek on Pleasants Valley Road. Just over the bridge, there is a county park where water and restrooms are available. Beyond the park, turn left on Putah Creek Road. This is where the short route rejoins. Putah Creek Road spends most of these last, flat miles winding through fruit and nut orchards, but also includes a brief run along the shore of the creek. Roll out these easy miles and cross back over the old bridge into downtown Winters. Now it's time to look around for a bistro where you can replace some of the calories you burned up on this nice ride.

MILEAGE LOG

0.0	From Winters Community Center, south on bike bridge over Putah Creek
0.2	Right to stay on Winters Rd. (now also Putah Creek Rd., briefly)
0.4	Bear left to stay on Winters Rd. (Putah Creek Rd. turns right)
5.1	Right on Allendale Rd.
6.5	Left on Timm Rd.
7.6	Right on Peaceful Glen Rd.
9.3	Becomes English Hills Rd.
10.5	Right on Cantelow Rd.
11.2	Bear right to stay on Cantelow Rd.
15.1	Left on Pleasants Valley Rd.; short route turns right

Short route:

15.1	**Right on Pleasants Valley Road**
21.0	**Right into Solano County Park (water, restrooms)**
21.2	**Left on Pleasants Valley Road; leave park, retrace**
22.0	**Left on Putah Creek Road; rejoin long route (see mile 64.0)**

21.5	Right on Cherry Glen Rd.
22.3	Right on Lyon Rd.; suburbs of city of Fairfield
24.6	Right on Hillborn Rd.
26.7	Right on Vista Grande Rd.
28.1	Right on Waterman Blvd.
28.5	Becomes Mankas Corner Rd.; leave Fairfield
29.4	Right to stay on Mankas Corner Rd. at Abernathy Rd. junction
30.8	Right on Clayton Rd.; village of Mankas Corner
30.8	Left on Gordon Valley Rd.
34.7	Left on Wooden Valley Cross Rd.
36.0	Right on Wooden Valley Rd.
41.8	Right on Hwy 121, also known as Monticello Rd.
47.3	Bear right on Hwy 128; Moscowite Corner (store)
57.6	Vista point overlooking Monticello Dam at Lake Berryessa
63.0	Right on Pleasants Valley Rd., cross Putah Creek
63.2	Solano County Park (water, restrooms)
64.0	Left on Putah Creek Rd.; short route rejoins here
68.8	Left on Winters Rd. (still Putah Creek Rd. as well)
69.0	Bear left to stay on Winters Rd. (Putah Creek Rd. turns right)
69.2	Finish in downtown Winters

50 DAVIS BIKE LOOP

Difficulty:	Easy
Time:	1 to 1.5 hours
Distance:	12 miles
Elevation gain:	Flat
Best seasons:	Spring and fall
Road conditions:	Most of loop is on bike trails. Some sections are on quiet neighborhood streets.

GETTING THERE: From downtown Sacramento, head west on I-80 approximately 15 miles to Davis. Drive 2 miles north on Hwy 113 to the W. Covell Blvd. exit, and head east on W. Covell for 1 mile to Oak Ave.; turn right. Drive 0.3 south on Oak Ave. to W. 14th St., turn left, and proceed to the parking lot at Davis High School.

The city of Davis, west of Sacramento, is justifiably famous in the bike world as a haven for cycling. It has all the requisite pieces in place. It's the home of UC Davis, a large university, so has that big pool of student and faculty riders, plus the activism and idealism that go with most good colleges, in this case often directed toward cycling issues. The local bike club and cycling advocacy organizations are large and vibrant, and even the city government is on board, to the degree that the city's logo is a bicycle: a classic high-wheeler. It is even the home of the US Bicycling Hall of Fame. Finally, the town is virtually flat, making cycling easy for everyone on any sort of bike. The city is frequently cited as one of the best biking towns in the United States.

The city earned those accolades with a great

To ride the Davis Bike Loop, simply follow the green directional graphics.

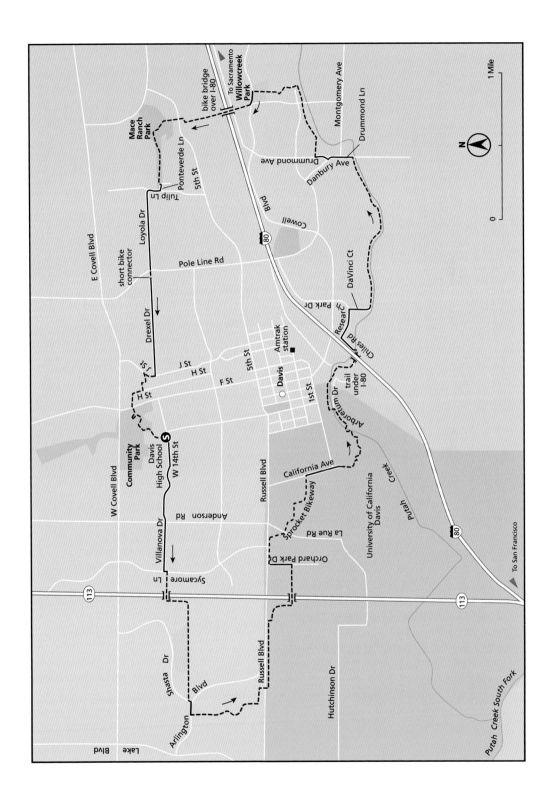

deal of planning and energy (and money) put into bike infrastructure. There are bike paths everywhere, featuring many bridges and tunnels over and under boulevards and freeways. This 12-mile ride is the crown jewel in the Davis bike-trail system. Known as the Davis Bike Loop, it's a circuit around the city, passing through the college campus and through numerous parks and greenbelts and incorporating most of the significant bridges and tunnels and other hallmarks and highlights of the city's bike environment. Planning began on the loop in the 1980s and has proceeded ever since. Older sections of trail were loosely linked first, and the city's general plan assured that new trail segments were included in all new developments. Finally, in 2007, with the loop essentially complete, it was marked with a distinctive set of green arrows featuring the town's signature high-wheeler logo.

The idea with the arrows is that anyone, without any prior local knowledge, should be able to navigate the full loop by simply following the markings. I put this to the test personally. My only prior experience of cycling in Davis was starting and finishing a few Davis Double Centuries at the high school. It was essentially *terra incognita* for me. I did my homework first, reading up on the system and getting the basic layout clear. Then I drove up to Davis and winged it. I climbed on my bike, joining hundreds of other riders going about their bike-transit business, and poked along the trails, keeping one eye on the scenery and one eye always watching for the green markers. And it worked! There were a couple of construction projects on campus where I had to follow unmarked detours and then puzzle my way back to the official path, but those were only minor difficulties, easily solved.

The loop is still a work in progress. Local cycling advocates and city planners are not done with their efforts to make the system better. For instance, I just learned that one section that was a public road when I did it is soon to be transformed into a bikes-only parkway (Arboretum Drive). But no matter how they tinker with the trails, they will keep the green arrows up-to-date. My mileage log may eventually become mildly out of date, but if you follow the arrows, you'll be okay. In fact, in this case, the log should *not* be the tail wagging the dog: when in doubt, ignore the log and follow the arrows. This write-up is more background about the trail than a turn-by-turn guide for how to tackle it. For that, in theory at least, all you need are the arrows.

I can tell you that, not only does the trail work with respect to finding your way along it, it also works as a pleasant cycling experience. About 2 out of the 12 miles run along quiet residential lanes, but the balance is entirely car-free and carefree. Some of the miles are a bit ho-hum, but the best miles—and there are many in this category—are delightful, with the well-engineered, well-maintained path meandering through wooded parklands and greenbelts and across the handsome university campus.

I've included this little loop in the book as a tip of the old cycling *chapeau* to the folks in Davis who have been such pioneers in bringing bikes into the mainstream, in elevating cyclists from some marginalized role to being a legitimate part of the community and the transit mix. You ride this loop and you realize: yes, this works; this is the way it's supposed to be, the way it could be everywhere.

MILEAGE LOG

0.0	From Davis High School, right on W. 14th St.
0.4	Becomes Villanova Dr.
0.9	Jog left on Sycamore Ln. to bike trail; follow green bike directional markings
1.1	Bridge over Hwy 113; left on trail after bridge

2.0	Left on Shasta Dr.
2.0	Cross Arlington Blvd. to bike trail on south side of road
2.2	Pass community garden
2.7	Cross Russell Blvd. and turn left on bike trail on south side of road
3.5	Bridge over Hwy 113
3.6	Right on Orchard Park Cir.
3.7	Left on Orchard Park Dr.
3.8	Right on bike trail; follow Sprocket Bikeway through UC Davis campus
4.6	Right on California Ave.
4.9	Follow bike trail to Lake Spafford and Arboretum
5.3	Left on Arboretum Dr.
5.5	Cross Putah Creek on old bridge to right on bike trail
6.2	Under I-80 to right on Research Park Dr.
6.5	Right on Da Vinci Ct. to bike trail at end of street
7.7	Left on Drummond Ln.
7.9	Right on Drummond Ave.
7.9	Straight, then right on bike trail from end of Drummond Ave.
8.8	Cross Cowell Blvd. to bike trail on north side of road
9.0	Bridge over I-80
10.0	Right on Ponteverde Ln. to right on Tulip Ln.
10.1	Left on Loyola Dr.
10.7	Cross Pole Line Rd. to short bike trail to right on Drexel Dr.
11.4	Jog right on J St. to left on bike trail
11.6	Right on H St. to left on bike trail, past ball fields, through community park
12.2	Finish at Davis High School

51   AMERICAN RIVER TRAIL

Difficulty:	Moderate
Time:	4 to 6 hours
Distance:	57 miles
Elevation gain:	1200'
Best seasons:	Spring and fall
Road conditions:	Pavement is good. Almost the entire ride is on bike trails.

GETTING THERE: From I-5 in Sacramento, exit at Garden Hwy and go east 0.3 mile. Turn right on Natoma Park Dr. and proceed to parking lot at end of road, near Jibboom St. Bridge.

The Jedediah Smith Memorial Trail, more commonly known as the American River Trail, is one of the longest purpose-built bike trails in the state, stretching for 32 miles from Sacramento to Folsom Lake. While the trail has run alongside the American River since the 1970s, it is no aging relic. The County of Sacramento keeps it in tip-top shape, with

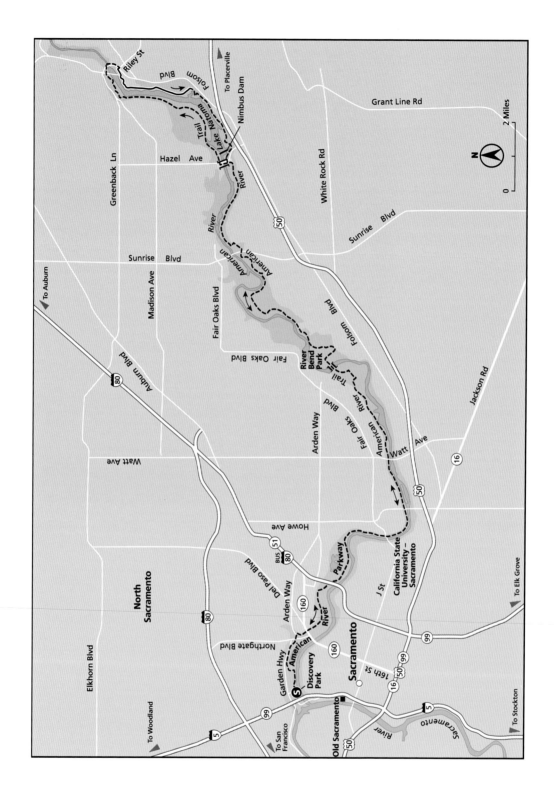

Riding next to Lake Natoma on the American River Trail,
one of the longest and best bike trails in California

new features added every year and with old elements upgraded or well maintained.

This ride does not quite sample the full trail. It heads east from Discovery Park, near downtown Sacramento, for 28 miles to the town of Folsom and Lake Natoma, a smaller, intermediate lake below Folsom Lake. At that point, it circles Lake Natoma before retracing the outward-bound run along the river. If you continue farther east, beyond the point where this route crosses to the other side of the lake, you could log another 7 miles (round-trip), up to the shore of the bigger lake and back. But some of those miles are a mixed bag and a bit confusing. So, in the interest of keeping it simple, I've omitted that last section. There are also 3 more miles of trail on the start/finish end of the journey (round-trip): across the Jibboom Street Bridge and along the Sacramento River frontage into Old Town

Sacramento. This is very much a tourist destination, but it still presents a reasonable facsimile of what it must have looked like when this was a bustling, riverfront town in the Gold Rush. In spite of its tourist trappings, I think it's worth a visit.

Being essentially an out-and-back, you can of course trim the route down to any comfort zone by lopping off as many miles as you need to. But the farther upstream you go, the better the trail and the scenery become. So if you want to do less than these 57 miles, find one of the parks upstream along the trail and start from there, dropping miles from the downtown end of the trail.

Navigation along the trail is usually simple. While there are many spur trails connecting to the main trail, including a few leading to bike bridges over the river, the main trail is easy to follow. It runs through a succession of parks, so access to water and restrooms is never a problem. While the trail is undoubtedly climbing in the outward-bound, upstream direction, the grade is so gentle that we're not bothering with an elevation profile. The average is less than 1 percent, with most of it nearly flat and just a few spots approaching the dam at Lake Natoma tilting up to perhaps 3 percent for brief pitches.

There are only two spots where navigation becomes complex. The first is at the Hazel Avenue Bridge at about mile 23. The trail approaches the bridge on the south bank. You are going to take a trail ramping up onto the west side of the bridge, where a beautiful new bike lane crosses the river next to the main bridge. On the north bank, loop around to cross underneath the bridge, now heading uphill, past Nimbus Dam, to the level run along the north shore of the lake. On the way back west, after circumnavigating Lake Natoma, use an underpass on the south bank to hook back up with the main trail.

The other tricky spot is where the trail loops around the top of the lake and heads down the south shore. You make a right turn onto an old box-truss bridge—now just for bikes and walkers—and then have to ride for a few blocks along the streets of the town of Folsom to reconnect to the trail on that side of the lake. The log should make this section plain, but if in doubt, stop another cyclist and ask. It would be a rare day when you would not see dozens of other trail users going by.

As noted above, the trail is extremely well maintained and also well thought out. There are two wide lanes, with a center stripe, and wide, compacted gravel shoulders in many areas for joggers and equestrians. In spite of being used by thousands of visitors every day, it doesn't feel crowded. There are a few areas where the turns along the trail are a little tight for faster bike speeds, but then you shouldn't be going that fast on a bike path anyway.

Sometimes the trail runs right along the river or the lake, but it often leaves the water to meander through pretty woods or grasslands in the almost uninterrupted sprawl of parks and preserves along the river. Some of the scenery is just so-so, with tract neighborhoods or shopping districts only a few yards away. But the best of the scenery is superb, and there are far more miles in this category than in the so-so department. Taking it all together—the quality of the trail and the handsome surrounding scenery—it adds up to a wonderful linear park, probably the best-loved and most-used recreational "facility" in the greater Sacramento area.

MILEAGE LOG

0.0	From Discovery Park, east on American River Parkway
7.9	Spur trail junction for Guy West Bridge to Sacramento State campus
13.8	Cross river to River Bend Park
22.8	Bear right, uphill, onto bike bridge over river, adjacent to Hazel Ave.
23.0	Loop around on trail to pass under Hazel Ave.; continue east on north bank of river
23.3	Pass Nimbus Dam and ride alongside Lake Natoma
28.3	Right on old bridge over river to circle back on other side of lake
28.6	Right at Scott St. signal, then left to continue on River Trail
28.7	Bear right on Leidesdorff St.; city of Folsom
28.9	Right on trail on west side of Folsom Blvd.
29.0	Left on River Trail
34.4	Cross under Hazel Ave. bridge; rejoin outward-bound route
57.2	Finish in Discovery Park

52 SACRAMENTO DELTA LOOP #1

Difficulty:	Moderate
Time:	3.5 to 5 hours
Distance:	56 miles
Elevation gain:	Almost flat
Best seasons:	April through October
Road conditions:	Some roads may be busy, but most are quiet. Most are narrow, with little or no shoulders. Pavement varies.

GETTING THERE: From I-80 near Fairfield, drive approximately 25 miles east on Hwy 12 to Rio Vista. Just before the Rio Vista Bridge, take the Front St. exit, then turn left on Front to small parking lot at foot of bridge.

Southwest of the city of Sacramento and northeast of San Francisco Bay lies the Sacramento–San Joaquin River Delta. It is the bathtub drain for all of California's enormous Central Valley. The Sacramento River and all of its tributary streams flow into the delta from the north, while from the south and east, all the rivers draining the Sierra come together in the San Joaquin and join the Sacramento in a vast, flat sprawl of channels and streams and sloughs meandering among myriad islands and marshes. It is the only substantial river delta in California, and its particular landscape makes for an entirely unique cycling experience.

This is one of two rides in this book that explore this special region (see also Ride 53). This is the longer of the two rides. Both can be combined into one ride of 92 miles.

The ride begins by putting your bike on your shoulder and walking up a flight of stairs, from the parking lot by a bridge to the bridge sidewalk. It's the only safe way to cross this busy bridge. East of the bridge, turn right and head south along the wide shoulder of Highway 160. After 2.5 miles, turn left on Brannan Island Road, also signed as heading to Twitchell Island. That's the last of the busy roads for a while.

Roads in the delta take two forms. They either run along the tops of the flood-control levees, next to waterways, or they travel across the low, flat farmlands behind the levees. Brannan Island is of the former sort and is a typical levee road except that it has more resorts for the boating crowd than any other road today. It runs for over 10 miles, twisting and turning to follow the course of whatever waterway the levee abuts.

That description could be repeated for every road on this loop, with the additional note that they are all essentially flat. The only changes in grade involve the modest transitions onto and off the levees.

There is not much point in describing every road and turn around this course. They are all much the same, and although it's a fairly complicated route, the mileage log does an adequate job of guiding you along. What I would rather do is discuss the general landscape and any points of interest along the way.

Excluding Rio Vista, there are four towns dotted along the route: Isleton, Walnut Grove, Locke, and Courtland. All of them share the same slightly dilapidated, laid-back look that seems a hallmark of little river towns the world over. All could be described

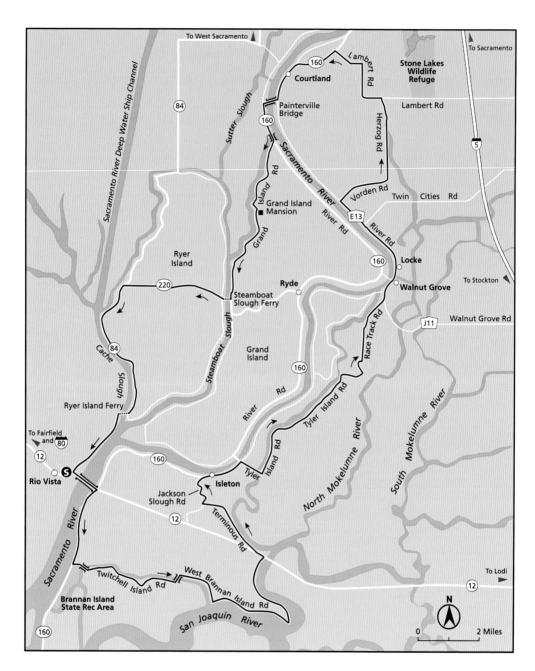

with the cliché, "a place that time forgot." No tract neighborhoods or shopping malls here. These towns are off the beaten path, and you get the impression their residents like it that way. Isleton comes up 3-plus miles

beyond Brannan Island. Walnut Grove is 11 miles farther along the route, with nothing in between but quiet, wandering lanes through the farm fields.

Walnut Grove is the biggest, busiest town

Two free ferry crossings are part of this ride through the watery world of the Sacramento River Delta.

on this ride, although still a lazy little burg, sprawled atop the levee along the main channel of the Sacramento River. Coming up at mile 26, it offers the best opportunity for a mid-ride break. Just beyond Walnut Grove is Locke. It's the smallest town out here but perhaps the most interesting. It was founded in 1915 and constructed entirely by and for the local Chinese community. It's now on the register of historic sites. You won't get the full flavor of this quaint little village if you just blow through on the highway. You need to take a loop along the town's main street, one block away. It's a fascinating place.

Another 9 miles of levees and farm fields lead to the town of Courtland, just as sleepy and laid-back as the other river towns out here. Two-and-a-half miles beyond the town, turn right over the river on the Painterville Bridge, and in another mile, cross another bridge to reach Grand Island, where a pleasant road runs for 5-plus miles along Steamboat Slough. Painterville Bridge is the spot where you could leave this route and splice onto the other, shorter delta ride (Ride 53) to create a much longer but still not-too-hard ride.

In contrast to the slightly down-at-heel towns along the route, this run along Grand Island Road offers up a number of handsome old homes overlooking the water. Most conspicuous among them is the Grand Island Mansion, a 58-room Italian Renaissance–style villa built in 1917. It now functions as a swank resort and a venue for weddings and parties on the grand scale.

With sloughs and rivers and streams on every side today, crossing them is part of what makes this ride interesting. The route crosses four significant bridges, which may at any time be raised for passing river traffic. There are two ferry crossings as well, the first of them at the south end of Grand Island. The little ferries run on a regular schedule and are free. The first ferry crosses Steamboat Slough just before mile 46 and the second one crosses Cache Slough just before mile 54. The run across Ryer Island between the two ferries features more of the same farm fields and levees that have been the bill of fare all day. After the second ferry, all that remains is a 2-mile run along the main river channel, back to Rio Vista.

0.0	Climb stairs to cross Hwy 12 bridge
0.6	Right on Hwy 160 S.
3.1	Left on Brannan Island Rd.; sign also points to Twitchell Island Rd.
3.5	Straight on Brannan Island Rd., becomes Twitchell Island Rd.
6.8	Right on West Brannan Island Rd.
13.9	Left on Hwy 12 to right on Terminous Rd.
16.2	Right on Jackson Slough Rd., becomes Jackson Blvd.
17.3	Left on Jackson Blvd.; town of Isleton
17.4	Right on 2nd St.
17.5	Jog left on C St. to right on Hwy 160 (River Rd.)
18.3	Right on West Tyler Island Bridge Rd.
19.1	Left on Tyler Island Rd.
23.8	Left on Race Track Rd.
26.2	Left on CR E13 (River Rd.) into town of Walnut Grove
27.3	Town of Locke; go off-course one block to see historic old main street
29.9	Right on Vorden Rd.
31.4	Left on Herzog Rd.
33.9	Left on Lambert Rd.
36.2	Left on Hwy 160 (River Rd.) into town of Courtland
38.9	Right on Painterville Bridge over Sacramento River; still Hwy 160
39.1	Left on Hwy 160
40.1	Bear left over bridge to right on Grand Island Rd.
42.9	Grand Island Mansion
45.6	Right to ferry over Steamboat Slough; across slough, straight ahead on Hwy 220 W. (Note: no mileage added for either ferry crossing.)
48.7	Left on Hwy 84 S.
53.4	Right to ferry over Cache Slough, then left (south) on Hwy 84 (River Rd.)
55.6	Left on North Front St., under Hwy 12 bridge; town of Rio Vista
55.7	Left into parking lot and finish

53 SACRAMENTO DELTA LOOP #2

Difficulty:	Easy/moderate
Time:	2 to 3 hours
Distance:	32 miles
Elevation gain:	Almost flat
Best seasons:	Spring and fall
Road conditions:	Most roads are low traffic. Most are well paved.

GETTING THERE: From I-5 south of Sacramento, take exit 512 for Pocket Rd., also marked "TO FREEPORT, HWY 160." Head west on Pocket Rd. about a quarter mile, then south on Hwy 160 to town of Freeport. Park in the gravel lot next to Freeport Bridge.

This is the second of two rides in the Sacramento–San Joaquin River Delta, southwest of Sacramento. For a little background on the Delta, see Ride 52. All of the general observations about the region mentioned there apply here as well. About the only difference between the two rides, aside from distance, is that while the other ride includes some moderately busy roads, this one is entirely on quiet, low traffic roads. Both can be combined into a 92-mile tour. These are quality bike adventures: not too hard (virtually flat throughout), consistently quiet and scenic, and unique. There is nothing else in Northern California quite like these Delta rides. I think of them as Levee Heaven.

Begin this one by crossing the Sacramento River on Freeport Bridge and turning right, north along the levee road next to the river.

The broad river will be on your right all the way to the next turn onto Babel Slough Road, a quiet, shady lane along a smaller tributary stream. This too is a levee road, with a dense canopy of trees overhanging the meandering lane. Out beyond the roadside trees are flat vineyards, produce fields, orchards and pastures. In general, this scenic mix stays constant throughout the ride.

Two straight, section-line roads follow: Highway 84, heading due south, and Willow Point Road, heading east into the town of Clarksburg. Coming up at 11 miles, Clarksburg is the only town on this ride. A few blocks of town streets will take you in one side of town and out the other, but you might want to stop at the Old Sugar Mill, a large brick refinery that has been reborn as a tourist destination, with shops and food and wine

Nestled behind the levees in the Sacramento River Delta are thousands of acres of prime vineyards.

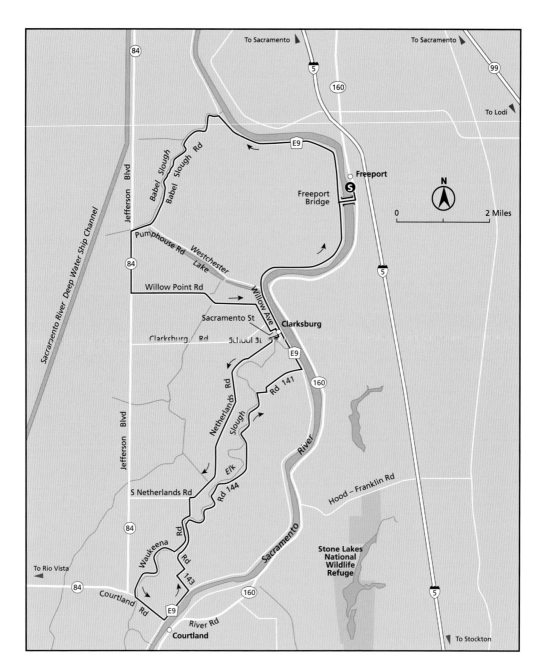

tasting. (Vineyards are a big deal in this part of the delta. You will be seeing them and their consort wineries all day.)

Leave Clarksburg on Netherlands Road, amid more vineyards and handsome old estates. Then, 4 miles on, turn left on Waukeena Road. This little lane climbs from the flat fields back up onto a levee, if you can call 20' up a climb. This levee runs along Elk Slough, bigger than Babel Slough but smaller than the main river channel. Waukeena hugs the sleepy slough for most of 3 miles—as quiet and out of the way as a road can be—before teeing into Courtland Road, which takes you back to the Sacramento River, briefly. When you tee into South River Road (County Road E9), you are about a mile north of Painterville Bridge, which is on the route of the other Delta ride. This is the easy, obvious spot for linking the two routes together.

After just a short section heading north along the river, turn left onto Road 143, which becomes 144 and 141 as it meanders back north along the opposite bank of Elk Slough. This side of the slough is the same as the other side (on Waukeena): a tiny levee road following the bends of the waterway, with the slough on the left, trees overhead, vineyards on the right, and no traffic anywhere.

Eventually the road drops off the levee and heads back across the fields to the next levee over: back to the one along the main channel of the Sacramento. This slightly busier highway—still fairly light on traffic—will finish off the route with 5 miles alongside the big river, back past Clarksburg and on up to Freeport Bridge, where the ride began.

MILEAGE LOG

0.0	South on Hwy 160, out of town of Freeport
0.1	Right across Freeport Bridge
0.2	Right on CR E9
3.8	Left on Babel Slough Rd.
6.8	Straight on Pumphouse Rd.
7.2	Left on Hwy 84 (also known as Jefferson Blvd.)
8.4	Left on Willow Point Rd.
11.0	Right on Willow Ave.; town of Clarksburg
11.7	Left on Sacramento St.
11.8	Right on School St.
11.9	Right on Netherlands Rd.
16.0	Left on Waukeena Rd.
18.9	Left on Courtland Rd.
19.7	Left on CR E9 (also known as South River Rd.)
20.5	Left on Road 143
21.4	Becomes Road 144
25.9	Right to continue on Road 144 (now also known as Road 141)
27.1	Left on CR E9
31.9	Right across Freeport Bridge
32.0	Left on Hwy 160; finish near Freeport Bridge

GOLD COUNTRY

In their frenzied search for gold, the Forty-Niners left some treasures behind: a densely tangled network of tiny roads through the gorgeous Sierra foothills, and scores of quaint old Gold Rush boomtowns, which now serve as the dots in our connect-the-dots voyages of discovery through this almost-perfect cycling landscape.

54 LUNCH IN NEVADA CITY

Difficulty:	Challenging
Time:	6 hours
Distance:	68 miles
Elevation gain:	Up to 5600'
Best seasons:	May through October

GETTING THERE: From I-80 at Auburn, drive 10 miles north on Hwy 49 to the Combie Rd. junction. Turn right on Combie and park in the CVS Drugs lot (or nearby).

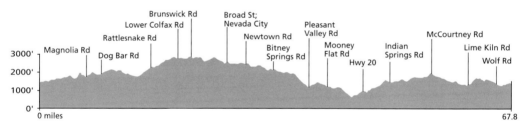

To complete this ride—and to have fun doing it—you will need to be comfortable with climbing and descending, and you will need to be handy with maps and mileage logs. But the effort put in on the hill work and the navigation should reward you with a great ride.

Combie Road begins amid the commercial clutter of shopping centers but quickly works its way out into more pleasant country scenery. It dodges around the edge of a housing development and golf course and then becomes Dark Horse Drive, a hilly scramble through a high-end housing tract, with enormous trophy homes back in the hills. Two little lanes at the end of Dark Horse connect to Magnolia Road, which becomes Dog Bar Road, as you head up into the foothills through a rural, wooded landscape.

The roads tilt uphill until Nevada City at mile 27, except for a rolling, downhill run between miles 10 and 14 and a few other, shorter dips. The biggest climb begins at mile 14.4 and carries on for 5 miles, gaining 1000', first on Dog Bar and then on Rattlesnake Road, always in the dappled shade of mixed forest. Just as the climb on Rattlesnake eases off, turn right on Lower Colfax Road.

This is on the outskirts of the city of Grass

Valley. To avoid suburban congestion, the route takes a circuitous, complicated dodge around the town, with twelve road changes in the 7 miles from here to Nevada City. I'm sorry to have to do this to you, but it's the best route through this maze. It's what local cyclists use. Some of the roads are quite pleasant and some less so. But they get you where you need to go.

So let's leap forward and catch up with the route as it homes in on Nevada City. You approach the town along Sacramento Street, passing The Tour of Nevada City Bicycle Shop, a regular port-of-call for riders in this area. Bear left on Pine and head steeply downhill to a creek, over the quaint old bridge, and uphill into quaint old Nevada City. This is one of the best preserved and most picturesque of

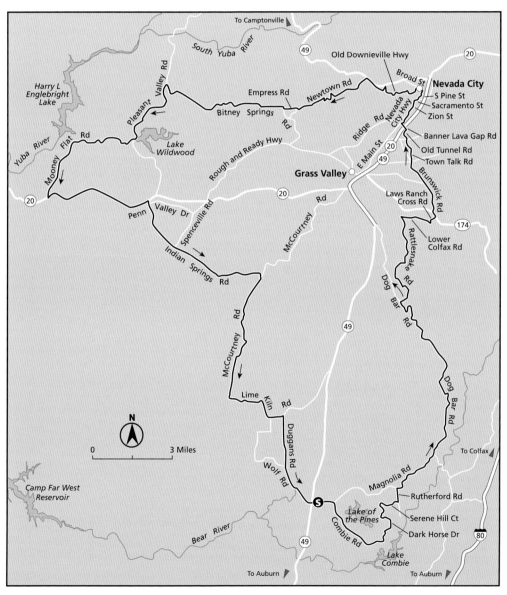

Bitney Springs Road meanders through a classic California foothills landscape of old oaks and golden meadows.

all the Gold Country boomtowns, with block after hilly block of exquisite gingerbread Victorian homes and storefronts. That's both the good news and the bad news: it is charming, but it is also often thronged with tourists.

The town has added interest for cyclists: it's the home of the Nevada City Classic, a prestigious pro bike race, which traces a hilly, challenging circuit through the old town. Established in 1960, it has been won by many famous pros. If you are going to take a lunch break here—highly recommended—you may discover colorful racing memorabilia in the local shops.

After lunch, the best bike route out of town is Old Downieville Highway, a tiny byway through the woods. After a brief bit of busy Hwy 49, turn left on Newtown Road, which marks the start of nearly 9 miles of almost constant descending, continuing from Newtown onto Empress and Bitney Springs roads. "Almost" is the key word: there are at least five little uphills on that run, but aside from those bumps, it is downhill and sometimes extravagantly so. In particular, Bitney Springs drops 750' in 2 hectic miles. The scenery, if you can spare it a glance while carving down the hillside, is as pretty as it can be: a mix of rocky meadows and pine, fir, and oak woods. Although the roads are remote and rustic, pavement is excellent.

When the wild descent ends, turn left on Pleasant Valley Road, climb a small hill, and descend past Lake Wildwood, a reservoir with a planned resort community around it. Turn right, away from the resort, on Mooney Flat Road, one of the best roads of the day. Roll up and down across the grassy hillside, then boogie downhill for a mile and a half through the woods, similar to the crazy-steep thrills on Bitney Springs. At the bottom of that free fall at mile 45, you hit the lowest elevation on the ride, about 2200' below the high point. The next 11 miles will be mostly uphill, although always gently and with a few little dips and flats mixed in.

At the end of Mooney Flat, turn left on Hwy 20. There is a small store at this corner where you can refill your bottles. Hwy 20 is busy, but a recent repaving has added enormous shoulders, nearly as wide as full lanes. Turn right off Hwy 20 on Penn Valley and right again on Indian Springs Road, climbing gently, all the way to McCourtney Road. This begins one of the best descents of the day: 5 miles of slinky curves and silky pavement, with just one little uphill blip to interrupt the fun. So far down the hillside now, we've left the pines and firs of the high country behind and are back into the classic foothills landscape of grassy meadows and scattered oaks.

McCourtney flows directly into Lime Kiln Road and—yikes!—tilts back uphill in a wicked pitch of over a mile. That's what I meant at the beginning about this ride: a ruggedly chunky topography that keeps coming at you, all day long. Never assume you're done climbing until you climb into your car at the finish. But then, you wouldn't have done this ride if you didn't like climbing, right?

MILEAGE LOG

0.0	From CVS parking lot, right on Combie Rd.
0.7	Right on Combie Rd. at Magnolia Rd. junction
3.3	Straight on Dark Horse Dr.
6.0	Straight on Serene Hill Ct.
6.2	Left on Rutherford Rd.
6.7	Right on Magnolia Rd.
8.8	Bear left on Dog Bar Rd.
16.1	Right on Rattlesnake Rd.
20.1	Right on Lower Colfax Rd.
21.4	Left on Laws Ranch Cross Rd.
21.6	Left on Hwy 174
21.8	Right on Brunswick Rd.
24.5	Right on Town Talk Rd.
24.9	Right on Old Tunnel Rd.
25.3	Left on Banner Lava Gap Rd.
25.4	Right on Nevada City Hwy
25.8	Cross Ridge Rd. to straight on Zion St.
26.4	Right on Sacramento St.
26.6	Left on S. Pine St.; tour of Nevada City Bicycle Shop
27.0	Left on Broad St.; town of Nevada City
27.2	Left on Bennett St.
27.3	Left on Monroe St.
27.6	Straight on Old Downieville Hwy
29.3	Left on Hwy 49
29.7	Left on Newtown Rd.
33.1	Right on Empress Rd.
33.7	Right on Bitney Springs Rd.
38.7	Left on Pleasant Valley Rd.
41.3	Right on Mooney Flat Rd.
46.5	Left on Hwy 20
49.9	Right on Penn Valley Dr.

50.7	Right on Indian Springs Rd.
56.3	Right on McCourtney Rd.
61.5	Straight on Lime Kiln Rd.
63.8	Right on Duggans Rd.
65.7	Left on Wolf Rd.
67.6	Cross Hwy 49 to Combie Rd.
67.8	Finish

55 IOWA HILL–FORESTHILL LOOP

Difficulty:	Epic
Time:	4.5 to 6 hours
Distance:	55 miles
Elevation gain:	7500'
Best seasons:	May through September
Road conditions:	Traffic varies but should not be too bad. Pavement varies but is usually decent.

GETTING THERE: On I-80 2 miles north of central Auburn, take the Foresthill exit. Turn right and immediately left on Lincoln Way, then right into shopping center parking lot.

This ride of 55 miles might seem a little short to earn the "epic" rating in this book. And in fact, almost all of it would be considered merely "challenging" were it not for one section of less than 2 miles. That's the climb out of the canyon of the American River on Iowa Hill Road. I'll talk about that in more detail when we get there.

The ride begins with a few miles of roads heading north near the interstate. There is one tricky corner at mile 2.7: the right on Lake Arthur Road. The sign at the junction says "DRY CREEK ROAD." That's actually the road to the left; although it doesn't say it on the street signs, the road to the right is Lake Arthur. At mile 4, tiny Pinewood Way turns away from I-80 and up into the hills. It cuts over to Placer Hills Road, which will carry you farther up into the piney woods for almost 10 miles, climbing very gently. Tokayana Way continues in the same vein—essentially the

same road—until you make a right on Rising Sun Street and descend into the town of Colfax. At mile 16, this makes a good spot for topping up your water.

On the far side of Colfax, cross under I-80, turn south on Canyon Way, and then turn left on Iowa Hill Road. At about mile 17, you have arrived at the reason why this ride is in the book. Iowa Hill is legendary among hardcore riders, and for sure, you have to be pretty hardcore to even consider tackling it. Look at the profile and notice the deep cleft between miles 17 and 21.5: that's the canyon of the North Fork American River, and it's quite the biking adventure. The descent is just shy of 3 miles and is about as much fun as a downhill can be, all wiggly S-bends and hairpins through the woods. It's just a lane-and-a-half wide, with no stripes, but the pavement is quite good. It's steep, but not so steep as to be scary.

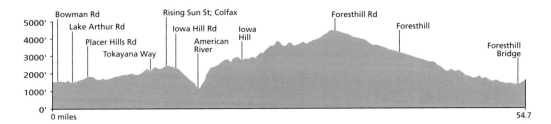

At the bottom, a new bridge crosses the wild river next to the rickety old suspension bridge that used to be in service here. You can still walk across the old span. Just beyond the bridge, the road tilts up into the ferocious ascent that earns this loop its "epic" rating. It gains 1200' in 1.8 miles as it claws its way up the rocky canyon wall. That's an average of 13 percent for almost 2 miles, but it's worse than that, with spots that approach 20 percent. It is *soooo* hard! Personally, I remember being absolutely maxed out on the steepest part, beginning to wonder if I would have to put

a foot down and rest a bit. But then, just at the worst, steepest, most leg-breaking, lung-baking moment of crisis, the grade eased off just the slightest bit, and I was able to sit back down and recover, if only for a few yards. That's nearly at the top of the nasty section. Just around the bend, it eases off considerably, and that easing ushers in over 17 miles of relatively easy uphill rollers. It's still a good workout, but nothing like those first 2 miles up from the river.

In the midst of this rolling uphill, you hit the sleepy village of Iowa Hill at mile 26, one

Yes, Iowa Hill Road, climbing out of the canyon of the American River, really is that steep.

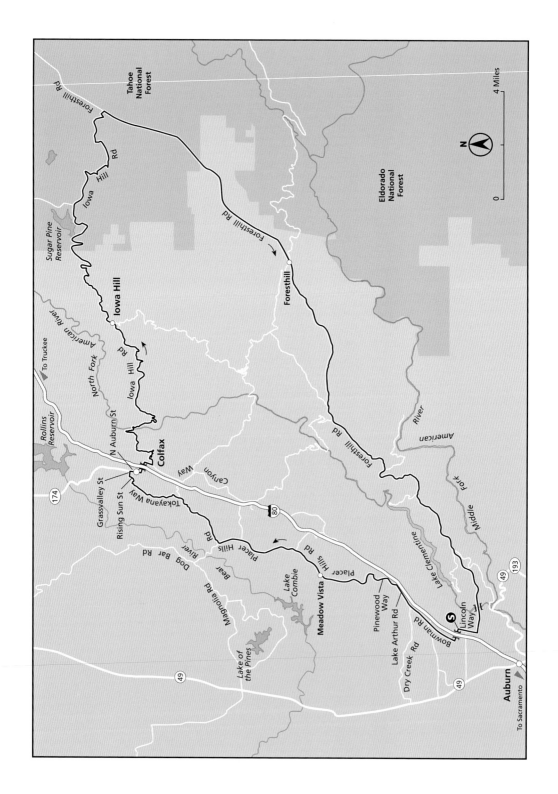

Tahoe National Forest

Eldorado National Forest

N

4 Miles

0

Foresthill Rd

Iowa Hill Rd

Sugar Pine Reservoir

Iowa Hill

American River

To Truckee

North Fork

Iowa Hill Rd

Foresthill Rd

Foresthill

Rollins Reservoir

N Auburn St

Colfax

Grassvalley St

Rising Sun St

Tokayana Way

Canyon Way

174

80

Dog Bar Rd

Bear River Rd

Placer Hills Rd

Magnolia Rd

Lake Combie

Lake of the Pines

Meadow Vista

Placer Hills Rd

Lake Clementine

American River

Middle Fork

49

193

Pinewood Way

Lake Arthur Rd

Bowman Rd

Dry Creek Rd

Lincoln Way

49

Auburn

To Sacramento

of the most primitive settlements this side of Appalachia. You can almost hear the dueling banjos off in the trees. This is really deep in the pine forest wilderness, and the town is entirely appropriate to its middle-of-nowhere setting, with just a few ramshackle structures, including a rustic store where you can find refreshments and a friendly word with the proprietor.

The gentle uphill run, with a few small downhill bits mixed in, continues almost to the next turn: a right on Foresthill Road at mile 38.6. You will be on this road all the way to the finish, and almost all of that 26-mile run will be downhill, losing 3200' along the way. Those numbers sound grand, but in fact it works out to a lazy grade of about 2 percent. The larger town of Foresthill comes up at mile 47, and if you didn't stop in Iowa Hill, you certainly should stop here.

Foresthill Road is a bigger, more modern road than Iowa Hill, with two wide lanes and big shoulders. It carries a fair amount of traffic, but is okay for bikes. It's not nearly as dramatic and exciting as Iowa Hill, but is a good road for closing the loop and for easing back down from the hardcore extremes of the earlier miles. It does have some drama, though. There is, first of all, the crossing of the Foresthill Bridge: at 731' above the Middle Fork American River, the highest bridge in California and fourth highest in the United States. (Quite a view over the side!) Then, beyond the bridge, there is one last little climb back to Lincoln Way and the finish. It's only half a mile but is double-digit steep. After all the lazy, downhill miles, it comes as a bit of a shock, right before the finish. Perhaps it will refresh your memory about the really brutal climb on Iowa Hill. That is, after all, the most significant impression you will take home from this ride. It's a fine ride, from start to finish, but it's those 5 miles in the American River canyon that will really define this journey.

MILEAGE LOG

0.0	From shoping center parking lot, right (north) on Lincoln Way
0.6	Left on Bowman Undercrossing, under I-80
0.8	Right on Bowman Rd.
2.7	Right on Lake Arthur Rd. (Sign at turn says "DRY CREEK ROAD," but that is the road to the left.)
4.0	Left on Pinewood Way
4.8	Left on Placer Hills Rd.
6.6	Community of Meadow Vista
13.5	Continue straight on Tokayana Way
15.6	Right on Rising Sun St.
15.9	Right on Grassvalley St.; town of Colfax
16.2	Bear right on Auburn St.
16.5	Left on Hwy 174, over I-80
16.6	Right on Canyon Way
16.9	Left on Iowa Hill Rd.
19.8	Cross North Fork American River
26.0	Town of Iowa Hill
38.6	Right on Foresthill Rd.
47.5	Town of Foresthill
53.7	Cross Middle Fork American River on Foresthill Bridge
54.7	Right on Lincoln Way, right into parking lot and finish

56 THE MOTHER LODE LOOPS

Difficulty:	Challenging
Time:	4.5 to 6 hours
Distance:	61 or 66 miles
Elevation gain:	5800' or 6500'
Best seasons:	April through October; midsummer can be hot
Road conditions:	Some of the main highways can be quite busy. Most have at least some shoulders. Some of the smaller roads are steep and narrow. Pavement is generally good.

GETTING THERE: From Hwy 50 at Shingle Springs, take North Shingle Rd., Green Valley Rd., and Lotus Rd. north 11.4 miles to Hwy 49. Turn right and go 0.6 mile to Marshall Gold Discovery State Historic Park parking lot.

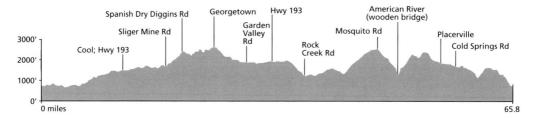

I might refer to this as the definitive Gold Country ride, if only because it starts and ends at Marshall Gold Discovery State Historic Park, the place where gold was first found in the tailrace of Sutter's Mill on the American River in 1848, one of the true tipping points in American history. But the ride also embodies all the classic Gold Country elements: pretty, wooded foothills; deep, steep-sided canyons; quaint pioneer towns; and, most of all, tiny, wickedly hilly roads. This loop includes the best parts of the Motherlode Century, staged each year in mid-May.

The first 17-plus miles are on Highways 49 and 193. Although scenic in the classic California foothills manner, these are main highways—especially Hwy 49—and carry a good bit of traffic. But they are still acceptable for bikes, usually with decent shoulders.

Both the longer and shorter options branch off from Hwy 193. The shorter route turns right off the highway onto Greenwood Road at mile 18.3. This quiet road descends lazily for 2 miles, climbs 400' in the next 2 miles, and finally descends to a junction with Marshall Road near the village of Garden Valley, where it rejoins the long route, saving exactly 5 miles.

The longer, hillier option turns left off Hwy 193 onto Sliger Mine Road at mile 17.5. This tiny lane climbs 200' in 2 miles and then joins Spanish Dry Diggins Road, which bumps up and down along a wooded ridgeline in a series of twisting, dancing gyrations that altogether may add another 600' of climb and an equal measure of frisky little descents before teeing back into Hwy 193. Turn left and roll uphill to the village of Georgetown, a well-preserved Gold Rush treasure. I've included a two-block detour for exploring the town. After

The rustic, wooden suspension bridge over the American River gorge is one of the marquee attractions on this spectacular, hilly loop. (Rick Gunn)

that diversion, take Main Street to a left onto Marshall Road and enjoy 4 miles of slinky descending through the trees to Garden Valley, where the short route rejoins.

Turn left on Garden Valley Road and roll along through pretty forest and meadows for most of 5 miles to a right on another section of Hwy 193. After 2 almost level miles, the well-paved highway plunges into a deep canyon, snaking down the hillside in a 2-mile tangle of kinked-up hairpins. Stay alert for the left onto little Rock Creek Road. It's well marked, but it comes up in the midst of that fast, frantic downhill.

Rock Creek and Mosquito roads will be your home for the next 19 miles, and these two little roads may be the best or at least most extraordinary miles of the loop. Narrow, twisty, and remote, they offer a real walk on the wild side. Rock Creek begins with 4 slightly uphill miles, descends 1.5 miles to a quaint old bridge over a rocky gorge, and finally climbs 1200' in 4 miles to a scattered,

rural subdivision, complete with an airstrip and a fire station around mile 47 (a good spot for water). Just beyond the airstrip, turn right on Mosquito Road and get ready for a wild ride: 1200' down in 3 miles, with most of the last mile over 15 percent, stacked up in a series of tight, cliff-hanging hairpins. As thrilling as this corkscrew squiggle may be, it is upstaged by what happens in the bottom of this rocky canyon: a crossing of the spectacular American River on a wooden, one-lane suspension bridge. You will want to stop and admire this antiquated wonder. It's special.

Being at the bottom of a deep gorge, you can guess what comes next: almost 1000' up in 2 miles, with some of it well over 10 percent. A short descent and a short climb follow. Finally, after all that work, you are rewarded with a 2-mile descent to the town of Placerville. This is another Gold Rush boomtown with an interesting old downtown but a sprawl of commercial clutter around its perimeter. A short run on the El Dorado Trail bike route

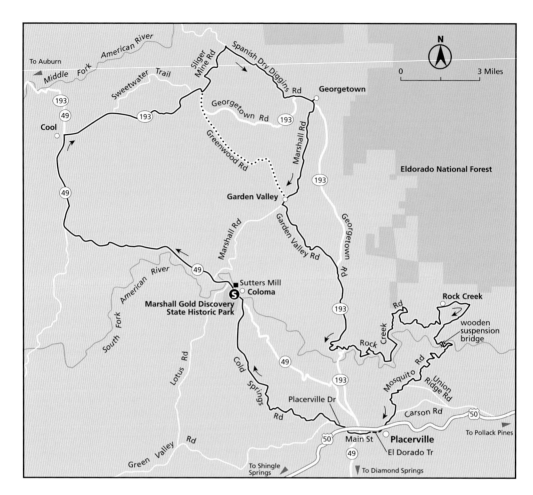

avoids some of that, and then you cruise downhill along the historic main drag and out the west end of town on Placerville Drive.

A little uphill bump and a swift, 2-mile downhill deliver you to a right on Cold Springs Road and the last real climb of the day: 500' up in a mile, now well clear of the Placerville suburbs. After that, Cold Springs rolls along the ridge through broadleaf forest and meadows, eventually toppling down the hillside in one last, fast descent to Hwy 49, Coloma, and the Marshall Gold Discovery State Historic Park where this rollicking adventure began. Once you've stowed the bike and put on some walking shoes, take the time to explore Sutter's Mill and contemplate what happened here, and what it has meant to the history of California and America.

MILEAGE LOG

0.0 From Marshall Gold Discovery State Historic Park , go north on Hwy 49

11.3 Right on Hwy 193 near the town of Cool

17.5 Left on Sliger Mine Rd.; short route stays on Hwy 193

Short route:
17.5   **Straight on Hwy 193**
18.3   **Right on Greenwood Rd.**
23.3   **Right on Marshall Rd.; rejoin long route (see mile 28.7)**
19.8   Right on Spanish Dry Diggins Rd.
23.4   Left on Georgetown Rd. (Hwy 193)
24.1   Left on Main St. into village of Georgetown
24.3   Turn around, retrace Main St. out of town
24.5   Left on Marshall Rd.
28.7   Left on Garden Valley Rd.; short route rejoins here
32.3   Right on Hwy 193
36.8   Left on Rock Creek Rd.
47.1   Right on Mosquito Rd.
49.9   At bottom of steep descent, cross American River on wooden suspension bridge
53.6   Right to stay on Mosquito Rd. at Union Ridge Rd. junction
55.5   Right to stay on Mosquito Rd. at Dimity Ln. junction
55.8   Bear right on Mosquito Rd., then immediately...
55.8   Jog right on Locust Ave. to left on El Dorado Trail (signed as bike route)
56.2   Jog left on Clay St. to right on Main St.; downtown Placerville
57.1   Becomes Placerville Dr.
57.8   Right on Cold Springs Rd.
65.5   Left on Hwy 49
65.8   Finish at Marshall Gold Discovery State Historic Park

57 PLYMOUTH–EL DORADO LOOPS

Difficulty:	Challenging
Time:	3.5 to 5.5 hours
Distance:	40 or 57 miles
Elevation gain:	4000' to 5000'
Best seasons:	Spring and fall
Road conditions:	Hwy 49 can be quite busy. Other roads are mostly remote and quiet. Pavement is generally good.

GETTING THERE: In Sacramento, exit Hwy 50 and drive 31 miles east on Hwy 16 and then 3.5 miles north on Hwy 49 to town of Plymouth. Turn left on Main St. and left on Locust St. Park near Amador County Fairgrounds or Plymouth Elementary School.

This is a classic California foothills ride, out at the western edge of the rolling hills tumbling down from the Sierra. Any farther west, and you'd be in the sprawling Central Valley; any farther east, and the hills would become mountains. It stages out of the town of Plymouth. Founded in 1871, it's not one of the most interesting of the Gold Country

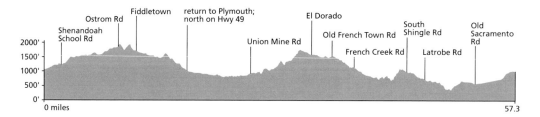

2000'
1500'
1000'
500'
0'

Shenandoah School Rd
Ostrom Rd
Fiddletown
return to Plymouth; north on Hwy 49
El Dorado
Old French Town Rd
South Shingle Rd
Old Sacramento Rd
Union Mine Rd
French Creek Rd
Latrobe Rd

0 miles
57.3

towns, although it does have some charm. But it's attractive for cyclists because of the many good biking roads in the nearby hills. The Sacramento Wheelmen's popular Sierra Century begins and ends at the fairgrounds, following roads we use on this ride and also on Rides 58 and 59.

There are two loops to this ride, joined near the start in Plymouth. Skipping the little loop would be easy to do, but I hope you won't, as those miles are some of the best of the day. To begin that small loop, head east out of Plymouth, crossing Highway 49 to Shenandoah Road and heading uphill. Just past mile 2, turn right on Shenandoah School Road and discover the Shenandoah Valley's main attraction: wineries. Vineyards and wineries

have been a part of this region almost since the Gold Rush, and there are vines here that are among the oldest in the state. The warm climate lends itself to the production of big, robust Zinfandels. For the next 7 miles, vineyards will dominate the landscape, as you meander through this pretty, peaceful valley.

By the time you turn onto Ostrom Road at mile 9, most of the vineyards are behind you and the scenery shifts back to the more typical foothills landscape: grassy meadows and oak woods. Ostrom begins with two short climbs sandwiched around a plunge into the little canyon of Big Indian Creek. These twin summits represent the high point of the ride and are about 1000' higher than the start in Plymouth. Most, but not all, of the miles to

Riding along Ostrom Road, in the hills above Shenandoah Valley (Linda Fluhrer)

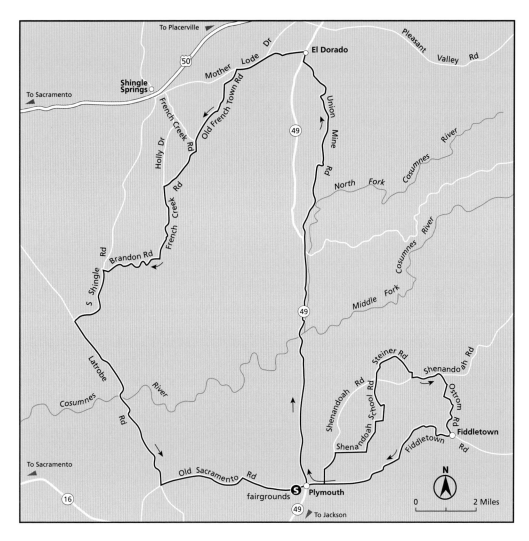

this point have been mildly uphill. Beyond that summit are 11 mostly downhill miles, beginning with one fast, twisty mile to the quaint village of Fiddletown. After turning right on Fiddletown Road, there are 3 miles of gentle descending, a half-mile climb, and then 2.5 miles of fast, smooth free fall back to Plymouth, closing out the little loop at 17 miles. Think about food and water here: you won't have another shot at them until El Dorado at mile 32.

Now you head north for 8 miles on Hwy 49, the main artery through the Gold Country. It has excellent pavement and pleasant scenery and is nearly level as it rolls along the wooded valley of the Cosumnes River. It's a fine road except for the volume of traffic it may carry. Sometimes it has shoulders but more often not. I recommend doing this ride on a weekday to avoid the heaviest tourist traffic.

At mile 25, turn onto Union Mine Road and escape whatever traffic there might have been on the main highway. This byway is an excellent cycling road: no traffic and pretty scenery. It climbs 800' in 5.5 miles. Most of that is easy, but there are two short, steep pitches, each followed by a little dip. When you top out on this road, you're into the residential fringe of the town of El Dorado. Turn right on Hwy 49 and roll down to the center of town, which isn't much of a place. There is a mini-mart here, and it's the last spot you can replenish your munchies for the rest of the ride (25 miles to go).

The next 2 miles along Pleasant Valley Road and Mother Lode Drive are the least scenic of the loop: a ragged straggle of commercial clutter. It's unavoidable but soon over, and when you turn onto Old French Town Road, you'll appreciate why I asked you to put up with those 2 messy miles. This is the reward: 9 miles of purest bike heaven along Old French Town, French Creek, and Brandon roads. The first 7.5 miles are mostly downhill in the nicest sort of way: steep enough to be fun but not white-knuckle. No traffic, decent pavement, dream-like beauty, and all of it scaled to the speed of a bike. It's dang near perfect.

There is a 1-mile, 400' climb on Brandon to wake your legs up again, but then the downhill fun resumes, with 6 miles along Brandon, South Shingle, and Latrobe roads, culminating in a speedy flier down to another crossing of the Cosumnes River. Of course that lands you in the bottom of the canyon, needing to climb back out. Latrobe tilts up at about 5 percent for a mile before easing off into false flats—up and down—before you turn onto Old Sacramento Road for the last run back to Plymouth. Latrobe is a faster, wider, more modern road, but Old Sacramento is what the name implies: an older, quieter road, with all those nicer touches we enjoy on better biking back roads. It climbs—mildly, painlessly—all the way to the town, where you can climb off the bike and take your appetite in search of a well-earned late lunch.

MILEAGE LOG

0.0	From Amador County Fairgrounds, north on Locust St.
0.1	Right on Main St.
0.5	Cross Hwy 49 to Shenandoah Rd.
2.1	Right on Shenandoah School Rd.
6.0	Cross Shenandoah Rd. to Steiner Rd.
8.0	Left on Shenandoah Rd.
9.0	Right on Ostrom Rd.
11.4	Right on Jibboom St. in village of Fiddletown
11.5	Right on Fiddletown Rd.
17.2	Right on Hwy 49 in town of Plymouth
25.1	Right on Union Mine Rd.
32.1	Right on Hwy 49 in town of El Dorado
32.3	Left on Pleasant Valley Rd.
33.5	Left on Mother Lode Dr.
34.7	Left on Old French Town Rd.
37.4	Left on French Creek Rd.
41.9	Right on Brandon Rd.
44.0	Left on South Shingle Rd.
46.2	Left on Latrobe Rd.
52.5	Left on Old Sacramento Rd.
57.1	Right on Locust St. in town of Plymouth
57.3	Finish at fairgrounds

58 FIDDLETOWN LOOPS

Difficulty:	Challenging
Time:	3.5 to 5 hours
Distance:	47 or 51 miles
Elevation gain:	4000' or 4500'
Best seasons:	Late spring and fall
Road conditions:	Pavement varies but is mostly decent. Traffic is light for most of the ride.

GETTING THERE: From Hwy 49 at Plymouth, head east 6 miles on Shenandoah Rd. and Fiddletown Rd. to Fiddletown. Park anywhere.

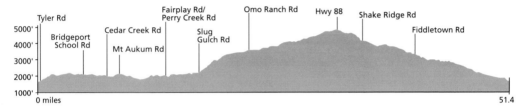

A few miles uphill from Highway 49 at Plymouth, the little village of Fiddletown slumbers in the woods. This rustic hamlet looks much as it must have over 100 years ago: a few stores and houses in the classic Old West style, including a kooky general store where you can get just about anything, as long as it's odd. The town is the site of a rest stop on the Sierra Century, a popular, early-summer ride, and this loop makes use of the some of the best roads from that event.

The ride begins by climbing out of Fiddletown on Tyler Road. For the next 9 miles, it wanders through the wooded hills on three narrow, up-and-down lanes serving thinly settled backcountry. It's a perfect venue for cycling: peaceful, attractive, and low traffic. At the end of this back-road reverie, turn right on busier Mount Aukum Road and roll up to the spot where the long and short routes diverge.

First, let's follow the short route to the point where the two routes rejoin. It's an easy tale to tell: Omo Ranch Road, all the way. For 9 miles, the road climbs into the Sierra foothills, gaining 1500'. That's only a 3 percent average, but the real-world climb varies from flat and even a little downhill to as much as 8 percent. Scenery includes vineyards and pastures at the bottom and solid forest higher up. The wide spot in the road that maps label as Omo Ranch has very little there beyond a few buildings and a school where you might find water.

The long route continues north on Mount Aukum Road, dropping briefly into a pastoral valley and then climbing to a junction with Fairplay Road. There is a small store at this corner. Turn right on Fairplay and immediately left onto Perry Creek Road, a little lane through the woods. It drops into a creek canyon and then begins climbing. A little over 3 miles into the uphill, turn left on Slug Gulch Road.

In comparing the long and short routes, the mileage and elevation numbers don't really do justice to the difference between

The sleepy village of Fiddletown hasn't changed much since the gold mines played out. (Linda Fluhrer)

them: just 4.5 miles and 500'. Hidden behind the numbers is the way those extra miles and feet are acquired: steeply. Slug Gulch is where "steeply" happens. This road is notorious in the cycling world, with a funky reputation to match its funky name. In the first 3.3 miles, it scrambles up a series of intimidating walls, gaining 1300'. That's a 7 percent average, but the steepest pitches are well up into double digits. When the Sierra Century goes up it, course workers are waiting at the top to present each gasping, wheezing rider with a medal that says, "I TAMED SLUG GULCH!"

After the steep section, the Slug shows some mercy, with only a few uphill rollers in the final 2 miles to the junction with Omo Ranch Road, where the routes rejoin. But don't congratulate yourself too soon on having beaten this hill: that is far from the end of the work. Omo Ranch continues to climb to the tune of another 1300' spread over nearly 10 miles of steady grade. Now you're really up in the

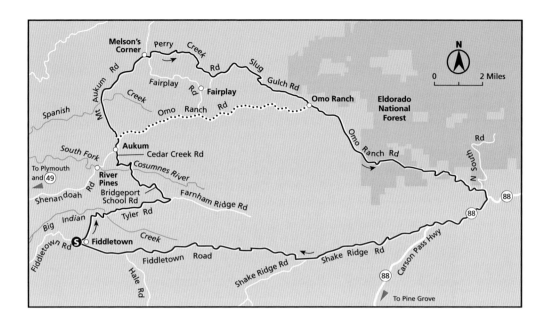

mountains—up to 4844'—and the scenery has an almost alpine quality to it, with a tidy understory of fragrant bear's clover beneath a soaring canopy of fir, pine, and cedar. Most of the time you're closed in among the trees, but occasionally you catch a vista out over distant, forested ridges.

Finally—near mile 32—you come to the end of all the climbing, and it's almost all downhill from here. Aside from one modest climb, the final 19 miles are all downhill excitement, beginning with a high-speed screamer down Hwy 88. This is a major highway—rolling down from Carson Pass—with the potential for heavy traffic. But there is a wide shoulder, and if you want to, you can bomb through these 3 miles almost as fast as the cars. It's wide open and beautifully paved. When I've toured here (twice), I've done this

fast, smooth descent absolutely car-free…the whole wide road, all to myself.

In the midst of that free fall, stay alert for a right onto Shake Ridge Road. Now you're back on dinky, two-lane byways for the duration. Shake Ridge begins with a mile-plus of speedy downhill, and after that one little uphill at mile 37, you'll drop 2300' in almost 14 miles on Shake Ridge and Fiddletown roads. All of it is perfect for a bike: steep enough to pile on a good turn of speed, but not steep enough to require much braking; flowing back and forth through endless S-bends, all well banked and well paved, and all through a pretty forest of leafy trees, with hardly a car on the road. This is cycling at the highest, purest level: transcendent bliss achieved through kinetic poetry. For me, this pretty well defines why I ride a bike.

MILEAGE LOG

0.0   From Fiddletown Rd., north on Tyler Rd.
5.0   Left on Bridgeport School Rd.
7.7   Left on Cedar Creek Rd.
9.0   Right on Mount Aukum Rd.

Short route:

| 9.4 | **Right on Omo Ranch Rd.** |
| 18.4 | **Bear right on Omo Ranch Rd.; rejoin long route (see mile 22.9)** |

14.0	Right on Fairplay Rd.
14.1	Left on Perry Creek Rd.
17.6	Left on Slug Gulch Rd.
22.9	Left on Omo Ranch Rd.; rejoin short route
32.5	Right on Hwy 88
35.3	Right on Shake Ridge Rd.
41.0	Right on Fiddletown Rd.
51.4	Finish in town of Fiddletown

59 SUTTER CREEK FIGURE-8

Difficulty:	Moderate/challenging
Time:	3 to 5 hours
Distance:	50 miles
Elevation gain:	4500'
Best seasons:	Spring and fall
Road conditions:	Pavement varies but is mostly decent. Traffic is light for most of the ride.

GETTING THERE: From Jackson, head north 3.2 miles on Hwy 49. Turn right on Old Hwy 49 to Sutter Creek. Turn right on Church St. and park at Minnie Provis Park.

This ride consists of two loops of 28 and 22 miles, with the town of Sutter Creek at the hub. Sutter Creek is one of the most interesting and attractive of the Mother Lode boomtowns. Over $40 million in gold was pulled out of the mines here, and when the gold ran out, the town continued to prosper with a lively lumber industry. Through good luck and good planning, it has preserved the best of its charming downtown core, where second- and third-floor balconies on the ornate Victorian storefronts overhang not only the sidewalks, but the narrow main street as well, giving the town an especially quaint, old-world look. Highway 49, the busy main road through the Gold Country, used to run right down this narrow main street, but in 2007 a bypass was completed, skirting the

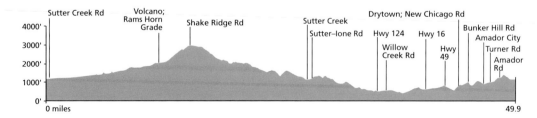

Willow Creek Road is just one of many quiet, attractive byways on this nice two-loop ride out of Sutter Creek. (Linda Fluhrer)

town on the west. Now the main street's traffic volume is more in keeping with the town's nineteenth-century heritage.

The first loop heads east, into the hills, toward the village of Volcano, along beautiful Sutter Creek. The road climbs gently for 12 miles, gaining 800'. It's pleasant work, under the shade of the surrounding broadleaf forest, often alongside the cascades and pools of the pretty stream. The main street of Volcano runs past the venerable St. George Hotel and turns hard right at the end of the block, becoming Rams Horn Grade as it leaves town and starts climbing. Rams Horn gains around 900' in 3 miles, which works out to a grade of over 5 percent. It's not killer but is steady work, tacking back and forth up the wooded hillside.

Right at the top of the climb—the high point on the ride—turn left on Shake Ridge Road and begin the run back to Sutter Creek.

Shake Ridge descends for most of 12.5 miles. There are some rollers and two half-mile climbs in there, but most of this run is a dream downhill, curling through the forest on smooth pavement.

Back in town, cross Main Street to tiny Hayden Alley and turn right on Spanish Street. This pleasant street runs parallel to the main drag and is lined with elegant old homes, most in states of pristine restoration. Spanish climbs a short hill to a left on Sutter–Ione Road, where a longer climb heads west out of town to begin the second loop.

Sutter–Ione is a fine cycling road. It crosses the new Hwy 49 bypass near the crest of the climb, runs along the ridge, and then glides downhill for 6 miles on smooth pavement, now out of the woods and into open meadows. Turn right onto Hwy 124 and head north—very slightly uphill—for 1 mile to a

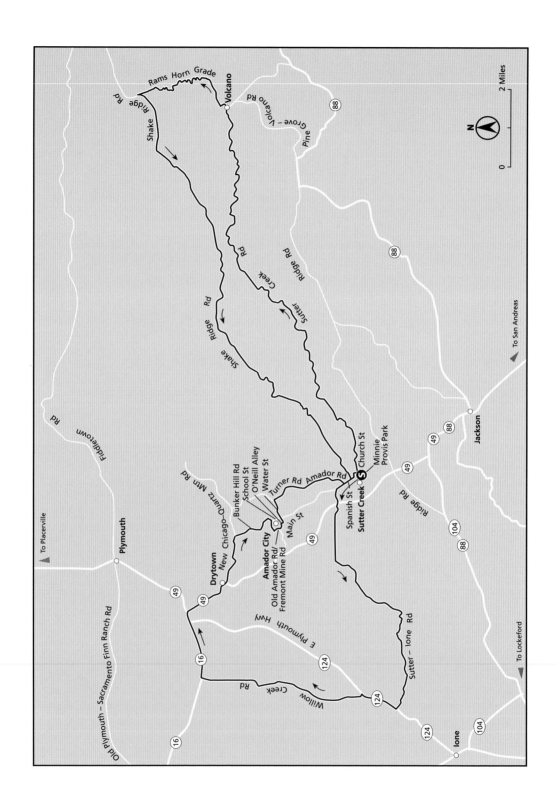

left on Willow Creek Road, another lovely, quiet road well suited to cycling. It rolls along for 4-plus miles, dipping into a couple of creek cuts and humping up over the hills in between, before teeing into Hwy 16. This is a rather busy highway, but with big shoulders—a straight, flat, fast link heading east out of Sacramento. It ends when it runs into Hwy 49. Turn south on Hwy 49 and zoom downhill for a little less than a mile before escaping from these busy highways by turning left into the hamlet of Drytown.

This begins a run of remote roads perfect for cycling. But these hidden treasures come at a cost: there are three chunky climbs in the next 5 miles which will add almost 1200' of gain to your day's total. In between the climbs are lovely little valleys...meadows and shady forest glades and handsome old barns. It's all very off-the-beaten-path and serene. Most of the time, the roads are little more than one lane wide, and yet they sport decent pavement (a common theme in the Gold Country).

The next hidden treasure is the drowsy village of Amador City, another quaint relic from the Gold Rush, with a cluster of nineteenth-century homes and storefronts just begging to be explored.

Leave town on Water Street and turn right, south, on Turner Road. Turner becomes Amador Road, climbs one last hill, and drops steeply back to the town of Sutter Creek. Cross Main Street to Amelia Street, which tees into Spanish Street. It's the same street you were on 21 miles ago, only this time you're going in the opposite direction, all the way to its southern end, where it squeezes between the tall Victorian storefronts and spills right out into the center of the historic old town.

Now it's time to stash the bikes and prowl the picturesque downtown on foot, including finding a nice spot for lunch.

MILEAGE LOG

0.0	From Minnie Provis Park in Sutter Creek, left on Church St.
0.3	Church St. becomes Sutter Creek Rd.
12.1	Right on Consolation St. in village of Volcano
12.4	Becomes Rams Horn Grade
15.2	Left on Shake Ridge Rd.
25.3	Bear right on Gopher Flat Rd. at Pine Gulch Rd. junction
27.8	Cross Main St. in town of Sutter Creek to Hayden Alley
27.9	Right on Spanish St.
28.4	Left on Sutter–Ione Rd.
35.3	Right on Hwy 124
36.2	Left on Willow Creek Rd.
40.5	Right on Hwy 16
42.1	Right on Hwy 49
43.5	Left on Main St. in village of Drytown (turn at crosswalk)
43.7	Becomes New Chicago–Quartz Mountain Rd. as it leaves Drytown
44.8	Right on Bunker Hill Rd.
46.0	Right to stay on Bunker Hill Rd. at School St. junction
46.3	Bear left on Old Amador Rd.; becomes Fremont Mine Rd.
46.6	Right on O'Neill Alley
46.6	Left on Main St., town of Amador City
46.7	Left (almost straight ahead) on Water St.
47.3	Right on Turner Rd.

48.3	Becomes Amador Rd. at Stringbean Alley junction
49.3	Cross Main St. in Sutter Creek to N. Amelia St.
49.4	Left on Spanish St.
49.7	Right on Main St.
49.9	Left on Church St./Sutter Creek Rd.
49.9	Finish at park

60 JACKSON LOOPS

Difficulty:	Challenging to epic
Time:	4.5 to 7.5 hours
Distance:	61 or 75 miles
Elevation gain:	6700' or 7500'
Best seasons:	Spring and fall
Road conditions:	Most roads are low traffic. Pavement varies from excellent to poor.

GETTING THERE: From downtown Jackson, drive 1 mile south on Hwy 49 and turn right on Clinton Rd. to Gold Country Center (a shopping center with a big parking lot).

This hilly loop in the heart of the Gold Country is a hard ride, but also a wonderful one, if you have the fitness to tackle it. There is a shorter option that cuts the challenge down to size a bit. Because the short option diverges right at the start, let's look at it first. Rather than heading north into the town of Jackson, as the long loop does, the short loop heads south on Highway 49 to a right on Middle Bar Road. A 1-mile descent, a 1-mile flat, and a final, shorter descent take the road down to a crossing of the Mokelumne River, where the road name changes to Gwin Mine. After a brief, level run along the river, Gwin Mine Road climbs 700' in 2 miles to the village of Paloma, where the short loop rejoins the long route. Both Middle Bar and Gwin Mine are primitive, rather decrepit roads, barely a lane wide, very remote and lightly traveled...and beautiful.

The long route begins with a run into and through the town of Jackson, managing to avoid most of the city's suburban sprawl by heading right through the center of the old, pioneer downtown, home to an impressive collection of stately old structures from the latter half of the nineteenth century.

The road out of town—Hoffman Street—starts with a steep climb. At the edge of town, the grade eases off, the road name changes to Stony Creek, and you embark on a great downhill run: 8 undulating miles through the rolling hills, almost always pleasantly and sometimes dramatically downhill.

In the last couple of miles of the descent, you start catching glimpses of Pardee Reservoir, and at mile 10 you fetch up on the shore of the lake. A mile later, turn left on Pardee Dam Road, running south along the lake. The road runs along the top of Pardee Dam, and you might want to stop and peer over the downstream side into the deep gorge of the Mokelumne River. It's impressive.

Just past mile 15, turn left on Campo Seco Road and in a mile, left on Paloma Road. This is all rolling terrain, but Paloma soon ramps up into a substantial climb: 800' in 4.4 miles.

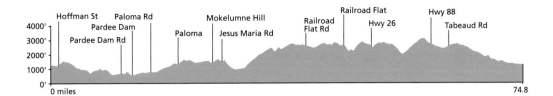

Up on the ridge, with lovely views over the surrounding hills and valleys, sits the little village of Paloma. This is where the short option joins the longer route, with about 13 fewer miles on the clock.

Beyond Paloma, 5 miles of lumpy ups and downs on Paloma Road, Hwy 26, and Campo Seco Turnpike take you to the pretty pioneer town of Mokelumne Hill. Founded around 1850, "Mok Hill" followed the same trajectory of many Gold Rush towns: an overnight boom, a brief heyday of sudden wealth, and, after the local gold was played out, a long slumber as a near ghost town. Now its few remaining blocks of Victorian storefronts and homes have a quiet charm, and the town survives as an historic tourist destination.

Wiggle through town on neighborhood streets and then turn left on Hwy 26, heading uphill. Watch for an obscure right turn onto Jesus Maria Road. After a brief rise, the road tilts downhill on a tangled, 1.5-mile plunge to Jesus Maria Creek. In spite of being a tiny, remote road, it has recently been repaved and is satin smooth. Roll along beside the pretty creek for a mile-plus before beginning the climb out of the canyon: 1500' up in 4.5 miles. This is serious work, and even though there are several small flats or saddles along the way to afford the occasional rest, the overall impact is severe. Over the top of the main climb, the road bumps up and down for several miles along the ridgeline, losing and gaining altitude in 100' to 300' chunks. The

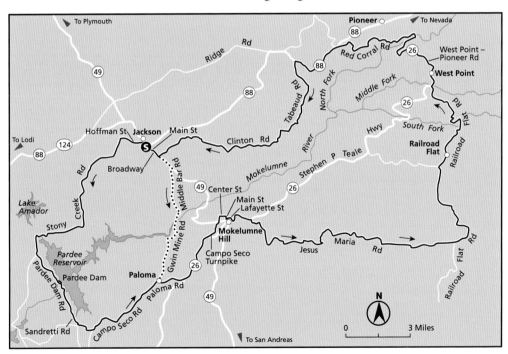

The Pardee Dam crossing—impounding the waters of the Mokelumne River—is one of the few flat spots on this ruggedly hilly ride. (Linda Fluhrer)

scenery here runs to mountain streams, granite boulders, forests of broadleaf and needle trees in great variety, and every so often an open, subalpine meadow. It's a wild, remote, rugged region.

Jesus Maria tees into Railroad Flat Road around mile 40. There is a market in the town of Railroad Flat at mile 46, your first crack at store-bought munchies since Mok Hill, 20 miles back. There will be another couple of small stores in the next 10 miles, but that's about it for civilization.

Up here in the mountains, the Mokelumne River spreads out into a network of tributaries, with each creek dancing down its own steeply walled canyon. Heading north on Railroad Flat and Hwy 26 (between miles 40 and 60), the route will cross at least five streams, dropping into the canyon and climb-

ing back up the other side of each one. All those little climbs add up, and the last of them might be the toughest of all. Beyond the town of West Point, the road plunges to the north fork of the Mokelumne and crosses the river above deep, green pools and granite boulders. Getting back out of this defile is a chore: 1000' up in 3.5 miles.

Once over the top of this grinder, you can recuperate for most of the remainder of the ride, and maybe even have some fun, beginning with a 3-mile downhill: 1 mile on Hwy 26 and 2 miles along the wide shoulder of Hwy 88. A half-mile climb leads to a left turn onto Tabeaud Road. Leave the highway behind and make the acquaintance of this sweet little road. Tabeaud (pronounced "taboo" locally) climbs gently for half a mile before embarking on a nearly perfect descent.

Tabeaud and Clinton Road, just below it, combine for 11 miles of fast, twisty downhill on generally excellent pavement. There are a few uphill bits in there, but the overall theme is low-level flying. It's a real treat, and a nice way to wrap up this big ride.

MILEAGE LOG

0.0	Depart Gold Country Center, cross Hwy 49; short route turns right on Hwy 49

Short route:

0.0	**Depart Gold Country Center, right on Hwy 49**
1.0	**Right on Middle Bar Rd.**
3.6	**Cross Mokelumne River to Gwin Mine Rd.**
6.9	**Left on Paloma Rd. in village of Paloma; rejoin long route (see mile 20.4)**

0.3	Left on Broadway
0.4	Left to stay on Broadway at Mission Blvd. junction
1.0	Cross Hwy 88, jog left on Water St. to right on Main St.; old town Jackson
1.2	Right on Hwy 49
1.3	Left on Hoffman St.; leave town, steeply uphill
2.2	Becomes Stony Creek Rd.
10.0	Cross Jackson Creek Spillway at Pardee Reservoir
10.8	Pardee Reservoir Recreation Area (water)
11.1	Left on Pardee Dam Rd. (sign says, "PARDEE DAM 2, VALLEY SPRINGS 7")
12.8	Cross Pardee Dam; name changes to Sandretti Rd. beyond dam
15.2	Left on Campo Seco Rd.
16.1	Left on Paloma Rd.
20.4	Town of Paloma; short route rejoins here
21.6	Left on Hwy 26
23.5	Left on Campo Seco Tpke.
25.2	Cross Hwy 49, continue on Campo Seco Tpke.
25.4	Right on Center St. into town of Mokelumne Hill
25.7	Right on Main St., left on Lafayette St.
26.2	Left on Hwy 26
27.3	Right on Jesus Maria Rd.
39.8	Fire station (water)
40.2	Left on Railroad Flat Rd.
45.0	Right to stay on Railroad Flat Rd.
45.6	Town of Railroad Flat
50.9	Right on Hwy 26
52.0	Bear left on Hwy 26 in town of West Point; sign points toward Hwy 88; Hwy 26 now also known as West Point–Pioneer Rd.
55.6	Cross Mokelumne River; Hwy 26 now also known as Red Corral Rd.
60.2	Left on Hwy 88; store near junction
62.9	Left on Tabeaud Rd.
69.6	Left on Clinton Rd.
74.6	Cross Broadway and Hwy 49 in town of Jackson
74.8	Finish at Gold Country Center

61 ANGELS CAMP LOOP

Difficulty:	Challenging
Time:	3 to 5 hours
Distance:	41 miles
Elevation gain:	4600'
Best seasons:	Spring and fall
Road conditions:	Most roads are quiet; pavement varies from excellent to terrible.

GETTING THERE: From downtown Angels Camp, drive 1 mile north on Hwy 49. Turn right on Murphys Grade Rd. and park at Bret Harte High School. A permit is required to park in the school lot while school is in session, so if you visit during school hours, park on the street nearby.

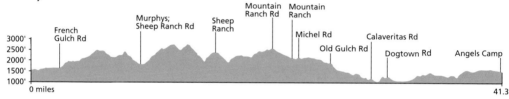

Angels Camp is another of the Gold Rush towns strung out along Highway 49. It has some residual charm from those boomtown days, but a fair amount of modern development too. It is best known for the Jumping Frog Jubilee in mid-May, when the town is swamped with tourists for a few crazy days. If you're looking for a peaceful back-road cycling experience, don't come near here on that weekend. Aside from that one caveat, you can hardly go wrong with this ride. It's a great loop. However, don't let the modest mileage fool you. Note the elevation gain: This is a stout challenge, with steep ups and downs, early and often.

Say good-bye to the town with a run east into the hills on Murphys Grade Road, a moderately busy highway. That run is gently uphill, but when you turn onto French Gulch Road at mile 2.6, the uphill becomes more serious: 850' in 3.4 miles. About a mile of that is nearly flat, so the climbing is concentrated in steeper pitches. Over the top at mile

6, descend for a mile-plus into the pretty village of Murphys. This too is a Gold Rush settlement, but unlike Angels Camp, it remains quaint and charming. It's one of the best of the small pioneer towns in the region. I loop the route around a couple of extra blocks here to encourage you to see more of the town.

Once you leave Murphys, you leave behind most of what passes for civilization for a while. The route heads out of town on Sheep Ranch Road, a rugged, ragged cycling challenge. Over its 14-mile length, there are six serious climbs, varying in length from less than a mile to almost 3 miles. Some of the pitches are over 10 percent. Total gain is over 2500'. What all those numbers add up to is a lot of hard work. Each of those climbs also comes with a descent, and some of them are above-average exciting: steep, twisty, and occasionally badly paved. (Pavement around this loop is a Jekyll-and-Hyde mix: some sections are smooth and others are primitive, patch-and-pothole minefields.)

The town of Sheep Ranch perches on the top of one of the six summits at about mile 16. Calling it a town is a bit of a stretch; there are just a few, clustered homes and no services. Small as it is, though, I got caught in a traffic jam in the middle of town: I had to ride through a large herd of sheep milling about in the road. Sheep Ranch, indeed.

The funky, chunky adventure that is Sheep Ranch Road finally ends at the junction with Mountain Ranch Road at mile 21, and in 2 miles you drop into the town of Mountain Ranch, where there is a good market, conveniently about halfway around the loop.

That junction at mile 21 also marks the last of the six summits. For the next 9 miles, the roads tilt downhill most of the time. Mountain Ranch, Michel, Old Gulch, and Calaveritas roads are a delight: never too steep but plenty steep enough to be big fun. All have at least decent pavement, and all twist and turn in ways that are scaled perfectly for bike speed. One of my favorite spots is on Calaveritas Road, near the end of this sassy run: the road scoots under a rough-hewn trestle and then zips right through the front yard of an old farmhouse. This is downtown Calaveritas, another mini-village, about the same size as Sheep Ranch.

This little settlement represents the lowest point on the loop. The final 12 miles—mostly along Dogtown Road—bounce up

The pump says gas is still 18¢ a gallon in downtown Sheep Ranch...definitely a throwback to an earlier time.

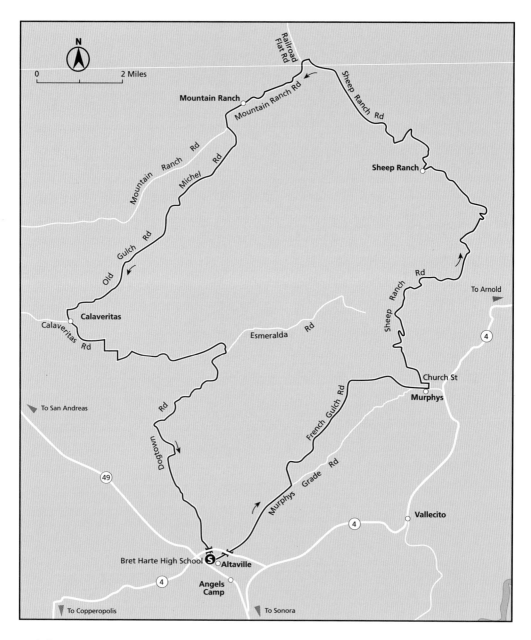

and down constantly, with a few more ups than downs. And "bounce" is the apt word, as Dogtown has some of the worst pavement of the loop...enough patches and cracks to rattle a few fillings loose.

I've been remiss in not mentioning the scenery on this ride. It's classic Gold Coun-

try fare: oaks and other broadleaf trees in the lower valleys, with scruffy pines eking out a living up on the rocky hillsides. And meadows...loads of lovely, sheep-cropped meadows, here and there, all day long.

Dogtown winds its lumpy, bumpy way right up to the edge of Angels Camp. Just as you come up on the first rank of tract houses at the city limit, turn left on Gardner Lane and nip back to Murphys Grade Road and the high school. This ride is plenty hard enough to have worked you up into a good lather by the end, especially if it's as hot as these foothills can be. If you don't have a motel room in town for a shower, you might be pleased to know there's a nice municipal swimming pool next to the school.

MILEAGE LOG

0.0	From Bret Harte High School, east on Murphys Grade Rd.
2.6	Left on French Gulch Rd.
7.1	Bear left (almost straight ahead) on Main St.; town of Murphys
7.4	Left on Church St.
7.5	Left to stay on Church St. at Surrey Ln. junction
7.6	Right on Santa Domingo; becomes Sheep Ranch Rd.
16.3	Town of Sheep Ranch
21.0	Left on Mountain Ranch Road
22.9	Town of Mountain Ranch
23.5	Left on Michel Rd.
26.2	Bear left on Old Gulch Rd.
29.9	Left on Calaveritas Rd.; town of Calaveritas
31.2	Right on Fricot City Rd.; becomes Dogtown Rd.
34.5	Bear right to stay on Dogtown Rd. at Esmeralda Rd. junction
40.7	Bear left on Gardner Ln. at Angels Camp city limit
41.2	Right on Murphys Grade Rd.
41.3	Finish at Bret Harte High School

62 SONORA–COLUMBIA LOOP

Difficulty:	Challenging
Time:	3 to 5 hours
Distance:	49 miles
Elevation gain:	4700'
Best seasons:	Spring and fall
Road conditions:	Most roads are quiet; pavement is good.

GETTING THERE: From Jamestown, take Hwy 49/108 east toward Sonora for approximately 2 miles. Take Hwy 49 north 1.6 miles into Sonora. Turn left on Washington St. (Hwy 49), left on Snell St. at mile 3.7, and right on School St. at mile 3.8. Park at the high school.

This classic Gold Country loop climbs from the lower foothills into an almost-Sierra mountain landscape. By starting low, 90 percent of the climbing is knocked off by mile 20, leaving the later miles for lively descending. Aside from the wonderful miles around

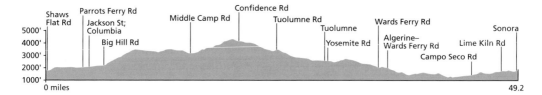

this loop, the special attraction today is a visit to Columbia State Historic Park, which comes up early in the ride.

The loop begins in Sonora. This pioneer town was known as the Queen of the Southern Mines and was the richest and wildest boomtown in the southern Mother Lode. After the gold played out, the town survived on lumber and other local industry, and it is still a modestly prosperous, bustling town. These days, its historic charms are mixed with modern development.

The ride leaves town on Shaws Flat Road, climbing steadily through a rural-residential fringe. Cross Highway 49 to Springfield and Parrots Ferry roads before rolling into the very special town of Columbia. Even though the ride has barely begun, you have to stop here and explore.

Columbia has been preserved in a state of something resembling its nineteenth-century beginnings, when for a brief boom in the 1860s it was the second largest city in California. The state parks department has been working to preserve and restore the town since the 1940s. People do still live here and all the stores are open for business, but everything is a living museum, a sort of Gold Rush

The almost perfectly preserved Gold Rush boomtown of Columbia is the centerpiece of Columbia State Historic Park.

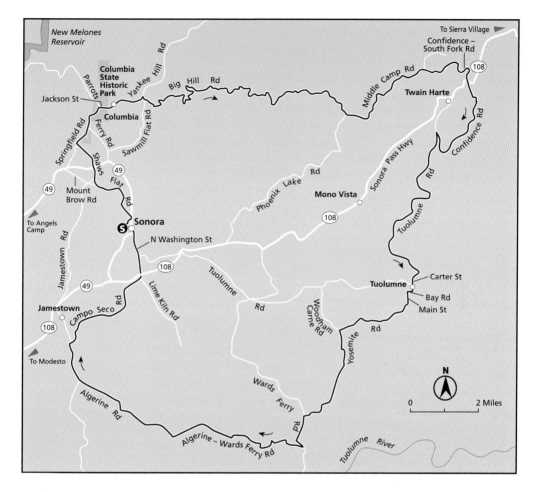

Williamsburg. On a weekend in the summer, the tree-lined streets can be teeming with tourists to a point where it resembles Main Street at Disneyland. But if you visit on a weekday or in the off-season, you should be able to cast yourself backward in time and recapture the flavor of that earlier era.

After your stop in Columbia, follow Yankee Hill Road out of town, heading mildly uphill. After 1 mile, jog right on Saw Mill Flat Road to a left on aptly named Big Hill Road. This is a significant climb: over 1300' in 3.5 miles, and another 200' in 2 miles after the pitch eases off. There are some great views out over the valley below. Over the top, you can recover on 3 miles of gentle downhill

through the forest before tackling the next big climb of the day on Middle Camp Road: 1000' in 4 miles.

Middle Camp can be a bit confusing. It carves a ragged arc around the town of Twain Harte, and is often intersected by neighborhood streets. Take your time at the intersections, follow your mileage log, and you'll get there. It takes you to Confidence–South Fork Road, the highest point on the ride. Confidence–South Fork becomes Confidence Road after crossing Hwy 108. This begins a great run of downhill thrills. Confidence is one fat lane wide, with no fancy frills, just a meandering lane through the woods, usually with decent pavement. It dances down the hillside for 3 saucy miles before a brief, level jog on Cedar Springs Road ties it into Tuolumne Road, where the descent resumes.

While Confidence is a narrow, slightly technical twister through the trees, Tuolumne Road is a fast, smooth highway, but still with plenty of turns to keep it interesting: 4.5 miles of full-tilt flying to the town of Tuolumne. Coming up at mile 29, Tuolumne is the obvious spot for a break.

While you've been busy descending, the scenery around you has been changing. Up around Middle Camp, it's fir and pine forest, a mountain landscape. Midway down Confidence, you enter a zone of mixed broadleaf and needle trees, with more open spaces between. Finally, beyond Tuolumne, you're into the classic valley environment of open meadows dotted with stands of oak. Moving through this transition at the speed of a fast descent makes it quite dramatic.

Head south and west out of Tuolumne, now on Yosemite Road. A mile beyond town, you bottom out at a crossing of Tuolumne Creek and face a moderate, 1-mile climb. After that little summit, glide downhill on an easy run of a mile to a T, where Yosemite Road turns left. In 3 miles, make another left on Wards Ferry Road, still descending. The next turn—a right onto Algerine–Wards Ferry Road—is going to be tricky. It comes up on a fast descent and is much more than a 90-degree turn, almost 180 degrees. There is a small street sign at the junction, but no advance warning. After your turn onto Wards Ferry Road, stay alert for it.

All of the roads on this ride are nice, but I think some of my favorites are the ones around the bottom of the loop, Algerine–Wards Ferry and Algerine roads: quiet, empty miles through the dappled shade of leafy woods and across rolling grasslands, with old farmhouses and barns here and there. Idyllic is the word that comes to mind. About a mile before the end of Algerine, as it nears Jamestown, the road widens, picks up a set of stripes, and starts looking like a busier highway. Turn right on Campo Seco Road, dodging around the edge of Jamestown, and head north toward Sonora. All of the last 11 miles are rolling, but with a mildly uphill bent.

At the far end of Campo Seco, turn left on Lime Kiln Road, cross Hwy 108, and roll into Sonora on Washington Street, where any number of cafés and restaurants are waiting for your lunch time trade.

MILEAGE LOG

0.0	From Sonora High School, north on W. School Rd.
0.1	Left on Washingston St.
0.2	Left on Shaws Flat Rd.
1.8	Bear right to stay on Shaws Flat Rd. at Mount Brow Rd. junction
3.2	Becomes Springfield Rd.
3.9	Left on Parrots Ferry Rd. (also known as Broadway in town of Columbia)
4.5	Right on Jackson St.; Columbia State Historic Park
4.7	Becomes Yankee Hill Rd.
6.0	Jog right on Sawmill Flat Rd., left on Big Hill Rd.
14.9	Bear right on Big Hill Rd. onto Longeway Rd. at Kewin Mill Rd. junction
14.9	Bear left on Longeway Rd. at Phoenix Lake Rd. junction
15.3	Becomes Middle Camp Rd. (also known as South Fork Rd. and Middle Camp–Sugar Pine Rd.)
19.1	Right on Confidence–South Fork Rd.
20.3	Jog left across Hwy 108 to right on Confidence Rd.

23.2	Right on Cedar Springs Rd.
23.6	Left on Tuolumne Rd.
28.1	Left to stay on Tuolumne Rd.
28.4	Becomes Carter St. in town of Tuolumne
29.0	Right on Bay St.
29.1	Left on Main St.; downtown Tuolumne
29.4	Becomes Yosemite Rd.
31.8	Bear left to stay on Yosemite Rd. at Woodham Carne Rd. junction
34.8	Left on Wards Ferry Rd.
35.8	Sharp right on Algerine–Wards Ferry Rd.
40.0	Becomes Algerine Rd.
44.4	Right on Jacksonville Rd., right again on Campo Seco Rd.
47.6	Left on Lime Kiln Rd.
47.7	Cross under Hwy 108; becomes Washington St. into town of Sonora
49.1	Left on Snell St.
49.2	Right on W. School St. to high school parking lot

63 WARDS FERRY–CHERRY LAKE LOOPS

Difficulty:	Epic
Time:	6 to 10 hours
Distance:	90 or 109 miles
Elevation gain:	11,500' or 14,000'
Best seasons:	Mid-May through mid-September
Road conditions:	Hwy 120 can be busy; other roads are remote and quiet. Pavement is generally good.

GETTING THERE: From Hwy 99 at Manteca, take Hwy 120 east for 65 miles to Groveland. Or from Yosemite National Park, take Hwy 120 west for 47 miles to Groveland. Park at Groveland Wayside Park.

This is a tough ride. The longer option may be the hardest ride in the book. But if you have the fitness and self-reliance to tackle it, you will be rewarded with a huge, amazing adventure. While the west end of the ride wanders the Gold Country foothills, the bulk of the loop is in the rugged mountains of the Sierra, in the Stanislaus National Forest.

Head west out of Groveland on Highway 120, turn right on Deer Flat Road, and right again on Wards Ferry Road at mile 2. It

doesn't take long for this ride to become exciting. After a half-mile climb on Deer Flat, the roads tilt downhill to the tune of over 2000' in almost 7 miles, plunging into the canyon of the Tuolumne River. It isn't one steady grade, but a mix of fast chutes, tight hairpins, and rollers. This is a perilous, dicey descent. The road is narrow and twisty and hangs by its fingernails off the side of a steep cliff. In some spots, the drop-offs into the canyon are almost sheer, with no guardrails. Going over

Wards Ferry Road is steep, narrow, twisty, and a literal cliffhanger. But that's par for the course on this loop, perhaps the most challenging in the book.

the edge here could quite possibly be a fatal error. Good skills and caution are needed in equal measure.

Good legs and lungs are needed for climbing out of the canyon on the other side: 1200' up in 3 miles, followed by another few miles of gentle uphill amid a classic foothills landscape of oaks and meadows. After a small summit, a 1-mile descent and gentle uphill lead into the town of Tuolumne at mile 17, a good spot for food and water. (There won't be another for 30 miles.) Head north through town and turn right on Buchanan Road, following signs to Cherry Lake. Buchanan Road climbs briefly and then topples off a cliff in a dizzy, 2-mile descent back into the canyon of the Tuolumne. The road is narrow but well paved.

At the bottom of the canyon, the road's name changes from Buchanan to Cottonwood, and it begins to climb. For 11 miles,

it ascends steadily, gaining 2600', passing through deep forest of fir, pine, incense cedar, and madrone. This is remote, empty wilderness. Unless you happen upon a log truck, you might ride for hours without encountering a single vehicle.

Over the summit, enjoy a 4.5-mile, 1400' descent, all slinky turns on nice pavement. You'll hit the bottom of the descent flying, but break it off here for a little sightseeing, as you cross the Clavey River on a high bridge. If I tell you the bridge is posted with "NO BUNGEE JUMPING" signs, would that give you some idea of how high the bridge is? It spans a beautiful canyon, with the whitewater river cascading from pool to pool far, far below.

From the bridge, there's more uphill ahead: 1900' in 12 miles for a relatively painless 3 percent average. The road tops out at 5600' around mile 48—high point of the ride—

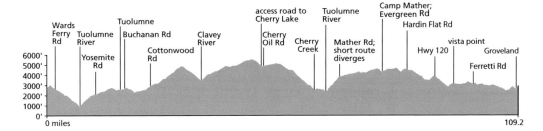

where there is a nice vista over Cherry Lake, and beyond the lake, the vast panorama of high mountains that crown Yosemite National Park.

At mile 49.5, you pass a road into a campground by the lake. As far as I know, this is the only spot for drawing water from a faucet for many miles around. It's a 1.4-mile round trip into the camp. This out-and-back is not included in the mileage totals, as you may or may not need to stop here.

Just downhill from the camp road is a stop sign where you turn right. This is Cherry Oil Road, although it isn't signed at the junction; there is a sign pointing to Hwy 120. The road climbs briefly and then tilts downhill. The descent begins modestly but soon picks up speed. For 8 miles, you'll be carving corners and ripping down straights at a great rate, dropping 2500' along the way.

At the bottom of the hill, you cross over Cherry Creek, another bungee-deep gorge. A mostly level run alongside an old aqueduct leads to another 1.5-mile descent. This time, the bridge you cross is straddling the main branch of the Tuolumne, with the Kirkwood hydro station sprawling over both banks of the river at the crossing. Finally, all the descending catches up with you and you have to do some serious climbing to get out of this canyon: 1500' in 3 miles, without one yard of relief in the whole painful package. This is a really serious wall, one that will test even the hardiest riders.

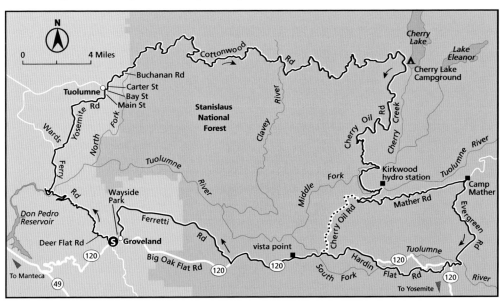

At the top of the ascent, the long and short routes diverge. The short route stays on Cherry Oil Road. The first mile at the top is level, rolling through pleasant forest, and then you're treated to another helping of frisky downhill, almost 4 miles long. You bottom out at a bridge over the South Fork Tuolumne before teeing into Hwy 120. This is where the long route rejoins.

When the short route goes straight on Cherry Oil, the longer loop turns left on Mather Road and follows it to Camp Mather, a large summer camp. There is a store here. Turn right on Evergreen Road and follow it to Hwy 120. Mather and Evergreen roads both include a few mild ups and downs, but nothing severe. Pavement and scenery are both excellent.

Continuing on the long route, turn right on Hwy 120 and quickly left onto Hardin Flat Road. This delightful little road bypasses the highway for over 6 miles, including a riotous downhill and then a short but stiff climb at the far end. Back on Hwy 120, cruise downhill for 3 miles to the Cherry Oil Road junction, where the routes rejoin.

Hwy 120 isn't an ideal cycling road, but it's tolerable. Most of the time there are wide shoulders, and the scenery is anywhere from good to excellent. At 2 miles west of Cherry Oil, there is a vista point overlooking the canyon of the Tuolumne, which, in addition to having the great view, has restrooms.

One last, small climb on Hwy 120 leads to a right on Ferretti Road, a quiet, 10-mile loop around Pine Mountain Lake and a nice bypass off the main highway. It descends gently through a rural-residential community around the lake and then tilts back up into two short climbs before returning to Hwy 120 near the town of Groveland and the finish of this wonderful, out-of-scale ride.

MILEAGE LOG

0.0	Right (west) on Hwy 120; leave Groveland Wayside Park
0.5	Right on Deer Flat Rd.
2.0	Right on Wards Ferry Rd.
11.5	Bear right on Yosemite Rd.
14.7	Bear right on Yosemite Rd. at Woodham Carne Rd. junction
17.0	Becomes Main St. in town of Tuolumne
17.3	Right on Bay St.
17.4	Left on Carter St.
18.0	Right on Buchanan Rd.; leave Tuolumne
22.7	Cross North Fork Tuolumne River; becomes FR 1N04
24.1	Becomes Cottonwood Rd. (still FR 1N04 as well)
49.5	Access road to Cherry Lake USFS camp (water); 1.4-mile round trip to camp
49.9	Right at stop sign on Cherry Oil Rd. (also known as Cherry Lake Rd. and FR 1N07)
67.6	Long route: Left on Mather Rd.; short route stays on Cherry Oil Rd.
	Short route:
67.6	**Stay on Cherry Oil Rd.**
73.0	**Right on Hwy 120; rejoin long route (see mile 92.4)**
75.2	Right on Evergreen Rd.; village of Camp Mather (store)
82.6	Right on Hwy 120
82.9	Left on Hardin Flat Rd.
89.1	Left on Hwy 120
92.4	Rejoin short route at Cherry Oil Rd. junction

94.2	Vista point with restrooms on right
98.6	Right on Ferretti Rd.
109.0	Right on Hwy 120 in Groveland
109.2	Finish at Groveland Wayside Park

64 COULTERVILLE LOOPS

Difficulty:	Challenging/epic
Time:	5 to 8 hours (long loop)
Distance:	34, 56, or 73 miles
Elevation gain:	3900' to 7300'
Best seasons:	May through October
Road conditions:	Numbered highways can be quite busy. Other roads are remote and quiet. Pavement varies.

GETTING THERE: From Hwy 99 at Modesto, take Hwy 132 east 55 miles to Coulterville. Park anywhere near downtown.

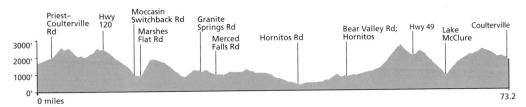

This is a challenging ride, although the two shorter options are quite manageable. The middle third of the big loop is out in the low, open grasslands where the Sierra foothills taper down to the Central Valley. But the other two-thirds scramble up and down over some serious hills, farther up into the mountains. The ride starts and ends in Coulterville, a pioneer town. It had a population of 5000 at the height of the Gold Rush but is now just a sleepy wide spot in the road with an interesting collection of old buildings.

Head uphill out of Coulterville on Greeley Hill Road for 2 miles to a left on Priest–Coulterville Road. This is a pretty, quiet back road: no traffic and no homes that might generate any traffic. It climbs for 2 miles, descends

for 3 miles, and finally climbs for another 3 miles to a junction with Highway 120.

Hwy 120 is all about descending: over 1500' in 5 miles. There is potential for traffic on this gateway to Yosemite, but on the twisty, 6 percent grade, most riders should descend as fast as the cars. (I've done it without interacting with a single car, all the way.)

At the bottom of the hill, jog left onto Moccasin Switchback Road (at the Old Priest Grade junction). It drops into the midst of Moccasin, the little community supporting the small hydro power plant at Moccasin Reservoir. Ride across the top of the reservoir's dam and turn left on Hwy 49.

Turn right off Hwy 49 on Marshes Flat Road (also known as Kelly Grade). Climb

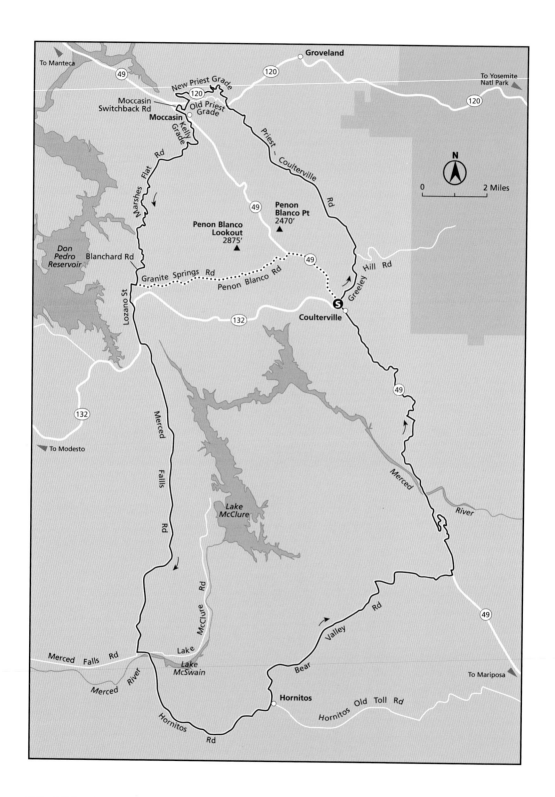

Cruise through these easy, almost-flat miles now; it gets harder later...

900' in 2 miles—that's the grade in Kelly Grade—then descend for most of 5 miles through rolling ranch lands dotted with oaks. After the descent, the road name changes to Blanchard—still the same road—and climbs to a junction with Granite Springs Road.

This is where the two short routes meet (or leave) the long route. The shortest option (the north loop) follows the course to this point and then takes Granite Springs and Penon Blanco roads back to Hwy 49 and Coulterville. This shortcut is mostly uphill, gaining almost 900' over 5 miles. It's a gentle grade at first, but quite steep at the end, with downhills and rollers on Hwy 49 into Coulterville. The longer short option (the south loop) uses the same shortcut but in the opposite direction, out from Coulterville to this junction on Granite Springs, then follows the long route around the southern end of the loop.

The long route turns right on Granite Springs and left on Lozano before teeing into Hwy 132. This is a modern, wide highway, but you're only on it for a mile and a half before turning left onto the more bike-friendly Merced Falls Road. At the outset the road climbs, gaining 300' in its first 5 miles in a series of rolling hummocks. Over the next 8 miles, it loses 700' in a similar series of rolling descents, all on smooth pavement. The scenery is lovely: low hills and meadows of waving grasses, with small stands of oak. The fields are filled with millions of jagged granite shards, standing on end, looking like ancient, weathered tombstones.

After almost 13 miles on this nice road, turn left onto Hornitos Road and then right—still on the same road—to cross the Merced River. Once over the bridge, the landscape becomes even more empty and treeless than it has been. The only dot on the map out here is the historic town of Hornitos. This little burg barely clings to life in the twenty-first century, but in the Gold Rush, it was a roaring hell-camp fueled by gold dust, boasting a population of 15,000 and supporting four hotels, six stores, numerous saloons, and a Wells Fargo office shipping out $40,000 in gold every day. Hard to imagine it all when you see the drowsy, dusty village now.

It's 7 miles from the Merced River to Hornitos and another 10 miles along Bear Valley Road to Hwy 49. About 15 of those miles are uphill. That bridge over the river represents the low point on the loop—around 360'—and Bear Valley climbs to over 2400' before descending to its junction with Hwy 49. As you climb, you leave the austere landscape around Hornitos and return to woods, with oaks and other broadleaf trees providing at least a little shade and color on the long climb.

Hwy 49 north of Bear Valley might resemble the view from the seat of a roller-coaster called the Big Dipper. This is a down-and-up monster on the way to Coulterville. So twisted is this stretch of Hwy 49 that it's known as the Little Dragon because of all the bends in its tail. Descend 1500' in 4 miles to cross one of the outer reaches of Lake McClure, then climb back up the other side of the canyon on a formidable grade: 1500' up in 6 miles. Coulterville is 700' lower than that highest summit on Bear Valley Road (before the junction), so in spite of all this tough climbing, there is actually more descending through this section. Much of that net loss of elevation comes in the final 5 miles into Coulterville, where Hwy 49 drops 500' in a mellow downhill cruise.

There are some nice places for a post-ride lunch in quaint old Coulterville. There is also a municipal swimming pool, which might look good if your ride has been a hot one.

MILEAGE LOG

0.0	Uphill on Greeley Hill Rd.; leave Coulterville

South loop short option:

0.0	**North on Hwy 49; leave Coulterville**
1.8	**Left on Penon Blanco Rd.**
6.3	**Becomes Granite Springs Rd.**
8.3	**Join long route at Granite Springs/Blanchard Rd. junction (see mile 25.2)**

2.0	Left on Priest–Coulterville Rd.
10.1	Left on Hwy 120/New Priest Grade (not left on Old Priest Grade)
14.7	Left on Moccasin Switchback Rd. at foot of Old Priest Grade
15.4	Cross dam at Moccasin Reservoir
15.5	Left on Hwy 49
15.8	Right on Marshes Flat Rd. (also known as Kelly Grade)
24.3	Becomes Blanchard Rd.
25.2	Right on Granite Springs Rd.; junction with both short options

North loop short option:

25.2	**Left on Granite Springs Rd.**
27.2	**Becomes Penon Blanco Rd.**
31.7	**Right on Hwy 49**
33.5	**Finish in Coulterville**

25.4	Left on Lozano St.
26.3	Right on Hwy 132
27.6	Left on Merced Falls Rd.
28.3	Don Pedro High School (water)
40.2	Left on Hornitos Rd.
40.6	Right on Hornitos Rd. across Merced River at Lake McClure Rd. junction
47.7	Left on Bear Valley Rd.; town of Hornitos (water)
58.1	Left on Hwy 49
73.2	Finish in Coulterville

SIERRA

The High Sierra, with its soaring peaks, plunging cascades, and pristine forests, is world-famous. However, this magnificent, empty wilderness doesn't contain all that many roads that can be bundled into bite-sized, bike-friendly packages. But the best of those few roads are here, and they show off this most spectacular of California landscapes to best advantage.

65 PORTOLA–GOLD LAKE–YUBA PASS LOOP

Difficulty:	Challenging
Time:	4 to 5 hours
Distance:	61 miles
Elevation gain:	4200'
Best seasons:	June through September
Road conditions:	Most roads are low traffic and bike friendly. All are well paved.

GETTING THERE: From I-80 at Truckee, take Hwy 89 approximately 46 miles north to Hwy 70 near Graeagle. Take Hwy 70 east from Hwy 89 10 miles to the center of Portola.

This loop is half hills and half flats. Ninety percent of the climbing is concentrated in two long, steady grades of 7-plus miles each. The rest of the ride rolls across flat, open meadows or rockets down the far sides of the two big climbs.

Before leaving the town of Portola, I want to recommend an off-the-bike attraction just off our route: the Western Pacific Railroad Museum. This is an old, sprawling switching yard for the Union Pacific Railroad that has been filled, over the years, with more and more old trains...a vast fleet of engines and rolling stock from all over the country. Many of the engines are still in good working order and can be seen rumbling around the yard or venturing out into the real, modern world. Unlike "look, but don't touch" museums, this one is very much a hands-on experience. You can clamber all over the trains, sit in the engineers' seats, pull on levers, and just generally act like a kid. If you have any interest in trains, this is a must, either before or after the ride.

The ride leaves town just beyond the museum and heads down the south side of the Feather River on McLears Road (County Road A15). It climbs slightly, does a couple of rolling miles on the top of the piney ridge, and then heads downhill in a hurry: first 2 miles of gentle grade, and then 2.5 miles of frisky, twisty free fall.

Turn right at the bottom of the hill and head north on Highway 89, rolling across an open meadow for 3 miles to a left turn on the Gold Lake Highway. This is the beginning of the first big climb: a gain of 2100' in 7.6 miles. It's a modern road with wide, smooth lanes, broad, sweeping curves, and no sudden changes in grade.

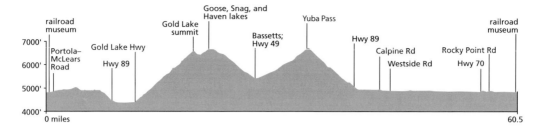

The higher the road climbs, the better the scenery becomes, passing great masses of naked granite standing tall out of the trees. Gold Lake summit itself is nothing too remarkable: just a flattening out of the grade. But what lies ahead is worth the work it took to get here. There is a first descent of 1 mile, with a short access road to Gold Lake right at the bottom, then a brief climb to a 1-mile level stretch. Gold Lake is the biggest of the small lakes clustered together here, but my personal favorites are along this level stretch:

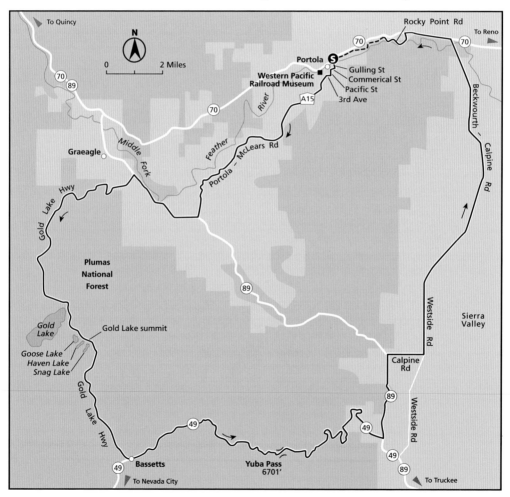

Goose, Haven, and Snag lakes, all just off the road to the right. They're all tiny, but each has a quiet, jewel-like beauty, with the jagged peaks of the Sierra Buttes reflected in their still waters. They're just visible from the road, but their special charms are mostly obscured. You have to get off your bike and walk a few yards through the trees to really see them. These lakes come up at around mile 21, which—coupled with the fact that you just completed a major climb—makes this an obvious spot for a rest stop.

After your lakeside reverie, it's time to shift gears—literally as well as figuratively—for just beyond the lakes, the road plummets off the mountain in a downhill flier, dropping over 1300' in 5 fast miles. If you like going fast, you'll love this one. The express-train downhill thrills don't stop until the road tees into Hwy 49 at Bassetts. There is a nice old café at the junction, where they dish up the biggest ice cream cones I've ever seen.

Now, at Hwy 49, you have to remember how to pedal again. Turn left and head uphill toward 6701' Yuba Pass. It's 7 miles from Bassetts to the pass, gaining 1300' over

that stretch for a 3.5 percent average, an easy, steady grade. This is nice riding, with the wild Yuba River never far away, splashing along beside the road, keeping you entertained with its happy chatter and pretty curves. And speaking of pretty curves, just wait until you crest the pass and start down the other side. This descent is even more fun than the one from Gold Lake, dropping 1800' in 7 kinky miles. Where the previous descent was all about high speed and hanging on for the ride, this one requires more in the way of handling skills. As it tumbles down the rocky mountainside, it twists itself up into a tangle of twitchy switchbacks and slithery S-bends.

At the bottom of this wild ride, turn left on Hwy 89 and head north for 3 flat miles through scattered stands of ponderosa pine. Turn right on Calpine Road and in a bit over a mile, left on Westside Road, which becomes Beckwourth–Calpine Road. Leave the pines behind and roll out across the wide, flat Sierra Valley, a classic eastern Sierra landscape: open, dry, austere, and lovely. Hayfields and ranch lands are most of what you see, with rugged

Beautiful alpine scenery abounds on this loop in the northern Sierra. (Dave Dietz)

hills ranging along the borders of the valley. There are a few very gentle ups and downs along this stretch, but it's as close to level as a mountain road can be.

At mile 55.8, turn left on Hwy 70. A mile and a half later, just before Hwy 70 tilts up into a long, tedious climb, turn left on a neat little bypass called Rocky Point Road, which hugs the bank of the Feather River in the bottom of a beautiful, rugged canyon, a quiet and enjoyable 2.6-mile escape from a busy highway and a big hill. Just before the road tees back into Hwy 70 on the far side of the hill, pick up the East Riverside Avenue bike trail, which runs along the river for the final mile to the finish in Portola.

MILEAGE LOG

0.0	From the center of Portola at Hwy 70, head south on S. Gulling St.
0.3	Right on Commercial St.
0.4	Left on Pacific St. (past Western Pacific Ave., road to railroad museum)
0.6	Right on 3rd Ave.
0.7	Bear left on Portola–McLears Rd. (CR A15)
8.4	Right on Hwy 89
11.4	Left on Gold Lake Hwy
19.0	First summit (6600')
19.9	Gold Lake access road
21.0	Second summit (6680'); Goose, Snag, and Haven lakes on right
26.8	Left on Hwy 49; Bassetts (store)
33.6	Yuba Pass (6701')
39.8	Left on Hwy 89
42.8	Right on Calpine Rd.
44.1	Left on Westside Rd.; becomes Beckwourth–Calpine Rd.
55.8	Left on Hwy 70 (Feather River Hwy)
57.3	Left on Rocky Point Rd.
59.6	Left on East Riverside Avenue bike trail
60.5	Finish in center of Portola

66 TRUCKEE OUT-AND-BACKS

Difficulty:	Moderate/challenging
Time:	4 to 5 hours
Distance:	Up to 44 miles
Elevation gain:	2100'
Best seasons:	Mid-June through September
Road conditions:	Some roads are busy; some are not. Pavement is good.

GETTING THERE: From I-80 in Truckee, take the Hwy 89 exit and proceed north and across Donner Pass Rd., following Frates Ln. to the Safeway shopping center.

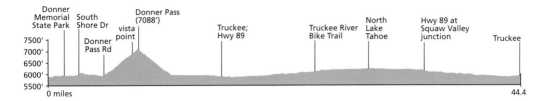

Donner
Memorial
State Park
South
Shore Dr
vista
point
Donner Pass
(7088')
Truckee;
Hwy 89
Truckee River
Bike Trail
North
Lake
Tahoe
Hwy 89 at
Squaw Valley
junction
Truckee
7500'
7000'
Donner
Pass Rd
6500'
6000'
5500'
0 miles
44.4

This ride is really two distinct out-and-backs from a hub on the western fringe of the mountain city of Truckee. One heads west to Donner Pass, while the other heads south to Lake Tahoe. Each could be done alone. The run down to Tahoe could also be combined with the ride along the west side of the big lake (Ride 67), as both rides meet at the northwest corner of the lake.

The day's adventure begins with the run west from Truckee on Donner Pass Road. The first mile-plus is commercial clutter on the edge of town, until the road crosses over I-80 and approaches Donner Lake. The route passes through Donner Memorial State Park, making use of the park's pretty access road and a short bike path to pass out of the park and connect to the road along the south shore of the lake. It's a beautiful park, here because of its natural setting on the shore of the lake, but it also commemorates the tragic Donner Party, an early pioneer expedition that was stranded here over the winter of 1846–47.

South Shore Drive rolls along on a mildly rolling course through dense mountain forest a little way back from the lakeshore, with

The view from Donner summit makes the climb up to it worthwhile. And then you get to ride back down to the lake.

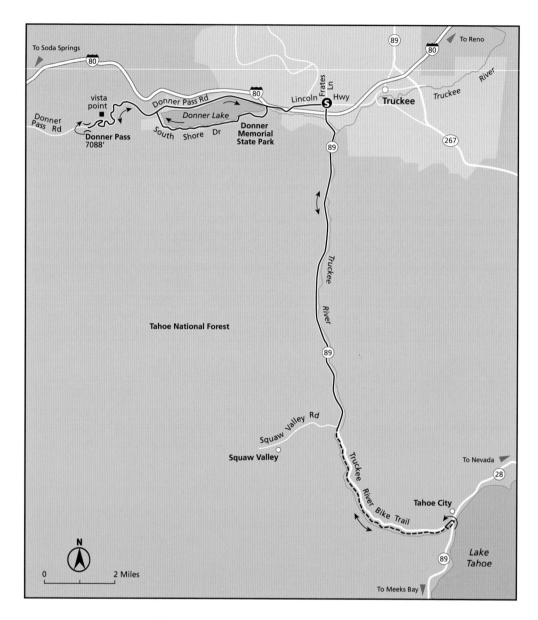

homes tucked into the trees between the road and the lake. That mild topography ends when you turn left on Donner Pass Road and head uphill toward the pass.

The climb begins just as you leave the lake, and right away the scenery improves, or at least the development tapers off abruptly, leaving you in a wild, scenic setting. The road

gains 1100' in 3.5 miles. None of it is brutally steep, but it is a substantial ascent. As you climb, the landscape becomes increasingly extravagant in its display of soaring granite cliffs and house-sized boulders... classic High Sierra geology that would look right at home in Yosemite. About a half mile below the summit, there is an official vista point, and I suggest you stop here on the way up. This is the big pay-off for the climb. The view back down to the lake and to the magnificent big-granite scenery on all sides is spectacular, and worth whatever effort you put in on the climb. Either make this the goal of your climb or stop first, enjoy the view, and then do the last bit to the summit. You only need to go to the actual 7088' summit to check Donner Pass off your personal been-there-done-that list and to wring the fullest measure of fun out of the 3.5-mile descent back to the lake, a really thrilling downhill.

When the descent bottoms out back at the lake, continue straight on Donner Pass Road, now on the north shore of the lake. The road is almost dead flat here and snuggles right up next to the lake, so views over the water predominate. Roll out that last mile back into Truckee and then turn south out of town on Highway 89, heading for Lake Tahoe.

Hwy 89 is a little too much of a big highway to be an ideal bike road, but it does have immense shoulders and the scenery is pleasant, with the Truckee River riffling along its rocky bed on the east side of the road. (It will be more visible on the return run, when you're over on that side of the road.) While this run south is an upstream run alongside

the river, it is about as gradual as a climb can be, gaining less than 400' in 13 miles. That will feel like a level road.

At mile 25, at the junction with the road to the Squaw Valley ski resort (home of the 1960 Winter Olympics), you leave the highway for the Truckee River Bike Trail, which meanders along beside the river the rest of the way to the lake. This trail is a gem. If the vista point was the big pay-off on the Donner Pass out-and-back, this trail is the prize on this part of the day's route. It's delightful.

When it ends, you are in North Lake Tahoe, suddenly immersed in another busy commercial zone, but with the lake dead ahead. There are a number of ways you can play around with your destination here at the lake. I suggest a loop that visits the historic gatehouse where the lake flows out into the river, and the park next to the gatehouse. But you can expand upon the basics by finding a spot for lunch or by riding down the west shore. (See the Ride 67 write-up for more details on that section.)

After your sojourn at the lake, all you have to do is ride back to Truckee: 5 miles on the wonderful bike trail and 9 miles along the wide shoulder of Hwy 89, now on the river side of the road.

MILEAGE LOG

0.1	From Safeway parking lot at Frates Ln., right (west) on Donner Pass Rd.
1.5	Left into Donner Memorial State Park on South Shore Dr.
2.7	Follow bike trail out of park at end of road
2.9	Pick up South Shore Dr. again after trail link
5.2	Left on Donner Pass Rd.
7.9	Left into vista point below Donner Summit Bridge; after break, continue uphill on Donner Pass Rd.
8.4	Donner Pass (7088'); turn around, head back down the hill (retrace Donner Pass Rd.)
16.3	Back in Truckee, left on Frates Ln.; becomes Hwy 89; pass through two traffic circles on way out of town, heading south for Lake Tahoe
25.0	At Squaw Valley junction, cross Hwy 89 to Truckee River Bike Trail
30.0	At North Lake Tahoe, exit trail and head south on Hwy 89
30.2	Cross Hwy 89 (West Lake Blvd.) and enter park near lake outflow; cross bridge at lake outflow to Gatekeeper's Museum and Park

30.3	Cross back over West Lake Blvd. on bike trail on south bank of river
30.6	Left on Truckee River Bike Trail; retrace trail to Squaw Valley
35.6	At Squaw Valley junction, right on Hwy 89, north to Truckee
44.3	In Truckee, cross Donner Pass Rd. to Frates Ln.
44.4	Finish at Safeway parking lot

67 LAKE TAHOE OUT-AND-BACK

Difficulty:	Moderate/challenging
Time:	2 to 3 hours (one way)
Distance:	24.5 (one way) or 49 (round trip)
Elevation gain:	Up to 3200'
Best seasons:	June through September
Road conditions:	Traffic can be heavy during tourist seasons; some of route is on bike trails.

GETTING THERE: From the Hwy 50/89 junction in South Lake Tahoe, head north on Hwy 89 3.2 miles to a right on access road to Kiva Beach Picnic Area.

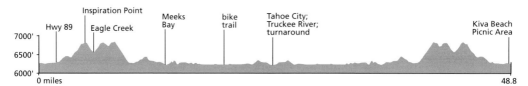

Lake Tahoe probably needs no introduction, but I'll make a quick stab at it anyway. It is a large alpine lake nestled into the dogleg crook along California's eastern border, with the Nevada state line running through the middle of the lake. It is the largest "alpine" lake in the United States, and the largest lake in California (unless you subtract the part that's actually in Nevada). Its depth of 1645' makes it the second deepest lake in the country, with only Crater Lake being deeper. And as is the case with Crater Lake, that depth and the purity of its snowmelt water conspire to render the lake a beautiful, deep blue color, much admired by all who see it. The lake's setting is much admired as well, with magnificent peaks on all sides: the Sierra Nevada

in the west and the Carson Range in the east.

This out-and-back ride explores the west shore of the lake, heading from the south end near South Lake Tahoe to the north end near Tahoe City. You could ride it one-way using a car shuttle, but I'm guessing most people will do the round-trip. Of course, as with any out-and-back, you can turn around whenever you've had your fill. The public parking lot on the south shore is just one of many similar park-related spots where you can stash a vehicle. Another option is to start at the north end and do the ride in reverse.

The first 2 miles are on a nearly level bike trail next to Highway 89. Then you have to get out on the highway and begin the biggest challenge of the day: climbing over three

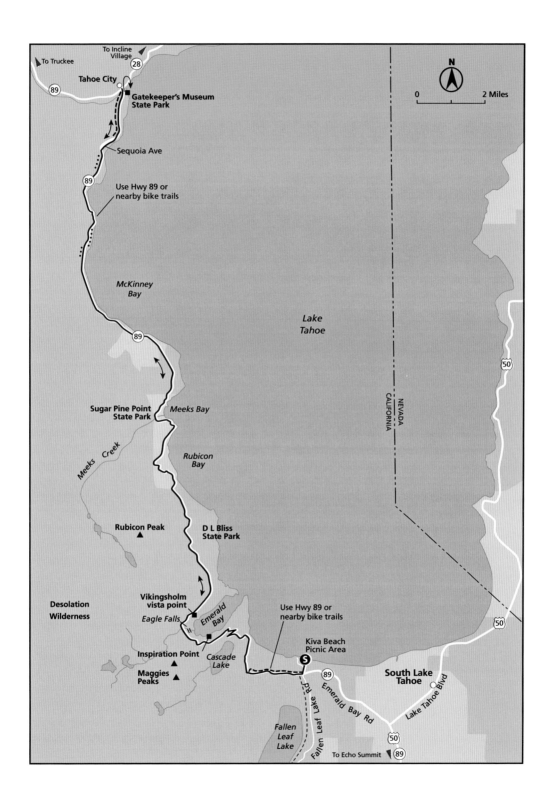

N

0   2 Miles

To Truckee

To Incline Village

28

Tahoe City

89

Gatekeeper's Museum State Park

Sequoia Ave

89

Use Hwy 89 or nearby bike trails

McKinney Bay

Lake Tahoe

89

NEVADA
CALIFORNIA

50

Sugar Pine Point State Park

Meeks Bay

Meeks Creek

Rubicon Bay

Rubicon Peak

D L Bliss State Park

Desolation Wilderness

Vikingsholm vista point

Eagle Falls

Emerald Bay

Use Hwy 89 or nearby bike trails

Kiva Beach Picnic Area

50

Inspiration Point

Cascade Lake

S

Maggies Peaks

89

South Lake Tahoe

Lake Tahoe Blvd

Emerald Bay Rd

Fallen Leaf Lake Rd

Fallen Leaf Lake

50

To Echo Summit

89

The bike trail along the west shore of Lake Tahoe is often closer to the water than the nearby road. (Nancy Yu)

summits on the way through Emerald Bay and D. L. Bliss state parks. These climbs (and descents) will of course be waiting for you at the end of your return trip too. I'm only going to cover the route going one-way, but don't lose track of the full picture if you're doing it as a round-trip.

The ascents are not that hard. The first one gains 550' in 2 miles, including some level or even mildly downhill bits. After a 1-mile descent, the second climb gains 250' in 1 mile. The last climb is the smallest: 100' up in a little over half a mile. What's more significant about these climbs than any measure of difficulty is where they take you. The road claws its way up and over the rocky headland in a most dramatic way, including a few tight hairpins that would look right at home on a famous *col* in the French Alps. Even more impressive than the road itself are the world-class views that open up from the higher summits, 500 or more feet above the lake. The most spectacular vistas are over Emerald Bay.

You can break off the climbs at any number of vista points along the way: give your legs a rest while you give your eyes a workout. I also recommend stopping where the road passes Eagle Falls, one of the prettiest mountain cascades around and easily accessible from the road.

After this larger-than-life scramble over the rocky headlands, the road descends through the pine forest back to near lake level near Meeks Bay at mile 13. For the remaining 11-plus miles to Tahoe City, the route stays approximately on the lakeshore, although it is as likely to be back in the trees as right out by the water. About 5 of those miles can be ridden on a bike trail that parallels the highway.

Whether you use the trail or stay on the main road is your choice and may depend on how heavy the traffic is on the road. On weekends in the summer tourist season, traffic can be a bit of a pain here, and then the trail makes a good alternative. If you're here on a weekday or in the off-season and the traffic isn't bad, the road may suit you.

North of Meeks Bay, there is more development: more residential districts—mountain cabins, ski lodges, and some elegant old estates—and more commercial enterprise, most of it tourist-oriented. Pine forest and Sierra granite are still much in evidence, and the overall ambience remains quite pleasant; it's just not as knock-your-socks-off gorgeous as the miles up on the rocky promontories in the state parks around Emerald Bay. One nice thing about the touristy stuff: there are loads of places to stop for lunch or munchies.

Note that this route meets the bike trail along the Truckee River that is featured in Ride 66; you might consider combining all or parts of both rides. There is another interesting out-and-back directly across Hwy 89 from today's start/finish site: a run up the shore of Fallen Leaf Lake, a 10-mile round-trip to the far end of the lake.

MILEAGE LOG

0.0	From Kiva Beach Picnic Area, south toward Hwy 89
0.3	Right on bike trail parallel to Hwy 89
1.9	Right on Hwy 89; leave trail
4.9	Inspiration Point; summit of first big climb
5.8	Eagle Creek
6.1	Vikingsholm vista point overlooking Emerald Bay
8.0	Final summit
13.3	Meeks Bay
19.4	Cross Hwy 89 and bear right onto bike trail (optional), parallel to highway
22.3	Right on Sequoia Ave.
22.7	Cross Hwy 89 to continue on Sequoia
23.3	Left on Hwy 89 or bike trail on west side of highway
24.4	Turnaround at Gatekeeper's Museum State Park near Truckee River

68 CALIFORNIA ALPS OUT-AND-BACKS

Difficulty:	Challenging
Time:	5 to 7 hours
Distance:	65 or 73 miles
Elevation gain:	Up to 8500'
Best seasons:	June through September
Road conditions:	Roads are mostly low traffic. Pavement is good.

GETTING THERE: From South Lake Tahoe, take Hwy 89 24 miles south to Markleeville.

This must be one of the easiest rides in the book…for navigation. It's mostly just one long out-and-back with a couple of minor wrinkles. But that's the only way this ride is easy. In terms of effort, it's a bit of a brute, with climbs that are both long and steep.

The ride begins and ends in Markleeville, the little town in Alpine County that is the

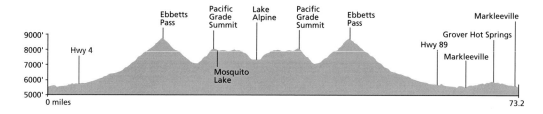

home of a popular midsummer ride called the Tour of the California Alps or, in common parlance, the Markleeville Death Ride. That big event does five huge Sierra climbs: both sides of 8314' Monitor Pass, both sides of 8730' Ebbetts Pass, and the east face of 8573' Carson Pass. Today, we're doing both sides of Ebbetts and also another pass beyond it, beyond where the Death Ride turns around: 8050' Pacific Grade. (We do Monitor Pass on our multi-day tour of the Sierra, Ride 75.)

Head south out of Markleeville on Highway 89 on a mildly uphill run along the East Fork Carson River, which tumbles along next to the road in a boulder-strewn wash amid stands of aspen and pine. At about mile 5, at the junction where Hwy 89 heads east over Monitor Pass, continue straight on Hwy 4. A mile later, the grade kicks up just a bit, from what had been little more than a false flat to a

Climbing to 8730' Ebbetts Pass amid the alpine grandeur of the High Sierra (Nancy Yu)

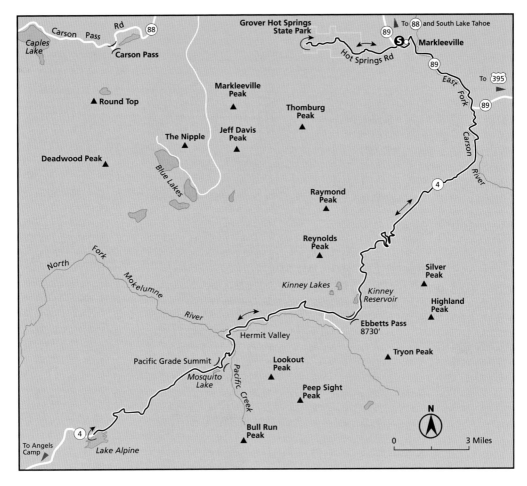

steady uphill, gaining around 900' in 6 miles (3 percent). At mile 12, the lazy grade gives way to a real alpine challenge, as the narrow road rears up on its hind legs and starts grappling up the granite cliff in a series of steep, tight hairpins. It's all hard work from here to the summit at mile 18: 2000' up in 6 miles (7 percent), with some spots a good deal steeper. This is now a classic High Sierra landscape: huge, chunky granite monoliths knuckling up around the road, with the cascades of Silver Creek splashing away nearby.

Over the summit, the road slithers down the rocky hillside for 5 miles, losing 1700'. At the bottom of this descent, it flattens out for most of a mile through a meadow known as Hermit Valley. This is where the Death Ride turns around, but our route is going to continue and take on one more big climb on our outward-bound leg, and what a climb it is! After crossing Pacific Creek—the headwaters of the Mokelumne River—the road tilts up into a ferocious pitch. The raw numbers don't really do justice to how fierce this is: 1000' up in 2.5 miles for an 8 percent average. But in the middle of the climb, just beyond mile 25, there is a set of steep switchbacks that must be flirting with 20 percent for a while. It eases off after that brutal wall and tops out at mile 26.

Just past Pacific Grade summit, the road descends gently to a rolling run along pretty

Mosquito Lake, where cute, rustic cabins perch along the rocky shore, just begging to have their pictures taken. From here 6 miles of rollers and easy downhills lead to Lake Alpine and our turn-around point at Lake Alpine Lodge, where a long, shady front porch overlooks the lake. This is the perfect spot to order lunch, put your feet up, and admire the lake and the surrounding alpine scenery.

Once you've stowed your lunch away, it's time to retrace the route to Markleeville. That means 6 miles of gently rolling uphill to Pacific Grade summit, 2.5 miles downhill into Hermit Valley—including those really steep pitches—5 miles of moderate climbing to Ebbetts Pass, and almost 17 miles of nonstop descending back into the valley of the Carson River. The last 11 miles of that run will be gentle roll-out, but prior to that, the first 6 miles are intense. Bold descenders will be lighting it up. But you don't want to be *too* bold. A few corners, including one notorious left-hand hairpin known as Cadillac Curve, are treacherous. Overcooking it here can have dire consequences.

Back in Markleeville, we have to think about our other, much smaller out-and-back. This is a run from town up to Grover Hot Springs State Park. It's about 4 mildly uphill miles to the park...8 miles round-trip. It's a beautiful park with a nice campground, but the main attraction is the hot springs, with a big pool steaming away, ready to soothe your aching muscles. You will have to decide if you want to ride up and back, with a dip in the pool in the middle, or drive up and back. Another option—one I have done—is to camp here and begin and end the ride here, making it a 73-mile day, with the hot springs beckoning at the end.

MILEAGE LOG

0.0	From Markleeville, south on Hwy 89
4.9	Straight on Hwy 4 toward Ebbetts Pass (Hwy 89 turns left toward Monitor Pass)
18.1	Ebbetts Pass (8730')
26.0	Pacific Grade summit (8050')
32.6	Lake Alpine: end of the line (lodge, food); retrace to Markleeville
65.2	Left on Hot Springs Rd. to Grover Hot Springs State Park (alternate start/finish site; add 4 miles to all figures)
69.2	Grover Hot Springs State Park; retrace to Markleeville
73.2	Finish in Markleeville

69 YOSEMITE VALLEY

Difficulty:	Easy/moderate
Time:	2 to 4 hours
Distance:	21 miles
Elevation gain:	Up to 1000'
Best seasons:	June through September (but especially September)
Road conditions:	Traffic can be heavy during tourist seasons; some of the route is on bike trails.

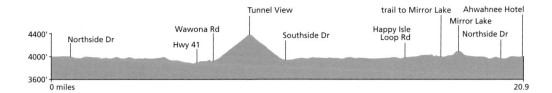

GETTING THERE: There are three routes into Yosemite Valley: Wawona Rd. from the southwest, El Portal Rd. from the west, and Big Oak Flat Rd. from the northwest. All feed onto Southside Dr., a one-way road into the valley center. Turn left on Northside Dr., right on Village Dr., and right on Ahwahnee Dr. to the Ahwahnee Hotel.

What can I say about Yosemite Valley that hasn't been said by hundreds of other writers, beginning with John Muir? It is probably the most famous, most iconic, most revered spot in California. Any flights of journalistic fancy I could cobble together would fail to do justice to this special place. Because it is so well known, I'm going to assume you don't need me to describe it. Instead, I want to discuss the best way to experience this magical valley on a bicycle.

The main valley—the more-or-less flat valley floor between the soaring cliffs—is about 14 miles long and rarely more than a mile

Caution: Riding in Yosemite Valley may result in a severe case of sensory overload.

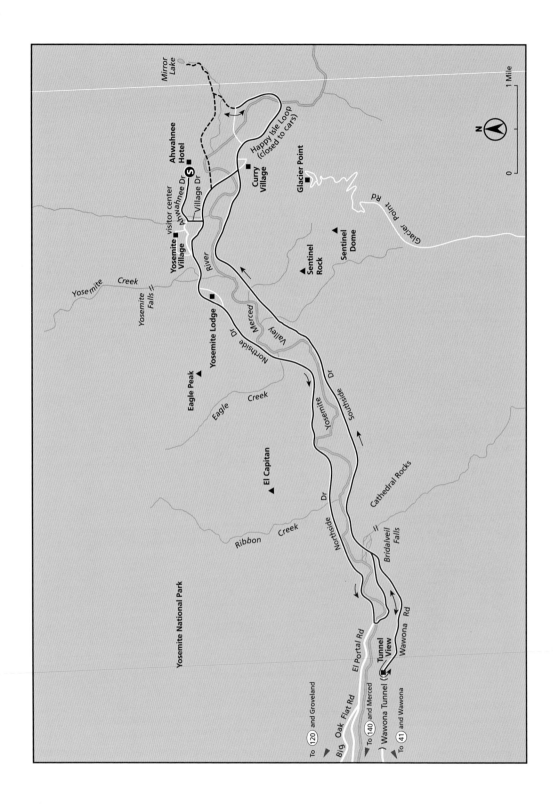

wide. Two main roads run the length of the valley: Northside and Southside drives, with the pretty Merced River in between. Most of the time, the two roads are one-way: Southside feeds into the valley (east, upstream) and Northside heads down the valley. A few roads cross the river. There are also quite a few smaller roads squiggled about, especially near the eastern end of the valley where most of the lodgings, campgrounds, and services are concentrated. And then there is a fairly complex tracery of paved nature trails available to bikes.

This ride consists primarily of the basic Northside–Southside counterclockwise loop, following the flow of the one-way roads, and I've added a few little embellishments to make the experience better. But you should not feel bound to follow this route precisely. You do generally have to follow the big one-way loop; that part is pretty much a no-brainer. But just as I have added a few flourishes here and there, so can you: if you see something interesting down a side road or trail, check it out.

We start from the Ahwahnee Hotel, one of my favorite spots in the valley. This grand old inn, opened in 1927, is among the greatest of America's great park lodges. Be sure to take a stroll through the public rooms after your ride.

The side road from the lodge leads out to Northside Drive, and before turning onto this busy road, I want to stop and talk about traffic. In spite of the best efforts of park planners to limit private vehicle traffic in the valley, there is still a lot of it. The best advice I can offer for dealing with traffic is not so much about where to ride but *when* to ride. I suggest the month of September, when the weather is still nice but the families have gone home to put the kids back in school. The

traffic flow drops off considerably then, and it gets even better if you can plan to be here on a weekday. All that said, you will still be sharing the roads with many automobiles and RVs and all the rest of the motorized horde. But be assured that cars and bikes can and do coexist here quite peacefully.

After circling the west end of the valley and beginning the run east on Southside, turn right for an out-and-back to the mouth of the tunnel on Wawona Road and the vista point next to it. The park literature refers to this spot as Tunnel View, a humble name for such a magnificent panorama. The whole of the valley is on display, looking as grand as only Yosemite can. The climb to the tunnel gains 450' in 1.5 miles, a 6 percent average. Yes, that is real work, but not brutal, and it's the only challenging element in the entire ride. The view is worth it.

There are many other scenic attractions around the valley. Read the park literature to learn more, but especially, look around.

At the east end of the canyon, Southside Drive feeds directly onto Happy Isle Loop Road. This road provides access to campgrounds, but beyond the camps is closed to cars; only bikes and park shuttle buses are allowed. There is a trail off this loop that runs up to Mirror Lake before merging back into Northside Drive, not far from the road that winds around to the Ahwahnee. Along with everything else in this valley, Mirror Lake is well worth a visit. It's just one example of the detours you can make as you explore Yosemite Valley. Find quiet spots where the cars can't go—Mirror Lake, for instance—and let this most beautiful, most mystical of all places smooth out the wrinkles in your spirit.

MILEAGE LOG

0.0	From the Ahwahnee Hotel parking lot, left on Ahwahnee Dr.
0.6	Left on Village Dr.
0.8	Right on Northside Dr.
6.4	Left on Hwy 140; follow sign to Wawona

7.3	Turn right on Hwy 41; follow sign to Wawona; climb ahead…
8.8	Wawona Tunnel vista point; turnaround, retrace to…
10.4	Bear right on Southside Dr., back in valley
15.5	Straight on Happy Isle Loop Rd. at Northside Dr. junction
16.1	Continue on Happy Isle Loop: becomes bikes and pedestrians only
17.1	Right from Happy Isle Loop on trail to Mirror Lake
17.5	Right to continue to Mirror Lake
18.0	Mirror Lake; retrace
19.7	Bear right on trail next to Northside Dr.
20.1	Right on Village Dr.
20.3	Right on Ahwahnee Dr.
20.9	Finish at Ahwahnee Hotel parking lot

70 JUNE LAKE LOOP

Difficulty:	Easy/moderate
Time:	2 to 3 hours
Distance:	28 miles
Elevation gain:	1700'
Best seasons:	Mid-June to October
Road conditions:	Some roads are busy; most are not. Pavement is good.

GETTING THERE: From Lee Vining, near the Hwy 120 junction, head south on Hwy 395 for 11 miles. Drive 4 miles west on Hwy 158 to June Mountain Ski Area parking lot, just downhill from the town of June Lake.

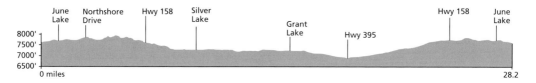

This little loop visits two glacial valleys below the steep, towering escarpment of the east face of the Sierra. It occupies a transition zone between the rugged granite mountains to the west and the open, dry, austere Basin and Range country stretching away to the east, out across Nevada. This route samples both of those landscapes.

June Lake has been a tourist destination since decent roads were laid down in the region in the early part of the twentieth century. It has always been both a destination in its own right and a stopover for travelers heading for the backdoor entrance to Yosemite: Tioga Pass, just a few miles north of here. There are four lakes along the loop: June, Gull, Silver, and Grant.

This ride begins with a smaller loop within the bigger loop. From the ski area parking lot, head uphill on Highway 158, past Gull and June lakes and the town of June Lake. This is

June Lake is one of four pretty lakes along this little loop on the eastern flank of the Sierra. (Bill Bushnell)

an easy climb, 300' in 3 miles. After turning left on Northshore Drive, you have a gentle, 1-mile downhill, a mile and a half of chunky rollers, including the high point of the ride (7887'), and finally a frisky 3-mile descent, almost all the way to Silver Lake. Scenery along this little loop is everything you would expect it to be in the shadow of the Sierra: rugged knuckles of granite muscling up along the road, the lakes glinting in the sun, off in the middle distance, and the majestic peaks of the Range of Light, clawing at the heavens in the west.

The only problem with the 3-mile downhill is the stop sign halfway down, where you turn from Northshore Drive back onto Hwy 158. When you bottom out at the end of the descent, around mile 8, you are into the part of the loop I like best: the run past Silver Lake. This lake is the prettiest of them all, and the roadside scenery is beautiful, with woods of pine and aspen. Charming mountain cabins and a few resort lodges are on display, either next to the road or back in the woods.

Heading north from Silver Lake, the landscape begins to change. The road passes through a deep, rocky canyon before emerging into more open country around Grant Lake. What had been dense, pretty forest near Silver Lake is at first replaced by random stands of trees and eventually by flora not much bigger than sagebrush and chaparral. Grant Lake is bigger than the other three lakes put together, but it didn't come by that bigness naturally. In the 1940s, the original lake was dammed by the Los Angeles Department of Water and Power as part of their grand scheme to siphon off Sierra water for the folks in the southland. So it looks a bit more like a reservoir than a classic, natural alpine lake.

For the 8 miles from south of Silver Lake to north of Grant Lake, Hwy 158 remains more or less flat. There are a number of rolling ups and downs along the way, but the elevation at the end of that section is almost the same as it was at the beginning. Past the dam at Grant Lake, that changes. The road slopes downhill, out across Pumice Valley and into the vast emptiness south of Mono Lake. You have just come face to face with the archetypal wide-open spaces of the American West. The road spools out straight ahead, mile after

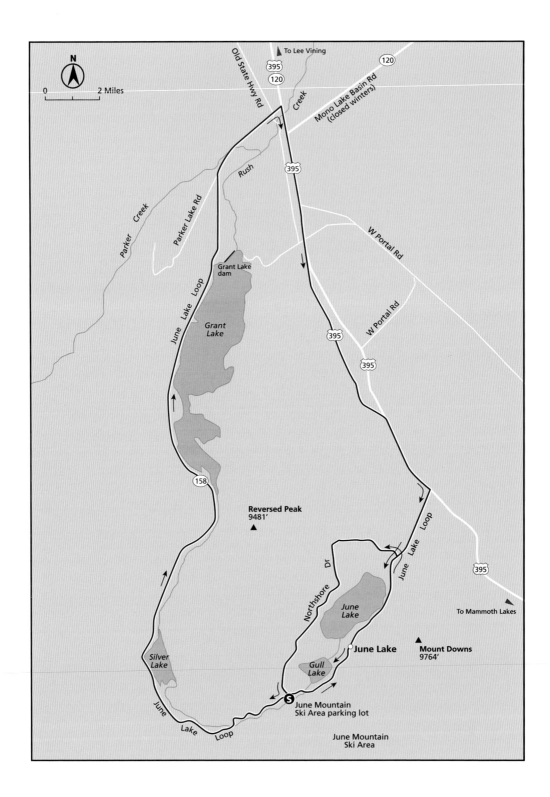

mile, like an illustration of the principle of perspective. For a puny cyclist, toiling along at bike speed, this can be troubling. You feel as if you're on rollers: pedaling away but not getting anywhere. For the 3 remaining miles on Hwy 158 and all 6 miles heading south on a mildly uphill grade along Hwy 395, this out-of-scale malaise persists.

Now, some cyclists don't seem to mind this. Witness all the riders who sign up for the Death Valley Double each year, or for the Eastern Sierra Double, which runs on these very roads. Others find it demoralizing. You will have to decide which sort of cyclist you are. If you like those forever horizons, go for it: keep chugging on around the loop. If you balk at all that barren, possibly boring emptiness, I suggest you turn around at the top of Grant Lake and ride back to the start on Hwy 158 through the cozily forested landscape around the smaller lakes.

If you do continue, you will eventually complete the run down Hwy 395 and will turn right onto Hwy 158 at its southern end, uphill from June Lake. All that remains is to head downhill to and through the town to the finish at the ski station. You will have been through the resort of June Lake twice now, so perhaps you will have spied out a good spot for an after-ride lunch.

MILEAGE LOG

0.0	From ski area parking lot, right on Hwy 158
1.0	Town of June Lake
2.7	Left on Northshore Dr.
6.3	Right on Hwy 158
9.3	Silver Lake
14.0	Grant Lake
18.3	Right on Hwy 395
24.4	Right on Hwy 158
27.2	Town of June Lake
28.2	Finish

71 MAMMOTH–MARY–MINARETS

Difficulty:	Challenging
Time:	4 to 5 hours
Distance:	40 miles
Elevation gain:	3900'
Best seasons:	Mid-June through September
Road conditions:	Traffic is generally low and pavement good.

GETTING THERE: From Hwy 395 about 37 miles north of Bishop, drive 3 miles west on Hwy 203 into Mammoth Lakes. Turn left on Old Mammoth Rd. and park at Mammoth Gateway shopping center.

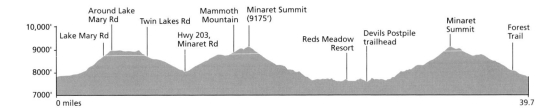

Mammoth Lakes is a resort village on the eastern flank of the Sierra. This ride offers two high-country treks near the town. Don't be deceived by the modest 40-mile distance. This is a fairly ambitious ride, but also a hugely spectacular one.

The journey begins with a 4-mile climb on Old Mammoth Road. The clutter of town falls away as the road tilts uphill and narrows to one lane, twisting through rocky, forested hills above the residential sprawl. It gains about 1000' over that run, most of it concentrated in the last 2.5 miles.

At 4 miles, turn left on Lake Mary Road, heading for the namesake lake. The road climbs for another half mile before flattening out at Around Lake Mary Road, which, as the name so clearly implies, makes a circuit around the lake. This loop is pretty and quiet, a mix of High Sierra wilderness and

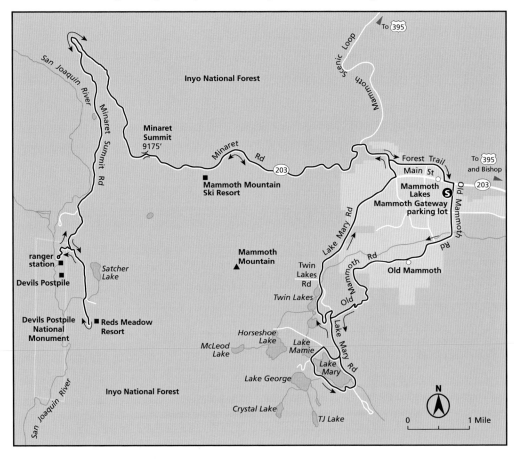

When you cross 9175' Minaret summit and look across the deep gorge of the San Joaquin River, the rugged peaks of the High Sierra are ranged out along the western skyline. (Bill Bushnell)

mountain cabins with docks for little boats. Once you've circumnavigated the lake, turn right on Lake Mary Road and retrace your route past the Old Mammoth junction. At 7.7 miles, turn left on Twin Lakes Road and follow a 1-mile detour snuggled up against the shore of Twin Lakes before returning to Lake Mary Road. After traversing the hillside, past ski resorts and loads of mountain cabins, the road plunges back to town on a fast, smooth flier.

Just before mile 11, you bottom out in town and turn left on Highway 203, also at this point known as Minaret Road. You're heading, first of all, for Mammoth Mountain, the premier ski resort in the area, a huge development. The road climbs, most of the time, between miles 11 and 16, passing the resort, usually on a moderate, steady grade that seldom exceeds 5 percent. Much of this section is quite pretty, deep in fir and pine forest. The resort itself sprawls over thousands of acres and is typical of ski resorts: attractive when covered in a blanket

of white, midwinter snow, but raw and bleak in the summer, just a bit less denuded than a strip mine.

But you're just passing through the ski area. The goal on this out-and-back is farther along: up and over the pass (9175' Minaret Summit, one of the highest passes in California) and down to Devils Postpile National Monument. This is a long dead end that plummets dramatically into the majestic gorge of the San Joaquin River, near the eastern border of Yosemite National Park, with the jagged Minarets and Ritter Range looming in snaggletooth glory on the far side of the gorge.

The road beyond the summit, down into the gorge, is restricted to just shuttle buses and bicycles. Private cars can travel here only under certain exceptions. (Read the Devils Postpile National Monument literature to learn more.) For the most part, you will have the road to yourself, except for the infrequent buses. The descent is a bit over 5 miles and is never too steep. It's perfect for smooth descending, and then, on the way back, not too brutal as a climb. The pavement is good or even very good, and the road is not overly engineered. It's old-fashioned in all the right ways that make biking fun. And it's all as magnificently scenic as you would expect a national park in the High Sierra to be.

The road rambles along down in the bottom of the canyon for 2 or 3 miles, passing pretty little lakes, before fetching up at Reds Meadow at around mile 25. There are a number of options here for off-the-bike activities. The simplest thing would be to have lunch in the nice café. If you have figured out how to get some walking shoes down here with you, you might consider a hike to Devils Postpile, a 1-mile round-trip, always easy. To really appreciate this geological marvel, you should take the trouble to hike up to the top of the cliff and walk out onto it. Glacial scouring has smoothed off the tops of the basalt columns so that it looks almost like a level floor of hexagonal tiles. The trail to the rocks takes off from a short side road, clearly marked on your map and noted on the mileage log. I have you rolling all the way to the end of the main road first, then hitting this side road and the (possible) hike on the way back.

After whatever adventures you tackle down in the canyon, eventually you have to get back out of this deep hole. That's not really as daunting as it might seem. The gradient is relatively moderate and the scenery along the way is superb, making it easy to forget the work you might be putting into the project. The climb is about 1500' over 5 miles (4 to 6 percent).

Once over the summit, you have that 5-mile descent back past the ski resort and down into the town of Mammoth Lakes. It's a fast, clean run, never technical or sketchy. Just let 'er rip. At the bottom, turn left on Forest Trail, a residential side road running parallel to Hwy 203. It gets you almost all the way to the finish without any urban congestion. If you didn't have lunch down in Reds Meadow, this resort town has an almost endless inventory of places to chow down.

MILEAGE LOG

0.0	From Mammoth Gateway parking lot, right (south) on Old Mammoth Rd.
4.0	Left on Lake Mary Rd.
4.7	Left on Around Lake Mary Rd.
6.5	Right on Lake Mary Rd.
7.7	Left on Twin Lakes Rd.
8.8	Right on Lake Mary Rd.
10.9	Left on Minaret Rd.; back in Mammoth Lakes
15.0	Mammoth Mountain ski resort
16.3	Ranger kiosk, Minaret summit (9175'), also known as Postpile Rd. and Minaret Summit Rd.
24.8	Reds Meadow Resort; turnaround, retrace to...
25.8	Left on side road to ranger station
26.3	Ranger station, Devils Postpile trailhead; retrace to...
26.8	Left on Minaret Summit Rd.
33.3	Ranger kiosk, summit
38.4	Left on Forest Trail; back in Mammoth Lakes
39.5	Left on Main St. (Hwy 203)
39.6	Right on Old Mammoth Rd.
39.7	Right into Mammoth Gateway Center and finish

72 BASS LAKE–GRIZZLY LOOP

Difficulty:	Challenging
Time:	5 to 7 hours
Distance:	76 miles
Elevation gain:	7100'
Best seasons:	Late spring to early autumn
Road conditions:	Pavement is good throughout. Traffic is light.

GETTING THERE: From Oakhurst, near the junction of Hwy 49 and 41, take Hwy 41 north 3.5 miles and turn right on County Road 222 toward Bass Lake. Take CR 222 south, then continue on CR 274 down the east shore of Bass Lake to the town of North Fork, 17.7 miles south of Hwy 41. Cross South Fork Rd. to Mono Dr. and turn left up the driveway to North Fork Elementary School.

Plotting this loop was a no-brainer: for the most part, it follows the course of the Sierra Vista National Scenic Byway (so designated by the US Forest Service). It also follows most of the route of a great autumn ride called the Grizzly Century. I've done the Griz several times, one of the best centuries in the state. The scenery is very nearly as grand as it is in nearby Yosemite Valley (Ride 69). The roads are well paved, and traffic is just about nonexistent. There is a great deal of High Sierra climbing, but it's never brutal. And the payback for all that climbing comes in the form of some of the best descending you will ever do.

The ride begins at the same place the century does: a school in the town of North Fork, near the southern end of Bass Lake. After a rolling run of 4-plus miles, the route passes the little settlement of South Fork and begins the first of many climbs along Mammoth Pool Road (Minarets Road), following the US Forest Service National Scenic Byway signs and signs to Mammoth Pool and Clover Meadow. For you geography buffs, this is within a mile of the spot designated as the geographical center of the state of California. (How you determine the exact center of a state shaped like a dogleg golf fairway, I have no idea, but they confidently make the claim and have a roadside marker to commemorate it.)

Minarets Road is really magnificent, mostly climbing, but also descending frequently, sometimes traversing flower-filled valleys and sometimes clinging to hillsides high above distant lakes and ridgelines. As you climb, you enter a zone of impressive sculpted granite

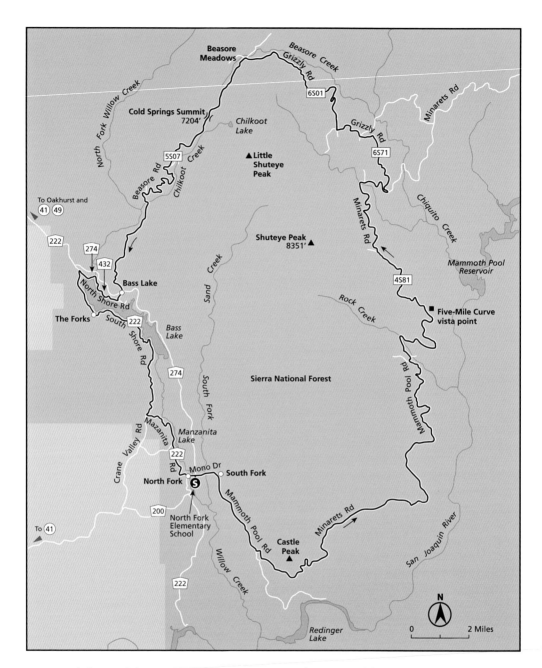

spires and domes. The Five-Mile curve vista point mentioned in the mileage log, overlooking Mammoth Pool Reservoir, is as spectacular as any national park panorama.

You have to pay attention for your next turn: a left on Grizzly Road, also known as Road 6S71 and later Road 6S01. This road is just as good as Minarets, with good paving, great scenery, no traffic, and with turns and ups and downs scaled to the speed of bike travel…pretty nearly perfect. Grizzly Road climbs for most of its 11 miles, with a

This ride is just south of Yosemite National Park, and the big-granite scenery so famous in the park is much in evidence here as well. (Rick Garner)

few level spots and small downhills thrown in. Overall, you gain well over 2000' before you get to the next turn onto Beasore Road, and the climbing doesn't end there. You climb for most of the next 3 miles to 7204' Cold Springs summit before launching off on a descent that's as good as they come: 4200' of twisting, twirling downhill frolic in 11 magical miles, all of it on excellent pavement. If there's a better downhill out there, please lead me to it!

At the bottom of this glorious run, jog right on busy Road 274 and then left onto smaller, less-traveled Road 432 to roll along the northeast shore of Bass Lake. There is a market here near mile 61, which will be your first access to food and drink on the whole ride. Head north along the east side of the lake, bend around the top, and roll south along the west shore. It's a pretty lake, about 4 miles long and a half mile wide, with a scatter of campgrounds and resorts along the shore, but also with the road hugging the shore most of the time. The west side is the nicer side for cycling, carrying much less traffic. The 10-mile run around the lake is about as close to level as any road in the mountains can be. Finally, with about 5 miles to go, the road leaves the lake and descends—most of the time—on a lively wiggle through the woods, past little Manzanita Lake and back into North Fork.

Really top-notch loop rides in the Sierra are a rarity, simply because there aren't that many paved roads in what amounts to a vast, trackless wilderness. This loop is one of the happy exceptions. I recommend it without reservation. It approaches cycling nirvana.

0.0	From parking lot of North Fork Elementary School, down the driveway
0.3	Right on Mono Dr. (Road 228)
0.3	Quick right on Mammoth Pool Rd. (also known as Minarets Rd.); follow sign to Mammoth Pool and Clover Meadow, also for Sierra Vista National Scenic Byway
27.2	Five-Mile Curve vista point overlooking Mammoth Pool
35.8	Left on Grizzly Rd. (also known as Road 6S71 and 6S01)
47.0	Left on Beasore Rd. (also known as Road 5S07)
49.6	Cold Springs summit (7304')
61.2	Jog right on Road 274 to left on Road 432 (also known as North Shore Rd.)
61.5	Stores on lakeshore
63.7	Left on Road 222 (also known as South Shore Rd.)
71.8	Bear left on Road 222 at Crane Valley Rd. junction. Sign says, "MANZANITA LAKE 2, NORTH FORK 4"
75.4	Left on Road 225 (also known as Mammoth Pool Rd.) in town of North Fork
75.7	Jog right on Mono Dr. to left on school driveway
76.0	Finish at school

MULTIDAY TOURS

Multiday tours are, for me, the very best sort of cycle-touring adventures. You leave your everyday cares behind for as long as the journey lasts, living in the moment, rolling from one new sensation to the next, mile after mile, day after day. And while a slog across the great plains of the Midwest might seem like the same old same old, day after day, in California, with its wonderfully varied tapestry of landscapes and scenery, every hour of every day offers something new and engaging...always entertaining, never boring. What's more, there are enough hours in each day, after the riding is done, for all sorts of other fun, from hiking to swimming, from exploring new towns to sampling the best local cuisine. And at the end of the long trek, you have that warm glow of accomplishment, of knowing you covered all that ground under your own power. They say getting there is half the fun, but in the case of cycle tours, getting there is all the fun.

These tours have been designed for overnights at indoor lodgings (not camping). In theory at least, this means you could do them while traveling light, carrying only minimal luggage. It is not within the scope of this book to either survey or review the quality or cost of the various inns and motels at the overnight locations. All I'm doing is guiding you to those locales and assuring you that lodgings exist there, and also that there is access to food: stores or restaurants.

73 MARBLE MOUNTAINS LOOP

Difficulty:	Challenging
Time:	3 days
Distance:	168 miles
Elevation gain:	12,700'
Best seasons:	May through September
Road conditions:	Pavement is good to excellent. Traffic is usually light.

GETTING THERE: From I-5 at Yreka, drive 15.5 miles south on Hwy 3 to Fort Jones.

This is a circuit around the Marble Mountain Wilderness in the far north of the state. It travels along three wild rivers: the Scott, Klamath, and Salmon. It is listed as "challenging" because of one big climb on the third day, but aside from that, it's a moderate proposition.

While I generally do not specify the lodgings on tour overnights, in this case, I have to: there is only the one place to stay each night, and because both are in remote locations, if you didn't know their names, you might have trouble finding them (on the Internet). Both offer kayaking opportunities on their respective rivers, and adding a day off the bike for such an adventure would be a great addition to this little loop.

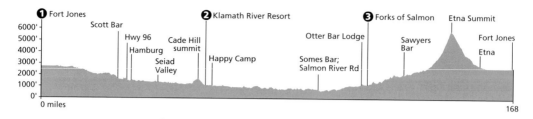

Stage 1. Fort Jones to Klamath River Resort: 59 miles, 3400'

Head west on Scott River Road, crossing pan-flat hay fields and pastures for 7 miles until you encounter the Scott River. For the next 24 miles, road and river will be braided together in happy harmony. This rolling run along the river is wonderful, sometimes skimming along right next to the rocky stream and sometimes riding high up on the canyon wall, with the river a ragged silver ribbon far below. Everything about this road is perfect for cycle-touring, including better-than-average pavement.

At mile 31, this great road tees into Highway 96. Turn left and head downstream along the Klamath River. This is a slightly busier highway, although still reasonably quiet. The pavement is good. The scenery is great. There are a couple of country stores along the way where you might pick up a snack. This downstream run along Hwy 96 is gently downhill, with a few modest rollers thrown in. But near the end of the stage, there is one significant climb, leaving the river and scrambling over a rocky headland to the tune of 500' in 2 miles. Then it's downhill all the way to the finish, losing 600' in 2-plus miles to the Klamath River Resort, 2 miles east of the town of Happy Camp.

MILEAGE LOG

0.0	West on Scott River Rd.
27.4	Town of Scott Bar
30.7	Left on Hwy 96
32.3	Town of Hamburg
41.8	Town of Seiad Valley
55.8	Cade Hill summit (1750')
58.4	Left to Klamath River Resort

Stage 2. Klamath River Resort to Otter Bar Lodge: 56 miles, 3500'

Continue along Hwy 96 and the Klamath River for another 40 miles, through Happy Camp and onward to the little town of Somes Bar. There are a few small climbs on this section: the biggest gains 200' in 1 mile, so not much, really. Sometimes you're rolling along on a gentle downgrade and sometimes flying on smooth, fast descents in the canyon, always on perfect pavement and always with the beautiful river nearby, growing bigger as it flows toward the sea.

At mile 40, just south of Somes Bar, turn upstream along the Salmon River. For the first few miles, Salmon River Road looks like a real highway, but soon loses its stripes, gives up any pretense at dignity, and hangs onto the cliff anywhere it can find a foothold. The gorge narrows, and great gray knuckles of rock grip the river in a stranglehold, forcing the stream over waterfalls and cascades between deep, green, glassy pools. Sometimes the road is only a lane wide, with a chunky rock face looming up on the right and the world dropping away abruptly

The run up the rugged Salmon River gorge is one of the best bike adventures anywhere. It's on Stage 2 of this 3-day loop. (Tom Helm)

at the edge of the pavement on the left, down into the deep canyon. It's wild and maybe a bit scary, and also stunningly beautiful. This is a cycling dream road, one of the best.

During this dramatic run up the gorge, you'll be so engrossed with the scenery and with staying away from the more alarming drop-offs into the chasm, you may forget to notice whether you're going up or down. You're doing a little of both, with more up as the day wears on, none of it too tough. For being in such a tortured canyon, the pitches are surprisingly moderate. This spectacular section takes you all the way to Otter Bar Lodge, on the right side of the road, 2 miles before the village of Forks of Salmon.

MILEAGE LOG

0.0	Left on Hwy 96
2.4	Town of Happy Camp; statue of Bigfoot
39.7	Town of Somes Bar
39.9	Left on Salmon River Rd.
55.4	Right to Otter Bar Lodge

Stage 3. Otter Bar to Fort Jones: 54 miles, 5800'
Now you arrive at the only really big climb of the tour, and yes, it is *really big*.

The stage begins at around 1300'. Etna summit, 31.5 miles ahead, tops out at over 5900'. Adding in a few ups and downs in the early miles, it works out to nearly 5000' of elevation gain over that distance. More precisely, it means 2000' on a rolling run along the Salmon River for the first 22-plus miles—all pretty and not too difficult—and then 3000' of steep, unrelenting toil for the final 9 miles. This monster would be rated *Hors Catégorie* (off the chart) in any Tour de France stage. It is a huge beast of a climb, and it seems to get harder the higher you go.

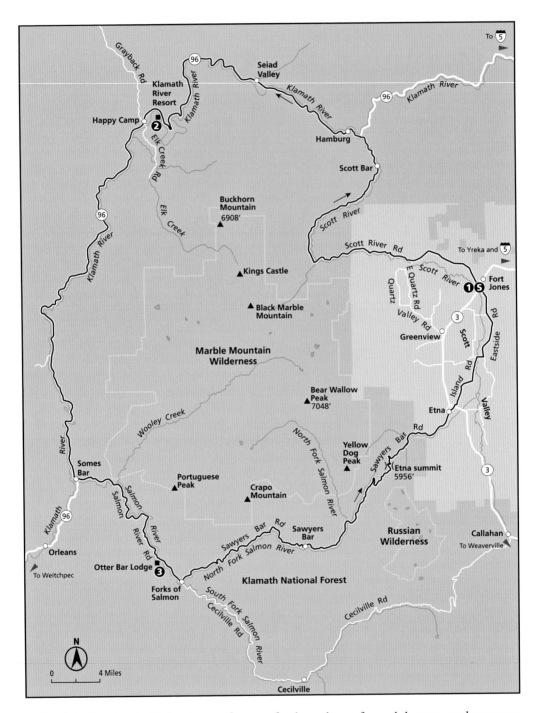

On the other hand, this has been a feature of at least three of our club tours, and everyone on every tour has finished it, including many moderate riders. It just takes chugging away at it, one turn of the pedals at a time.

The early miles on the stage are not nearly that daunting, rolling along the Salmon River through Forks of Salmon. Bear left here on Sawyers Bar Road and head upstream along the North Fork of the river for several miles on a gently rising grade, passing through the tiny village of Sawyers Bar. This section of the river is not quite as spectacular as the rocky gorge below Forks of Salmon, but it's still pleasant for cycling.

Eventually, the river veers off up a side canyon and you continue along the banks of Russian Creek. It's at this point that things become difficult. On the map, you can see a couple of hairpin switchbacks along this section. As you come around one of them, you can look up across the canyon and see the summit, *waaaaay* off in the distance. We had a support vehicle parked there on one of our tours, and the big van looked like a tiny white dot against the immensity of rock and sky…most discouraging!

But eventually you do get there, up to that lofty summit, and the payoff is panoramic views in every direction. The other big payoff is the descent off the north face of this giant *col*. It's huge, and if you're a bold descender, you'll be livin' large for the next little while, carving down the mountain for 11 busy, dizzy miles, all the way to the town of Etna at mile 42. After a break in the town, cross Hwy 3 and follow a series of quiet farm roads north along the east rim of the nearly flat Scott River Valley for 12 mellow miles back to Fort Jones.

MILEAGE LOG

0.0	Right on Salmon River Rd.
1.0	Bear left on Sawyers Bar Rd.; town of Forks of Salmon
15.0	Town of Sawyers Bar
31.6	Etna summit (5956')
41.7	Town of Etna
42.2	Cross Hwy 3 to Island Rd.
47.0	Right on Eller Ln.
47.6	Left on Eastside Rd.
53.8	Finish in Fort Jones

74 CALIFORNIA COAST

Difficulty:	Challenging
Time:	7 days
Distance:	448 miles
Elevation gain:	30,000'
Best seasons:	May through October

GETTING THERE: From San Francisco, head north on Hwy 101 approximately 377 miles to Brookings, Oregon. Turn left on W. Benham Ln. and proceed 1 mile to a district of motels along the waterfront.

Whenever one thinks of multiday tours in Northern California, the route that comes to mind first is the north–south journey from Oregon to San Francisco, on or near the coast. In broadest outline, this means a run down Highways 101 and 1, but it's rarely that simple. At times, Hwy 101 becomes a *de facto* freeway, and bypassing it requires creative navigation. The route leaves Hwy 1 occasionally as well, not to avoid traffic, but for the fun of exploring smaller roads nearby. Each diversion improves the quality of the experience but adds to the complexity of the route.

Stage 1. Brookings to Klamath: 50 miles, 2300'

The tour begins near motels in Brookings, Oregon, and soon crosses into California. Over the border, 10 miles of pleasant side roads crossing the flat, verdant valley of the Smith River deliver you to Crescent City. It takes 5 miles to ride through town, including a pretty run along the beach. Then it's all Hwy 101 for the last 20 miles, up and over a big, forested headland in Del Norte Coast Redwoods State Park and down to an overnight in the town of Klamath.

MILEAGE LOG

0.0	South on Lower Harbor Rd.; becomes Benham Ln.
0.3	Right on Wenbourne Ln.; becomes Oceanview Dr.
3.8	Right on Hwy 101
4.7	Cross into California
5.3	Left on Ocean View Dr.
10.9	Cross Hwy 101 to continue south on Sarina Rd.
11.4	Bear left on 1st St.
12.4	Right on Fred D. Haight Dr.
15.6	Right on Hwy 101
16.1	Right on Lake Earl Dr. (CR D3); becomes Northcrest Dr.
24.3	Right on Madison Ave.
24.9	Left on Arlington Dr.
25.3	Right on Washington Blvd.
26.7	Left on Pebble Beach Dr.
29.1	Bear right on Taylor St., left on 5th St.
29.3	Right on B St.
29.5	Left on Front St.
30.1	Right on Hwy 101; downtown Crescent City
49.9	Jog left on Ehlers Ave., right on Klamath Blvd.
50.0	Finish in town of Klamath

Stage 2. Klamath to Eureka: 66 miles, 3700'

The most complicated stage of this ride for navigation begins simply, with a 5-mile run down Hwy 101 and 10 miles of beautiful side roads through state and national parks, climbing and descending two big ridges along the way. Another 5 miles on Hwy 101, 4 hilly miles on a funky old side road, another 10 miles on 101 (also rather hilly), and then things become complex: in the last 34 miles, there are twenty-eight lines of directions in the mileage log. But trust me: they're all necessary and beneficial.

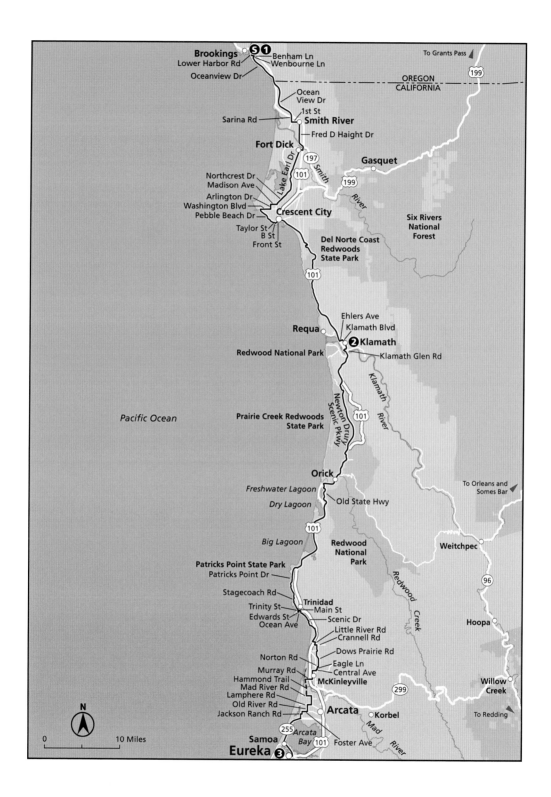

Brookings
Lower Harbor Rd
Benham Ln
Wenbourne Ln
Oceanview Dr

To Grants Pass

OREGON
CALIFORNIA

199

Ocean
View Dr
1st St
Sarina Rd
Smith River
Fred D Haight Dr

Fort Dick

197

Gasquet

Northcrest Dr
Madison Ave
Arlington Dr
Washington Blvd
Pebble Beach Dr

101

199

Crescent City

Taylor St
B St
Front St

Del Norte Coast
Redwoods
State Park

Six Rivers
National
Forest

101

Ehlers Ave
Requa
Klamath Blvd
Klamath

Redwood National Park

Klamath Glen Rd

Newton Drury Scenic Pkwy

Prairie Creek Redwoods
State Park

101

Pacific Ocean

Orick

Freshwater Lagoon

Dry Lagoon
Old State Hwy

To Orleans and
Somes Bar

101

Big Lagoon

Redwood
National
Park

Weitchpec

Patricks Point State Park
Patricks Point Dr

96

Stagecoach Rd

Trinidad
Trinity St
Main St
Edwards St
Scenic Dr
Ocean Ave
Little River Rd
Crannell Rd
Dows Prairie Rd

Hoopa

Norton Rd
Eagle Ln
Murray Rd
Central Ave
Hammond Trail
McKinleyville
Mad River Rd
Lamphere Rd
Old River Rd
Jackson Ranch Rd

299

Willow
Creek

Arcata
Korbel

To Redding

255
Arcata
Bay
101
Foster Ave

Samoa
Eureka

N

0   10 Miles

This side-road stretch begins with Patricks Point State Park, leading down to and through the quaint village of Trinidad. More quiet back roads, including one steep climb, meander down to the town of McKinleyville. A few residential streets and a nice bike trail and bridge see riders clear of town and over the Mad River, and the final 12 miles are a wandering odyssey across the flat, green pastures north of Humboldt Bay. Finish up in Eureka's historic downtown.

MILEAGE LOG

0.0	South on Klamath Blvd.
0.7	Right on Klamath Glen Rd., under Hwy 101 to left on Hwy 101 south
5.2	Right on Newton Drury Scenic Pkwy. into Prairie Creek Redwoods State Park
14.4	Right on Hwy 101
19.5	Town of Orick
20.5	Left on Old State Hwy
24.1	Left on Hwy 101
34.4	Right on Patricks Point Dr.
38.0	Right on Stagecoach Rd.
40.6	Becomes Trinity St. in town of Trinidad
40.7	Left on Edwards St. (Trinidad harbor)
40.8	Left on Ocean Ave.
41.0	Right on Main St.
41.1	Right on Scenic Dr.
44.3	Merge left onto Hwy 101 south
45.0	Take exit 725 toward Crannell Rd.
45.4	Left on Clam Beach Dr. over Hwy 101, bear right on Little River Rd.
45.7	Bear left on Crannell Rd., right on Dows Prairie Rd.
49.5	Right on Norton Rd., left on Eagle Ln.
50.1	Left on Central Ave.; town of McKinleyville
50.2	Right on Murray Rd.
51.4	Straight ahead, then left on Hammond Trail; head south on bike trail and local streets to bike bridge over Mad River
53.8	Bear left (south) on Mad River Rd.
56.2	Right on Lamphere Rd.
56.7	Left on Seidel Rd.
57.8	Right on Foster Ave.
59.7	Right on Samoa Blvd. (Hwy 255); unmarked, a wider highway just past RR tracks
63.7	Left on Hwy 255 on bridge over bay; follow sign to Eureka
65.6	Right on 3rd St.; city of Eureka
65.8	Jog left on O St., right on 3rd St.
65.9	Right on M St.; finish in front of Carson House at corner of M and 2nd streets

Stage 3. Eureka to Garberville: 80 miles, 4300'

This is the longest stage but it is never too difficult, with many small climbs but nothing brutal. After a comfortable transit of Eureka and another section of Hwy 101, you embark on a fairly complicated trek to and through the historic village of Ferndale and onward through Scotia to

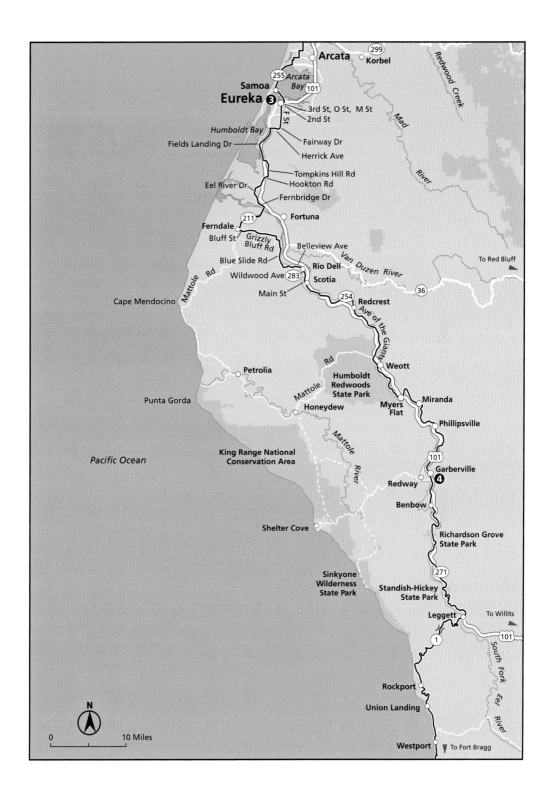

Humboldt Redwoods State Park. (See Rides 1 and 2 for more details about these miles.) Of the final 39 miles, 32 are on the beautiful Avenue of the Giants, beneath the towering trees, often near the Eel River, almost always within state or national parks. The final 6 miles to Garberville are back on Hwy 101 and feature the biggest climb of the day.

MILEAGE LOG

0.0	South on 2nd St.
0.4	Left on F St.
3.2	Becomes Fairway Dr., then Herrick Ave.
5.0	Left to merge onto Hwy 101 south
7.3	Right on exit 699 to Fields Landing Dr.; merge back onto Hwy 101 at 7.9
8.8	Right on exit 698, under freeway
9.2	Right on Tompkins Hill Rd.
11.8	Right on Hookton Rd.
11.9	Right on Eel River Dr.; unmarked, follow sign for Hwy 101 south
16.6	Right on Fernbridge Dr.
17.1	Right on Hwy 211, on bridge over Eel River; follow sign to Ferndale
21.3	Becomes Main St. in town of Ferndale
21.9	Left on Bluff St.
22.7	Right on Grizzly Bluff Rd.; becomes Blue Slide Rd.; then Belleview Ave.
34.2	Right on Wildwood Ave. (Hwy 283); town of Rio Dell
35.2	Cross Eel River to Main St., town of Scotia
37.1	Jog left, then right to head south on Hwy 101
41.3	Take exit 674, follow sign to Pepperwood and Ave. of the Giants
41.4	Left under highway on Ave. of the Giants (Hwy 254)
48.0	Town of Redcrest
60.5	Town of Myers Flat
66.5	Town of Miranda
70.4	Town of Phillipsville
73.3	Merge onto Hwy 101 south
79.2	Take exit 639B; follow sign to Garberville
79.3	Left on Redwood Hwy; follow sign to Garberville
79.7	Finish in Garberville

Stage 4. Garberville to Fort Bragg: 68 miles, 6400'
This stage contains the last and perhaps most uncomfortable sections along Hwy 101. Recent improvements have made it a better biking experience than it used to be, but it will still feel good to put this behind you. The first 24 miles are on the big highway, except for a 4-mile bypass on quiet Hwy 271. All of these miles are busily up and down, as the roads tumble along in the deep canyon of the Eel River.

Prepare for a challenge when you finally turn onto Hwy 1: a 4-mile, 1100' ascent out of the river canyon and over the ridge toward the ocean. That hard work is well rewarded with a long run of almost constant descending: 1800' down in 9 miles. A 2-mile, 700' climb and matching descent follow, and then chunky rollers along the coast take you through the town of Westport and on to Fort Bragg. Finish up with a couple of miles on a state park bike trail into town.

It's no exaggeration to say that the rugged coastline of Northern California is as spectacular as any stretch of coastline, anywhere. (Jof Hanwright)

MILEAGE LOG

0.0	South on Redwood Dr., right on Sprowl Creek Rd. to Hwy 101 south
8.3	Richardson Grove State Park and nearby store
8.9	Right on Hwy 271
14.8	Left to merge onto Hwy 101 south
22.2	Store across from Standish-Hickey State Park
23.7	Right on Hwy 1
51.2	Town of Westport
63.5	Right on Cleone Heights Rd. into MacKerricher State Park (signed as "BIKE ROUTE, SCENIC ALTERNATE")
64.3	Pass under bike bridge, then left on spur to access trail, southbound
66.6	Cross bridge over creek; becomes Old Haul Rd., then Elm St.
67.1	Right on Main St. (Hwy 1); town of Fort Bragg
67.6	Finish in downtown Fort Bragg

Stage 5. Fort Bragg to Gualala: 62 miles, 4800'

Today's ride is all small ups and downs as Hwy 1 scrambles over bluffs and headlands and dives into coves and river canyons. Three scenic *divertimenti* early on: first a 3-mile detour on Point Cabrillo Drive, then a 2-mile visit to the famous village of Mendocino, and finally a little nip

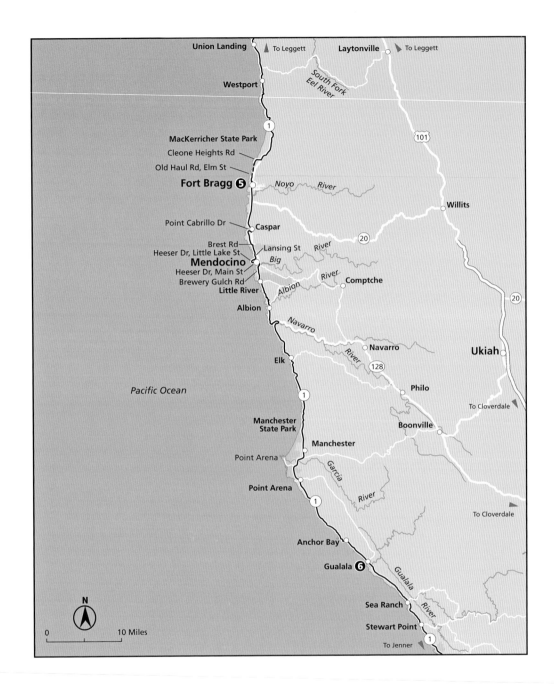

Union Landing
To Leggett
Laytonville
To Leggett
Westport
South Fork Eel River
①
MacKerricher State Park
Cleone Heights Rd
Old Haul Rd, Elm St
Fort Bragg ❺
Noyo River
Willits
Point Cabrillo Dr
Caspar
20
Brest Rd
Heeser Dr, Little Lake St
Lansing St
River
Mendocino
Big
Heeser Dr, Main St
River
Brewery Gulch Rd
Comptche
Little River
Albion
Albion
Navarro
Navarro
Ukiah
Elk
River
20
128
Philo
To Cloverdale
Pacific Ocean
①
Manchester State Park
Boonville
Manchester
Point Arena
Garcia
River
To Cloverdale
Point Arena
①
Anchor Bay
Gualala ❻
Gualala
Sea Ranch
River
N
Stewart Point
①
0   10 Miles
To Jenner

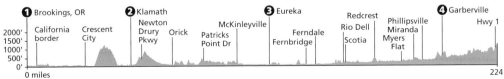

❶ Brookings, OR   ❷ Klamath   ❸ Eureka   ❹ Garberville
                                                                                          Redcrest   Phillipsville   Hwy 1
              California   Crescent   Newton   McKinleyville   Rio Dell   Miranda
2000'   border   City   Drury   Orick   Ferndale   Myers
1500'   Pkwy   Patricks   Scotia   Flat
1000'   Point Dr   Fernbridge
500'
0'
0 miles   224

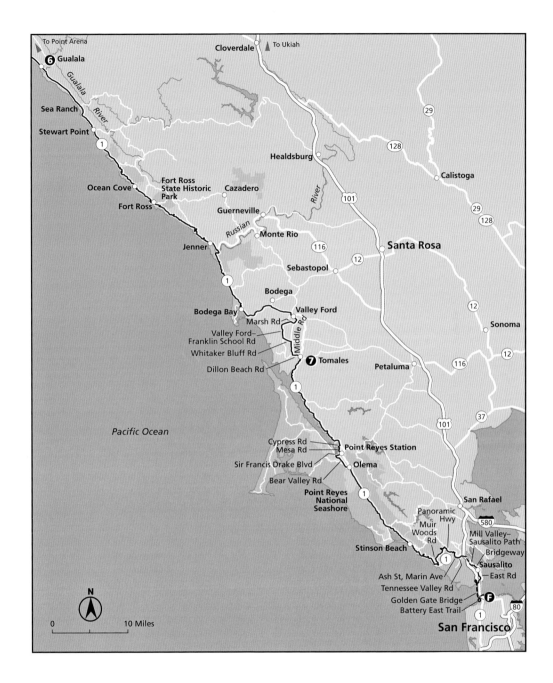

To Point Arena

6 Gualala

Cloverdale · To Ukiah

Gualala River

Sea Ranch

Stewart Point

1

Ocean Cove

Fort Ross State Historic Park

Cazadero

Fort Ross

Healdsburg

Calistoga

29

128

Guerneville

Russian River

Jenner

Monte Rio

116

Santa Rosa

1

Sebastopol

12

29

128

Bodega

Bodega Bay

Valley Ford

Marsh Rd

Valley Ford–Franklin School Rd

Whitaker Bluff Rd

Middle Rd

12

Sonoma

Dillon Beach Rd

7 Tomales

Petaluma

116

12

Pacific Ocean

1

Cypress Rd

Mesa Rd

Sir Francis Drake Blvd

Bear Valley Rd

Point Reyes Station

Olema

101

37

Point Reyes National Seashore

1

San Rafael

Panoramic Hwy

Muir Woods Rd

580

Mill Valley–Sausalito Path

Bridgeway

Sausalito

East Rd

Stinson Beach

1

Ash St, Marin Ave

Tennessee Valley Rd

Golden Gate Bridge

Battery East Trail

F

80

1

N

San Francisco

0   10 Miles

| Hwy 1 summit (1894') | **5** Fort Bragg | **6** Gualala | **7** Tomales | Golden Gate Bridge |

Westport · Navarro River; Hwy 128 · Anchor Bay · Stewarts Point · Ocean Cove · Fort Ross · Bodega Bay · Pt Reyes Station · Sausalito · Muir Woods

Mendocino · Point Arena · Manchester · Elk · Jenner · Valley Ford · Marshall · Stinson Beach · Olema

2000'
1500'
1000'
500'
0'

224 miles   448

off the main road south of Mendocino...all worth doing. (See Ride 4 for more details on some of today's miles.) From mile 13.6 on, it's simple: 48 heavenly miles on Hwy 1, almost always with the blue Pacific on your right. Relatively light traffic, wonderful scenery, perhaps even a tailwind.

MILEAGE LOG

0.0	South on Hwy 1
6.2	Right on Point Cabrillo Dr.
9.2	Jog left on Brest Rd., right on Hwy 1 South
10.2	Right on Lansing St.; follow sign to Mendocino Headlands State Park
10.7	Right on Heeser Dr.; becomes Little Lake St.
11.7	Right on Heeser St.; becomes Main St.; town of Mendocino
12.5	Right on Hwy 1
13.0	Right on Brewery Gulch Rd.
13.6	Right on Hwy 1
15.2	Town of Little River
29.0	Town of Elk
41.8	Town of Manchester
47.4	Town of Point Arena
58.0	Town of Anchor Bay
61.5	Finish in town of Gualala

Stage 6. Gualala to Tomales: 66 miles, 4500'

This is another day for simple navigation, with all but the final 9 miles on Hwy 1. Those first 53 miles are a reprise of yesterday's ride, dancing along the coastal cliffs, up and down, over and over. Almost the only notations on the mileage log are those for the little towns popping up at regular intervals all day. (You don't have to worry about running out of water or snacks.)

If you've never been there, plan for a stop at Fort Ross State Historic Park, the site of the only colonial outpost of Tsarist Russia on this coast. It comes up at mile 26, a good spot for a mid-ride break and well worth a visit. South of Fort Ross are the biggest climbs of the day: back-to-back ascents of a few hundred feet, each followed with a big descent. Smaller climbs and descents take you through the town of Jenner and on down the coast to Bodega Bay and Valley Ford, where the route finally leaves the main highway. These last miles offer a quiet, remote detour off Hwy 1. Not that the main road is bad; it's not. But these roads are better...more scenic and more fun. (Read more about this section and the early miles of Stage 7 in Ride 22.)

MILEAGE LOG

0.0	South on Hwy 1
11.4	Stewarts Point Store
21.2	Ocean Cove Store
24.5	Fort Ross Store
26.0	Fort Ross State Historic Park

37.5	Town of Jenner
48.0	Town of Bodega Bay
56.6	Town of Valley Ford
56.9	Right on Middle Rd.
57.8	Right on Marsh Rd.
58.7	Left on Valley Ford–Franklin School Rd.
61.3	Left on Whitaker Bluff Rd.
62.7	Right on Middle Rd. (unmarked)
64.6	Left on Dillon Beach Rd.
65.7	Finish in town of Tomales

Stage 7. Tomales to San Francisco: 56 miles, 4000'

From Tomales, Hwy 1 unrolls more dream miles for most of the day. Several of the early miles run along Tomales Bay (See Ride 22), down to the town of Point Reyes Station. Side roads are used for 5 miles, into the town and beyond it, swinging through the Point Reyes National Seashore. At Olema, at mile 20.4, you return to Hwy 1 for the next 20 miles, through more of the National Seashore, along Bolinas Lagoon, through the town of Stinson Beach (at mile 34, a good spot for a break), and on down the spectacular coastal cliffs to a turn inland toward Muir Woods. (For more details about these miles, read Ride 24.)

Beyond Muir Woods is the biggest climb of the day: 600' in 2 miles. This is followed by an even bigger descent: 750' in 2.5 miles. When you roll out at the bottom of that bad boy, you need to put your thinking cap on, as the remaining 9 miles are tricky. You'll be dodging around Mill Valley, drilling right through Sausalito, and climbing to the Golden Gate Bridge through Fort Baker (a former Army base and now part of a beautiful park). Be assured that thousands of cyclists do this every day. If you're confused, don't be afraid to ask another rider for help.

The run up to and across the bridge is magnificent. It's a perfect way to wrap up this grand tour. I end the route at the south end of the bridge, but you will need to continue to wherever you're holing up in the city. I can't know where that will be, but it may help you to get there if you read about routes to and from the bridge in Rides 25 and 30.

MILEAGE LOG

0.0	South on Hwy 1
8.0	Town of Marshall
15.5	Right on Cypress Rd.
16.0	Right on Mesa Rd.
17.1	Right on Hwy 1; town of Point Reyes Station
17.3	Right on Sir Francis Drake Blvd.
18.1	Left on Bear Valley Rd. into Point Reyes National Seashore
20.4	Town of Olema
34.2	Town of Stinson Beach
40.5	Left on Muir Woods Rd.
44.4	Right on Panoramic Hwy
45.3	Left on Hwy 1
47.1	Right on Ash St.

47.2   Left on Marin Ave.; bear left on Marin Ave. at 47.8
47.9   Left on Tennessee Valley Rd.
48.2   Right on Hwy 1
48.7   Jog left, then right to head south on Mill Valley–Sausalito Path
49.4   Continue south on Bridgeway into city of Sausalito; follow main road through town (becomes Alexander Ave. south of town)
52.3   Right on Marin Bike Route 5 to cross under Alexander to East Rd. into Fort Baker
53.4   Left on Moore Rd.; becomes Conzelman Rd. on climb to Golden Gate Bridge
54.1   Right on west walkway of Golden Gate Bridge (Hwy 1 and Hwy 101)
55.8   Right on bike trail to Battery East Trail
56.2   Finish tour at Lincoln Blvd., or continue to destination in San Francisco

75 CALIFORNIA PEAKS

Difficulty:	Challenging/epic
Time:	9 days
Distance:	548 miles
Elevation gain:	34,000'
Best seasons:	July through September

GETTING THERE: From Sacramento, take I-5 north approximately 225 miles to the town of Mount Shasta. Exit at Lake St. and head east to the city center.

GETTING BACK: From Yosemite Valley, head west on Hwy 120 approximately 110 miles to Hwy 99 at Manteca (or 115 miles, past Manteca, to I-5). Take either Hwy 99 or I-5 north approximately 60 miles to Sacramento.

From the southern end of the Cascades to the heart of the High Sierra, this journey down the length of California's backbone is a grand, out-of-scale adventure. It begins in the shadow of mighty Mount Shasta and ends in the holy temple of Yosemite Valley. In between are many other mountains, but also quiet miles across open valleys and alpine meadows, and along deep blue lakes and dancing streams. If you're ready for it, this tour will reward your efforts with the ride of a lifetime.

Stage 1. Mount Shasta to Fall River Mills: 60 miles, 2600'
After departing the town of Mount Shasta, settle in for a long but gradual climb to 4478' Snowmans Hill summit (1000' in 5.5 miles). A 4.5-mile, 1200' descent ends with you flying past the town of McCloud and onward along Highway 89 on a rolling, mildly uphill run of 22 miles to another summit, always buried in the forest. The next 8 miles of chunky ups and downs lead to a turn onto McArthur Road and a smooth descent into lovely, tranquil Fall River Valley. The final 15 miles are almost dead flat, cruising along near the pretty Fall River.

0.0   From Lake St. in Mount Shasta, south on Mount Shasta Blvd.
1.9   Merge onto Hwy 89, following signs to Hwy 89 S. and McCloud
7.6   Snowmans Hill summit (4478')
12.0   Town of McCloud
33.6   Dead Horse summit (4533')
41.2   Left on McArthur Rd.
53.1   Right on Brown Rd.; town of Glenburn
53.4   Left on Glenburn Rd.
58.8   Cross Hwy 299 to Bridge St.
59.3   Left on Main St. to finish in town of Fall River Mills

Stage 2. Fall River Mills to Mineral: 84 miles, 6000'

Ideally, there would be a grand old lodge for an overnight in Lassen Volcanic National Park, somewhere around mile 65. But there isn't, so we have to stretch it out today and ride all the way through the park and down to the town of Mineral. But consider: your work is done when you cross 8512' Lassen summit at mile 67. The last 17 miles are all downhill, and about as good a downhill as you could imagine. (Read Ride 7 for more about this wild descent.)

The ride begins with 15 miles on quiet back roads along the Pit River, with a little climbing to wake you up, and then easy miles back to Hwy 89. (Read Ride 6 for more on this section.) In the next 30 miles along 89, you gain 3000' (a very gradual ascent). That puts you well into the national park, amid its magnificent scenery. A twisting, 3-mile descent sets you up for the big challenge: over 16 miles up to Lassen summit…and the big descent that follows.

MILEAGE LOG

0.0   From Hwy 299 in Fall River Mills, south on Main St.
0.2   Straight on River St., continue on Cassel–Fall River Rd.
11.7   Left on Cassel Rd.
14.9   Left on Hwy 89
31.8   Old Station (store)
45.3   Left into Lassen Volcanic National Park (still on Hwy 89)
46.4   Loomis Visitor Center
66.9   Lassen summit (8512')
73.9   Kohm Yah-mah-nee Visitor Center
79.3   Right on Hwy 36
83.8   Finish in town of Mineral

Stage 3. Mineral to Greenville: 51 miles, 1900'

This stage is short and easy, but still good fun, beginning with Hwy 172, a nearly perfect bike road. (See Ride 7.) Over 23 rolling miles through the forest on Hwy 89 are next. That brings you to the Lake Almanor Recreation Trail, running through the woods near the lake. After the section of trail listed in this route, you can either use Almanor Drive or more sections of trail (if you can find them), but eventually, you return to Hwy 89, heading down the west side of the lake and then slithering downhill along Wolf Creek to the town of Greenville.

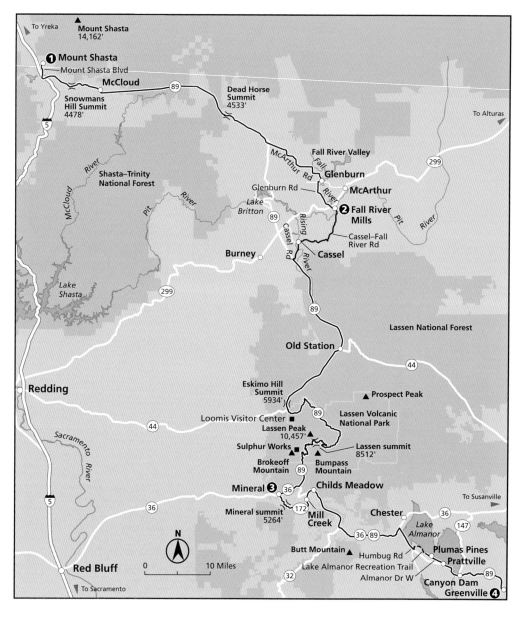

To Yreka

Mount Shasta
14,162'

❶ **Mount Shasta**
Mount Shasta Blvd

McCloud

89

Snowmans
Hill Summit
4478'

Dead Horse
Summit
4533'

5

To Alturas

McCloud River

Shasta–Trinity
National Forest

Pit River

McArthur Rd

Fall River Valley

Glenburn

Glenburn Rd

McArthur

Lake
Britton

89

Cassel Rd

Rising River

❷ **Fall River
Mills**

Cassel–Fall
River Rd

Pit River

299

Burney

Cassel

Lake
Shasta

299

89

Lassen National Forest

Old Station

44

Eskimo Hill
Summit
5934'

▲ **Prospect Peak**

Redding

Loomis Visitor Center ■

89

**Lassen Volcanic
National Park**

44

Lassen Peak
10,457' ▲

Sacramento River

Sulphur Works ■

▲ Lassen summit
8512'

**Brokeoff
Mountain**

89

Bumpass
Mountain

Mineral ❸

36

Childs Meadow

To Susanville

Mineral summit
5264'

172

**Mill
Creek**

Chester

36

Lake
Almanor

147

5

36

36 89

Butt Mountain ▲

Humbug Rd

Plumas Pines

Red Bluff

N

0   10 Miles

32

Lake Almanor Recreation Trail

Almanor Dr W

Prattville

Canyon Dam

89

Greenville ❹

To Sacramento

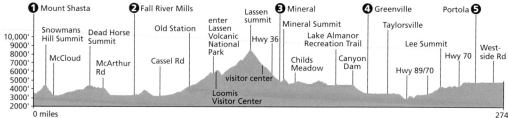

❶ Mount Shasta   ❷ Fall River Mills   Lassen summit   ❸ Mineral   ❹ Greenville   Portola ❺

Snowmans
Hill Summit   Dead Horse
Summit   Old Station   enter
Lassen
Volcanic
National
Park   Hwy 36   Mineral Summit   Taylorsville   West-
side Rd

10,000'
9000'
8000'
7000'
6000'
5000'
4000'
3000'
2000'

McCloud   McArthur
Rd   Cassel Rd   visitor center   Childs
Meadow   Canyon
Dam   Hwy 89/70   Lee Summit   Hwy 70

Loomis
Visitor Center

Lake Almanor
Recreation Trail

0 miles

274

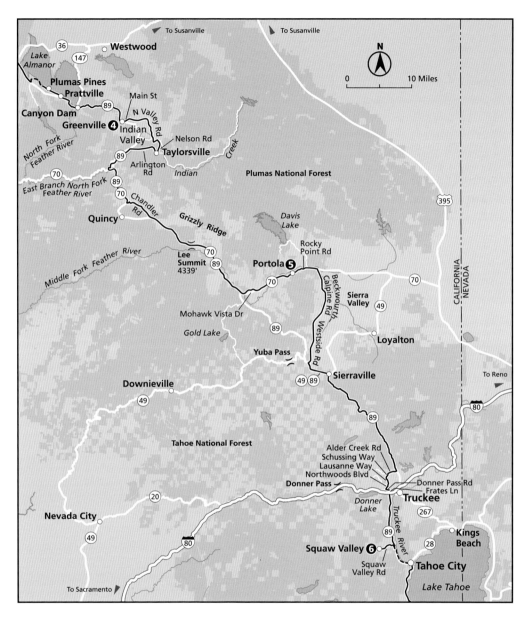

To Susanville

To Susanville

Westwood

Lake Almanor

36

147

N

0   10 Miles

Plumas Pines

Prattville

Main St

Canyon Dam

89

N Valley Rd

Greenville ❹

Indian Valley

Nelson Rd

89

Taylorsville

Arlington Rd

Indian

Creek

Plumas National Forest

North Fork Feather River

395

East Branch North Fork Feather River

70

89

70

Chandler Rd

Grizzly Ridge

Davis Lake

Quincy

Rocky Point Rd

Middle Fork Feather River

Lee Summit 4339'

70

89

Portola ❺

70

Beckwourth Calpine Rd

Sierra Valley

49

70

Mohawk Vista Dr

89

Westside Rd

Gold Lake

Yuba Pass

Loyalton

Downieville

49

49 89

Sierraville

To Reno

80

89

Tahoe National Forest

Alder Creek Rd
Schussing Way
Lausanne Way
Northwoods Blvd

Donner Pass

Donner Pass Rd
Frates Ln

Truckee

CALIFORNIA
NEVADA

20

Donner Lake

267

Truckee River

Nevada City

49

80

89

Kings Beach

28

Squaw Valley ❻

Squaw Valley Rd

Tahoe City

To Sacramento

Lake Tahoe

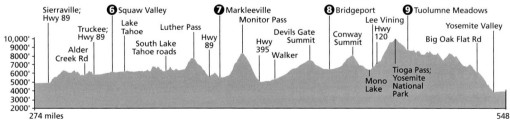

Sierraville; Hwy 89

❻ Squaw Valley

❼ Markleeville
Monitor Pass

❽ Bridgeport

❾ Tuolumne Meadows

Truckee; Hwy 89

Lake Tahoe

Luther Pass

Hwy 89

Lee Vining
Hwy 120

Yosemite Valley

Alder Creek Rd

South Lake Tahoe roads

Hwy 395

Devils Gate Summit

Conway Summit

Big Oak Flat Rd

10,000'
9000'
8000'
7000'
6000'
5000'
4000'
3000'
2000'

Walker

Mono Lake

Tioga Pass; Yosemite National Park

274 miles   548

0.0	East on Hwy 172
2.3	Mineral summit (5264')
8.9	Right on Hwy 89/36
9.9	Childs Meadow Resort (store)
15.9	Fire Mountain (store)
28.0	Right on Hwy 89 (Hwy 36 goes straight into Chester)
32.3	Left to Lake Almanor Recreation Trail at Humbug Rd. junction
34.8	Left on Almanor Dr. W.
35.2	Plumas Pines Resort (store)
38.0	Left on Hwy 89
42.0	Town of Canyon Dam
50.6	Finish in town of Greenville

Stage 4. Greenville to Portola: 63 miles, 3900'
This ride starts out with a 16-mile dream run down Indian Valley. (See Ride 9 for more on this lovely region.) After returning to Hwy 89, a 6-mile descent in the rocky canyon of Indian Creek bottoms out at a junction with Hwy 70. Climb out of the canyon and then, at mile 29, dodge off the highway for a 6-mile bypass on tiny Chandler Road, skirting congestion around the town of Quincy. Back on Hwy 89/70, chug up a 7-mile grade to Lee summit, then bounce along an up-and-down run above the Middle Fork Feather River for 13 miles. Turn east and head for Portola, first on a little uphill back road and then on 6 rolling miles along Hwy 70.

0.0	East on Main St.
0.9	Bear right on N. Valley Rd.
10.7	Right on Nelson St.
11.7	Right on Arlington Rd.; town of Taylorsville
16.4	Left on Hwy 89
22.6	Left on Hwy 89/70
28.9	Left on Chandler Rd.
34.9	Left on Hwy 89/70
36.8	Roadside rest area (water, restrooms)
42.3	Lee summit (4339')
53.3	Straight on Hwy 70 (Hwy 89 turns right)
54.3	Left on Mohawk Vista Dr.
56.7	Left on Hwy 70
62.9	Finish in town of Portola

Stage 5. Portola to Squaw Valley: 61 miles, 3200'
Head east out of Portola on a lovely little road along the Feather River, then cross the wide, peaceful Sierra Valley on the way back to another helping of Hwy 89. (Read more about these miles in Ride 65.) Beyond the town of Sierraville at mile 24 are 21 mountainous miles

On the long climb to 8512' Lassen summit on Stage 2
of this magnificent tour through California's mountains

heading for the town of Truckee. This section will be challenging because of the climbs and—possibly—the traffic. Bail off the highway at the first opportunity and plot a bypass that avoids most of Truckee. A mile of clutter is unavoidable, but soon over, and the last leg of the stage runs down Hwy 89 to the Squaw Valley ski area and the lodgings that go with the resort.

MILEAGE LOG

0.0	From Portola (Gulling St. junction), east on Hwy 70
0.8	Right on Rocky Point Rd.
3.2	Right on Hwy 70
4.7	Right on Beckwourth–Calpine Rd.; becomes Westside Rd.
20.2	Left on Hwy 89/49
24.1	Right on Hwy 89; town of Sierraville; Hwy 49 goes straight
45.0	Right on Alder Creek Rd.
46.4	Left on Schussing Way
47.9	Left on Lausanne Way
48.8	Left on Northwoods Blvd.
49.7	Left on Donner Pass Rd.; town of Truckee
50.3	Right on Frates Ln.; becomes Hwy 89 S when road passes under I-80
59.0	Right on Squaw Valley Rd.
61.1	Finish at Squaw Valley Village

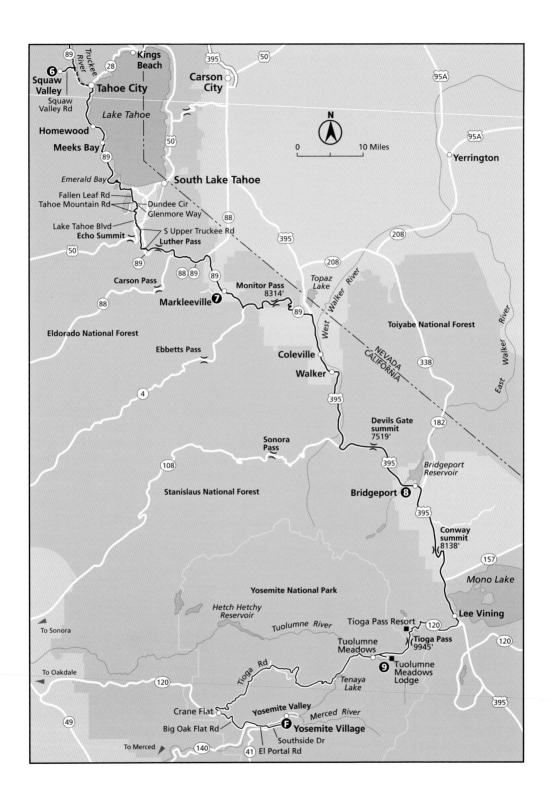

Stage 6. Squaw Valley to Markleeville: 63 miles, 4000'

Begin with 5-plus miles on the Truckee River Bike Trail. This delivers you to the northwest corner of Lake Tahoe for a cruise down the west shore. (To learn more about the bike trail and the ride along the lake, see Rides 66 and 67.) South of the vista points above beautiful Emerald Bay, leave the lake for a complex detour around South Lake Tahoe, through a mix of mountains and suburbs. A secluded, wooded lane carries you clear of the neighborhoods and up to the long climb to 7740' Luther Pass, once again on our old friend Hwy 89.

A frisky 8-mile descent from the pass, down the rocky defile of the Carson River, brings you to the last leg of the journey: 3 miles of easy climbing and 3 miles of fast descending to the quaint mountain town of Markleeville.

MILEAGE LOG

0.0	From Squaw Valley Village, retrace Squaw Valley Rd.
2.1	Cross Hwy 89, turn right on Truckee River Bike Trail
7.1	Right on bike bridge over river, right on Tahoe Rim Trail
7.6	Right on Hwy 89 (W. Lake Blvd.) or nearby bike trail; numerous spots for food and water along lake; also many vista points
31.3	Right on Fallen Leaf Rd.
33.3	Left on Tahoe Mountain Rd.
33.8	Right on Dundee Circle
34.0	Jog right on Glenmore Way, left on Tahoe Mountain Rd.
35.1	Right on Lake Tahoe Blvd.
36.4	Right on North Upper Truckee Rd.
38.7	Jog left on Hwy 50, right on South Upper Truckee Rd.
43.5	Cross Hwy 89 to continue on South Upper Truckee Rd.
44.5	Left on Hwy 89
47.8	Luther Pass (7740')
50.4	Left on Hwy 88/89
56.2	Right on Hwy 89 (Hwy 88 goes straight)
62.5	Finish in town of Markleeville

Stage 7. Markleeville to Bridgeport: 63 miles, 4800'

One last installment of Hwy 89: south out of town along the Carson River, up and over massive Monitor Pass (8314'), and down the eastern flank of the Sierra to Hwy 395 (over 9 miles and 3400' down). On the eastern side of the mountains, the landscape is more arid and austere, but never bleak or barren. It's a different sort of beauty. Hwy 395 runs south along the Walker River, past rows of venerable cottonwoods, climbing gradually—2500' in 29 miles—to Devils Gate summit. Finish up with a lazy, 11-mile glide down to Bridgeport.

MILEAGE LOG

0.0	South on Hwy 89
4.9	Left on Hwy 89
13.1	Monitor Pass (8314')
22.5	Right on Hwy 395

28.0	Coleville High School (water)
29.0	Meadowcliff Resort (store)
31.7	Town of Walker
51.4	Devils Gate summit (7519')
62.9	Finish in town of Bridgeport

Stage 8. Bridgeport to Tuolumne Meadows Lodge: 45 miles, 4600'

A short stage, but you won't mind that after you've crawled in the upstairs attic window of Yosemite National Park: the 12-mile, 3200' grind up to 9945' Tioga Pass. But there are other miles to do before that, beginning with the gentle grade along Virginia Creek, from Bridgeport to 8138' Conway summit. Beyond that ridge, there is the panoramic vista over Mono Lake and then the 8-mile flier down to the shore of the briny lake. A small climb to the town of Lee Vining sets up the big climb to Tioga.

Once you've conquered the huge ascent and are reveling in the glorious landscape that is Yosemite's high country, all that remains is a snappy, 6.5-mile descent toward Tuolumne Meadows. *Toward* but not quite *to*: we stop a mile short of the actual alpine meadow to turn into the only lodgings in this part of the park (other lodgings just outside the park are noted in the log).

MILEAGE LOG

0.0	South on Hwy 395
13.1	Conway summit (8138')
24.7	Mono Lake visitor center
25.2	Town of Lee Vining
25.7	Right on Utility Rd.
26.6	Right on Hwy 120 (Tioga Rd.)
35.6	Tioga Pass Resort (store, lodging)
37.7	Tioga Pass (9945'); entrance to Yosemite National Park
44.2	Left on Tuolumne Meadows Lodge Rd.
44.8	Finish at lodge

Stage 9. Tuolumne Meadows Lodge to Yosemite Valley: 58 miles, 2700'

What a fitting way to end this nine-day mountain odyssey: dropping from the high country into the famous valley, snuggled in beneath its majestic granite ramparts. Soaking up the scenery will be your first order of business today. I'm not going to list all the highlights and vista points you'll encounter. You can't miss them. So let's take all that as a given and talk about the biking.

With the end of the ride almost 5000' lower than the start, you can figure descending will dominate. However, there are at least seven climbs in the first 37 miles, some of them quite substantial. But with about 20 miles to go, you start tilting downhill for good on the exhilarating plunge into the valley. After 13 miles of Newtonian bliss, you hit the valley and head upstream along the Merced River to wherever you plan to stay tonight. I've broken off the route at a corner near Curry Village. Other lodgings are farther along, near Yosemite Village. (For more information on biking in the valley, read Ride 69.)

0.0	Retrace Lodge Rd.
0.6	Left on Hwy 120 (Tioga Rd.)
1.3	Tuolumne Meadows
40.8	Left on Big Oak Flat Rd. toward Yosemite Valley; Crane Flat (store)
50.3	Left on Hwy 140 (El Portal Rd.) into Yosemite Valley
52.1	Straight on Southside Dr.
57.3	Junction of Southside Dr. and roads to various lodgings

RESOURCES

CYCLING CLUBS

BAY AREA
Almaden Cycle Touring Club, www.actc.org
Alto Velo Racing Club, www.altovelo.org
Benicia Bicycle Club,
    www.beniciabicycleclub.org
Berkeley Bicycle Club, www.berkeleybike.org
Delta Pedalers, www.deltaped.org
Diablo Cyclists, www.diablocyclists.org
Different Spokes, www.dssf.org
Fremont Freewheelers,
    www.fremontfreewheelers.org
Grizzly Peak Cyclists,
    www.grizzlypeakcyclists.org
Oakland Yellow Jackets,
    www.oaklandyellowjackets.org
San Jose Bicycle Club, www.teamsanjose.org
Santa Cruz County Cycling Club,
    www.santacruzcycling.org
Valley Spokesmen Bicycle Club,
    www.valleyspokesmen.org
Western Wheelers, www.westernwheelers
    bicycleclub.memberlodge.com

CENTRAL VALLEY
Chico Velo Cycling Club,
    www.chicovelo.org
Cycle Folsom, www.cyclefolsom.com
Davis Bike Club, www.davisbikeclub.org
Sacramento Bike Hikers,
    www.bikehikers.com
Sacramento Wheelmen,
    www.sacwheelmen.org
Shasta Wheelmen, www.shastawheelmen.org
Stockton Bicycle Club,
    www.stocktonbikeclub.org

GOLD COUNTRY/SIERRA
Alta Alpina Cycling Club,
    www.altaalpina.org
Plumas-Sierra Bicycle Club, www.facebook
    .com/PlumasSierraBicycleClub

Sierra Express Bicycle Club,
    www.sierraexpress.org

NORTH BAY
Eagle Cycling Club,
    www.eaglecyclingclub.org
Marin Cyclists, www.marincyclists.com
Santa Rosa Cycling Club,
    www.srcc.memberlodge.com

NORTHWEST
Bigfoot Bicycle Club,
    www.bigfootbicycle.org

ADVOCACY
Butte Bicycle Coalition (Central Valley),
    www.buttebicyclecoalition.org
California Bicycle Coalition, www.calbike.org
California Association of Bicycling
    Organizations, www. cabobike.org
Davis Bicycles! (Central Valley),
    www.davisbicycles.org
Bay Area Bicycle Coalition (Bay Area),
    www.bayareabikes.org
East Bay Bicycle Coalition (Bay Area),
    www.ebbc.org
Lake Tahoe Bicycle Coalition (Sierra),
    www.tahoebike.org
Marin County Bicycle Coalition (North
    Bay), www.marinbike.org
Napa County Bicycle Coalition (North Bay),
    www.napabike.org
Sacramento Area Bicycle Advocates (Central
    Valley), www.sacbike.org
San Francisco Bicycle Coalition (Bay Area),
    www.sfbike.org
Silicon Valley Bicycle Coalition (Bay Area),
    www.bikesiliconvalley.org
Sonoma County Bicycle Coalition (North
    Bay), www.bikesonoma.org

EVENTS

Most of these events are either centuries or double centuries, and most are put on by local bike clubs. Typically, the organizers will offer a 100-mile route, but also a 100-K and occasionally a 200-K, or perhaps a shorter, "fun ride."

APRIL

Cinderella Century (Bay Area), Valley Spokesmen, valleyspokesmen.org/

Devil Mountain Double (Bay Area), Quackcyclists, quackcyclists.com/

Tierra Bella Century (Bay Area), Almaden Cycle Touring Club, tierrabella.org/

Wildflower Century (Central Valley), Chico Velo, chicovelo.org/

MAY

Davis Double Century (Central Valley), Davis Bike Club, davisbikeclub.org /annual_events/organized_rides/davis _double_century

Delta Century (Central Valley), Stockton Bicycle Club, stocktonbikeclub.org/docs /dc/delta_century.htm

Grizzly Peak Century (Bay Area), Grizzly Peak Cyclists, grizz.org/century/

Motherlode Century (Gold Country), motherlodecentury.com/

Tour of the Unknown Coast (Northwest), tuccycle.org/

Wine Country Century (North Bay), Santa Rosa Cycling Club, srcc.memberlodge .com/WCC

JUNE

Alta Alpina Double (Sierra), altaalpina.org /challenge/

Eastern Sierra Double (Sierra), Planet Ultra, planetultra.com/portfolio/eastern-sierra -double-century/

Ride Around Lake Tahoe (Sierra), bikethewest.com/americas-most -beautiful-bike-ride/

Sequoia Century (Bay Area), Western Wheelers, westernwheelersbicycleclub .memberlodge.com/sequoia

Sierra Century (Gold Country), Sacramento Wheelmen, sacwheelmen.org /sierracentury.org

Terrible Two (North Bay), Santa Rosa Cycling Club, srcc.memberlodge.com/TT

JULY

Fall River Century (Northeast), fallrivercentury.com/

Tour of the California Alps, the Death Ride (Sierra), deathride.com/

AUGUST

Marin Century (North Bay), Marin Cyclists, marincyclists.com/Default .aspx?pageId=143302

Mount Tam Double (North Bay), Marin Cyclists, marincyclists.com/Default .aspx?pageId=143302

Tour of Napa Valley (North Bay), Eagle Cycling Club, eaglecyclingclub.org/tour

SEPTEMBER

Knoxville Double Century (North Bay), Quackcyclists, quackcyclists.com/

OCTOBER

Foxy's Fall Century (Central Valley), Davis Bike Club, davisbikeclub.org /annual_events/organized_rides/foxys _fall_century

Grizzly Century (Sierra), grizzlycentury.org/

Levi's GranFondo (North Bay), levisgranfondo.com/

RECOMMENDED READING

Forester, John. *Effective Cycling.* Cambridge: MIT Press, 2012.

Fournel, Paul. *Need for the Bike (Besoin de Vélo).* Lincoln: University of Nebraska Press, 2001.

INDEX

ABOUT THE AUTHOR

(Gordon Stewart)

Bill Oetinger was born and raised in Portland, Oregon, but has lived most of his adult life in the San Francisco Bay Area. He has been cycling for all of that adult life, rolling out well over 200,000 miles so far.

For more than twenty years, he has been the ride director and newsletter editor for the Santa Rosa Cycling Club, one of the larger bike clubs in Northern California. In that capacity, he has planned and coordinated thousands of rides around the Bay Area. Farther afield, he has organized many tours for the club, adding up to over two hundred stages scattered throughout California and Oregon, as well as in other states and abroad. For the tour participants, he prepares descriptive previews of each stage, similar to the write-ups in this volume.

Bill has been writing a monthly column at BikeCal.com since 1999, ranging across the full spectrum of bike topics, from touring to racing to advocacy. (Over 180 past essays are archived at the site.)

Since 1992, Bill has been either chair or co-chair of the prestigious Terrible Two Double Century, one of the most challenging one-day rides in America. He has completed many double centuries and more than four hundred centuries. Long, hard rides aside, he is happiest knocking off a 60-mile tour stage with his friends.

Bill lives with his wife, Kathy, on a rural acre outside the little town of Sebastopol, Sonoma County, 60 miles north of the Golden Gate... prime cycling country.

recreation • lifestyle • conservation

MOUNTAINEERS BOOKS is a leading publisher of mountaineering literature and guides—including our flagship title, *Mountaineering: The Freedom of the Hills*—as well as adventure narratives, natural history, and general outdoor recreation. Through our two imprints, Skipstone and Braided River, we also publish titles on sustainability and conservation. We are committed to supporting the environmental and educational goals of our organization by providing expert information on human-powered adventure, sustainable practices at home and on the trail, and preservation of wilderness.

The Mountaineers, founded in 1906, is a 501(c)(3) nonprofit outdoor activity and conservation organization whose mission is "to explore, study, preserve, and enjoy the natural beauty of the outdoors." One of the largest such organizations in the United States, it sponsors classes and year-round outdoor activities throughout the Pacific Northwest, including climbing, hiking, backcountry skiing, snowshoeing, bicycling, camping, paddling, and more. The Mountaineers also supports its mission through its publishing division, Mountaineers Books, and promotes environmental education and citizen engagement. For more information, visit The Mountaineers Program Center, 7700 Sand Point Way NE, Seattle, WA 98115-3996; phone 206-521-6001; www.mountaineers.org; or email info@mountaineers.org.

Our publications are made possible through the generosity of donors and through sales of more than 500 titles on outdoor recreation, sustainable lifestyle, and conservation. To donate, purchase books, or learn more, visit us online:

MOUNTAINEERS BOOKS
1001 SW Klickitat Way, Suite 201 • Seattle, WA 98134
800-553-4453 • mbooks@mountaineersbooks.org • www.mountaineersbooks.org

 Mountaineers Books is proud to be a corporate sponsor of the Leave No Trace Center for Outdoor Ethics, whose mission is to promote and inspire responsible outdoor recreation through education, research, and partnerships. • The Leave No Trace program is focused specifically on human-powered (nonmotorized) recreation. • Leave No Trace strives to educate visitors about the nature of their recreational impacts and offers techniques to prevent and minimize such impacts. • Leave No Trace is best understood as an educational and ethical program, not as a set of rules and regulations. • For more information, visit www.lnt.org or call 800-332-4100.